Jaguar Books on Latin America

Series Editors

WILLIAM H. BEEZLEY, Neville (
    American Studies, Texas Chris
COLIN M. MACLACHLAN, Prof
    of History, Tulane University

Volumes Published

John E. Kicza, ed., *The Indian in Latin American History: Resistance, Resilience, and Acculturation* (1993). Cloth ISBN 0-8420-2421-2
Paper ISBN 0-8420-2425-5

Susan E. Place, ed., *Tropical Rainforests: Latin American Nature and Society in Transition* (1993). Cloth ISBN 0-8420-2423-9   Paper ISBN 0-8420-2427-1

Paul W. Drake, ed., *Money Doctors, Foreign Debts, and Economic Reforms in Latin America from the 1890s to the Present* (1994).
Cloth ISBN 0-8420-2434-4   Paper ISBN 0-8420-2435-2

John A. Britton, ed., *Molding the Hearts and Minds: Education, Communications, and Social Change in Latin America* (1994).
Cloth ISBN 0-8420-2489-1   Paper ISBN 0-8420-2490-5

Darién J. Davis, ed., *Slavery and Beyond: The African Impact on Latin America and the Caribbean* (1995). Cloth ISBN 0-8420-2484-0
Paper ISBN 0-8420-2485-9

David J. Weber and Jane M. Rausch, eds., *Where Cultures Meet: Frontiers in Latin American History* (1994). Cloth ISBN 0-8420-2477-8
Paper ISBN 0-8420-2478-6

Gertrude M. Yeager, ed., *Confronting Change, Challenging Tradition: Women in Latin American History* (1994). Cloth ISBN 0-8420-2479-4
Paper ISBN 0-8420-2480-8

Linda Alexander Rodríguez, ed., *Rank and Privilege: The Military and Society in Latin America* (1994). Cloth ISBN 0-8420-2432-8
Paper ISBN 0-8420-2433-6

Eileen ten Schink

Slavery
and
Beyond

Slavery and Beyond

The African Impact on Latin America and the Caribbean

Darién J. Davis
Editor

Jaguar Books on Latin America
Number 5

A Scholarly Resources Inc. Imprint
Wilmington, Delaware

© 1995 by Scholarly Resources Inc.
All rights reserved
First published 1995
Printed and bound in the United States of America

Scholarly Resources Inc.
104 Greenhill Avenue
Wilmington, DE 19805-1897

Library of Congress Cataloging-in-Publication Data

Slavery and beyond : the African impact on Latin America and the
    Caribbean / Darién J. Davis, editor.
        p.   cm. — (Jaguar books on Latin America ; no. 5)
    Includes bibliographical references.
    Filmography.
    ISBN 0-8420-2484-0 (alk. paper). — ISBN 0-8420-2485-9 (pbk. :
alk. paper)
        1. Latin America—Civilization—African influences. 2. Caribbean
Area—Civilization—African influences. 3. Blacks—Latin America—
History. 4. Acculturation—Latin America—History. 5. Latin
America—Race relations. I. Davis, Darién J., 1964–   .
II. Series.
F1408.3.S515   1995
980—dc20   94-32739
                                                                    CIP

⊛ The paper used in this publication meets the minimum requirements
of the American National Standard for permanence of paper for printed
library materials, Z39.48, 1984.

Acknowledgments

Many people have helped bring this volume to fruition. I am indebted to the editors of the Jaguar Books on Latin America series, William Beezley and Colin MacLachlan, for their critical and helpful suggestions. Special thanks go to Colin who read an earlier version of the introduction and forced me to provide a more precise conceptualization of the African dimension of Latin America.

I would also like to express my gratitude to Linda Pote Musumeci, Project Editor, and the staff at Scholarly Resources Inc. for their assistance and patience during the entire editorial process.

About the Editor

Darién J. Davis is assistant professor of history at Middlebury College, Middlebury, Vermont. He has conducted extensive research on race relations in Latin America, with particular emphasis on Brazil and Cuba, and has carried out various projects in Mexico, Paraguay, Colombia, Peru, and the Dominican Republic. His recent work explores the relationship between race, national identity, and intellectual history.

Contents

Introduction: The African Experience in Latin America— Resistance and Accommodation

Darién J. Davis

The African diaspora had a major demographic and cultural impact on all areas of Latin America, from Mexico to the Bahamas to Chile and Brazil. Although it is unusual today to observe African features among the populations of many Latin American nations, it should not be assumed that the genetic contribution was slight. In some parts of colonial Latin America, Africans outnumbered Europeans by a margin of 15 to 1. Almost one half of the populations of colonial Buenos Aires, Lima, and Mexico City reflected varying degrees of African ancestry.

European familiarity and experience with Africa occurred long before contact with the New World in 1492. Many Africans had been involuntarily settled in the Iberian peninsula prior to the conquest of the Western Hemisphere. In 1455, Pope Nicolas V gave the Portuguese the right to reduce to slavery the inhabitants of the southern coast of Africa who resisted the introduction of Christianity, thus in theory becoming the enemies of Christ. As a consequence, the Iberians began a modest slave trade on the western coast of Africa. The Portuguese set up factories, or trading posts, to deal with local middlemen and tribal chiefs. Africans contributed to the diversity of Iberian cities such as Seville and Lisbon, which were already inhabited by Jews, Arabs, and Christians. Small communities of Afro-Iberians thus emerged.

The slave market in Seville, while still relatively small, became one of the most active in Europe. Many called the city the "New Babylon." Northern and sub-Saharan Africans comprised more than 50 percent of the inhabitants of several of Seville's neighborhoods. The African populations became so socially and politically important that in 1475 the Crown appointed Juan de Valladolid, its royal servant and mayoral, to represent Seville's Afro-Iberian community. Churches and charities catered to its spiritual and material needs.

African slavery met a steady but limited demand in Europe. Neither Spain nor Portugal could absorb profitably a large number of slaves into its peninsular economy. European-African relations thus did not revolve around the institution of slavery. Indeed, the Portuguese recognized the independent sovereign existence of many African rulers and sought to establish political and cultural alliances with them. The institution of slavery, although long established both in Europe and Africa, continued to occupy a relatively minor position in both regions.

At the same time, the flora, the fauna, and the many complex societies of sub-Saharan, or black, Africa fascinated European explorers. Characterized by distinct ethnic groupings with varying religions, customs, and practices, West Africa's inhabitants included the Ashanti, the Yoruba, the Ibo, and the Dahomey, all of whom subsequently affected culture in the Western Hemisphere. Tribes from the Muslim area of North Africa, such as the Hausa, the Amalinke, and the Mandingo, in addition to tribes from the central Congo region, such as the Bantu, also influenced culture in the New World.[1]

The role of Africans in the New World varied both in time and place. The initial period of conquest relied upon Africans residing on the peninsula to supplement the limited number of Europeans in their effort to reduce the native population of the New World to the altered economic and political order. Indigenous groups recognized them as part of the conquering party. Miguel León Portilla, the prominent Mexican historian, reported that Aztecs referred to the Afro-Iberians who arrived with the Spaniards in Mexico as "soiled gods."[2] The Spanish respected and rewarded their contribution. Thus, Juan Valiente, a fugitive slave who had fought alongside the conquistadors in Chile, received an encomienda in the 1550s for his bravery. Other men of African ancestry, such as Juan Beltrán and Juan Fernández, also took part in the conquest of Chile.

Juan Garrido, known simply as "Handsome John," participated in the conquest of Mexico. Both Manuel Orozco y Berra and Bernal Díaz del Castillo noted his arrival with the conquistadors.[3] Garrido, who lived in Castile and considered himself a devout Christian, went to Santo Domingo. After participating in several exploratory trips to other islands, he traveled to New Spain with one of the first groups of conquistadors. While he did not receive the same rewards or honors as those of other Spanish conquistadors, he nevertheless, in 1525, became a respected *vecino* (citizen). In Chapter 1, Peter Gerhard examines Juan Garrido's life in Mexico and provides an assessment of the extent of African participation in the conquest and development of Latin America.

Following the conquest, the new overlords began the task of constructing colonial economies and societies. At the same time, cultural disruption, exploitation of the indigenous populations, and epidemic diseases caused a drastic decline in the native American populations, resulting in a severe shortage of labor and retarding the rate of European development and exploitation of the newly conquered territories. In some areas, such as Brazil, it became evident that the native populations could not be transformed into efficient laborers to meet the needs of the Portuguese-controlled economy. Consequently, Europeans turned to African slavery, in some areas as a supplement to scarce indigenous labor and in other areas as the main source of workers. Henceforth, European-African relations centered on slavery and the slave trade, a reality that endured for over three hundred years.

The institution of slavery adapted to the needs of the particular region, the demographic reality, and the nature of the work being performed. A variety of tasks, from pearl fishing, mining, and carpentry to sharecropping and domestic chores, depended on African labor. Slavery in Mexico, Argentina, and Chile differed substantially from the plantation economies of the Caribbean and Brazil. Urban slave labor also differed from plantation life, which had its own set of laws. In both urban and rural areas, it is important to be aware of the distinction between laws and actual practices. Enforcement of the laws of manumission and marriage as well as the general treatment of slaves depended on regional and local considerations rather than on abstract laws or theoretical codes of conduct. Verena Martínez Alier, author of several works that focus on slavery in Cuba, has pointed out, for example, that although there were rigid laws that prohibited interracial marriage, widespread cohabitation and other sexual arrangements occurred.[4]

Slaves were not passive victims of the system. They struggled to improve their well-being in personal ways, including sexual alliances and the establishment of ties of loyalty that enabled them to mitigate the impersonal cruelty of slavery. The African's survival depended on his or her ability to resist or manipulate, collectively and individually, a common institutional structure. Many slaves resisted their European oppressors through suicide, escape, sabotage, and the defiance of the laws of social conduct and religion. Others sought to preserve their own culture while accommodating themselves to the new social and cultural order. Chapter 2 gives an inside view of slavery in the words of Estéban Montejo, who recounts life on a Cuban plantation. Montejo comments on the racial complexity of Cuban slave society as well as on ethnic distinctions among the main African groups on the island.

The strength of African culture, despite the oppressive impact of slavery, is demonstrated by the re-creation of African societies in the areas of the New World that remained beyond the control of the Europeans. The most famous Afro-Creole settlement was the Republic of Palmares (1630–1682), established by runaway slaves in a remote region of Portuguese America. At least twenty thousand people lived within its boundaries, governed by West African customs (particularly Bantu) and cultural elements drawn from the Portuguese slave society from which they had fled. Other Afro-Creole settlements ranged from the small encampment of runaways to the *palenques* in Spanish America, the *quilombos* in Portuguese America, and the maroons in Jamaica and Guyana. A lesser known example of adaptation, not only to an independent existence but also to a hostile environment, was the re-creation of African societies on the coast of Ecuador. In Chapter 5, Norman E. Whitten, Jr., explores the communities created by Afro-Creoles on the frontier region of the South American Pacific lowlands. Whitten has written one of the few studies on the Afro-Ecuadorian communities on the Pacific coast, providing an important contribution to the literature on the frontier. His research underscores the fact that Africans successfully struggled not only against a dominant culture but also, in the case of the frontier, against the harsh environment in which they forged a civilized existence.

Miscegenation, or the commingling of the races, inevitably accompanied the development of the New World. Contact among Europeans, aborigines, and Africans created a mixed people—Afro-Creoles—and facilitated a distinct New World culture through *mestizaje*, or the combining of elements of distinct cultures. Extensive miscegenation between the native populations and Africans in some regions forced the Spanish to create a legal category for them: the *zambos*. The Portuguese called them *cafuzos*. In colonial Mexico the Spanish felt so threatened by intermarriage between natives and Africans that they declared it illegal.

Rebecca B. Bateman, in Chapter 3, examines the identity of two communities that share African and aboriginal roots in the Americas. Honduras and Belize are home to the majority of the Black Carib, exiles from St. Vincent commonly called by their Carib name, *Garífuna*. The Black Seminole, originally from Florida, share many customs and patterns of migration with the *Garífuna*.

Portuguese and Spanish authorities often promoted miscegenation as a population policy in underpopulated regions. This policy stressed the importance of assimilating the African into the broader mestizo, or racially mixed, society. As a result, a psychologically important caste system emerged, based on color, in which blacks occupied the lowest rung and which collided with a developing class system based on economic considerations. As a result, miscegenation engendered a "flexibility" in which race as well as an individual's socioeconomic position determined social status.

Most Latin American societies had become decidedly mestizo or mulatto by the end of the nineteenth century. Mestizos formed the majority in areas with high concentrations of indigenous communities, such as the Andes, Central America, and Mexico. In regions with small native populations, including newly formed Spanish cities, mulattoes became a dominant force. In these regions many mulattoes and mestizos achieved middle-class status and served as a buffer between the lower oppressed classes of blacks and natives and those who identified themselves as upper-class whites, many of whom were mestizos or mulattoes. However, class could not be strictly defined along racial lines. Dark mulattoes, *morenos*, and *pardos* and people of a wide hue of colors crossed class and social boundaries.[5]

Demographic data for the nineteenth century attest to the importance of miscegenation and the proliferation of the mixed population. Their contribution to major Latin American institutions such as the military needs to be examined. In cities such as Buenos Aires, Caracas, and Lima, mulattoes constituted a high percentage of those men who enlisted into the military, one of the few institutions that afforded Afro-Creoles some mobility within the broader society. Afro-Creoles played a significant role in the national struggles for independence throughout the nineteenth century. They fought valiantly on behalf of their emerging nations, side by side with their Creole counterparts. George Reid Andrews, in Chapter 4, investigates the participation of Afro-Creoles in Argentina's military service. Mulatto support, in particular, was sought enthusiastically by government officials.

Ideological leanings and political agendas influenced Latin American writers' and historians' views on miscegenation. In the nineteenth century, liberal elites preferred to focus on development issues rather than on race relations or racial origins. Most did not question the premise of inferior and superior races but hoped that miscegenation would eliminate the issue. They opposed slavery for economic reasons and believed that European immigration would promote progress and alleviate racial problems. The Brazilian notion of *branqueamento*, the whitening process, and becoming more European appeared to be the way to overcome the negative legacy of slavery. Thus, liberals such as Joaquim Nabuco advocated an end to slavery in Brazil because, among other factors, it repelled potential European immigration. Moreover, without slavery, Nabuco believed that his country could have been another Canada or Australia. Nabuco's arguments are reflected in the writings of a wide range of Latin American commentators, who ignored the contribution of the native American and the African to the building of their societies. Their desire to modernize and attract investment reinforced the prejudice toward the nonwhite sectors of the region.

In the 1920s nationalist writers recognized the contribution of previously ignored racial sectors to the formation of national identity. Latin Americans began to project positive racial images, celebrating the *mestizaje* of native, European, and African traits. In this era the Mexican José Vasconcelos noted that miscegenation had created what he called a "cosmic race."[6] Similar theories arose in the 1920s and 1930s throughout Latin America. Writers such as the Brazilian Gilberto Freyre and the Cuban Elías Entralgo wrote about miscegenation between Europeans and Africans in an approving manner. These views, in part, reflected the twentieth-century nationalists' attempt to see their Latin American identity and development in positive terms.[7]

Despite their lack of political and economic power, Afro-Creoles nonetheless have influenced many aspects of regional and local society. While music and food are the most obvious examples to the casual observer, Afro-Creoles have exerted a strong force on the social values and attitudes often conveyed through religious beliefs and practices. The Cuban Fernando Ortiz was one of the first Latin Americans to explain African transculturation, or the transfer of cultural values and rituals from Africa to the New World. Yoruba slaves from Angola brought with them to Brazil a philosophy and concept of the cosmos that provided the religious basis of *shangó*, *umbanda*, and *candomblé*.

In Africa the Yoruba people used anthropomorphic images to interpret and organize their world, a practice continued in the Americas and facilitated by Catholicism's organization of the saints in a pantheon similar to that in the Yoruba religion. While forced to acknowledge European saints and follow the Roman Catholic liturgical calendar, they associated African deities with Catholic saints. Santería, derived from Yoruba practices, provides another example of religious flexibility that preserved core beliefs while accommodating Catholic practices. Different Santería deities can be associated with various Catholic saints in the Caribbean, depending on the region. Many Yoruba customs and expressions that no longer exist in Africa persist in Cuba; Cuban Santería employs eighteenth-century Yoruba terms and prayers, for example.

Afro-Creole religions constitute powerful sources of inner strength, enabling believers to reaffirm their African identity. Priests and priestesses play an important role in Afro-Creole society, as religion and spiritual notions touch every aspect of daily life. The Dahomey, like the Yoruba, believed in a supreme god who governed a divine pantheon. Each divinity allowed men and women to serve as consorts, thereby providing believers with an active spiritual life in close association with powerful deities. Dahomey religious philosophy is clearly seen in voodoo. In the Fon language of Dahomey and Togo, vodun refers to a spirit or deity; and while the uninformed associate vodun or voodoo with sorcery and witchcraft, voodoo is a sophisticated, complex, and thriving religion.

Scholars frequently study the African aspect of Latin American religions in the context of syncretism—the fusion of two religions or faiths in the creation of a new religion—with the dominant European religion, Catholicism. In many cases, however, what is erroneously called syncretism is simply a loose association of Catholic saints with African deities. Many Latin Americans, for example, associate Yemanja, the Yoruba goddess of the sea, with Our Lady of Glory, Our Lady of Conception, or Our Lady of Carmen, depending on the region. Nonetheless, Yemanja retains all of the human characteristics afforded to her by the Yoruba and little or none of the European traits of the Virgin Mary. Luc de Heusch (Chapter 6) investigates African religious practices, concluding that Catholicism has very little influence in voodoo. His study of Haitian voodoo suggests the need for a reevaluation of the syncretic process.

Music also has provided an important channel for the cultural and social values essential to the survival of a sense of community. For Afro-Creoles, music reestablished and recreated the ancestral bond with Africa. It provided, as did religion, a mechanism by which people of African descent could reaffirm and celebrate their identity. Africa is the home of a wealth of musical instruments—xylophones, flutes, harps, bells, horns, and drums—which produce complex musical sounds. Drumming, in particular, is a highly sophisticated activity in Africa; almost every ethnic group has its own type of drum, and different drums are used for different purposes. Some are sacred and used only in religious ceremonies, while others accompany various instruments in rhythmic ensembles. Africans brought to the Americas their unique blend of rhythms and musical practices, which they adapted to the new environment.

The musical experience, like other social experiences, reflects a distinct pattern of interaction. African music entered Latin American society at the lowest social levels and, therefore, was not accepted by the elites in its pure form. However, musicians adjusted to make it palatable to the upper classes. In the case of the Argentine tango, the Brazilian samba, or the Dominican merengue, the musical form was appropriated by mainstream society and celebrated as a national symbol.

Even though African rhythms have influenced all aspects of popular Latin American music, the contemporary term "black music," or, alternatively, "Afro-Latin music," refers to those forms in which the drumming is dominant. Peter Wade (Chapter 7) studies the Afro-Colombian music from the Caribbean coast of Colombia. Wade discusses the connotations of "black music," arguing that the term is misleading because Africans have influenced many aspects of "Latin music." Simultaneously, he demonstrates the importance of Afro-Colombian music as an artistic and a social experience. Many Colombians regard black music as sensual and exotic, yet for Afro-Colombians on the Caribbean coast this music reaffirms their identity in a country that has, in the past, refused to recognize them in official census reports. West Indian migration to Central and South America in the nineteenth and twentieth centuries has increased Afro-Creole cultural influences within the wider Caribbean basin. Panama is now the creative center for Jamaican-born reggae music in Spanish.[8]

Although Africans were cocreators of a new culture, they had come to the Americas as workers. After the abolition of slavery, Afro-Creole labor never ceased to have important economic consequences for the region. A competitive social order developed, but this did not ensure Afro-Creole participation in the modernization, given the debasing effects of slavery, pauperism, and isolation. The growing pool of unemployed workers provided a cheap labor supply and drove down real wages, and the rapid expansion and industrialization that began at the turn of the century were assured at a low cost.

Foreign investment in Latin America increased with the construction of railroads and utilities and the purchase of land by multinational agricultural corporations such as the United Fruit Company. Demographics within the region also began to shift as workers migrated to centers of industrialization or to the large multinational plantations across national barriers. International investors looked for transportation routes that would facilitate exchange throughout the region. Consequently, the most miraculous and economically important project, the Panama Canal, was under way.

The Panama Canal provided a new commercial passage through the Americas. Construction did not begin until the United States had arranged the independence of Panama from Colombia. The 1903 Panama Canal Treaty, often referred to as the Isthmian Canal Convention, gave the United States permission to construct the canal and rights to govern the Canal Zone as if it were its territory. Because of the magnitude and urgency of the project, a massive number of workers would be needed in a relatively short time. The United States turned to the West Indies to find the ideal workers: English-speakers accustomed to the temperate climate who could be trained easily and who could be relocated cheaply. Thus began a migratory pattern that would change demographics on the isthmus.

West Indian migration to Central and South America has increased cultural connections within the wider Caribbean basin. Well-known Afro-Creoles, such as the Costa Rican writer Quincy Duncan and Jamaican-born Marcus Garvey, have West Indian roots. Garvey, like many West Indians, traveled to the isthmus to work on the expanding banana plantations. Just as European migration changed the face of countries such as Uruguay and Argentina by the early twentieth century, so too did West Indian migration change Central America. Today, the Caribbean coast of Central America shows marked Afro-Creole influences. The West Indian population at first settled in the Canal Zone areas such as Colon City, but by the 1930s this migration had changed the demographics of Panama City. Michael Conniff (Chapter 8) examines the political negotiations between Panamanian officials, the United States, and the islands in the West Indies and the complex social and economic system that developed during the period of the construction of the canal.

In Puerto Rico, the Afro-Puerto Rican socialist José Luis González traces the formation of the nation by emphasizing the contribution of the Afro-Creoles and their relationship to subsequent immigrants to the island (Chapter 9). Africans formed the base of Puerto Rican nationhood, according to González, because they developed a unique sense of patriotism and attachment to the island due to their condition of bondage. González provides a provocative point of departure for a discussion on the nature of race relations and national identity in Latin America.

Twentieth-century cultural rejuvenation and racial and ethnic pride represent another dimension of modern race relations. The writings of intellectuals such as the Cuban Nicolás Guillén, the Martinican Aimé Césaire, and the Brazilian Abdias do Nascimento have been instrumental in raising black consciousness. Cultural movements such as Negritude, Negrismo, and Rastafarianism have bound Afro-Creoles together. The period following World War I saw the rise of popular Afro-Creole social movements that challenged the status quo. Their emergence was due to a combination of international and national factors. Since then, black consciousness movements have emerged in virtually every region of the Americas. Chapter 10 provides examples from the French-speaking Caribbean, the English-speaking Caribbean, and Brazil.

One of the most celebrated exponents of Negritude in the Francophone Caribbean is the poet and politician from Martinique, Aimé Césaire. As cofounder of the Negritude movement, he provides a poignant indictment of European colonization. In the English-speaking Caribbean the philosophy of the Jamaican-born Marcus Garvey became very influential. As a precursor to the Negritude movement, Garvey began the Universal Negro Improvement Association in 1922. Previously, he had worked on a banana plantation owned by the United Fruit Company on the Caribbean coast of Costa Rica, where he founded the newspaper *La Nacionale*. From Costa Rica he traveled to Panama, Guatemala, Nicaragua, and several of the South American republics before settling in Harlem. Garvey emphasized the solidarity of Afro-Creoles throughout the Americas, a theme that other social and cultural movements from the 1930s to today continue to stress.

The third selection in Chapter 10 also describes the grass-roots religious and cultural movement that Garvey inspired. The Rastafarians followed Garvey when he said, "Look to Africa where our new king will be crowned." In 1930, Ras Tafari was crowned King Haile Selassie of Ethiopia. Rastafarians claim the divinity of Haile Selassie and advocate a spiritual return to Africa. Leonard Barrett discusses their history, customs, and beliefs.

The Afro-Brazilian activist Abdias do Nascimento followed in the tradition of Garvey and Césaire. Nascimento was one of the founders of the Teatro Experimental do Negro (T.E.N.), which became the major consciousness-raising organization of the 1940s and 1950s. Although the agenda and programs of T.E.N. emerged out of the uniquely Brazilian milieu, Nascimento saw a connection with other types of cultural activity throughout the diaspora. His essay, the fourth within Chapter 10, underscores the relationship among all Afro-Creole consciousness movements in the hemisphere.

Chapter 11 examines the participation of Afro-Brazilian women in civil rights and political movements in the twentieth century. Not always supported by their male counterparts, women forged their own agenda within and outside of organized movements. The participation of artists, activists, and popular-class women in the transformation of the sociopolitical process in Brazil remains only partially explored.

As a result of the increased participation of Afro-Creole men and women in social, cultural, and political activity, governments in Latin America have begun to understand what the United States has long appreciated: Afro-Creoles are a powerful interest group. Nevertheless, in all Latin American societies, people of darker pigmentation occupy the lowest rung of the economic ladder and are often ignored by official government statistics, including national census reports. Consequently, the actual size of the Afro-Creole population in the hemisphere and its influence are misrepresented. Jack W. Hopkins's statistics on Latin America's population represent one of the more accurate compilations for the 1980s (Table 1).

Rodolfo Monge Oviedo's statistics on the Afro-Creole populations in Latin America underscore the difficulty in obtaining reliable figures

(Table 2). Ethnic or racial classification may change depending on the perceptions of the person collecting the data. Moreover, individual nations, as well as regions within countries, may use different categories to classify people of African descent. Indeed, many nations do not include ethnicity or race in their census reports. All of these factors make it

Table 1. The Nations, Population, and Social Composition of Latin America, 1983[a]

Nation	Population (000)	Percentage of Total[b]	Race and Ethnic Group (%)				
			Amerind	Mixed	White	Black	Other
Argentina	28,174	7.9		15	85		
Antigua/ Barbuda	77	<1			1	99	
Bahamas	215	<1			10	80	10
Barbados	251	<1			4	80	17
Belize	149	<1	19	33	3	11	35
Bolivia	5,600	1.6	55	35	6		4
Brazil	120,507	33.8	2	30	60	8	
Chile	11,292	3.1	7	62	31		
Colombia	26,425	7.4	4	58	20	18	
Costa Rica	2,340	<1	<1	90	6	2	<1
Cuba	9,865	2.7			37	11	52[c]
Dominica	74	<1	<1			99	
Dominican Republic	5,592	1.5		73	16	11	
Ecuador	8,605	2.4	25	55	10	10	
El Salvador	5,087	1.4	4	95	1		
Grenada	110	<1			1	99	
Guatemala	7,477	2.1	55	45			
Guyana	796	<1	4		1	43	52[d]
Haiti	5,104	1.4		1		99	
Honduras	3,818	1.1	2	95	1	1	1
Jamaica	2,194	<1			1	76	23[e]
Mexico	71,215	20.0	29	55	16		
Nicaragua	2,777	<1	5	69	17	9	
Panama	1,877	<1	7	70	8	14	1
Paraguay	3,057	<1	4	95	1		
Peru	17,031	4.7	35	47	15	1	2
Puerto Rico*	3,251	<1		73	2	25	
Saint Lucia	119	<1			1	90	9
Saint Vincent	115	<1	2	1	4	86	6
Suriname	356	<1	3	31	1	11[f]	65[g]

Trinidad/							
Tobago	1,203	<1		14	1	43	42[h]
Uruguay	2,929	<1		5	90	5	
Venezuela	16,500	4.6	2	67	21	10	
Averages or							
Totals	364,182	100[i]	10.7	41.4	35.5	6.2	2.4

Source: *Latin America: Perspectives on a Region*, ed. Jack W. Hopkins (New York: Holmes & Meier, Inc., 1987), 40. ©1987 by Holmes & Meier, Inc. Reprinted by permission of the publisher. [Editor's note: Due to rounding off, race and ethnic group figures may total more or less than 100 percent.]

[a]Estimates based on *World Bank World Development Report, 1983* and Global Studies, *Latin America, 1983.*

[b]Percentage of total Latin American population: <1 is less than one percent of total Latin American population.

[c]Includes mulattos (51%), Chinese (1%).

[d]Includes East Indians (51%), Chinese (1%).

[e]Includes Chinese, East Indians.

[f]Maroons (11%).

[g]East Indians (38%), Indonesians (16%).

[h]East Indians.

[i]Total rounded off.

*U.S. associated state.

Table 2. Statistics on the Afro-Creole Populations of Latin America, 1992

Country	Population (thousands)		Percent of total	
	Min.	Max.	Min.	Max.
Brazil	9,477	53,097	5.9	33.0
United States	29,986	29,986	12.1	12.1
Colombia	4,886	7,329	14.0	21.0
Haiti	6,500	6,900	94.0	100.0
Cuba	3,559	6,510	33.9	62.0
Dominican Republic	847	6,468	11.0	84.0
Jamaica	1,976	2,376	76.0	91.4
Peru	1,356	2,192	6.0	9.7
Venezuela	1,935	2,150	9.0	10.0
Panama	35	1,837	14.0	73.5
Ecuador	573	1,147	5.0	10.0
Nicaragua	387	559	9.0	13.0
Trinidad & Tobago	480	516	40.0	43.0
Mexico	474	474	0.5	0.5
Guyana	222	321	29.4	42.6

Guadaloupe	292	292	87.0	87.0
Honduras	112	280	2.0	5.0
Canada	260	260	1.0	1.0
Barbados	205	245	80.0	95.8
Bahamas	194	223	72.0	85.0
Bolivia	158	158	2.0	2.0
Paraguay	156	156	3.5	3.5
Suriname	146	151	39.8	41.0
St. Lucia	121	121	90.3	90.3
Belize	92	112	46.9	57.0
St. Vincent & Grenadines	94	105	84.5	95.0
Antigua & Barbuda	85	85	97.9	97.9
Grenada	72	81	75.0	84.0
Costa Rica	66	66	2.0	2.0
French Guiana	37	58	42.4	66.0
Bermuda	38	39	61.0	61.3
Uruguay	38	38	1.2	1.2
Guatemala	*	*	*	*
Chile	*	*	*	*
El Salvador	**	**	**	**
Argentina	zero	**	zero	**
Total	64,859	124,332	9.0	17.2

Source: Rodolfo Monge Oviedo, "Are We or Aren't We?" *NACLA Report on the Americas* 25, no. 4 (February 1992): 19. © 1975 by the North American Congress on Latin America. Reprinted by permission of the publisher.
*The presence of blacks is acknowledged but no figures are given.
**No figures are available.

difficult to determine the exact number of Afro-Creoles in Latin America. By checking information from the *Britannica Yearbook* against other published sources, Monge Oviedo has provided two figures for Afro-Creoles from thirty-six countries: a maximum and a minimum. Based on data for 1992, the minimum (*Min.*) represents the smallest number recorded for Afro-Creoles in the indicated countries, while the maximum (*Max.*) denotes the largest.

The complexity of the African dimension is also difficult to grasp. Few works offer scholars and students of Latin America a comprehensive framework in which to study and analyze the legacy of Africans and Afro-Creoles to the region's history. Franklin Knight was one of the first scholars in the United States to examine the African experience in broad socio-economic terms.[9] Richard Jackson's work on the contribution of people of African descent to Latin American literature is also valuable.[10] Recent research in anthropology, ethnohistory, and social history have unveiled new ways of approaching old documents that allow us to understand more fully the African presence in the region. Nevertheless, slavery and its bitter aftermath remain the focus of the majority of works that examine the African experience in Latin America. Scholars and students continue to debate differing interpretations of the institution and its lingering influence. Following in the footsteps of two of the forerunners of research on slavery and race relations—Frank Tannenbaum and Stanley Elkins[11] —historians, ethnographers, and sociologists have studied the similarities and differences between slavery in the United States and that in Latin America. Tannenbaum maintained that slavery in Latin America was more benign than it was in the United States because, in the former, the slave was recognized as a human being. Elkins agreed, arguing that slavery in the United States reflected a rampant capitalism, while in Latin America the presence of the Church and laws of manumission countered the tendency to reduce slaves to the status of a commodity. Manuel Moreno Fraginals later recognized the presence of many other factors in determining the nature of slavery but nevertheless argued that it was primarily an economic institution. Consequently, Latin Americans eventually abolished slavery because of the incompatibility of slave labor and technology.[12]

Florestan Fernandes is among the few scholars who have looked at the relationship between race and economic opportunity in Latin America. He examined the plight of blacks in the urban areas of São Paulo during the period of rapid modernization between World War I and World War II. As the new competitive economic order emerged, it did not eradicate to any significant extent the traditional social system. Participation in the modernization process required material and psychological skills as well as technological elements that neither the black nor the mulatto possessed, given their debasement by slavery, pauperism, and isolation.[13]

Despite their merits, such comparisons overlook the fact that the African experience is not a static one that can be defined easily by economic, political, or social paradigms. The dynamic African presence touched all aspects of society, as it continues to do today. Afro-Creoles, as active participants in the development of societies in the Americas, work within the social system yet also struggle to modify their negative circumstances and to safeguard their well-being.

Brazil and the countries that make up the Caribbean basin, including the islands and the littoral countries of South America from Colombia to the Guianas, show a different pattern of development from other regions. Based on a plantation economy and with a relatively small indigenous population, this region relied heavily on slave labor as did the southern United States. While most countries had abolished slavery by 1860, Cuba and Brazil held on to the institution until the late 1880s. Because of the duration of the system and the number of slaves introduced—exceeding the number that arrived in the United States—the African presence is most strongly felt in these two countries. It is also dominant in the English- and French-speaking Caribbean, where the ratio of African to European was very high.

In recognition of their historical and social relationship, both Brazil and Cuba have attempted to forge diplomatic, cultural, and political ties with nations in Africa. Cuba's willingness to become actively involved in Africa during the Cold War stemmed, in part, from this perceived rela- tionship. Armando Entralgo and David González López (Chapter 12) give an overview of the Cuban policy in Africa from 1960 to 1990.

Africa has played an essential part in the creation of Latin American societies. Nevertheless, much remains to be done if we are to understand fully that contribution. The purpose of this volume is to help students of Africa and Afro-Creole culture and history to move away from a static view of the African contribution to Latin America and to attempt to reconstruct the past and continuing impact of the diaspora with all its complexities.

Notes

1. Philip D. Curtin, in *Atlantic Slave Trade: A Census* (Madison: University of Wisconsin Press, 1969), identified the eight major regions in West Africa: Gambia and Senegal; Sierra Leone; the Ivory Coast and Liberia; the Gold Coast— modern-day Ghana; Togo and Dahomey; the Bight of Biafra; Angola; and South- ern Africa.

2. Miguel León Portilla, *Broken Spears: The Aztec Account of the Conquest of Mexico* (Boston: Beacon Press, 1992), 34.

3. Francisco de Icaza, ed., *Diccionario autobiográfico de conquistadores y pobladores de Nueva España* (Madrid, 1923), 1: entry no. 169. See Hubert Howe Bancroft, *History of Mexico*, 6 vols. (San Francisco, 1883–1886), 2:423n. Some scholars report that Cortés's expedition included four hundred Spaniards and three hundred blacks. In *La corona española y los foráneos en los pueblos de indios de América* (Stockholm, 1970), Magnus Mörner argues that many more blacks participated.

4. Verena Martínez Alier, *Marriage, Class, and Colour in Nineteenth-Century Cuba: A Study of Racial Attitudes and Sexual Values in a Slave Society* (Ann Arbor: University of Michigan Press, 1989), 12.

5. The origin of the mulatto class dates back to the colonial years, and mulat- toes were often referred to as free people of color. Many slaves who bought their freedom or who gained it through manumission formed part of this class. Mar- riage and concubinage offered other forms through which one's child could as- cend the socioeconomic ladder.

6. José Vasconcelos, *La raza cósmica: Misión de la raza Ibero-Americana* (México: Aguilar S.A. de Ediciones, 1961).

7. See Gilberto Freyre's Brazilian classic *The Masters and the Slaves* (1933) (reprinted ed., 1986 [Berkeley: University of California Press]), in which he developed his theory of Lusotropicalism, crediting Portugal's racial tolerance as critical to its colonization efforts. Elías Entralgo proposed his ideas about *mestizaje* and miscegenation in *La liberación étnica cubana* (Havana, 1953).

8. West Indies is the general term applied to the islands of the Caribbean basin because Columbus was intent on sailing west to find the "Indies of the East." Used without political implications, the term is synonymous with the Caribbean or Antilles. The term is especially used by the English-speaking Caribbean.

9. Franklin Knight, *The African Dimension of Latin America* (New York: Macmillan, 1974).

10. Richard Jackson, *Black Literature and Humanism in Latin America* (Athens: University of Georgia Press, 1988).

11. Frank Tannenbaum, *Slave and Citizen: The Negro in the Americas* (New York: Vintage Books, 1946), 112; and Stanley Elkins, *Slavery: A Problem in American Institutional and Intellectual Life* (Chicago: University of Chicago Press, 1959).

12. Manuel Moreno Fraginals, *El ingenio* (Havana: Editorial de las Ciencias Sociales, 1978), 30–32.

13. Florestan Fernandes, *The Negro in Brazilian Society*, trans. Jacqueline D. Skiles (New York: Columbia University Press, 1969), 132–34.

1

A Black Conquistador in Mexico

Peter Gerhard

*The Iberian experience in America passed through two stages: explora-
tion and conquest in the 50 years after Columbus's voyage; and colonization over the next 250 years, in which Spaniards and Portuguese began
the transfer of their culture and institutions to the New World. This chapter looks at the role of Africans during the era of exploration. From the
beginning the encounter brought together the peoples of three worlds—
Europe, Africa, and America. The earliest Spanish expeditions included
freed blacks from the vibrant black communities in the Iberian peninsula,
especially from Seville, the "New Babylon," and prominent conquistadors traveled with retinues that included numerous black slaves. Although
their presence during the era is evident, little is known about these individuals of African descent.*

Peter Gerhard, an independent scholar well known for A Guide to
the Historical Geography of New Spain *(1972), pieced together the following sketch of Juan Garrido, one of the conquistadors who accompanied Hernán Cortés in the conquest of Mexico. Gerhard reported that
Garrido was one of a substantial number of Africans in New Spain during these years. Cortés's expedition to Baja California, for example, re-
portedly consisted of four hundred Spaniards and three hundred blacks.
Gerhard's sketch of Garrido's career offers a direction for further research on African participation in the first fifty years after the encounter
between these different worlds. Above all, his essay suggests the outlines
of race relations before the demands for plantation slave labor dominated Spanish-African interaction.*

While the role played by the people of equatorial Africa in the
colonization of Latin America is relatively well known, it is for
the most part an impersonal history that emerges from the contemporary

From *Hispanic American Historical Review* 58, no. 3 (August 1978): 451–
59. © 1978 by Duke University Press. Reprinted by permission of Duke University Press.

documents: the establishment of a Negro slave trade as a result of the demand for labor to replace a devastated native population; the employment of these black slaves in the more arduous tasks throughout the colonies; and, in most areas, their gradual assimilation through miscegenation with natives (and to a far lesser extent with Europeans). Information about individual blacks is usually confined to a brief statement of age, physical characteristics, and degree of acculturation at the moment of sale or the taking of estate inventories; less frequently, the place of origin of a slave is indicated. Only rarely do we hear about a Negro slave who achieved distinction in some way. Two examples that come to mind are Juan Valiente, the conquistador of Chile,[1] and Yanga, the famed maroon leader in Veracruz.[2]

Although most blacks who came to America in early years were slaves, records of the Casa de Contratación show that a good many black freedmen from Seville and elsewhere found passage on westward-bound ships.[3] Some of them settled in the Caribbean region, and others followed the tide of conquest to Mexico and Peru, identifying themselves no doubt as Catholic subjects of a Spanish king, with much the same privileges and ambitions as white Spaniards. "Benito el Negro" and "Juan el Negro" (the latter's real name seems to have been Juan de Villanueva) were encomenderos in the province of Pánuco and thus they should not have been slaves, but we cannot be sure of their origin.[4] Spaniards might call anyone with a very dark skin "negro," and indeed the fact that Villanueva was from Granada makes it seem likely that he was a morisco. On the other hand there is record of an African who apparently crossed the Atlantic as a freeman, participated in the siege of Tenochtitlán and, in subsequent conquests and explorations, tried his hand as an entrepreneur (with both Negro and Indian slaves of his own) in the early search for gold, and took his place as a citizen in the Spanish quarter of Mexico City. His name was Juan Garrido, and he was still alive in the late 1540s when he wrote or dictated a short résumé of his services to the Crown:

> Juan Garrido, black in color . . . says that he, of his own free will, became a Christian in Lisbon, [then] was in Castile for seven years, and crossed to Santo Domingo where he remained an equal length of time. From there he visited other islands, and then went to San Juan de Puerto Rico, where he spent much time, after which he came to New Spain. He was present at the taking of the city of Mexico and in other conquests, and later [went] to the island with the marquis. He was the first to plant and harvest wheat in this land, the source of all that there now is, and he brought many vegetable seeds to New Spain. He is married and has three children, and is very poor with nothing to maintain himself.[5]

The early chronology of this statement is vague, but working backward from the fall of Tenochtitlán (1521), one can assume that Garrido arrived in America about 1510. It is perhaps more than a coincidence that a Spaniard called Pedro Garrido landed in Santo Domingo with his family and entourage in 1510, and later accompanied Cortés to Mexico.[6] Slaves were often given the surnames of their masters, and while we do not know whether Juan Garrido was ever a slave it seems most probable that he was at least a protégé of a Spaniard at one time. However, this is pure conjecture, and we might also consider the possibility that the subject of this essay was named for his physical appearance (Juan Garrido can be roughly translated as "Handsome John"). In fact, the matter of how and when Garrido got to Mexico, and what part he played in the conquest, are something of a mystery. The *Diccionario Porrúa*, perhaps relying on an inconclusive passage in Bernal Díaz, says that he arrived with Juan Núñez Sedeño, who accompanied Cortés's 1519 expedition in his own ship with a large retinue that included "un negro"; Manuel Orozco y Berra has him crossing a year later with the army of Pánfilo de Narváez.[7] Magnus Mörner, after claiming that "many" hispanicized and Spanish-speaking blacks took part in the conquest, leaves us without any details,[8] nor does one find any mention of Garrido by name in the various contemporary accounts of the siege and surrender of Tenochtitlán (indeed the same might be said of many Spaniards who were there). His name appears for the first time in the proceedings of Mexico City's cabildo on March 8, 1524, when that body granted a piece of land for the establishment of a smithy on the Tacuba causeway "going out of this city, just past the chapel [*hermita*] of Juan Garrido."[9] Lucas Alamán identifies this as the church subsequently rebuilt and dedicated to San Hipólito de los Mártires, occupying the site where so many of Cortés's men died as they fled from Tenochtitlán on the Noche Triste.[10] It may have been the brief statement in Alamán that gave rise to a somewhat embellished and much-repeated version, of which the following is an example:

> *San Hipólito* . . . Historically and sentimentally this is one of the most interesting churches in the city. In front of the spot where it now stands there existed in the year 1520 the second line of defenses on the causeway (now the street occupied by the horse railway to Tacuba) that connected the Aztec city with the main-land westward. At this point was the greatest slaughter of the Spaniards during the retreat of the memorable Noche Triste (July 1, 1520). After the final conquest of the city, one of the survivors of that dismal night, Juan Garrido, having freshly in mind its bloody horrors, built of adobe at this place a little commemorative chapel.[11]

Terry's guide [to Mexico], drawing on the story as told by Orozco y Berra, identifies Garrido as "one of the Conquistadores [who] undertook to recover the bodies of his slaughtered countrymen and to erect a chapel wherein they could be buried with religious rites."[12]

While his role in the Tenochtitlán episode remains obscure, Garrido took part in at least one of the expeditions sent out by Cortés after the conquest of the Triple Alliance to secure control and investigate the economic potential of outlying areas. According to a *relación geográfica* of 1580, "a Negro . . . who called himself Juan Garrido" accompanied Antonio de Caravajal and three other Spaniards to the hot country of Michoacán and the coast of Zacatula, most likely in 1523–1524. This little group was received hospitably by the Tarascans of Zirándaro, after which it proceeded across the Sierra Madre del Sur "on a deserted trail through a cold rugged area with lions and tigers and snakes and other animals."[13] Zirándaro belonged to the Tarascan empire which in 1522 had accepted Spanish rule practically without resistance, while the more truculent Indians of the coast had recently surrendered to the army of Gonzalo de Sandoval, which may explain how a small force could emerge unscathed from such an expedition.[14] In fact, Caravajal's mission was to introduce Christianity to the natives (although there was no priest in his party) and to make a careful census of the communities visited, noting the mineral wealth and the tribute-paying capacity of each, for the guidance of Cortés in the first distribution of encomiendas. We do not know whether Garrido stayed with Caravajal throughout the visitation of Michoacán, which lasted about a year; in any event, we find him once again in Mexico City early in August 1524.[15]

It must have been before he went off with the Caravajal party that Garrido became the first wheat farmer on the American continent. The importance to the expatriate Spaniards, both as a matter of taste and as a measure of social status, of having wheat bread rather than casava or maize tortillas, can hardly be overstressed.[16] According to the conquistador Andrés de Tapia, "after Mexico was taken, and while [Cortés] was in Coyoacán, they brought him a small amount of rice, and in it were three grains of wheat; he ordered a free Negro [*un negro horro*] to plant them."[17] The Negro referred to by Tapia is identified in a parallel account by the seventeenth-century chronicler Gil González Dávila as "Juan Garrido, a servant [*criado*] of Hernando Cortés."[18] Both sources agree that the tiny crop harvested by Garrido at this time was the first in New Spain, and that all wheat subsequently grown came from its seed.

The conquistador community moved from Coyoacán to the rebuilt Mexico City at the beginning of 1524. If, as we surmise, Garrido was still occupied in the reconnaissance of Michoacán when this move took place, it was perhaps a year or so earlier that the pious black conquistador built his hermitage, next to which he lived and had a garden plot or *huerta* (undoubtedly a *chinampa*) where he could continue his horticultural experiments.[19] We can be sure that foremost among such activities was the cultivation of grapevines and the manufacture of wine, a product not only greatly desired by the Spanish laity but also desperately needed by the clergy for the celebration of mass. Before long, Cortés ordered all encomenderos to have wheat and other useful European plants grown in their villages, and by late 1525, wheat and grapes cultivated by Indians in the vicinity of Mexico City were no longer a curiosity.[20]

Juan Garrido's position in the close-knit conquistador society of Mexico-Tenochtitlán in those early years can only be imagined, but surely he must have been considered a rarity because of his color. There were as yet relatively few free blacks in the colony (indeed as far as we know Garrido was the only Negro *vecino* in Mexico City in the 1520s), and the social complications of *mestizaje* had really not begun. At first, as we have seen, Garrido made his home outside the city limits or *traza* on a piece of land perhaps formed as the waters of the lake receded (a dry spell set in shortly after the conquest), adjacent to both the Tacuba causeway and the aqueduct bringing fresh water from Chapultepec. His may well have been the first of a great many *huertas* in the old lake bed west of the city acquired and developed by Spaniards beginning in the mid-1520s.[21] However, nearly all the conquistadors forming the original body of citizens (*vecinos*) had *solares* or house lots within the *traza*, and there is a suggestion of stigma in the fact that Garrido initially settled outside the Spanish quarter, and was not officially received as a *vecino* until February 10, 1525. At that time, he was assigned a house site within the *traza* on Calle de la Agua, although he retained his country property.[22] The move may have been merely a matter of convenience, after all, to make it easier for Garrido to carry out his duties as doorkeeper (*portero*) of the city's cabildo, a position that he seems to have held from 1524 to the end of 1526.[23] This was not a particularly lucrative post, the salary being a mere thirty gold pesos annually. However, for a few months Garrido was also made responsible for taking care of the Chapultepec aqueduct with a stipend of fifty pesos a year, and he may have acted simultaneously as town crier (*pregonero*), starting the still-honored tradition of "moonlighting."[24]

During the years 1526–1527, frequent changes in the Spanish power structure in Mexico brought about equally frequent reversals of personal fortune among the adherents and the enemies of Cortés, and thus it is quite conceivable that Juan Garrido lost his small sinecures as a result of this factional strife. Specifically, an unsuccessful effort on Cortés's part to "pack" the Mexico City cabildo at the beginning of 1527 coincided with the appointment of a new *portero-pregonero*.[25] Whatever the reason, Garrido decided to leave the city and seek his fortune in the gold fields, in the same region which he had visited with Caravajal years earlier. By the spring of 1528, he had acquired on credit a gang of slaves and mining equipment and was reported to be in the province of Zacatula, perhaps in the famous placers of the Motines area, the objective of many Spaniards and the grave of literally millions of Indians in those terrible years.[26] The gold rush was at its peak, but Garrido does not seem to have enjoyed much success as a miner. In October 1528, he was back in Mexico City and had still not paid a debt of twelve pesos, the value of "certain washing pans," when he incurred a new debt for some pigs that he had purchased.[27] The anti-Cortés faction was soon to be considerably reinforced by the president and judges of the first *audiencia*, and Garrido no doubt retired to his *chinampa* farm to await better times.

In 1530, Cortés returned to Mexico from Spain with a title (marquis), ample resources, and great ambition, but only a shadow of his former political power. New Spain was ruled by a hostile *audiencia*, Guatemala by the ungrateful Alvarado, and New Galicia by the marquis's greatest enemy, Nuño de Guzmán. Cortés, frustrated and bitter, sulked in his marquisate and surrounded himself with lawyers and malcontents. The king had wisely provided a remedy for this dangerous situation by giving him a commission to search the shores of the Pacific for new lands and riches.

By the early 1530s, the gold rush was almost finished, and while favored Spaniards in Mexico were living munificently on Indian tribute, and others were building fortunes in the newly discovered silver mines, there was a growing body of restless young men looking for adventure and profit. Many of them from 1532 to 1536 headed for the conquest of Peru, and indeed Cortés himself had prepared two ships to sail southward from Tehuantepec when he heard that another of his vessels had discovered an "island" in the north supposed to be rich in gold and pearls and the home of the legendary Amazons.[28] The island was in fact a peninsula, the southern tip of Lower California. Learning that Guzmán had seized the returning ship and its treasure, Cortés ordered his flotilla to the north and marched overland to join it, gathering recruits on the way.[29] By the time he reached Chametla, a port in Guzmán's territory opposite the newly discovered "island," the charismatic marquis was accompanied by a formidable retinue which apparently included Juan Garrido. A contemporary witness testified that Cortés's followers numbered four hundred Spaniards and three hundred Negroes;[30] most of the latter must have been slaves intended for work in the gold mines and oyster beds. Garrido was no doubt in a privileged category, and in fact it would seem that he had his own complement of Negro and Indian slaves at this time.[31]

The Lower California expedition was Cortés's last great venture and it was a disaster, an heroic undertaking carried out against impossible odds. There were far too many people and horses to be transported across the stormy gulf (the fleet had to make several trips to take them all), and once on that desolate shore they had to be fed with provisions brought from great distances. The nearest mainland was controlled by Guzmán, and in any event it produced little surplus as the native population on the whole west coast of Mexico was at this very time being decimated by a fearful epidemic. Thus, the settlers were dependent on what they could find locally (mostly fish) and supplies from the highlands of central Mexico, which had to be carried to the coast and shipped out of ports as far south as Huatulco.[32] Even the marquis's vast revenues were not enough to keep the colony going. The remarkable fact is that some Spaniards remained in the vicinity of La Paz, in a desert and surrounded by extraordinarily primitive Indians, for more than a year and perhaps two, from May 1535 to late 1536 or early 1537. Cortés himself, however, returned to Mexico via Acapulco in the spring of 1536, accompanied by a few California Indians and some of the colonists, including Juan Garrido, who was in Mexico City by July of that year.[33]

We know very little indeed about the further career of this unusual black man. How he made a living after his return from California, the details of his marriage, what role (if any) he played in the aborted black slave uprising of 1537 and its grisly aftermath, may some day come to light.[34] Twice in 1536, Garrido gave a power of attorney to the municipal *procurador de causas* in Mexico City in connection with some unspecified suit, perhaps a claim for unpaid back salaries as the cabildo doorkeeper which was finally settled in November 1538.[35] Garrido's *hoja de servicios* was part of a group of such documents prepared between 1547 and 1550, and since it bears the notation "es ya muerto," it would seem that he died sometime during those years.[36]

Notes

1. Peter Boyd-Bowman, "Negro Slaves in Early Colonial Mexico," *The Americas*, 26 (Oct. 1969), 150–151. Robert Brent Toplin, *Slavery and Race Relations in Latin America* (Westport, Conn., 1974), 16.

2. Gonzalo Aguirre Beltrán, *El señorío de Cuauhtochco—luchas agrarias en México durante el virreinato* (México, 1940).

3. Ruth Pike, "Sevillian Society in the Sixteenth Century: Slaves and Freedmen," *Hispanic American Historical Review*, 47 (Aug. 1967), 358.

4. *Papeles de Nueva España publicados de orden y con fondos del gobierno mexicano por Francisco del Paso y Troncoso, director en misión del Museo Nacional*, 7 vols. (Madrid, 1905–1906), I, nos. 566, 572–573. Francisco de Icaza, ed., *Diccionario autobiográfico de conquistadores y pobladores de Nueva España*, 2 vols. (Madrid, 1923), no. 1165.

5. Icaza, *Diccionario*, no. 169.

6. Peter Boyd-Bowman, *Indice geobiográfico de cuarenta mil pobladores españoles de América en el siglo XVI*, 2 vols. (Bogotá, 1964 and México, 1968), I, 15.

7. *Diccionario Porrúa de historia, biografía y geografía de México* (México, 1964), 357, 597. Bernal Díaz del Castillo, *Historia verdadera de la conquista de la Nueva España*, ed. by Joaquín Ramírez Cabañas, 2 vols. (México, 1960), I, 87, 92. Baltasar Dorantes de Carranza, *Sumaria relación de las cosas de la Nueva España con noticia individual de los descendientes legítimos de los conquistadores y primeros pobladores españoles* (México, 1902), 384. In an earlier version of his list of conquistadors, Orozco y Berra does not specify how Garrido reached Mexico: cf. *Diccionario universal de historia y de geografía*, 7 vols. (México, 1853–1855), II, 499.

8. Magnus Mörner, *La corona española y los foráneos en los pueblos de indios de América* (Stockholm, 1970), 94.

9. *Actas de cabildo de la ciudad de México* (hereafter cited as *AC*), Mar. 8, 1524 (since there are several published editions, I shall refer only to the date).

10. Lucas Alamán, *Disertaciones sobre la historia de la república mejicana desde la época de la conquista que los españoles hicieron a fines del siglo XV y principios del XVI de las islas y continente americano hasta la independencia*, 3 vols. (México, 1844–1849), II, 285–287. Cf. Francisco Cervantes de Salazar, *Crónica de la Nueva España* (Madrid, 1914), 494, where the chapel's builder is identified as Juan Tirado.

11. Thomas A. Janvier, *The Mexican Guide*, 4th ed. (New York, 1890), 206–207.

12. T. Philip Terry, *Terry's Mexico—Handbook for Travellers* (London, 1909), 335–337.

13. *Relaciones geográficas de la diócesis de Michoacán, 1579–1580*, 2 vols. (Guadalajara, 1958), II, 40. J. Benedict Warren, *La conquista de Michoacán, 1521–1530* (Morelia, 1977), 88.

14. Donald D. Brand et al., *Coalcomán and Motines del Oro: An Ex-distrito of Michoacán, Mexico* (The Hague, 1960), 56–58.

15. *AC*, Aug. 12, 1524. Warren, *La conquista de Michoacán*, 87–89.

16. Pierre Chaunu, *L'Amérique et les Amériques* ([Paris], 1964), 86.

17. Joaquín García Icazbalceta, ed., *Colección de documentos para la historia de México*, 2 vols. (México, 1858–1866), II, 592–593.

18. Gil González Dávila, *Teatro eclesiástico de la primitiva iglesia de las Indias occidentales, vidas de sus arzobispos, obispos, y cosas memorables de sus sedes*, 2 vols. (Madrid, 1649–1655), I, 8.

19. *AC*, Mar. 15 and Sept. 30, 1524; Aug. 11, 1525. Angel Palerm, *Obras hidráulicas prehispánicas en el sistema lacustre del valle de México* (México, 1973), 154–157. Cf. Manuel Toussaint, Federico Gómez de Orozco, and Justino Fernández, *Planos de la ciudad de México, siglos XVI y XVII* (México, 1938), 96–97.

20. Hernán Cortés, *Cartas y documentos*, ed. by Mario Hernández Sánchez-Barba (México, 1963), 349. García Icazbalceta, *Colección*, I, 488.

21. *AC*, passim.

22. *AC*, Feb. 10 and Aug. 11, 1525.

23. *AC*, Aug. 12, 1524; Jan. 13, Feb. 28, June 2, and Dec. 15, 1525; Aug. 17 and Dec. 10, 1526.

24. *AC*, Aug. 26 and Dec. 29, 1524; Jan. 4, 1525; Jan. 4, 1527.

25. C. Harvey Gardiner, *The Constant Captain, Gonzalo de Sandoval* (Carbondale, Ill., 1961), 178–179.

26. Agustín Millares Carlo and José I. Mantecón, *Indice y extractos de los protocolos del Archivo de Notarías de México, D.F.*, 2 vols. (México, 1945–1946), I, no. 1263. Brand et al., *Coalcomán*, 64.

27. Millares Carlo and Mantecón, *Indice*, I, nos. 1664, 1674.

28. Woodrow Borah, "Hernán Cortés y sus intereses marítimos en el Pacífico: El Perú y la Baja California," *Estudios de Historia Novohispana*, 4 (1971).

29. Cortés, *Cartas*, 524–527.

30. Hubert Howe Bancroft, *History of Mexico*, 6 vols. (San Francisco, 1883–1886), II, 423n; William H. Prescott, *The Conquest of Mexico*, 2 vols. (London, 1957), II, 352.

31. Millares Carlo and Mantecón, *Indice*, II, no. 1889.

32. Woodrow Borah, *Early Colonial Trade and Navigation between Mexico and Peru* (Berkeley, 1954), 22–25.

33. Millares Carlo and Mantecón, *Indice*, II, no. 1828.

34. Cf. Edgar F. Love, "Negro Resistance to Spanish Rule in Colonial Mexico," *Journal of Negro History*, 52 (Apr. 1967), 96.

35. *AC*, Nov. 19, 1538. Millares Carlo and Mantecón, *Indice*, II, nos. 1828, 2090.

36. Icaza, *Diccionario*, no. 169. *Epistolario de Nueva España, 1505–1818, recopilado por Francisco del Paso y Troncoso*, 16 vols. (México, 1939–1942), V, 8–9. Perhaps Garrido died in the great plague that was raging in 1547. On the other hand, someone called Juan Garrido was alive in Cuernavaca in March 1552; cf. Millares Carlo and Mantecón, *Indice*, II, no. 2647.

2

A Cuban Slave's Testimony

Estéban Montejo

The experience of Juan Garrido and other black conquistadors differed significantly from that of the majority of Africans, who came to the New World in bondage. Slavery, more than simply a labor system, affected all aspects of society and, at times, was responsible for unspeakable atrocities. Nevertheless, understanding this historical episode requires moving away from rigid explanations of Africans as victims and Europeans as oppressors. Slavery was a dynamic institution with complex regional, occupational, and urban-rural differences. Slaves had varied experiences and, despite the cruelty often inflicted upon them, tried to work out bearable lives within the constraints of their situation.

Recognizing that Africans were not passive victims of the slave system attests to their resilience as individuals. During the years before abolition an important distinction developed between law and practice. The rigid code that prohibited interracial marriages in Cuba, for example, did not preclude widespread concubinage. Recovering the history of slavery from the perspective of these dispossessed people has proven difficult though not impossible. Testimonies serve as one especially valuable source but require careful handling and must be placed in context through the use of other evidence. Because they are deeply personal accounts, not histories, they have a particular bias and rich nuances. Moreover, the editor or recorder may influence the recollection.*

In the following excerpt from The Autobiography of a Runaway Slave *(1968), Miguel Barnet has reconstructed the poignant testimony of Estéban Montejo, a Cuban slave. Montejo fully understood the harsh options*

From *The Autobiography of a Runaway Slave*, ed. Miguel Barnet (New York: Pantheon Books, 1968), 15–44. © 1968 by The Bodley Head, Ltd. Reprinted by permission of Pantheon Books, a division of Random House, Inc.

*Verena Martínez Alier, *Marriage, Class, and Colour in Nineteenth-Century Cuba: A Study of Racial Attitudes and Sexual Values in a Slave Society* (Ann Arbor: University of Michigan Press, 1989), 12.

*available to him on the plantation and chose instead life as a fugitive.
Besides recounting the oppressive nature of slavery, his story reveals an
awareness of the ethnic complexity that resulted from the subtle but real
distinctions among the African tribes brought to Cuba.*

There are some things about life I don't understand. Everything about
Nature is obscure to me, and about the gods more so still. The gods
are capricious and wilful, and they are the cause of many strange things
which happen here and which I have seen for myself. I can remember as
a slave I spent half my time gazing up at the sky because it looked so
painted. Once it suddenly turned the colour of a hot coal, and there was a
terrible drought. Another time there was an eclipse of the sun which started
at four in the afternoon and could be seen all over the island. The moon
looked as if it was fighting with the sun. I noticed that everything seemed
to be going backwards—it got darker and darker, and then lighter and
lighter. Hens flew up to roost. People were too frightened to speak. Some
died of heart failure and others were struck dumb.

I saw the same thing happen again in different places, but I never
dreamed of trying to find out why. You see, I know it all depends on
Nature, everything comes from Nature, even what can't be seen. We men
cannot do such things because we are the subjects of a God; of Jesus
Christ, who is the one most talked about. Jesus Christ wasn't born in
Africa, he came from Nature herself, as the Virgin Mary was a señorita.

The strongest gods are African. I tell you it's certain they could fly
and they did what they liked with their witchcraft. I don't know how they
permitted slavery. The truth is, I start thinking, and I can't make head or
tail of it. To my mind it all started with the scarlet handkerchiefs, the day
they crossed the wall. There was an old wall in Africa, right round the
coast, made of palm-bark and magic insects which stung like the devil.
For years they frightened away all the whites who tried to set foot in
Africa. It was the scarlet which did for the Africans; both the kings and
the rest surrendered without a struggle. When the kings saw that the
whites—I think the Portuguese were the first—were taking out these scarlet
handkerchiefs as if they were waving, they told the blacks, "Go on then,
go and get a scarlet handkerchief", and the blacks were so excited by the
scarlet they ran down to the ships like sheep and there they were captured. The Negro has always liked scarlet. It was the fault of this colour
that they put them in chains and sent them to Cuba. After that they couldn't
go back to their own country. That is the reason for slavery in Cuba. When
the English found out about this business, they wouldn't let them bring
any more Negroes over, and slavery ended and the other part began: the
free part. It was some time in the 1880s.

I haven't forgotten any of this. I lived through it all. I even remember my godparents telling me the date of my birth. It was the 26th of December 1860, St. Stephen's Day, the one on the calendars. That is why I am called Stephen [Estéban]. One of my surnames is Montejo, after my mother who was a slave of French origin. The other is Mera. But hardly anyone knows this. Well, why should I tell people, since it is false anyway? It should really be Mesa, but what happened is that they changed it in the archives and I left it that way because I wanted two names like everyone else, so they wouldn't call me "jungle boy." I stuck to this one and, well, there you are! Mesa was the name of a certain Pancho Mesa who lived in Rodrigo. It seems this gentleman cared for me after I was born. He was my mother's master. I never saw him, of course, but I believe this story because my godparents told it to me, and I remember every word they told me.

My godfather was called Gin Congo and my godmother Susanna. I got to know them in the Nineties before war began. An old Negro from their sugar plantation who knew me gave me the introduction to them, and took me to see them himself. I got into the way of visiting them in Chinchila, the district where they lived near Sagua la Grande. As I had never known my parents, the first thing I did was ask about them, and that was when I found out their names and other details. They even told me the name of the plantation where I was born. My father was called Nazario and he was a Lucumi* from Oyó. My mother was Emilia Montejo. They told me too that they had both died at Sagua. I would very much like to have known them, but if I had left the forest to find them I would have been seized at once.

Because of being a runaway I never knew my parents. I never even saw them. But this is not sad, because it is true.

Like all children born into slavery, *criollitos*† as they called them, I was born in an infirmary where they took the pregnant Negresses to give birth. I think it was the Santa Teresa plantation, but I am not sure. I do remember my godparents talking a lot about this plantation and its owners, people called La Ronda. My godparents were called by this name for a long time, till slavery left Cuba.

Negroes were sold like pigs, and they sold me at once, which is why I remember nothing about the place. I know it was somewhere in the region where I was born, in the upper part of Las Villas, Zulueta, Remedios, Caibarién, all the villages before you come to the sea. Then the picture of another plantation comes to mind: the Flor de Sagua. I don't know if that

*Cuban name for a Negro slave who came from Nigeria or the Gulf of Guinea.
†Little Creole. Creole was a first-generation Cuban, black or white.

was the place where I worked for the first time, but I do remember running away from there once; I decided I'd had enough of that bloody place, and I was off! But they caught me without a struggle, clapped a pair of shackles on me (I can still feel them when I think back), screwed them up tight and sent me back to work wearing them. You talk about this sort of thing today and people don't believe you, but it happened to me and I have to say so.

The owner of that plantation had a funny name, one of those long ones with lots of parts. He was everything bad: stupid, evil-tempered, swollen-headed . . . [Barnet's ellipses] He used to ride past in the fly with his wife and smart friends through the cane-fields, waving a handkerchief, but that was as near as he ever got to us. The owners never went to the fields. One odd thing about this man: I remember he had a smart Negro, a first-rate driver, with gold rings in his ears and everything. All those drivers were scabs and tale-bearers. You might say they were the dandies of the coloured people.

At the Flora de Sagua I started work on the *bagasse** wagons. I sat on the box and drove the mule. If the wagon was very full I stopped the mule, got down and led it by the rein. The mules were hardmouthed and you had to bear down on the reins like the devil. Your back began to grow hunched. A lot of people are walking around now almost hunchbacked because of those mules. The wagons went out piled to the top. They were always unloaded in the sugar-mill town, and the *bagasse* had to be spread out to dry. It was scattered with a hook, then it was taken, dried, to the furnaces. This was done to make steam. I suppose that was the first work I did. At least, that's what my memory tells me.

All the indoor parts of the plantation were primitive; not like today with their lights and fast machinery. They were called *cachimbos*, because that is the word for a small sugar-mill. In them the sugar was evaporated and drained. There were some which did not make sugar, but syrup and pan sugar. Almost all of them belonged to a single owner; these were called *trapiches*. There were three sugar-boilers in the *cachimbos*—big copper ones with wide mouths. The first cooked the cane-juice, in the next the froth was taken off, and in the third the treacle was boiled till ready. *Cachaza* was what we called the froth which was left over from the cane-juice. It came off in a hard crust and was very good for pigs. When the treacle was ready, you took a ladle with a long wooden handle and poured it into a trough and from there into the sugar-locker, which stood a short distance from the boilers. That was where they drained the

---

*The fibers left after the juice has been extracted from sugarcane.

muscovado, or unrefined sugar, which had most of the syrup left in it. In those days the centrifuge, as they call it, did not exist.

Once the sugar in the locker had cooled, you had to go in barefoot with spade and shovel and a hand barrow. One Negro always went in front and another behind. The barrow was to take the hogsheads to the *tinglado*, a long shed with two beams where the hogsheads were stacked to drain the sugar. The syrup which drained off the hogsheads was given to the mill-town people and was given to the pigs and sheep. They got very fat on it.

To make refined sugar there were some big funnels into which the raw sugar was poured to be refined. That sugar looked like the sort we have today, white sugar. The funnels were known as "moulds".

I know that part of sugar-making better than most people who only know the cane as it is outside, in the fields. And to tell the truth I preferred the inside part, it was easier. At Flor de Sagua I worked in the sugar-locker, but this was after I had got experience working with *bagasse*. That was spade-and-shovel work. To my mind even cane-cutting was preferable. I must have been ten years old then, and that was why they had not sent me to work in the fields. But ten then was like thirty now, because boys worked like oxen.

If a boy was pretty and lively he was sent inside, to the master's house. And there they started softening him up and . . . [Barnet's ellipses] well, I don't know! They used to give the boy a long palm-leaf and make him stand at one end of the table while they ate. And they said, "Now see that no flies get in the food!" If a fly did, they scolded him severely and even whipped him. I never did this work because I never wanted to be on closer terms with the masters. I was a runaway from birth.

All the slaves lived in barracoons. These dwelling-places no longer exist, so one cannot see them. But I saw them and I never thought well of them. The masters, of course, said they were as clean as new pins. The slaves disliked living under those conditions: being locked up stifled them. The barracoons were large, though some plantations had smaller ones; it depended on the number of slaves in the settlement. Around two hundred slaves of all colours lived in the Flor de Sagua barracoon. This was laid out in rows: two rows facing each other with a door in the middle and a massive padlock to shut the slaves in at night. There were barracoons of wood and barracoons of masonry with tiled roofs. Both types had mud floors and were as dirty as hell. And there was no modern ventilation there! Just a hole in the wall or a small barred window. The result was that the place swarmed with fleas and ticks, which made the inmates ill with infections and evil spells, for those ticks were witches. The only way to get rid of them was with hot wax, and sometimes even that did not work. The masters wanted the barracoons to look clean outside, so they were whitewashed. The job was given to the Negroes themselves. The master would say, "Get some whitewash and spread it on evenly". They prepared the whitewash in large pots inside the barracoons, in the central courtyard.

Horses and goats did not go inside the barracoons, but there was always some mongrel sniffing about the place for food. People stayed inside the rooms, which were small and hot. One says rooms, but they were really ovens. They had doors with latchkeys to prevent stealing. You had to be particularly wary of the *criollitos*, who were born thieving little rascals. They learned to steal like monkeys.

In the central patio the women washed their own, their husbands' and their children's clothes in tubs. Those tubs were not like the ones people use now, they were much cruder. And they had to be taken first to the river to swell the wood, because they were made out of fish-crates, the big ones.

There were no trees either outside or inside the barracoons, just empty solitary places. The Negroes could never get used to this. The Negro likes trees, forests. But the Chinese! Africa was full of trees, god-trees, banyans, cedars. But not China—there they have weeds, purslane, morning-glory, the sort of thing that creeps along. As the rooms were so small the slaves relieved themselves in a so-called toilet standing in one corner of the barracoon. Everyone used it. And to wipe your arse afterwards you had to pick leaves and maize husks.

The bell was at the entrance to the mill. The deputy overseer used to ring it. At four-thirty in the morning they rang the Ave Maria—I think there were nine strokes of the bell—and one had to get up immediately. At six they rang another bell called the line-up bell, and everyone had to form up in a place just outside the barracoon, men one side, women the other. Then off to the cane-fields till eleven, when we ate jerked beef, vegetables and bread. Then, at sunset, came the prayer bell. At half-past eight they rang the last bell for everyone to go to sleep, the silence bell.

The deputy overseer slept inside the barracoon and kept watch. In the mill town there was a white watchman, a Spaniard, to keep an eye on things. Everything was based on watchfulness and the whip. When time passed and the *esquifación*, the slaves' issue of clothing, began to wear out, they would be given a new one. The men's clothes were made of Russian cloth, a coarse linen, sturdy and good for work in the fields—trousers which had large pockets and stood up stiff, a shirt, and a wool cap for the cold. The shoes were generally of rawhide, low-cut with little straps to keep them on. The old men wore sandals, flat-soled with a thong around the big toe. This has always been an African fashion, though white women wear them now and call them mules or slippers. The women were given blouses, skirts and petticoats, and if they owned plots of land they bought their own petticoats, white ones, which were prettier and smarter. They also wore gold rings and earrings. They bought these trophies from the Turks and Moors who sometimes came to the barracoons, carrying boxes slung from their shoulders by a wide leather strap. Lottery-ticket-sellers also came round, who cheated the Negroes and sold them all their most expensive tickets. If any of the tickets came up on the lottery you wouldn't see them for dust. The *guajiros*, or white countrymen, also came to barter milk for jerked beef, or sell it at four cents a bottle. The Negroes used to buy it because the owners did not provide milk, and it is necessary because it cures infections and cleans the system.

These plots of land were the salvation of many slaves, where they got their real nourishment from. Almost all of them had their little strips of land to be sown close to the barracoons, almost behind them. Everything grew there: sweet potatoes, gourds, okra, kidney beans, which were like lima beans, yucca and peanuts. They also raised pigs. And they sold all these products to the whites who came out from the villages. The Negroes were honest, it was natural for them to be honest, not knowing much about things. They sold their goods very cheap. Whole pigs fetched a doubloon, or a doubloon and a half, in gold coin, as the money was then, but the blacks didn't sell their vegetables. I learned to eat vegetables from the elders, because they said they were very healthy food, but during slavery pigs were the mainstay. Pigs gave more lard then than now, and I think it's because they led a more natural life. A pig was left to wallow about in the piggeries. The lard cost ten pennies a pound, and the white countrymen came all week long to get their portion. They always paid in silver half-dollars. Later it became quarter-dollars.

Cents were still unknown because they had not crowned Alfonso XIII king as yet, and cents came after his coronation. King Alfonso wanted everything changed, right down to the coinage. Copper money came to Cuba then, worth two cents, if I remember right, and other novelties in the way of money, all due to the King.

Strange as it may seem, the Negroes were able to keep themselves amused in the barracoons. They had their games and pastimes. They played games in the taverns too, but these were different. The favourite game in the barracoons was *tejo*. A split corn-cob was placed on the ground with a coin balanced on top, a line was drawn not far off, and you had to throw a stone from there to hit the cob. If the stone hit the cob so that the coin fell on top of it, the player won the coin, but if it fell nearby, he didn't. This game gave rise to great disputes, and then you had to take a straw to measure whether the coin was nearer the player or the cob.

Tejo was played in the courtyard like skittles, though skittles was not played often, only two or three times altogether that I can remember. Negro coopers used to make the bottle-shaped skittles and wooden balls to play with. This game was open to all comers, and everyone had to go, except the Chinese, who didn't join in much. The balls were rolled along the ground so as to knock down the four or five skittles. It was played just like the modern game they have in the city except that they used to fight over the betting money in those days. The masters didn't like that at all. They forbade certain games, and you had to play those when the overseer was not looking. The overseer was the one who passed on the news and gossip.

The game of *mayombe** was connected with religion. The overseers themselves used to get involved, hoping to benefit. They believed in the witches too, so no one today need be surprised that whites believe in such things. Drumming was part of the *mayombe*. A *nganga*, or large pot, was placed in the centre of the patio. The powers were inside the pot: the saints. People started drumming and singing. They took offerings to the pot and asked for health for themselves and their brothers and peace among themselves. They also made *enkangues*, which were charms of earth from the cemetery; the earth was made into little heaps in four corners, representing the points of the universe. Inside the pot they put a plant called star-shake, together with corn straw to protect the men. When a master punished a slave, the others would collect a little earth and put it in the pot. With the help of this earth they could make the master fall sick or bring some harm upon his family, for so long as the earth was inside the pot the master was imprisoned there and the Devil himself couldn't get him out. This was how the Congolese revenged themselves upon their master.

The taverns were near the plantations. There were more taverns than ticks in the forest. They were a sort of store where one could buy everything. The slaves themselves used to trade in the taverns, selling the jerked beef which they accumulated in the barracoons. They were usually allowed to visit the taverns during the daylight hours and sometimes even in the evenings, but this was not the rule in all the plantations. There was always some master who forbade the slaves to go. The Negroes went to the taverns for brandy. They drank a lot of it to keep their strength up. A

---

*African word meaning evil spirit; hence name given to the branch of the Stick Cult . . . which concentrates on black magic.

glass of good brandy costs half a peso. The owners drank a lot of brandy too, and the quarrels which brewed were no joke. Some of the tavern-keepers were old Spaniards, retired from the army on very little money, five or six pesos' pension.

The taverns were made of wood and palm-bark; no masonry like the modern stores. You had to sit on piled jute sacks or stand. They sold rice, jerked beef, lard and every variety of bean. I knew cases of unscrupulous owners cheating slaves by quoting the wrong prices, and I saw brawls in which a Negro came off worse and was forbidden to return. They noted down anything you bought in a book; when you spent half a peso they made one stroke in the book, and two for a peso. This was the system for buying everything else: round sweet biscuits, salt biscuits, sweets the size of a pea made of different-coloured flours, water-bread and lard. Water-bread cost five cents a stick. It was quite different from the sort you get now. I preferred it. I also remember that they sold sweet cakes, called "caprices", made of peanut flour and sesame seed. The sesame seed was a Chinese thing; there were Chinese pedlars who went round the planta-tions selling it, old indentured labourers whose arms were too weak to cut cane and who had taken up peddling.

The taverns were stinking places. A strong smell came from all the goods hanging from the ceiling, sausages, smoked hams, red mortadellas. In spite of this, people used to hold their games there. They spent half their lives at this foolishness. The Negroes were eager to shine at these games. I remember one game they called "the biscuit", which was played by putting four or five hard salt biscuits on a wooden counter and striking them hard with your prick to see who could break them. Money and drinks were wagered on this game. Whites and blacks played it alike.

Another competition was the jug game. You took a large earthenware jug with a hole in the top and stuck your prick into it. The bottom of the jug was covered with a fine layer of ash, so you could see whether a man had reached the bottom or not when he took it out again.

Then there were other things they played, like cards. It was prefer-able to play with oil-painted cards, which are the correct ones to play with. There were many types of card games. Some people liked playing with the cards face up, others with them face down, which was a game where you could win a lot of money, but I preferred *monte*, which began in the private houses and then spread to the countryside. *Monte* was played during slavery, in the tavern and in the masters' homes, but I took it up after Abolition. It is very complicated. You have to put two cards on the table and guess which of the two is the highest of the three you still have in your hand. It was always played for money, which is what made it attractive. The banker dealt the cards and the players put on the money.

You could win a lot of money, and I won every day. The fact is, *monte* was my weakness; *monte* and women. And with some reason, for you would have had to look hard to find a better player than me. Each card had its name, like now, except that the cards today are not so colourful. In my day they had queens, kings, aces and knaves, and then came all the numbers from two to seven. The cards have pictures on them of men on horseback or wearing crowns, obviously Spaniards, because they never had fellows like that in Cuba, with those lace collars and long hair. They had Indians here in the old days.

Sunday was the liveliest day in the plantations. I don't know where the slaves found the energy for it. Their biggest fiestas were held on that day. On some plantations the drumming started at midday or one o'clock. At Flor de Sagua it began very early. The excitement, the games, and children rushing about started at sunrise. The barracoon came to life in a flash; it was like the end of the world. And in spite of work and everything the people woke up cheerful. The overseer and deputy overseer came into the barracoon and started chatting up the black women. I noticed that the Chinese kept apart; those buggers had no ear for drums and they stayed in their little corners. But they thought a lot; to my mind they spent more time thinking than the blacks. No one took any notice of them, and people went on with their dances.

The one I remember best is the *yuka*. Three drums were played for the *yuka*: the *caja*, the *mula*, and the *cachimbo*, which was the smallest one. In the background they drummed with two sticks on hollowed-out cedar trunks. The slaves made those themselves, and I think they were called *catá*. The *yuka* was danced in couples, with wild movements. Sometimes they swooped about like birds, and it almost looked as if they were going to fly, they moved so fast. They gave little hops with their hands on their waists. Everyone sang to excite the dancers.

There was another more complicated dance. I don't know whether it was really a dance or a game, because they punched each other really hard. This dance they called the *maní* or peanut dance. The dancers formed a circle of forty or fifty men, and they started hitting each other. Whoever got hit went in to dance. They wore ordinary work clothes, with coloured print scarves round their heads and at their waists. (These scarves were used to bundle up the slaves' clothing and take it to the wash: they were called *vayajá* scarves.) The men used to weight their fists with magic charms to make the *maní* blows more effective. The women didn't dance but stood round in a chorus, clapping, and they used to scream with fright, for often a Negro fell and failed to get up again. *Maní* was a cruel game. The dancers did not make bets on the outcome. On some plantations the masters themselves made bets, but I don't remember this happening at Flor de Sagua. What they did was to forbid slaves to hit each other so hard, because sometimes they were too bruised to work. The boys could not take part, but they watched and took it all in. I haven't forgotten a thing myself.

As soon as the drums started on Sunday the Negroes went down to the stream to bathe—there was always a little stream near every plantation. It sometimes happened that a woman lingered behind and met a man just as he was about to go into the water. Then they would go off together and get down to business. If not, they would go to the reservoirs, which were the pools they dug to store water. They also used to play hide-and-seek there, chasing the women and trying to catch them.

The women who were not involved in this little game stayed in the barracoons and washed themselves in a tub. These tubs were very big and there were one or two for the whole settlement.

Shaving and cutting hair was done by the slaves themselves. They took a long knife and, like someone grooming a horse, they sliced off the woolly hair. There was always someone who liked to clip, and he became the expert. They cut hair the way they do now. And it never hurt, because hair is the most peculiar stuff; although you can see it growing and everything, it's dead. The women arranged their hair with curls and little partings. Their heads used to look like melon skins. They liked the excitement of fixing their hair one way one day and another way the next. One day it would have little partings, the next day ringlets, another day it would be combed flat. They cleaned their teeth with strips of soap-tree bark, and this made them very white. All this excitement was reserved for Sundays.

Everyone had a special outfit that day. The Negroes bought themselves rawhide boots, in a style I haven't seen since, from nearby shops where they went with the master's permission. They wore red and green *vayajá* scarves around their necks, and round their heads and waists too, like in the *maní* dance. And they decked themselves with rings in their ears and rings on all their fingers, real gold. Some of them wore not gold but fine silver bracelets which came as high as their elbows, and patent leather shoes.

The slaves of French descent danced in pairs, not touching, circling slowly around. If one of them danced outstandingly well they tied silk scarves of all colours to his knees as a prize. They sang in patois and played two big drums with their hands. This was called the French dance.

I remember one instrument called a *marímbula*, which was very small. It was made of wickerwork and sounded as loud as a drum and had a little hole for the voice to come out of. They used this to accompany the Congo drums, and possibly the French too, but I can't be sure. The *marímbulas* made a very strange noise, and lots of people, particularly the *guajiros**, didn't like them because they said they sounded like voices from another world.

As I recall, their own music at that time was made with the guitar only. Later, in the Nineties, they played *danzones†* on pianolas, with accordions and gourds. But the white man has always had a very different music from the black man. White man's music is without the drumming and is more insipid.

More or less the same goes for religion. The African gods are different, though they resemble the others, the priests' gods. They are more powerful and less adorned. Right now if you were to go to a Catholic church you would not see apples, stones or cock's feathers. But this is the first thing you see in an African house. The African is cruder.

I knew of two African religions in the barracoons: the Lucumi and the Congolese. The Congolese was the more important. It was well known at the Flor de Sagua because their magic-men used to put spells on people and get possession of them, and their practice of soothsaying won them the confidence of all the slaves. I got to know the elders of both religions after Abolition.

I remember the *Chicherekú‡* at Flor de Sagua. The *Chicherekú* was a Congolese by birth who did not speak Spanish. He was a little man with a big head who used to run about the barracoons and jump upon you from behind. I often saw him and heard him squealing like a rat. This is true. Until recently in Porfuerza there was a man who ran about in the same way. People used to run away from him because they said he was the Devil himself and he was bound up with *mayombe* and death. You dared not play with the *Chicherekú* because it could be dangerous. Personally I don't much like talking of him, because I have never laid eyes on him again, and if by some chance . . . [Barnet's ellipses] Well, these things are the Devil's own!

The Congolese used the dead and snakes for their religious rites. They called the dead *nkise* and the snakes *emboba*. They prepared big pots called *ngangas* which would walk about and all, and that was where the secret of their spells lay. All the Congolese had these pots for *mayombe*. The *ngangas* had to work with the sun, because the sun has always been the strength and wisdom of men, as the moon is of women. But the sun is more important because it is he who gives life to the moon. The Congo-

*Peasants, originally white settlers, but by this time black and mulatto also.
†*Danzón*: a slow, stately Cuban dance popular in the last century.
‡African word for bogey-man.

lese worked magic with the sun almost every day. When they had trouble with a particular person they would follow him along a path, collect up some of the dust he walked upon and put it in the *nganga* or in some little secret place. As the sun went down that person's life would begin to ebb away, and at sunset he would be dying. I mention this because it is something I often saw under slavery.

If you think about it, the Congolese were murderers, although they only killed people who were harming them. No one ever tried to put a spell on me because I have always kept apart and not meddled in other people's affairs.

The Congolese were more involved with witchcraft than the Lucumi, who had more to do with the saints and with God. The Lucumi liked rising early with the strength of the morning and looking up into the sky and saying prayers and sprinkling water on the ground. The Lucumi were at it when you least expected it. I have seen old Negroes kneel on the ground for more than three hours at a time, speaking in their own tongue and prophesying. The difference between the Congolese and the Lucumi was that the former solved problems while the latter told the future. This they did with *diloggunes*, which are round, white shells from Africa with mystery inside. The god Eleggúa's* eyes are made from this shell.

The old Lucumis would shut themselves up in rooms in the barracoon and they could rid you of even the wickedness you were doing. If a Negro lusted after a woman, the Lucumis would calm him. I think they did this with coconut shells, *obi*, which were sacred. They were the same as the coconuts today, which are still sacred and may not be touched. If a man defiled a coconut, a great punishment befell him. I knew when things went well, because the coconut said so. He would command *Alafia*† to be said so that people would know that all was well. The saints spoke through the coconuts and the chief of these was Obatalá, who was an old man, they said, and only wore white. They also said it was Obatalá who made you and I don't know what else, but it is from Nature one comes, and this is true of Obatalá too.

The old Lucumis liked to have their wooden figures of the gods with them in the barracoon. All these figures had big heads and were called *oché*. Eleggúa was made of cement, but Changó and Yemaya were of wood, made by the carpenters themselves.

They made the saints' marks on the walls of their rooms with charcoal and white chalk, long lines and circles, each one standing for a saint,

*Eleggúa, Obatalá, Changó, Yemaya: gods of the Yoruba, a Nigerian tribe, worshipped in Cuba by the followers of Santería.

†Lucumi expression meaning "all goes well," used particularly in the system of divination with sacred coconuts.

but they said that they were secrets. These blacks made a secret of everything. They have changed a lot now, but in those days the hardest thing
you could do was to try to win the confidence of one of them.

The other religion was the Catholic one. This was introduced by the
priests, but nothing in the world would induce them to enter the slaves'
quarters. They were fastidious people, with a solemn air which did not fit
the barracoons—so solemn that there were Negroes who took everything
they said literally. This had a bad effect on them. They read the catechism
and read it to the others with all the words and prayers. Those Negroes
who were household slaves came as messengers of the priests and got
together with the others, the field slaves, in the sugar-mill towns. The
fact is I never learned that doctrine because I did not understand a thing
about it. I don't think the household slaves did either, although, being so
refined and well-treated, they all made out they were Christian. The household slaves were given rewards by the masters, and I never saw one of
them badly punished. When they were ordered to go to the fields to cut
cane or tend the pigs, they would pretend to be ill so they needn't work.
For this reason the field slaves could not stand the sight of them. The
household slaves sometimes came to the barracoons to visit relations and
used to take back fruit and vegetables for the master's house; I don't know
whether the slaves made them presents from their plots of land or whether
they just took them. They caused a lot of trouble in the barracoons.
The men came and tried to take liberties with the women. That was the
source of the worst tensions. I was about twelve then, and I saw the whole
rumpus.

There were other tensions. For instance, there was no love lost between the Congolese magic-men and the Congolese Christians, each of
whom thought they were good and the others wicked. This still goes on in
Cuba. The Lucumi and Congolese did not get on either; it went back to
the difference between saints and witchcraft. The only ones who had no
problems were the old men born in Africa. They were special people and
had to be treated differently because they knew all religious matters.

Many brawls were avoided because the masters changed the slaves
around. They kept them divided among themselves to prevent a rash of
escapes. That was why the slaves of different plantations never got together with each other.

The Lucumis didn't like cutting cane, and many of them ran away.
They were the most rebellious and courageous slaves. Not so the Congolese; they were cowardly as a rule, but strong workers who worked hard
without complaining. There is a common rat called Congolese, and very
cowardly it is too.

In the plantations there were Negroes from different countries, all different physically. The Congolese were black-skinned, though there were many of mixed blood with yellowish skins and light hair. They were usually small. The Mandingas were reddish-skinned, tall and very strong. I swear by my mother they were a bunch of crooks, too! They kept apart from the rest. The Gangas were nice people, rather short and freckled. Many of them became runaways. The Carabalís were like the Musungo Congolese, uncivilised brutes. They only killed pigs on Sundays and at Easter and, being good businessmen, they killed them to sell, not to eat themselves. From this comes a saying, "Clever Carabalí, kills pig on Sunday". I got to know all these people better after slavery was abolished.

◆　◆　◆

All the plantations had an infirmary near the barracoon, a big wooden hut where they took the pregnant women. You were born there and stayed there till you were six or seven, when you went to live in the barracoons and began work, like the rest. There were Negro wet-nurses and cooks there to look after the *criollitos* and feed them. If anyone was injured in the fields or fell ill, these women would doctor him with herbs and brews. They could cure anything. Sometimes a *criollito* never saw his parents again because the boss moved them to another plantation, and so the wet-nurses would be in sole charge of the child. But who wants to bother with another person's child? They used to bathe the children and cut their hair in the infirmaries too. A child of good stock cost five hundred pesos, that is the child of strong, tall parents. Tall Negroes were privileged. The masters picked them out to mate them with tall, healthy women and shut them up together in the barracoon and forced them to sleep together. The women had to produce healthy babies every year. I tell you, it was like breeding animals. Well, if the Negress didn't produce as expected, the couple were separated and she was sent to work in the fields again. Women who were barren were unlucky because they had to go back to being beasts of burden again, but they were allowed to choose their own husbands. It often happened that a woman would be chasing one man with twenty more after her. The magic-men would settle these problems with their potions.

If you went to a magic-man to ask his help in getting a woman, he would tell you to get hold of a shred of her tobacco, if she smoked. This was ground together with a Cantharis fly, one of the green harmful ones, into a powder which you gave to the woman in water. That was the way to seduce them. Another spell consisted of grinding up a hummingbird's heart to powder and giving this to a woman in her tobacco. If you merely wanted to make fun of a woman, you only had to send for some snuff from the apothecary's. This was enough to make any woman die of shame. You put it in a place where they used to sit down, and if only a little touched their bums they started farting. It was something to see these women with cosmetics all over their faces farting about the place!

The old Negroes were entertained by these carryings-on. When they were over sixty they stopped working in the fields. Not that any of them ever knew their ages exactly. What happened was that when a man grew weak and stayed huddled in a corner, the overseers would make him a doorkeeper or watchman stationed at the gate of the barracoon or outside the pigsties, or he would be sent to help the women in the kitchen. Some of the old men had their little plots of ground and passed their time working in them. Doing this sort of job gave them time for witchcraft. They were not punished or taken much notice of, but they had to be quiet and obedient. That much was expected.

I saw many horrors in the way of punishment under slavery. That was why I didn't like the life. The stocks, which were in the boiler-house, were the cruellest. Some were for standing and others for lying down. They were made of thick planks with holes for the head, hands and feet. They would keep slaves fastened up like this for two or three months for some trivial offence. They whipped the pregnant women too, but lying face down with a hollow in the ground for their bellies. They whipped them hard, but they took good care not to damage the babies because they wanted as many of those as possible. The most common punishment was flogging; this was given by the overseer with a rawhide lash which made weals on the skin. They also had whips made of the fibres of some jungle plant which stung like the devil and flayed the skin off in strips. I saw many handsome big Negroes with raw backs. Afterwards the cuts were covered with compresses of tobacco leaves, urine and salt.

Life was hard and bodies wore out. Anyone who did not take to the hills as a runaway when he was young had to become a slave. It was preferable to be on your own on the loose than locked up in all that dirt and rottenness. In any event, life tended to be solitary because there were none too many women around. To have one of your own you had either to be over twenty-five or catch yourself one in the fields. The old men did not want the youths to have women. They said a man should wait until he was twenty-five to have experiences. Some men did not suffer much, being used to this life. Others had sex between themselves and did not want to know anything of women. This was their life—sodomy. The effeminate men washed the clothes and did the cooking too, if they had a "husband". They were good workers and occupied themselves with their plots of land, giving the produce to their "husbands" to sell to the white farmers. It was after Abolition that the term "effeminate" came into use, for the practice persisted. I don't think it can have come from Africa, because the old men hated it. They would have nothing to do with queers. To tell the truth, it never bothered me. I am of the opinion that a man can stick his arse where he wants.

Everyone wearied of the life, and the ones who got used to it were broken in spirit. Life in the forest was healthier. You caught lots of illnesses in the barracoons, in fact men got sicker there than anywhere else. It was not unusual to find a Negro with as many as three sicknesses at once. If it wasn't colic it was whooping cough. Colic gave you a pain in the gut which lasted a few hours and left you shagged. Whooping cough and measles were catching. But the worst sicknesses, which made a skeleton of everyone, were smallpox and the black sickness. Smallpox left men all swollen, and the black sickness took them by surprise; it struck suddenly and between one bout of vomiting and the next you ended up a corpse. There was one type of sickness the whites picked up, a sickness of the veins and male organs. It could only be got rid of with black women; if the man who had it slept with a Negress he was cured immediately.

There were no powerful medicines in those days and no doctors to be found anywhere. It was the nurses who were half witches who cured people with their home-made remedies. They often cured illnesses the doctors couldn't understand. The solution doesn't lie in feeling you and pinching your tongue; the secret is to trust the plants and herbs, which are the mother of medicine. Africans from the other side, across the sea, are never sick because they have the necessary plants at hand.

If a slave caught an infectious disease, they would take him from his room and move him to the infirmary and try to cure him. If he died they put him in a big box and carried him off to the cemetery. The overseer usually came and gave instructions to the settlement to bury him. He would say, "We are going to bury this Negro who had done his time". And the slaves hurried along there, for when someone died everyone mourned.

The cemetery was in the plantation itself, about a hundred yards from the barracoon. To bury slaves, they dug a hole in the ground, filled it in and stuck a cross on top to keep away enemies and the Devil. Now they call it a crucifix. If anyone wears a cross around his neck it is because someone has tried to harm him.

Once they buried a Congolese and he raised his head. He was still alive. I was told this story in Santo Domingo, after Abolition. The whole district of Jicotea knows of it. It happened on a small plantation called El

Diamante which belonged to Marinello's father, the one who talks a lot about Martí.* Everyone took fright and ran away. A few days later the Congolese appeared in the barracoon; they say he entered very slowly so as not to scare everyone, but when people saw him they took fright again. When the overseer asked what had happened, he said, "They put me in a hole because of my cholera and when I was cured I came out". After that, whenever anyone caught cholera or another disease, they left him for days and days in the coffin until he grew as cold as ice.

These stories are true, but one I am convinced is a fabrication because I never saw such a thing, and that is that some Negroes committed suicide. Before, when the Indians were in Cuba, suicide did happen. They did not want to become Christians, and they hanged themselves from trees. But the Negroes did not do that, they escaped by flying. They flew through the sky and returned to their own lands. The Musundi Congolese were the ones that flew the most; they disappeared by means of witchcraft. They did the same as the Canary Island witches, but without making a sound. There are those who say the Negroes threw themselves into rivers. This is untrue. The truth is they fastened a chain to their waists which was full of magic. That was where their power came from. I know all this intimately, and it is true beyond a doubt.

The Chinese did not fly, nor did they want to go back to their own country, but they did commit suicide. They did it silently. After several days they would turn up hanging from a tree or dead on the ground. They did everything in silence. They used to kill the very overseers themselves with sticks or knives. The Chinese respected no one. They were born rebels. Often the master would appoint an overseer of their own race so that he might win their trust. Then they did not kill him. When slavery ended I met other Chinese in Sagua la Grande, but they were different and very civilised.

*[José] Martí, often known as the "Apostle" or "the Father of Cuba," was the leader of Cuba's national War of Independence and also a poet and essayist of great influence in the Spanish-speaking world. Juan Marinello, one of Cuba's leading Communists, is an important critic of Martí's literary work.

3

Africans and Indians: A Comparative Study of the Black Carib and Black Seminole

Rebecca B. Bateman

Miscegenation characterized the Iberian colonies, in contrast to the pattern in North America, where English families established settlements. Defined loosely as the mixing of races, it has taken many forms in Latin America, from rape, cohabitation, and concubinage to marriage. It became a common feature of the encounter among Europeans, Africans, and indigenous peoples because the vast majority of the dominant Spaniards and Portuguese were males who turned to subordinate indigenous or black women as mates and companions. La Malinche, the indigenous woman who was Cortés's mistress, has become the symbol of the females who endured this experience. Extensive racial intermixing has been used to explain more tolerant race relations in Latin America, nineteenth-century underdevelopment, and an emergent "cosmic race," depending on the racial attitudes and ideological commitments of the authors.

Miscegenation has created a complex spectrum of pigmentation in Latin America, distinct from the rest of the world. Studies of this process tend to rely on demographic data that support the cosmic race theory, without considering sociopolitical relations such as prejudice. Moreover, most examinations limit discussions of miscegenation to the mixing of Europeans and blacks or Europeans and Indians, ignoring the intermingling of other ethnic groups that resulted, for example, in Cuba's Afro-Chinese population.

The following selection offers a corrective to narrow discussions of miscegenation through the comparative study of Black Carib and Black Seminole communities. These groups, from the Caribbean basin

From *Ethnohistory* 37, no. 1 (Winter 1990): 1–24. © 1990 by Duke University Press. Reprinted by permission of Duke University Press.

and southern Florida, respectively, show similar patterns in their struggle for survival, organization, and identity. This essay emerged from the author's much larger investigation among Seminole Freedmen in Oklahoma undertaken at Johns Hopkins University.

This history of European mercantile and colonial expansion in the Americas is one of destruction, dispersal, and dispossession of native populations and forced transport and enslavement of African peoples. Ironically, the very processes responsible for the decimation of many cultural groups of the Americas led to ethnogenesis, the birth of new ones. Survivors of native societies ravaged by disease and warfare recombined with others to form new cultural groups; Africans and Afro-Americans escaped bondage to form new societies on the fringes of the plantation economies in which they had been enslaved.

Blacks and Indians sometimes found themselves allied in a mutual fight against Euro-American domination; at other times, the "divide and rule" policies of whites pitted the two groups against each other. The contacts between blacks and Indians brought about by the expansion of the frontier also led to the ethnogenesis of new "colonial tribes" (Helms 1969), such as the Miskito Indians of Central America, the Black Carib (currently also of Central America, but with roots in the Caribbean), and the Black Seminole, whose origins lie in the southeastern United States, primarily Florida. These groups differ from one another in the nature of the relationships that existed between Africans and Indians, but all three have structural and functional similarities that can best be demonstrated through comparative study (Helms 1977: 170).

In the discussion that follows, I will deal with the last two of these examples, the Black Carib and the Black Seminole.[1] My interest in the latter has resulted in fieldwork and historical research among a community of Black Seminole, the Seminole Freedmen of Oklahoma. I was struck by the similarities in the histories of the Black Seminole and Black Carib and undertook a comparison of the histories and social structures of these two groups to increase my own understanding of the Black Seminole in particular, but also to contribute to a better understanding of the cultural and historical processes involved in ethnogenesis.

Origins: Africans and Indians

The Black Carib

Though the exact origins of the Black Carib remain uncertain, ethnohistorical evidence indicates that some blacks on the Lesser Antilles island of St. Vincent in the seventeenth century included the survivors of the wreck of a slave ship that took place in the mid-1600s, while other Africans may have been captured from slave ships and European-settled islands by the Island Carib (Conzemius 1928: 187; Taylor 1951: 18; Craton 1982: 147). Some sources suggest that the Indians enslaved the blacks (Young 1971 [1795]: 6), while others maintain that the Africans formed their own separate colony on St. Vincent, intermarrying with the Indians and adopting their language and customs (Conzemius 1928: 188).

By the time European visitors to St. Vincent first described the island's inhabitants early in the eighteenth century, the Black Carib, as they came to be called, were already more numerous than the Island, or "Red" or "Yellow," Carib. The natural increase in their population was augmented by a steady influx of escaped slaves from the neighboring islands of Guadeloupe, Barbados, and Martinique. By the early eighteenth century, the Black and Island Carib formed two territorially and politically distinct groups, the former occupying the windward side and the latter the leeward side of the island. As the century progressed, conflicts with one another and with Europeans increased as the French and English played the two Carib groups against each other to further their colonial objectives.

The Black Seminole

The escaped slaves who fled into Florida in the eighteenth century encountered not one group of aboriginal inhabitants in situ but a diverse aggregation of native southeastern peoples. Some were survivors of native societies decimated and scattered by disease and warfare, while others were self-exiled members of the so-called Creek Confederacy. These peoples coalesced into the Florida Seminole in the mid-eighteenth century (see Sturtevant 1971 and Wright 1986 for extensive discussions of Seminole origins).

Black slaves had been escaping from the English colony of South Carolina into Spanish-controlled Florida since the late seventeenth century. A Spanish royal decree in 1693 encouraged such escapes by promising asylum to all black deserters from the British who fled to St. Augustine and converted to Catholicism. However, severe penalties for those who were caught, along with Indian slave catchers employed by the British, apparently discouraged large numbers of slaves from marooning (fleeing their owners) to Florida during this period (TePaske 1975: 3–4). Lower Creek towns were also encouraged by the Spanish to move into northern Florida to serve as buffers against British expansion to the south. Several towns did so, and all became early components of the Seminole (Sturtevant 1971: 101).

Throughout the mid-1700s, border conflicts between the British and Spanish and their respective Indian and black allies continued. Spain ceded Florida to Britain in 1763, and many of the survivors of Indian tribes indigenous to southern Florida left with the departing Spanish, as did most of the black population of Florida (Fairbanks 1974: 155–56).

During the period of British control of Florida (1763–1783), and especially during the American Revolution, blacks became an important element among the Creek and Seminole (Porter 1971: 209). British agents rewarded Creeks who served in the Revolution with slaves; other blacks were captured by the Indians through raids on plantations or joined the British and their allies on promises of freedom. With the departure of the British and the cession of Florida back to Spain in 1783, slaves fleeing from South Carolina and Georgia plantations began to take refuge among the Seminole (ibid.: 207–8).

Conflict and Removal

The Black Carib

In 1763, St. Vincent, like Florida, had been ceded to Britain by the terms of the Treaty of Paris. At that date, the Black Carib numbered some two thousand individuals, and the Island Carib only about a hundred families. French settlers and their slaves outnumbered both the Black and the Red Carib but were confined to the leeward side of the island (Kerns 1983: 23–25).

The British immediately began to make plans to colonize St. Vincent and to sell land to British colonists. Black and Indian resistance to incursions into their territories led the British to consider a plan whereby the Carib, both Black and Red, would be shipped off to the nearby island of Bequia or be granted areas of their own choosing within a specified region of St. Vincent. They were to be compensated for their lands and given five years to relocate (Craton 1982: 149–50). Both the Black and the Island Carib rejected this offer, and conflicts with settlers continued. In 1772, the British devised a military and naval plan to force the Carib into signing a treaty similar to one signed with Jamaican maroons in 1739. News of this plan leaked out, and settlers and Carib alike became convinced that military forces were converging on the island to exterminate the Carib population. The blacks and Indians resolved to stand their ground, and the result was a "full-scale Indian war"—the First Carib War— that ended in stalemate (ibid.: 150–51).

In 1773, a peace treaty was finally signed between the Black and Island Carib and the British. Those Caribs who desired to stay would be allowed to govern themselves, to fish around St. Vincent, and to sell their produce on any British island. They would also be required to return any runaway slaves in their possession and to refrain from encouraging any maroons to escape or harboring any who did, under penalty of forfeiture of their lands. If they chose, Caribs could also leave the island (ibid.: 151–52).

Two decades of peace ensued, punctuated by Black Carib participation in the French capture of St. Vincent in 1786, but the island was returned to the British three years later (Kerns 1983: 27). In 1795, another Black Carib-French alliance started the Second Carib War, a revolt that ended a year later with the surrender of more than five thousand Black Carib men, women, and children to the British (Craton 1982: 205–6).

Along with some Red Caribs, the Black Caribs were removed from St. Vincent in 1796 to the island of Baliseau. Overcrowding, lack of fresh water, disease, and inadequate food there reduced their numbers from 4,195 to 2,248 before they were transported early in 1797 to Roatan Island, off the coast of what is now Honduras. The Spanish garrison there surrendered without a shot, and the British left the Black Carib with one ship, the captured Spanish barracks, some provisions, and expectations that they would form a permanent colony on Roatan (Gonzalez 1983: 148–49).

The Black Seminole

References to blacks among the Seminole begin in 1812 with the failed attempt of the Georgia Patriots to seize control of Florida. The intervention of free maroon settlements and blacks living among the Indians prevented the fall of St. Augustine (Porter 1971: 209–12). In 1813–14, Andrew Jackson and his forces entered Alabama to put down an uprising by the anti-American Red Stick Creek. After a number of military victories against Jackson, the Red Sticks and their black allies were finally forced to flee into northern Florida.

Promises of free land in the West Indies and protection from return to their masters attracted fugitive slaves to Florida, where British agents, with the acquiescence of the Spanish, sought to recruit an army of fugitive Indians and runaway slaves. Many of these blacks and Indians were established at a fort built by the British at Prospect Bluff, at the mouth of the Apalachicola River in the Florida Panhandle (ibid.: 215–16). American slaveowners along the Florida border were very uneasy over this "negro fort," and in 1816 it was destroyed by two American gunboats dispatched from New Orleans (ibid.: 218–20). Black and Seminole towns then mobilized for the First Seminole War (1817–18), and hundreds of

Red Sticks, Seminoles, and blacks began to engage American troops in skirmishes across northern Florida. Jackson and his forces invaded Florida in 1818, destroying black and Indian towns, engaging both groups in battle, and ultimately capturing Pensacola (ibid.: 221–32).

Jackson's invasion forced the Indian and black population of Florida farther south, into virtually inaccessible swamps. Some blacks fled to the coastal areas of southern Florida; many continued on to Andros Island in the Bahamas by dugout canoe or were taken there by British ships (ibid.: 233–34; Porter 1945; Goggin 1946; Kersey 1981). Unopposed by the Spanish, Jackson continued to destroy Indian and maroon towns, execute British subjects, and capture Spanish forts. In 1821, Florida was formally ceded to the United States by the Spanish (Porter 1971: 234).

The years between the takeover of Florida by the Americans and the beginning of the costly and protracted Second Seminole War in 1835 saw a change in Indian policy from confining Indian tribes to reservations in the East to removing them west of the Mississippi. In 1823, some Seminole leaders were coerced into signing a treaty accepting a reservation in Florida; they were admonished to be vigilant and return any runaway slaves. In typical "divide and rule" fashion, the Indians were warned that the blacks cared nothing for them but only wanted protection from their former owners (McReynolds 1957: 98–99, 116). When Indian removal became the official policy of the Jackson administration, a few Seminole leaders were once again coerced into signing treaties, this time providing for their removal to what is now Oklahoma; but the Seminoles who signed the treaties had no real authority to speak for the majority of the Seminole. Most opposed removal, especially the blacks, for they feared that removal meant enslavement. Seminole-American relations deteriorated, and in 1835 America's costliest Indian war broke out in Florida.

Major General Sidney Jesup emphasized in 1836 that the Second Seminole War was "a negro, not an Indian War" (Porter 1971: 238). Though part of the general policy of Indian removal, the removal of the Seminole was more importantly an effort to rid Florida of the blacks. By this time, the black population of Florida included "Seminole negroes" (blacks who were closely associated with the Indians, wore Seminole dress, and fought alongside Seminole warriors) and slaves who had been captured in raids on Florida plantations, as well as recently marooned slaves. Those blacks still enslaved on Florida plantations smuggled goods to the Indians and maroons and provided intelligence regarding white activities. Some of these slaves had relatives among the Seminole and were acquainted with the Indians well enough to have acquired at least limited knowledge of their language (ibid.: 263). Recalcitrant Seminole leaders such as Wildcat and Osceola recruited heavily from the plantations, adding more and more black fighters to their ranks (ibid.: 280–84).

By 1838, many black and Indian warriors had been captured or had surrendered to American troops. Some Seminole blacks who had served as interpreters, advisers, and spies for the Seminole now cooperated with government agents to encourage hostile factions to surrender (ibid.: 258–59). The long, bloody, and costly war ended in 1842, and the majority of the Seminole and almost all of the blacks were gradually removed to Indian Territory. Attempts by the military to identify and return to their owners more recently marooned or captured blacks had to be abandoned—to do so would have prolonged the conflict and hampered removal (ibid.: 284–85; Littlefield 1977: 36).

The Post-Removal Period

The Black Carib

After the departure of the British ships from Roatan in 1797, the Spanish, who saw the landing of the Black Carib as a British invasion, sent a small war party from Trujillo to recapture the island. Encountering two hundred armed Caribs on the shore, the Spanish decided to parley rather than fight and negotiated capitulation terms with the Black Carib. In 1798, most of the Black Carib were transferred to Trujillo by the Spanish (Gullick 1976: 28–29). From there, the Black Carib settlements spread out to the west and eastward along the Honduran coast. As had been their custom on St. Vincent, the Black Carib established their villages in remote settings, limiting contact with outsiders. The few Europeans who did venture into their territory described the Black Carib as friendly, peaceable, and industrious, a marked change from the hostility they had exhibited toward whites on St. Vincent. Carib settlements were located close to the coast. The men hired themselves out for months at a time as mahogany and logwood cutters (Roberts 1965 [1827]: 274) and also as sailors, smugglers, hunters, and fishermen; the women cultivated cassava and other crops, some of which they sold in Trujillo and Belize to purchase clothing and other goods (Kerns 1983: 32–33), and raised hogs, fowl, and other small stock.

Having to adjust to new geographic and economic conditions, the Black Carib also found themselves affected by changing political circumstances. Two events prior to 1832 particularly affected them. First, they were classified as Negroes rather than Indians by the constitution of the Republic of Central America in 1823. Second, they became involved in the wars between liberals and conservatives in the countries that made up the Republic, principally Guatemala, Honduras, and Nicaragua. Conflicts between Guatemala and Honduras led to a continual shifting of political control over Trujillo between them. In 1832, encouraged by the Spanish, the Black Carib staged a rebellion against the governments of the formerly Spanish-controlled countries of Honduras and Nicaragua in an effort to reestablish Spanish rule. It failed, and many Black Caribs fled to British Honduras (Gullick 1976: 31).

The Black Carib came into contact with a number of different peoples following their relocation in Central America, including British and Spanish colonists, Maya Indians, blacks, and, after their flight into British-controlled areas, Miskito Indians. British colonists soon realized that the Black Carib could be valuable as military allies and laborers. Following the failed rebellion, Black Caribs who did not flee to British Honduras or Miskito territory were allowed to remain in Spanish-speaking areas of Central America, though they were regarded with suspicion. By the end of the nineteenth century, relations between the Black Carib and Spanish-speaking Central Americans could be described as indifferent, if not hostile (ibid.: 39–41). Relations between the Black Carib and other Afro-Americans were marked by conflict and mutual antagonism. Creole blacks looked upon the Carib as inferior, while the Black Carib considered themselves culturally distinct from other blacks and maintained their social distance from them (ibid.: 42).

The Black Seminole

Upon occupying their assigned lands in Indian Territory, the Seminole and blacks faced still more problems. Their lands were located in the area reserved for the Creek, and many Creeks owned black slaves. Settlements of Seminole blacks were raided by Creek slavehunters; some blacks, under the leadership of Gopher John or John Horse, sought the protection of the U.S. Army at Fort Gibson, while others continued to reside near the Seminole (Mulroy 1984: 42). In 1850, a group of Indians and blacks under Gopher John and the Seminole Wildcat left Indian Territory for Mexico, hoping at last to find a place where they could live in peace (Littlefield 1977: 147; Mulroy 1984: 42). The Mexican government granted the Indians and blacks lands in exchange for their assistance in military campaigns against the so-called wild Indians (Comanche, Lipan Apache, and Tonkawa), who plagued the northern regions of Mexico (Porter 1971: 426–29). The Seminole settlers proved to be skillful fighters, but pressure groups within Mexico in the late 1850s began to agitate for the removal of both groups. By 1861, most of the Seminole Indians had returned to Indian Territory, but the blacks remained in the settlement at Nacimiento de los Negros in Coahuila (ibid.: 457–58). Their descendants continue to live there and in Múzquiz and across the Rio Grande in Brackettville, Texas.

Black Seminoles who remained in Indian Territory were next affected by the Civil War, which unequivocally ended the controversy over the status of blacks in the Seminole nation. The Seminole were divided in their loyalties during this conflict; the full-bloods remained loyal to the Union for the most part, while other Seminoles cast their lot with the Confederacy. About two thirds of the tribe, and most of the blacks, fled to Kansas to join other refugees, while other pro-Union blacks took refuge among the Cherokee or sought protection at Fort Gibson. The Confederate Seminoles passed a law enslaving all free blacks in the Seminole nation and confiscated their property. The Confederate sympathizers took their slaves forcibly to the Red River in the Chickasaw nation to prevent their escape northward (Littlefield 1977: 183).

At the conclusion of the war, the pro-South faction continued for a while as a separate political entity in the southern part of the Seminole nation, but it finally allowed "its" blacks to move off and form their own settlements. In the meantime, the loyalist faction and the blacks with them rejoined the nation, founding settlements in the northern part of the reservation (Mulroy 1984: 601). In the treaty of 1866 between the Seminole and the federal government, the Seminole blacks, now known as the Seminole Freedmen, were granted all the rights and privileges accruing to tribal members (ibid.: 567).

After the Civil War, two events in particular greatly affected the Seminole Freedmen. The first was the allotment of the Seminole reservation under the terms of the Dawes Act in the late 1890s, and the second was the achievement of statehood for Oklahoma in 1907. Under the terms of allotment, Indians and Freedmen alike received parcels of land that totaled nearly 350,000 acres (McReynolds 1957: 344). Members of the two Freedmen bands took their allotments in the communities they had formed both before and after the war, clustering primarily around present-day Wewoka, Sasakwa, and Seminole, Oklahoma. Only a few years after allotment, restrictions that had prevented members of the Seminole tribe from alienating their lands were lifted for Freedmen and some mixed-bloods, with the result that many Freedmen fell victim to the schemes of unscrupulous white land grafters who had moved into the old reservation area in large numbers. Many Freedmen had their lands stolen from them (see also Debo 1940).

After Oklahoma became a state, Freedmen began to experience racial discrimination as Jim Crow laws were enacted by the new state government. Prior to that time, Freedman children had attended Indian or mixed schools, but the new laws classified Indians as white and prohibited mixing of whites and blacks in schools and other social settings. Freedmen found themselves lumped together with Afro-Americans whom they regarded as strangers and outsiders. Blacks had come into Indian Territory in large numbers following their emancipation, and while the Seminole Freedmen helped many of these newcomers by renting them land to farm and lending them seed and farm equipment, the Freedmen considered themselves culturally distinct from "State raised" blacks and in the early years of contact avoided intermarriage with them. Their attitudes softened in time, so that many Freedmen today are also of non-Freedman heritage (Foster 1935; Gallaher 1951).

Black Seminoles in Texas, descendants of Black Seminoles from Mexico who became Indian scouts for the U.S. Army in the mid-1800s, found themselves in a similar situation. Texas state laws also lumped the Seminole (as the Texas people call themselves) with other blacks, whom the Seminole, like the Freedmen, regarded as foreigners.[2] They also looked with disfavor upon marriages between members of their community and "American race" outsiders (Foster 1935: 49). Mexican Black Seminoles sought to maintain their distinctiveness from other peoples by using the term *índios máscogos* to refer to themselves, an indication of their Muskogean origins (Sturtevant, pers. corr., 1986).

Black Seminoles in the Andros Island communities of the Bahamas, visited in 1937 by John Goggin, had retained an oral tradition of their migration from Florida that contained a reference to a long period of time during which they remained separate and aloof from the blacks of the east coast of Andros, whom they called "Congos" or "Longas." Eventually, the two groups did begin to intermarry, and Goggin (1946: 203–4) concluded that the "culture of the Andros Island Seminole is only a variation of the typical Bahaman negro culture."

Summary and Discussion

A point of contrast between the Black Carib and Black Seminole is that the former became more Indian, culturally, than the blacks did among the Seminole. One reason for this is that the African maroons who were the ancestors of the Black Carib were, quite literally, "just off the boat," were predominantly male, and probably had little in common, culturally or linguistically. These black men raided Island Carib villages to abduct women (Labat 1970: 137), who then raised their children according to Carib custom and in the Carib language (Bastide 1971: 82).[3]

The blacks who became associated with the Seminole in Florida most likely shared a plantation slave culture, practiced a form of Afro-Christian faith, and spoke an English-based creole language.[4] We know that this last point is plausible because linguist Ian Hancock (1975, 1977, 1980) discovered that older Seminoles of Brackettville, Texas, had retained knowledge of an English-based creole, which Hancock termed "Afro-Seminole Creole," that was very similar to Gullah. The evidence indicates that this creole was also spoken in the Oklahoma and Mexico communities, and probably in the Andros Black Seminole settlement as well. The blacks spoke Creek/Seminole with the Indians but probably the creole within their own communities. Thus, the Black Seminole, while they did adopt some Seminole cultural practices, retained a significant degree of cultural, linguistic, and political autonomy throughout their history.[5]

The status of blacks among the Seminole seems to have been one of vassalage; black protégés, as Kenneth Porter (1971: 302–3) has termed them, supplied agricultural products in return for protection from enslavement. While historical sources usually refer to the blacks living among the Seminole as the Indians' slaves, the relationship between the two groups never resembled the chattel slavery that existed in other slaveholding tribes. Black Seminoles settled in separate towns, both before and after removal, fought alongside Indians in the Florida wars, and were important as advisers, interpreters, spies, and go-betweens in Indian-white dealings both in Florida and in Indian Territory.

A striking similarity between the Black Carib and Black Seminole is their staunch defense of their uniqueness and independence and their resistance to outside categorizations based solely on their physical appearance. Throughout their histories both groups have fought to preserve their distinctive ways of life while adjusting to new social, political, and economic environments. Today, the Black Carib and Black Seminole recognize their affinity with other Afro-Americans: a young Black Carib man emphasizes the "Afro-Caribbean" component of his heritage (Gonzalez 1983: 161–62); a woman of the Black Seminole community of Red Bays, Andros Island, proudly proclaims, "I be Africa descended" (Sturtevant, pers. corr., 1986); and Seminole Freedmen in Oklahoma prominently display portraits of Martin Luther King, Jr., in their homes. Yet these examples do not represent a loss or rejection of their Indian heritage; rather, they reflect the many years during which both the Black Carib and the Black Seminole have been treated by the larger societies in which they reside as *blacks* and have responded by forging social and political bonds with other Afro-Americans. For the Black Seminole, who have historically identified themselves as black people affiliated with but not the same as the Seminole Indians, this growing solidarity with other blacks represents an expansion of their ethnic identity.[6] For the Black Carib, their developing awareness and recognition of their African roots and their relatedness to other Afro-American societies seem like a more radical departure from their long-standing identity as an Indian group, but it would be foolhardy to predict a complete rejection or loss of their "Caribness," given their long history of fiercely protecting their ethnic uniqueness.

The ability of any group to retain its ethnic distinctiveness largely depends on its members' ability to maintain ties to one another and to their communities and thus to preserve a sense of group identity that transcends even geographic dislocations. The domestic organization of a society, the makeup of its families and communities and the relationships among its members, therefore is crucial to our understanding of how ethnicity is preserved and maintained.

Black Carib and Black Seminole Domestic Organization

The Black Carib

A considerable body of literature on Black Carib domestic organization has been written, primarily by Nancie Gonzalez (1969), Mary Helms (1976, 1981), and Virginia Kerns (1983). A central focus of these writings is the presence among the Black Carib of the so-called consanguineal household, comprising related women and their children to whom men, in the roles of husbands and fathers, are attached. Helms (1976, 1981: 77), who has argued for the antiquity of this domestic form, asserts that contemporary Black Carib domestic organization, with both the consanguineal household and the practice of polygyny, shows strong structural similarities both to earlier forms among the Black Carib and to Island Carib domestic arrangements as recorded in the mid-seventeenth century. She undertook her study in response to Gonzalez's (1969: 9–11) assertion that the consanguineal household as it exists today among the Black Carib "arises in certain systems as a functional result of the group's attempt to adapt to a modern economy" and is particularly a feature of societies Gonzalez (1970) has termed "neoteric," that is, those that have supposedly "shallow cultural roots" that have formed recently (ibid.). Moreover, Gonzalez believes that contemporary Black Carib culture as a whole should be viewed as a variant of a generalized West Indian culture rather than as related to any particular Indian group (Solien 1959).

Helms agrees that the current mode of domestic organization of the Black Carib is well adapted both to the diversity of their economic pursuits and to the conditions of economic marginality necessitating such diversity, but she sees no reason to assume that current economic conditions created the consanguineal household. Rather, she views Black Carib domestic organization as traditional Carib marital and residential patterns in modern form (Helms 1981: 84–85). The problem with this emphasis on household composition is that the dynamism and adaptiveness of household membership is obscured (Ryan 1982: 126), illustrating Carol Stack's (1971) observation that the household is not always the most useful unit of study for trying to understand the actual interactions of family members. It is the fluidity of Black Carib (and Black Seminole) domestic arrangements that has enabled them to adapt to new socioeconomic conditions.[7]

Polygyny, like household composition, has historical roots among the Island Carib that extend back at least to the seventeenth century, when European observers described it. At that time most Carib men had only one wife; polygyny, though not uncommon, was practiced primarily by village and family headmen. A few of these men had several wives, some living on different islands; ideally, a husband was expected to visit his wives on a rotational basis (Helms 1981: 81). Polygyny was reported among the Black Carib from the late eighteenth through the twentieth centuries, and white observers noted that Black Carib fathers were conscientious about the care of their children, even if the mother and father had split. The husband generally kept his wives in separate houses and yards and was supposed to divide both his time and any gifts he made equally among them (ibid.: 82–83). In the early decades of this century, polygyny continued to be practiced in much the same way, with the exception that a man rarely had more than one wife in the same village. Today, some Black Carib men associate with several common-law wives, sometimes concurrently. Helms (ibid.: 84) terms this pattern "polygyny in contemporary guise."

Again, we find differing opinions on the continuity between past and present in regard to domestic forms. Gonzalez (1969: 72) refers to the taking of common-law wives as a form of "modified monogamy," because, she says, this form of "marriage" is not considered ideal by the Black Carib, and because the women involved usually do not accept each other.[8] She notes, though, that some women do like and accept the arrangement, visit back and forth, share goods, and help each other with household duties. A man is expected to recognize the children of both women equally and to assert his paternity legally by registering the children as his with municipal authorities. By doing so, he enables the children to inherit from him (ibid.: 79). If a father fails to support his children, a woman can go to court and demand a minimum allowance for each child recognized by the father (ibid.: 72).[9]

Each Black Carib community, whether in Belize, Guatemala, Honduras, or Nicaragua, is separate and autonomous from every other Black Carib community, and an individual considers his place of birth his lifetime home, regardless where he might later live. Indeed, one's birthplace is a fundamental aspect of a Black Carib's social identity (Kerns 1983: 56). Historically, Black Carib villages, both on St. Vincent and in Central America, were established in isolated settings, and while men in particular were very mobile and pursued wage work outside the village, life inside Black Carib communities centered on food production carried out primarily by the women (ibid.: 32–33). An individual's community was a place to come back to, no matter how far he might have traveled in search of employment or how long he might have lived in another village or town.

The Black Seminole

Comparable literature on domestic organization for any of the Black Seminole communities is virtually nonexistent except for certain sections in Gallaher 1951 and Mulroy 1984. The following discussion is therefore based on my own fieldwork among the Seminole Freedmen of Oklahoma and on an admittedly preliminary analysis of documentary sources, primarily census and annuity rolls and probate and civil court records.[10]

An important distinction between the Seminole Indians and the Black Seminole is the absence among the latter of the matrilineal clan system, the basis of Seminole kinship and social relations (see Gallaher 1951: 111–13). Though blacks were sometimes incorporated into Indian clans to participate in dances and ceremonials, the Freedmen, as one elderly Freedman expressed it, "didn't pay no attention to anything like that [the prohibition against intraclan marriage], 'cause we figures you ain't related unless it is blood kin" (ibid.: 112).

The most valuable sources in studying domestic organization among the Seminole Freedmen are the censuses and annuity payment rolls, where individuals were grouped according to "household." However, it is often difficult or impossible to ascertain what a household was and what social units the groups of names represent. Also, given the caveats mentioned above regarding the use of the household as a unit of study, these documents tend to reify domestic arrangements that were, like those of the Black Carib, quite fluid. They also provide few clues as to the actual interactions of people within Freedman communities or to the relationships of family members. However, when we compare these rolls with one another, we have the opportunity to see how the groupings of individuals changed through time.

Household groupings composed of related women and their children appear on these records, with no men listed; some of these women had their children by several different men. Many of these female-headed households are seen to break up as the women form new relationships with men; they and their children then appear in male-headed households. In other cases, the husbands/fathers are listed as single individuals, with other wives and children, or with their natal families.

Husbands/fathers who were non-Seminole, whether black, Indian, or white, usually do not show up on tribal censuses and rolls at all, even though they may have been present in the household with their wives and children. Thus, the assertion can be made that the consanguineal household existed among the Freedmen, and such domestic groupings no doubt were not uncommon. But the documents alone do not suggest a father's role, nor do they illuminate a woman's relationship with the family or families of the man or men by whom she had children, or the assistance and support she received from her own kin. The memories of informants are much more useful for these purposes.

Some elderly Freedmen today recall growing up in large families headed by two parents, while others describe households made up of two or more generations of women and their children with no husbands/fathers permanently present. Still other Freedmen remember living in several different households while growing up, owing to the death of one or both parents or the breakup of a marriage, and being raised by relatives. Household composition, then, was fluid, while Freedman communities were characterized by sharing and cooperation among family members residing in different households.

During the period after removal and prior to Oklahoma's achieving statehood, some Freedman communities relied heavily upon hunting, fishing, and gathering, with agriculture supplying supplemental food. While the women did most of the gardening, the men helped out with the plowing and planting of large plots (ibid.: 33). Other communities relied more upon the raising of cattle and other stock. Just prior to and after statehood, the influx of white and black settlers to the area depleted the game supply, and the Freedmen came to rely more and more upon agriculture for their subsistence. As game became scarce, the men turned more of their attention to farming and tending livestock (ibid.: 35). After allotment and the massive loss of land that ensued, both men and women were forced to seek wage work outside their communities as laborers, field hands, and domestics. The family cooperation crucial in a subsistence economy based on agriculture and cattle raising now adapted itself to this new economic pattern: a woman's mother or sisters tended her children as she went off to work, and male relatives and neighbors cooperated in cutting and hauling lumber for sale. The self-sufficiency of the Freedman community prior to allotment, the result of abundant land, began to decline, however, as many Freedmen found themselves landless and what little land they retained was turned to the planting of such cash crops as cotton.

One explanation for the appearance of some of the female-headed households on censuses is the practice of polygyny among the Black Seminole, which they shared with the Indians. While most Seminole men had only one wife, older and wealthier men were frequently polygynous; in most cases the wives were sisters and resided in the same house with the husband. When the wives were not sisters, they usually were maintained by the husband in separate dwellings. Polygyny continued to be practiced by the Seminole until the early 1900s (Swanton 1928: 79; Spoehr 1942: 92). Among the Freedmen, this pattern also existed. As one Freedman put it, "As long as you put them womens up in a house of they own, and fed and take care of them, they wuz you wives, and no one else could bother them. At least, they wuzn't sposed to bother them" (Gallaher 1951: 56). Among the blacks, a man was expected to provide separate houses for his wives and their children and to visit them in turn (ibid.). He was also expected to provide for the support of his wives and children. A centenarian Freedwoman, describing the practice of separate dwellings for wives, said that if one wife got sick, the other, along with neighbor women, would go to the sick woman's house and cook, iron, clean, and wash for her. When the husband butchered a cow or hog, he would distribute the meat among the wives and their children. This informant reported "no fussin' or fightin' or nothin' " between the wives, and other Freedmen similarly described cordial and even sisterly relations among wives, though no one knew of any cases in which the wives actually were sisters.

Most of the cases of polygyny I have documented come from the period between the last two decades of the nineteenth and the first decade or so of the twentieth century. The men involved fit the description of the typical polygynous male among the Seminole: all were men of some prominence and/or wealth and included band leaders and tribal council representatives, lighthorsemen, and leaders in Freedman churches. Women may have been attracted to polygynous relationships with these individuals: most of these men had jobs that paid them cash wages, and in a subsistence economy, a man with cash could provide more store-bought goods to his wives. After Oklahoma achieved statehood, Seminole Freedwomen, like the Black Carib, began to use the legal system to ensure paternal support for their offspring.[11]

Until the first decade or so of this century, marriages among the Seminole Freedmen could be made or broken with relative ease, though many lasted for many years.[12] The fluidity of relationships between men and women in Freedman communities, their tendency (until fairly recently) to avoid marriages with non-Freedmen, and the fact that, until substantial numbers of Freedmen began to leave the native communities after the First World War, children generally settled near their parents (ibid.: 63–64) all contributed to the creation and maintenance of communities made up of several large, extended families. These communities tended to be relatively insular. An individual's ties to his community were strong and remained so even if he ventured far away in search of a livelihood. Freedmen continue to return to the now mostly depopulated rural communities for church homecomings, family reunions, funerals, and their own interment in Freedman cemeteries (ibid.: 77).

The division of the entire Freedman population into just two bands for purposes of representation on the Seminole tribal council brought the residents of the various Freedman communities together to attend band meetings and discuss political action and tribal affairs. Intermarriage among the Freedman communities has also bound all Freedmen to one another through complex ties of kinship. Freedmen today will say that they are all related; a glance at any individual's genealogy shows that this statement is no exaggeration.

Community/Domestic Organization and Ethnicity

The Black Carib and Black Seminole have in common aspects not only of cultural history but also, at a deeper structural level, of family composition, attachment to birthplace, and marital practice. But to what extent have these social-structural features enabled both groups historically to maintain their distinctiveness?

It should be reemphasized that among both the Black Carib and the Black Seminole (specifically, the Seminole Freedmen), communities tend to be largely separate and autonomous and their inhabitants to have a very definite sense of their superiority to, or at least distinctiveness from, those of other settlements. This is true for the Black Carib today (Kerns 1983: 6, 56–57) and, to judge from my fieldwork, also for the Freedmen historically. The residents of a community were bound to one another by complex ties of kinship, owing in no small measure to the fact that so many men and women had children by more than one mate (ibid.: 116).

The association of the Seminole Freedmen with the Seminole tribe and their representation by bands on the tribal council cut across community distinctions, and this relationship with the Seminole has served as an important integrating mechanism tying all Freedmen to one another. At times, they have found themselves at odds with the Seminole, when the political or economic interests of the Indians diverged from theirs. In fact, the relationship between the Seminole and Black Seminole throughout their history can best be described as ambivalent. There have been periods in which the Indians endeavored to separate themselves from the Freedmen by excluding them from membership and participation in the tribe. To date their efforts have all failed, because they have not been able to circumvent the 1866 treaty that granted the blacks all rights of tribal membership. Ironically, the Seminole's attempts to exclude the blacks have served to unite the Freedmen in a common cause, illustrating that their relationship to the tribe that would cast them out continues to be an important focus of their identity.[13]

Black Carib communities cooperate with each other only on one occasion each year, Settlement Day, which commemorates the arrival of the first Black Carib settlers in Belize (ibid.: 57). There are no formal ties, political or economic, that tie the communities together (ibid.: 6). In contrast to the Black Seminole, the Black Carib do not have to struggle to maintain their ties to an Indian group. Rather, they identify themselves and are identified by others as an Indian people, who speak an Indian language and have cultural practices that are uniquely the result of their Indian origins. Because so many Black Carib, particularly males, work outside their communities of birth, to return "home" is to reaffirm their identities as Caribs by speaking the Carib language and following Carib cultural practices that distinguish them from "other races" (ibid.).

For both the Black Carib and Black Seminole, an extensive kin network provided a support system to rely on in times of need. Whether or not a woman had a man to help support her and her children, she had relatives nearby who could help her with child care or financial assistance or could take her and her children in for a period of time. For the Black Carib, a high incidence of local endogamy, and the tendency of women to continue to reside in their birthplace after forming unions with "strangers" from other villages, contributed to a prevalence of mothers and daughters residing in the same community (ibid.: 109). A preliminary analysis of residence patterns for the Oklahoma Black Seminole suggests a similar pattern, with some communities tending to be more endogamous than others (see Mulroy 1984: 630). Couples generally resided near their families after marriage, resulting in a similar pattern of daughters and their children remaining near their mothers.[14] In the few cases of intermarriage that did occur during the early period of contact with "State" blacks, Freedmen rarely left the native communities (Gallaher 1951: 89). After allotment and the massive loss of lands among the Freedmen, a married couple sometimes was obliged to live outside the native communities on property retained by relatives or to lease land from white or Indian owners.

Uxorilocal residence, by providing a core of consanguineal women to tie separate families together even if husbands/fathers are absent or not members of the group, contributes to the maintenance of cultural identity through continued local expression of traditional forms of kinship, generosity, and general cultural patterns (Helms 1968: 461). Kerns's (1983) work demonstrates that this is very much the case of the Black Carib, and, as we have seen, the pattern of male out-migration and the uncertainty of their labor and the amount and frequency of the cash contributions they can make to their families have contributed to the preservation of the consanguineal household, polygyny, and matrilocality among the Black Carib (Helms 1981: 84). The Black Seminole, while not strictly matrilocal, can also be said to exhibit a similar pattern of women playing the important role of preservers and transmitters of cultural patterns. An individual's identity as a Black Seminole and his band membership are inherited through his mother, which, as Gallaher (1951: 113) has suggested, probably parallels the matrilineal emphasis on clan membership among the Seminole. An individual whose mother was a "State" woman, for example, would not be considered Freedman, even if his father were. In addition, strong bonds between mothers and daughters are often expressed by older Freedwomen, especially when the husband/father was not a permanent presence in the household.

Conclusions

My purpose here has been to compare two Afro-Indian groups, though it should be quite clear that the Black Carib and Black Seminole differ substantially in the degree to which they were and are culturally Indian. The slaves who fled into Florida did not, in most cases, become culturally Indian but formed societies that were distinct blends of Afro-American and Indian cultural practices. Because the Seminole were themselves an amalgam of peoples of diverse cultural and linguistic background, the blacks who settled and allied with them became an integral part of the Seminole people (Wright 1981: 277). For the African maroons of St. Vincent, historical circumstances led to the ethnogenesis of a uniquely New World people, phenotypically African but culturally owing much to the Island Carib.[15] Continued investigation and comparative study of these "New Peoples" (Ribeiro 1968: 110) will bring ethnohistorians to a better understanding of how Europeans, Indians, and Africans interacted in the Americas to create a truly new world.

Notes

1. "Black Carib" has been the standard designation in published ethnographic and historical works, but the names applied to the St. Vincent maroons throughout history have changed. In the eighteenth century, the British referred to the "free negroes of St. Vincent," "Black Indians," "Wild Negroes," and "Black Charibbs" (Kerns 1983: 12–13). Young (1971 [1795]: 8) states that this last term was the one chosen by the maroons themselves. Kerns (1983: 12) found that most Black Caribs she knew never used "Black Carib" among themselves but referred to themselves as Caribs or as *Garífuna*, depending on what language, English or Carib, they used. Seminole blacks have also been called various things by whites, including "Seminole Negroes," "Indian negroes," and, after the Civil War, "Seminole Freedmen." This last term, along with "native," is used by the Oklahoma blacks to refer to themselves, but other Black Seminole communities in Texas and Mexico use other terms. Richard Price and William Sturtevant have suggested that Seminole blacks in all of their communities might best be termed "Seminole maroons," an "etymological doublet" (Sturtevant 1979: 917), since both *Seminole* and *maroon* are derived from the same Spanish word, *cimarrón*. I have chosen to use "Black Seminole" mainly because, like "Seminole maroons," it suggests that, their close affiliation with the Seminole Indians notwithstanding, the Afro-American heritage of the blacks played a strong role in the formation of a unique Black Seminole culture.

2. The Black Seminole of Texas, long separated from the Seminole tribe, use the designation "Seminoles" to distinguish themselves from other blacks and also to emphasize their pride in their unique history. These descendants of the Seminole Negro Indian Scouts, noted for their bravery and skill as scouts for the U.S. Army on the Texas frontier, are fiercely proud of their ancestors and have formed the Seminole Indian Scout Cemetery Association to maintain the cemetery near Brackettville that is the resting place of many of the scouts, including four Congressional Medal of Honor winners.

3. Michael Craton (1986: 112–13) suggests that the Island Carib first thought of blacks as intruders fit to be slaughtered or enslaved, the same as whites or Arawaks, but came to regard them as allies and by 1700, at the latest, had begun to encourage black runaways to settle with them, make common cause, and intermarry. He attributes this change in attitude to the sharp decline in the Island Carib population after 1500, as well as to a long-standing pattern among the Carib of forming alliances to resist European encroachments.

4. From his examination of advertisements for groups of runaway slaves that appeared in the Charleston, South Carolina, newspapers from 1799 to 1830, Michael Johnson (1981) has determined that many of these groups, especially those made up of slaves from rural areas, were composed of individuals who were related; the most common rural family group included a husband and wife, often accompanied by one or more children (ibid.: 433). Other maroon groups included members of the same community or work group. While it is very difficult, if not impossible, to determine whether or not slaves mentioned in these advertisements made their way into Florida, Johnson's study illustrates that maroons who did reach Florida may have arrived in family and/or community groups and been able to build their new communities around kin and their shared experiences of slave-quarter culture and language.

5. The Black Carib continue to speak an Indian language within their own communities, but few if any Black Seminoles today can speak any Seminole, and Afro-Seminole Creole survives only among a small number of mostly elderly individuals. Intermarriage with non-Seminole blacks, out-migration from Black Seminole communities, social stigma attached by outsiders to the speaking of "broken English," and, for the Oklahoma blacks, the historical process of gradual replacement of Creek/Seminole by English among both blacks and Indians have all contributed to the decline in use of these languages, making it all the more difficult for Black Seminoles to assert their distinctiveness from other Afro-Americans.

6. A quote that Kenneth Porter (1971: 3) collected from an elderly Black Seminole woman of Brackettville, Texas, succinctly illustrates this point: "We's cullud people. I don't say we don't has no Injun blood, 'cause we has. But we ain't no Injuns. We's cullud people!"

7. Helms's work suggests that this same type of dynamic composition of domestic units may have enabled the Island Carib to adapt to and survive rapid population declines as the result of European incursions.

8. Virginia Kerns (1983: 113) describes such unions as "secondary," because in cases where men support and alternately reside with two women, one has a secondary status from the community's point of view. Most women, she says, disapprove of such relationships, because they nearly always lead to conflict between the two women, especially if they both have young children and depend heavily on their common husband for support.

9. Gonzalez's evidence suggests strongly that the pattern of the coexistence of monogamous and polygynous unions among the Black Carib persists, and that men and women involved in polygynous relationships have learned to use the legal system to ensure that fathers meet their obligations to their children. While polygynous unions may not be socially recognized as a desirable form of marital union, the taking of multiple spouses functions in much the same way.

10. Of the census materials, the Dawes roll, compiled when the Seminole and Freedmen lands were allotted in the late 1890s, is the most useful, because information available from the original census cards lists the parents of each individual, the band membership and owner (if any) of each individual and his or her parents, the location of the allotment, post office (a valuable indicator of residence), and age. Individuals listed together on a census card represent some sort of family or household grouping, though it is not clear in all cases whether or not these households were actually residential units. Probate court records, especially when the testimony in probate cases can be found, provide an invaluable source of genealogical information, because detailing relationships among individuals in such cases was extremely important. Heirship depositions are particularly rich sources of genealogical information, though their accuracy should always be checked with informants when possible.

11. After Oklahoma achieved statehood, polygyny became more and more problematic legally as new inheritance laws went into effect. Determining the legitimacy of the offspring of polygynous unions, especially those formed prior to statehood, created problems for local courts, so that some cases involving polygynous Seminole Freedmen went to the state supreme court. Complicating matters was the fact that no fewer than three sets of laws (tribal, Arkansas state, and Oklahoma state), plus a few special agreements made between the Seminole

tribe and the federal government, were in effect at various times; each affected inheritance differently. Under tribal law, for instance, if a minor died, his or her property would be inherited by the mother or siblings and their heirs rather than by the child's father, while under Oklahoma state law, a father was allowed to inherit. Because children also received allotments of land, the right of a father to inherit from his child became quite important, so the establishment of the legitimacy of a child became a much graver issue. Fathers sought to establish their paternity legally as well, so that their children would be able to inherit from them. Mothers brought suit to have their children included in the distribution of the estate in the event that they had not been legally recognized. Figuring out what sets of laws and agreements were in effect when, and which set applied in any particular case, caused headaches for the courts and must have been nearly incomprehensible to the majority of Seminole and Freedmen, who were, for the most part, illiterate.

12. Informants refer variously to the women involved in what I am terming polygynous relationships; it often depends on the informant's age. Younger individuals tend not to regard all of the women as wives but generally refer to them as a man's "women." Elderly Freedmen, on the other hand, are more likely to refer to these women as a man's wives. Individuals also differ in their attitudes toward such unions, particularly toward the men involved. Again, elderly people tend to be less critical of such relationships, while younger people find it hard to understand how the women could accept them. These differences of opinion indicate that the acceptance of polygyny as an alternative to monogamy has declined over time, owing in no small part to the legal problems associated with polygyny (see n. 11). In addition, Art Gallaher (pers. corr., 1986) has suggested that the racial discrimination aimed at the Freedmen and other blacks since statehood led to their downplaying cultural practices that they feared might be considered "heathen," a reaction that might lead to even more discrimination and reprisals from whites.

13. Currently, the Freedmen and Seminole are still struggling over the disbursement of funds awarded by the Indian Claims Commission some ten years ago for lands ceded by the Seminole in Florida prior to removal. This multimillion-dollar award is to be divided between the Oklahoma and Florida Seminole (who have been unable to agree between themselves how to divide the funds equitably). The original disbursement plan excluded the Freedmen, who challenged it before a congressional committee. The Freedmen contended that their ancestors were indeed an integral part of the Seminole tribe in Florida, and that therefore the Freedmen should be included in the distribution of funds. They enlisted the aid of the congressional Black Caucus and won the support of some Oklahoma congressmen. Though some groups within the Seminole tribe of Oklahoma support the cause of the Freedmen (if only to end the stalemate and get on with the disbursement of the much-needed funds), many Seminoles do not, contending that the ancestors of the Freedmen were only the slaves of the Seminole while in Florida, and that the Freedmen were not made members of the tribe until the 1866 treaty. It appears that an agreement is still a long way off.

14. While I know of no specific preference for uxorilocal residence, my informants reported that the initial aversion to intermarriage with "State" blacks was expressed particularly in regard to Freedwomen marrying non-Freedman men and thus being taken away from their families and native communities.

15. Regrettably, Nancie Gonzalez's 1988 book on *Garífuna* history and ethnogenesis, a major contribution to Black Carib studies, was published too late to be included in this article.

References

Bastide, Roger
   1971 *African Civilizations in the New World*. New York: Harper and Row.
Conzemius, Eduard
   1928 "Ethnographical Notes on the Black Carib (Garif)." *American Anthropologist* 30: 183–205.
Craton, Michael
   1982 *Testing the Chains: Resistance to Slavery in the British West Indies*. Ithaca: Cornell University Press.
   1986 "From Caribs to Black Caribs: The Amerindian Roots of Servile Resistance in the Caribbean." In *In Resistance: Studies in African, Caribbean, and Afro-American History*. Gary Y. Okihiro, ed. 96–116. Amherst: University of Massachusetts Press.
Debo, Angie
   1940 *And Still the Waters Run: The Betrayal of the Five Civilized Tribes*. Princeton: Princeton University Press.
Fairbanks, Charles
   1974 *Ethnohistorical Report on the Florida Indians* 3. New York: Garland.
Foster, Laurence
   1935 "Negro-Indian Relationships in the Southeast." Ph.D. diss., University of Pennsylvania.
Gallaher, Art
   1951 "A Survey of the Seminole Freedmen." M.A. thesis, University of Oklahoma.
   1986 Correspondence with author, December 9.
Goggin, John
   1946 "The Seminole Negroes of Andros Island, Bahamas." *Florida Historical Quarterly* 24: 201–6.
Gonzalez, Nancie L. Solien
   1969 *Black Carib Household Structure: A Study of Migration and Modernization*. Seattle: University of Washington Press.
   1970 "The Neoteric Society." *Comparative Studies in Society and History* 12: 1–13.
   1983 "New Evidence on the Origin of the Black Carib, with Thoughts on the Meaning of Tradition." *New West Indian Guide* 57: 143–72.
   1988 *Sojourners of the Caribbean: Ethnogenesis and Ethnohistory of the Garífuna*. Urbana: University of Illinois Press.

Gullick, C. J. M. R.
    1976 *Exiled from St. Vincent.* Malta: Progress.
Hancock, Ian
    1975 "Creole Features in the Afro-Seminole Speech of Brackett-
          ville, Texas." *Society for Caribbean Linguistics Occasion-
          al Papers*, No. 3. Mona, Jamaica: Society for Caribbean
          Linguistics.
    1977 "Further Observations on Afro-Seminole Creole." *Society for Car-
          ibbean Linguistics Occasional Papers*, No. 7. Mona, Jamaica:
          Society for Caribbean Linguistics.
    1980 "Texan Gullah: The Creole English of the Brackettville Afro-
          Seminoles." In *Perspectives on American English.* J. L. Dillard,
          ed. 305–33. The Hague: Mouton.
Helms, Mary
    1968 "Matrilocality and the Maintenance of Ethnic Identity: The
          Miskito of Eastern Nicaragua and Honduras." In *Verhandlungen
          des achtunddrei-ßigsten internationalen Amerikanisten
          Kongresses*, 459–64. Stuttgart.
    1969 "The Cultural Ecology of a Colonial Tribe." *Ethnology* 8: 76–
          84.
    1976 "Domestic Organization in Eastern Central America: The San Blas
          Cuna, Miskito, and Black Carib Compared." *Western Canadian
          Journal of Anthropology* 6: 133–63.
    1977 "Negro or Indian? The Changing Identity of a Frontier Popula-
          tion." In *Old Roots in New Lands: Historical and Anthropologi-
          cal Perspectives on Black Experiences in the Americas.* Ann M.
          Pescatello, ed. 155–72. Westport, CT: Greenwood.
    1981 "Black Carib Domestic Organization in Historical Perspective:
          Traditional Origins of Contemporary Patterns." *Ethnology* 20:
          77–86.
Johnson, Michael
    1981 "Runaway Slaves and the Slave Communities in South Carolina,
          1799–1830." *William and Mary Quarterly* 38: 418–41.
Kerns, Virginia
    1983 *Women and the Ancestors: Black Carib Kinship and Ritual.*
          Urbana: University of Illinois Press.
Kersey, Harry A., Jr.
    1981 "The Seminole Negroes of Andros Island Revisited: Some New
          Pieces to an Old Puzzle." *Florida Anthropologist* 34: 169–76.
Labat, Jean-Baptiste
    1970 *The Memoirs of Père Labat.* John Eaden, trans. and ed. London:
          Frank Cass.
Littlefield, Daniel F., Jr.
    1977 *Africans and Seminoles: From Removal to Emancipation.*
          Westport, CT: Greenwood.

McReynolds, Edwin
1957 *The Seminoles.* Norman: University of Oklahoma Press.
Mulroy, Kevin
1984 "Relations between Blacks and Seminoles after Removal." Ph.D. diss., University of Keele.
Porter, Kenneth
1945 "Notes on Seminole Negroes in the Bahamas." *Florida Historical Quarterly* 24: 56–60.
1971 *The Negro on the American Frontier.* New York: Arno.
Ribeiro, Darcy
1968 *The Civilizational Process.* Betty J. Meggers, trans. Washington: Smithsonian Institution Press.
Roberts, Orlando
1965 [1827] *Narrative of Voyages and Excursions on the East Coast and in the Interior of Central America.* Gainesville: University of Florida Press.
Ryan, Kathleen
1982 "Black Carib Household Structure: A Study of Migration and Modernization," by Nancie L. Solien Gonzalez [review]. *L'Homme* 22: 125–27.
Solien, Nancie
1959 "West Indian Characteristics of the Black Carib." *Southwestern Journal of Anthropology* 16: 144–59.
Spoehr, Alexander
1942 "Kinship System of the Seminole." *Field Museum Anthropological Series* 33: 37–113.
Stack, Carol
1971 *All Our Kin: Strategies for Survival in a Black Community.* New York: Harper and Row.
Sturtevant, William
1971 "Creek into Seminole." In *North American Indians in Historical Perspective*, Eleanor B. Leacock and Nancy O. Lurie, eds. 92–128. New York: Random House.
1979 "Africans and Seminoles: From Removal to Emancipation," by Daniel F. Littlefield, Jr. [review]. *American Anthropologist* 81: 916–17.
1986 Correspondence with author, November 15.
Swanton, John R.
1928 "Social Organization and Social Usages of the Indians of the Creek Confederacy." In *Bureau of American Ethnology Forty-second Annual Report, 1924–25.* 23–472. Washington: U.S. Government Printing Office.
Taylor, Douglas
1951 "The Black Carib of British Honduras." *Viking Fund Publications in Anthropology,* No. 17. New York: Wenner-Gren.

TePaske, John
  1975 "The Fugitive Slave: Intercolonial Rivalry and Spanish Slave
        Policy, 1687–1764." In *Eighteenth-Century Florida and Its Bor-
        derlands*. Samuel Proctor, ed. 1–12. Gainesville: University of
        Florida Press.
Wright, J. Leitch, Jr.
  1981 *The Only Land They Knew: The Tragic Story of the American
        Indians in the Old South*. New York: Free Press.
  1986 *Creeks and Seminoles: The Destruction and Regeneration of the
        Muscogulge People*. Lincoln: University of Nebraska Press.
Young, William
  1971 [1795] *An Account of the Black Charaibs in the Island of St.
        Vincent's*. London: Frank Cass.

4

The Black Legions of Buenos Aires, Argentina, 1800–1900

George Reid Andrews

Latin American armies served from the wars of independence throughout the nineteenth century as a critical Creole institution that recruited Americans from all ethnic, racial, and socioeconomic backgrounds. The military often provided a means of social mobility, offering regular employment and civic acceptance to African and Afro-Creole soldiers. Armed service, moreover, provided a way for these individuals to express their nationalism and personal pride. Slave and free blacks, mulattoes, and mestizos enlisted in the independence and regional conflicts—such as the War of the Triple Alliance (1865–1870) and the War of the Pacific (1879–80)— during the nineteenth century. The first republic in the region emerged when Afro-Creoles Toussaint Louverture and Jean-Jacques Dessalines called for slaves to take up arms and claim independence for Haiti. Mexico and Spain's South American colonies later achieved independence through wars fought by popular forces, including many black men. As did other leaders, Simón Bolívar, the liberator of northern South America, promised freedom to slaves who enlisted in his campaign for independence.

The following excerpt examines the Afro-Creoles in Argentina. It describes the African contributions usually neglected in this society, where Afro-Argentines numbered about one third of the population at Independence but seem to have "disappeared" during the nineteenth century. Moreover, the Argentine experience reveals patterns also characteristic of Venezuela, Brazil, and Cuba. George Reid Andrews, currently professor of history at the University of Pittsburgh, received honorable mention

From *The Afro-Argentines of Buenos Aires, 1800–1900* (Madison: University of Wisconsin Press, 1980), 113–37. Reprinted by permission of the University of Wisconsin Press.

from the Conference on Latin American History for The Afro-Argentines
of Buenos Aires, 1800–1900 *(1980), from which this material was taken.
He continued his study of the African presence in South America in* Blacks
and Whites in São Paulo, Brazil, 1888–1988 *(1991). In the selection that
follows, he elucidates the role of Argentina's black legions, providing a
fresh perspective on the African dimension of the military.*

The phenomenon of armed black men has always been a troublesome
one for the multiracial societies of the Americas. The spectacle of
present or former bondsmen, or their descendants, organized into disciplined fighting units inevitably suggests the possibility that those units
may acquire institutional autonomy and strike against the very government and society that created them. Armed forces always present this
threat, but especially so when the members of those forces belong to a
class or social group consistently exploited and confined to a subordinate
position. Even if the black soldiers never use their power to redress their
legitimate grievances, the fear that they will do so is a constant in the
mind of the greater society.

Another drawback of black participation in the armed forces is that
the services rendered the state by its black soldiers entitle those men, and
the rest of the black population as well, to recognition and repayment of
the collective debts owed them by their nation. Black assistance in defending the country against invasion can form the basis for demands that
official and unofficial discrimination against black people be ended. This
assistance, plus the potential of mutiny or rebellion if the demands are
not met, can provide black people with the bargaining power to force
societal change.

Thus, while black military units have proved useful and even irre-
placeable as defenders of various North, South, and Central American
states, their very existence has implied a force potentially hostile to the
social bases on which those states rest. The problem of black men serving
in the armed forces has therefore proved to be an extremely complex and
delicate issue, not only for military policymakers, but for historians as
well. To acknowledge black participation in a nation's military history is
to acknowledge the contributions which entitle black citizens to equality
with whites. Such acknowledgment is obviously undesirable in societies
dedicated to maintaining racial inequality.[1]

Perhaps it is for these reasons that the role of the Afro-Argentines in
fighting their country's wars remains so little known and poorly understood. Few Argentine historians have failed to mention the importance of
black soldiers in the nation's military past, but their participation in that
past has been misrepresented in a variety of ways. Inaccuracies abound in

the writings on Afro-Argentine military history, ranging from fairly innocuous mistakes concerning which regiments were black and which were white to far more serious misconceptions concerning the nature of segregation in the armed forces, death and desertion rates, and the very existence of the black officer corps. This chapter is an effort to set straight the confused and confusing record of Buenos Aires's black legions.

It is particularly important to correct these inaccuracies because of the pervasive influence of military activity and institutions in the life of Buenos Aires as a whole and its black community in particular. Embroiled in an almost continuous series of foreign and civil wars between 1810 and 1870, Buenos Aires underwent the "militarization" of its society and political system common to most Spanish American states in the postindependence period.[2] Military institutions assumed tremendous importance in the social and political affairs of the province, and black men were disproportionately represented in those institutions, though seldom at very exalted levels. Afro-Argentines were subject not only to racially discriminatory draft decrees but also to other laws aimed at rounding up as many of the province's nonelite masses as possible and impressing them into service. Legislation in effect between 1823 and 1872 required all men convicted of vagrancy, gambling, carousing, idleness, or carrying a firearm to serve four-year terms in the regular army, twice as long as terms for volunteers. The embattled Rosas administration, straining to fight simultaneous wars in Uruguay and the interior of Argentina, stretched those terms considerably: its courts regularly handed down sentences of ten to fifteen years of military service, while women convicts could receive sentences of ten years or more as military seamstresses, sewing uniforms for Rosas's troops.[3] Once enlisted, soldiers could be sentenced to additional years of service for infractions of military discipline, and cases of soldiers being illegally forced to reenlist were common.[4]

Given the province's never-ending quest for men to fuel its war machine, military service was an experience that virtually every black man who reached adulthood in nineteenth-century Buenos Aires could count on having. Few indeed are the memoirs of life in the city that do not include a vision of the province's black troopers, and one cannot help but be struck by the way in which the Afro-Argentines themselves dated events in their lives in relation to military happenings. The will of Federico Mendizábal recalled how his wife Ermenegilda deserted him in 1851 to follow Rosas's army in the Campaign of the South. Mendizábal himself died in 1867 while fighting as a lieutenant in the Paraguayan War.[5] In an 1852 lawsuit brought by the female members of the Mayombé nation against the males, the women recalled that the origins of their dispute dated from the calling up of the men for the 1840 campaign.[6]

Battalions and Regiments

Afro-Argentines served in a succession of units in colonial and nineteenth-century Buenos Aires. As early as the 1660s, black men formed segregated militia units in the province; by 1801 black troops formed 10 percent of the city's 1,600-man militia.[7] These troops were easily overcome by a British expeditionary force which occupied the city in 1806, but when the British were driven out six weeks later, free and slave Afro-Argentines fought side by side with white militiamen. A second British invasion a year later was defeated by a defending force of some 5,000 men, of whom 876 belonged to the Corps of Indians, Pardos, and Morenos.[8]

Officers and enlisted men from these black militia units went on to fight in the independence wars. Free black troops from Buenos Aires constituted two all-black units in the revolutionary army—the Sixth Infantry Regiment of Pardos and Morenos, and the Battalion of Pardos and Morenos of Upper Peru. Both units distinguished themselves against the Spanish in Uruguay, Bolivia, and northwestern Argentina before being mauled at the Battle of Sipe-Sipe in November 1815. In the worst defeat suffered by Argentine arms during the revolution, over one thousand men were killed, wounded, and captured, while the Spanish suffered twenty dead and three hundred wounded. The surviving Afro-Argentines were sent back to Buenos Aires to recuperate; they saw no further action against the Spanish.[9]

Another black unit, the Seventh Infantry Battalion, also fought at Sipe-Sipe, but the Seventh was of a very different type from the free black units, being composed entirely of slaves bought by the state or donated by their owners. In 1813 the government initiated the first of a series of *rescates* (possible translations of this word include ransom, redemption, and exchange), decrees by which owners were required to sell their able-bodied slaves to the state in varying proportions, depending on the economic use to which the slaves were being put. Owners of domestic slaves were to contribute one third of their holdings, owners of bakeries and *fábricas* one fifth, and owners of slaves engaged in agriculture one eighth. In Buenos Aires province, this draft produced 1,016 slave soldiers, who were organized into two battalions, the Seventh and the Eighth Infantry. Subsequent *rescates* in 1815, 1816, and 1818 yielded 1,059 more *libertos*, who were aggregated to the Eighth Infantry and the Second Battalion of *Cazadores* (literally, Hunters).[10]

When Englishman Emeric Vidal wrote an account of his trip to Buenos Aires, as part of his discussion on the humaneness of *porteño* slavery he mentioned a particularly benevolent government program by which slaves could be sold to the state as soldiers, whereupon they would be free men.[11]

In one respect Vidal was quite right: slaves were free as soon as they entered the armed forces, acquiring *liberto* status which they would retain for the duration of their military service, afterward becoming completely free men. This program therefore had obvious attractions for Buenos Aires's male slaves, though there is no record of their responding to it as enthusiastically as the slaves of Santiago, Chile, three hundred of whom hired a lawyer in 1813 to sue the government for their right to enter the army and win their freedom.[12] Instances of slave resistance to the *rescate* program in Buenos Aires were rare, much rarer than those of owner resistance. After an initial flurry of enthusiasm in which a number of *porteño* families donated slaves to the state as a patriotic gesture, slave owners began to flood government offices with petitions for exemptions for their slaves, usually based on their economic dependence on the slave's labor. Many owners resorted to the crime of spiriting their slaves out of the city and hiding them in the countryside, where law enforcement was looser. By 1816 the government had decreed the uncompensated expropriation of slaves belonging to any master caught illegally withholding eligible slave males, and an especially long term of service for any slave who failed to turn himself in when called for service. Slaves who informed on such recalcitrant owners would be released from service after a mere three-year term of duty, considerably less than the hitches served by the other *libertos*.[13]

Vidal's description of the *rescate* system as a benevolent one is a bit wide of the mark. The *libertos'* freedom came neither easily nor frequently. Those drafted earliest signed up for the comparatively short term of five years; later decrees required *liberto* troops to serve until two years after the cessation of hostilities before acquiring complete freedom.[14] To what extent these original terms were honored is unclear. Many *libertos* died during the campaigns and thus never lived to claim their freedom. The numerous *libertos* discharged for medical reasons before completing their term of service did not always win their freedom, but rather were frequently returned to their owners—whether as slaves or *libertos* is not clear.[15]

Many other *libertos* deserted to escape the miserable conditions of campaign life. Those who succeeded in this enterprise may have won a precarious freedom which conceivably could have proved permanent, but those who were recaptured were usually sentenced to lengthy terms of extra service as punishment.[16] In any case, deserting *libertos* forfeited hopes of legally winning their freedom through the originally established mechanism of service. There is even serious doubt that the remnants of the revolutionary regiments that made it back to Buenos Aires after years of campaigning were allowed to enjoy the freedom they so richly deserved. An official history of the *liberto* Eighth Infantry Regiment reports that when its few survivors returned to Buenos Aires in 1824 after eight years of campaigning in Chile, Peru, and Ecuador, they were promptly incorporated into regiments preparing for the approaching War with Brazil, an incorporation which must have been forced on them since it is impossible to imagine that those broken survivors would have gone off voluntarily to fight in yet another war.[17]

Despite the shortcomings of the *rescate* program from the Afro-Argentines' point of view, it was undeniably successful in furnishing the revolutionary armies with much-needed manpower. Following the destruction of the free black battalions at Sipe-Sipe, the Afro-Argentine representation in the armed forces consisted almost entirely of *libertos*. When General José de San Martín led his army across the Andes into Chile in 1816 to liberate that country from Spanish rule, half of his invading force consisted of ex-slaves recruited from Buenos Aires and the provinces of western Argentina and organized into the all-black Seventh and Eighth Infantry Battalions and the integrated Eleventh Infantry.[18] San Martín's conquest of Chile and Peru is the stuff of which military legend is made. Leading his small army with a rare combination of skill and luck, he succeeded in throwing off Spanish rule in two centers of royalist resistance and sympathy. Even more remarkable was the career of the black battalions that accompanied him. Between 1816 and 1823 they fought and won battles in Chile, Peru, and Ecuador in an odyssey of campaigning that took them as far north as Quito, thousands of miles from their homes in Argentina. By the time they were finally repatriated, fewer than 150 men remained out of the approximately 2,000 black soldiers who had crossed the Andes with San Martín.[19]

No other black unit ever experienced a Calvary quite so long and difficult as that suffered by those ill-fated battalions. The only other *liberto* unit fielded by Buenos Aires, the Second Battalion of Cazadores, sat out the war doing garrison duty in the city. It later saw action against the federalists who invaded the province in 1819 and in the Indian wars of the 1820s.[20] The Fourth Battalion of Cazadores, established in 1826 at the outset of the War with Brazil, also spent the war in Buenos Aires, seeing minor service in the civil disturbances of 1829. Dissolved in 1831, its members were assigned to the Argentine Guard, an all-black battalion of the Rosas period.[21] Other black units prominent in Rosas's army were the Provisional Battalion and the Restorer Battalion, named after Rosas's self-imposed title of Restorer of the Laws.[22]

Following Rosas's fall in 1852, segregation was eliminated in the regular army by the national Constitution of 1853 and the provincial Constitution of 1854, but it continued to exist in the militia. Black militia units remained a constant in Buenos Aires's military establishment throughout the nineteenth century, evolving from the colonial Corps of Indians, Pardos, and Morenos and Battalion of Castes into the Civic Regiment of Men of Color (established in 1811), the Third Battalion of the Native Legion (1820), the Fourth Militia Battalion (1823), the Defenders of Buenos Aires (1830), various units established during the Rosas years, and the Fourth Battalion of the National Guard (established in 1852 and reorganized into the Second Battalion of the Third National Guard Regiment in 1858). A slave militia, the Argentine Auxiliaries, also served during the independence wars.[23]

A focus on the all-black regiments, however, obscures the importance of Afro-Argentines in integrated units. Though segregation of the military was more strictly observed during the colonial period than after independence, there is considerable evidence that even prior to 1810 black and white soldiers served side by side in the local militias. It was not unusual, for instance, for well-to-do merchants or professionals to send their slaves to substitute for them at militia drills and in actual combat, so that a de facto integration resulted through slaves' serving in supposedly all-white units.[24] Sometimes integration was officially condoned. During the English invasions a company of free mulattoes was attached to the First Squadron of Hussars, a prestigious white cavalry unit. At least two petitions survive from black officers in this company appealing to the viceroy to allow them to continue to serve in "this distinguished unit" rather than be transferred back to the Battalion of Castes. So badly did these two men want to stay in the white unit that they both offered to serve without pay, supplying their armament and horses at their own expense. Despite their pleas, both men were reassigned to the Castes.[25]

Given the liberal rhetoric of the revolution, integration of regular army units was almost inevitable. At first the revolutionary junta sought to keep Afro-Argentine companies in separate battalions, allowing only the Indians to serve with the whites, but eventually they relented, and in 1811 several companies of free Afro-Argentines were aggregated to the Second Infantry Regiment. These companies were later separated from the regiment to form the basis of the Tenth Infantry, another integrated unit.[26] The Eleventh Infantry, which accompanied the black Seventh and Eighth Battalions on their eight-year campaign through the Andean countries, was also integrated.

The true extent of integration in Buenos Aires's nineteenth-century regiments is only hinted at by official military legislation. Although several units were established by decrees that explicitly described their integrated or segregated racial nature, the majority were not. Only by studying enlistment records from the period and seeing to which regiments soldiers of given races were assigned can one arrive at an accurate impression of the racial composition of Buenos Aires's army. Such investigation indicates that the province did not field one single battalion or regiment in the 1810–1860 period that did not have black soldiers. In some of these units black representation was minimal, 1 or 2 percent. Examples of these would be the Buenos Aires Artillery Division (1853–1860),* the Ninth Infantry Regiment (1816), the Infantry Legion of Cazadores (1853–1860), and the Artillery Regiment of the Fatherland (1814–1817). But in other units the representation was substantial, especially when one takes into account the Afro-Argentines probably concealed among the *trigueños* that appear in the enlistment records. Table 1

Table 1. Enlistees in Selected Military Units from Buenos Aires Province, 1813–1860, Tabulated by Race

| | Enlistees | | | | Percent |
Unit	Black	White	Trigueño	Total	black
Third Infantry Regiment (1813–1817)[a]	14	25	36	75	18.6
Second Infantry Regiment (1813–1815)	23	28	37	88	26.1
Tenth Infantry Regiment (1814–1818)	65	15	7	87	74.7
Seventeenth Cavalry Regiment (1826–1828)	34	60	40	134	25.4
Buenos Aires Artillery Battalion (1824–1828)	12	24	49	85	14.0
First Infantry Battalion (1853–1860)	200	224	264	688	29.1
Second Infantry Battalion (1853–1860)	43	97	80	220	19.5
Third Infantry Battalion (1853–1860)	56	91	60	207	27.1
Second Cavalry Regiment (1853–1860)	12	26	26	64	18.8
Fifth Regiment of Mounted Grenadiers (1853–1860)	10	12	11	33	30.3

Source: Archivo General de la Nación, 3 59-1-1, 59-1-6, 59-2-1, 59-2-4, 59-2-7.
[a]Dates in parentheses indicate the years for which enlistment records survive.

*The numbers in parentheses indicate the years for which enlistment records survive.

is a tabulation of the enlistments recorded for ten units in the 1813–1860 period. Those enlistments appeared in five volumes of such documents chosen at random from a total of about twenty.[27] The importance of black soldiers in integrated units, even before integration was instituted in Buenos Aires's army, is obvious. Black troops constituted more than a quarter of the soldiers in six of the ten units considered; in one of them, the Tenth Infantry Regiment, they made up three quarters of the enlistments. The *trigueño* enrollment was even larger, outnumbering the white in four of the ten units, including the largest, the First Infantry Battalion.

There is also evidence that units established as black were in fact integrated, though the number of whites in them was very small. Even the *liberto* Seventh Infantry Battalion of 1813–1815 showed two white enlistees, as did the Fourth Cazadores. In the Rosas period there were instances of white criminals being sentenced to service in such black units as the Restorer Battalion and the Argentine Guard, just as there were black prisoners sentenced to serve in white units.[28] This accounts for a surprising incident in 1847, when the commander of the Restorer Battalion, asked to nominate noncommissioned officers for promotion to two vacant sublieutenancies in the battalion, nominated two white men, both of whom had served in the unit for ten years.[29]

Death, Desertion, and Disease

A potentially explosive question concerned with segregation and the existence of all-black units is the possibility that commanders used them as assault troops in preference to white units, consciously killing off Argentine's black population while achieving military objectives. No Argentine historian has suggested in print that such genocidal policy existed, but several mentioned it in conversation as one explanation for the demographic decline of the Afro-Argentines. Simón Bolívar, the liberator of northern South America, once argued frankly in favor of such a policy:

> Is it right that only free men die to free the slaves? Would it not be just for the slaves to win their rights on the battlefield and diminish their dangerous number by this powerful and legitimate means? In Venezuela we have seen the free population die and the slaves remain; I do not know if this is politic, but I do know that if in [Colombia] we do not make use of the slaves [as soldiers] the same thing will happen.[30]

Let it stand to Argentina's credit that there is no evidence of such thought or practice in the country's military history. Although black males were drafted in numbers disproportionate to their representation in the population, it does not appear that they were singled out for consistently hazardous duty. It is true that the Seventh and Eighth Infantry Battalions eventually melted away to nothing during their years of campaigning, but the white units that accompanied them did no better. The First Cazadores was almost completely destroyed at the Battle of Maipú, and very few of the Mounted Grenadiers ever returned from Peru to Buenos Aires.[31] No casualty counts are available for the disaster at Sipe-Sipe, but a list of officers killed and captured suggests that the mainly white Ninth Infantry suffered more heavily than the two black regiments combined. The Ninth lost fifteen officers, while the Sixth and Seventh Infantry between them lost six.[32] Or consider the Fourth Cazadores, which quietly sat out the War with Brazil in Buenos Aires while the integrated regiments battled Brazilians and the cold in Uruguay.

A comparison of the 1810–1815 roll calls of several battalions on active duty against the Spanish indicates that the white units actually lost more men than the black.[33] Since these roll calls are fragmentary in nature and vary considerably in coverage from month to month, monthly death rates (number of deaths divided by number of men in the unit at the beginning of the month) were computed and the sum of those rates then divided by the number of months to produce a mean monthly death rate for the period in question. That mean monthly death rate was then multiplied by twelve to produce a yearly death rate.

Three units that campaigned together in Bolivia and northwestern Argentina from 1812 to 1814 were the Battalion of Pardos and Morenos of Upper Peru and the white Second and Eighth Battalions of Peru, all Argentine units despite their names. During the 1810–1813 period the Battalion of Pardos and Morenos suffered an annual death rate of 91.2 men per 1,000, a very high rate indeed. However, the roll calls of the white Second Battalion, which survive only for 1813, show a death rate of 253.2 per 1,000. By comparison, the black battalion's death rate in 1813 alone was 114.6 per 1,000. The white Eighth Battalion also fought in the 1813 campaign in northwestern Argentina, but roll calls survive for only two of the twelve months of that year, so their results should be treated with caution. They produce an annual death rate of 201.6 per 1,000.

Three other units that served together in the northwest were two Afro-Argentine units, the Sixth Infantry Regiment and the Seventh Infantry Battalion, and the white Ninth Infantry Regiment. These units had much lower losses. In an eighteen-month period in 1814–15 (a period which does not include the Battle of Sipe-Sipe; the army was so shattered after its defeat there that no roll calls were taken), the Ninth had an annual death rate of 38.4 per 1,000, the Sixth slightly lower at 37.2, and the newly created *liberto* Seventh Battalion had 27.6.

These losses vary somewhat from the traditional image of Argentina's blacks dying in heaps on the battlefield, going to their deaths by the thousands in the cause of the *patria*, the fatherland. There is no writer on the subject of the Afro-Argentines who does not sound this familiar theme, and some carry it to ghoulish extremes. One Argentine poet and writer of popular history recalls at length how the Afro-Argentines served as cannon fodder from one end of the country to the other, leaving their bleaching bones, which he employs as a recurring image, everywhere they went.[34] The image of the bones is a striking one: as used by that author, who focuses on the contrast between the black skin of the Afro-Argentines and the whiteness of their bones, it becomes a subtle metaphor for the whitening of the Afro-Argentines. They did their duty to their country, died in the process, and left as their memorial a heap of bones, which redeem the memory of the Afro-Argentines not only through the heroism they represent but also by the fact that the soldiers' blackness has disappeared, replaced by pure and gleaming white.[35]

The bone motif appeared in another of the many popular magazine features that have reinforced the theme of the Afro-Argentines' being killed in the wars. An 1898 interview with a veteran of the independence wars yielded the following grisly anecdote:

> One time we were marching to San Juan, and with me in the advance guard was a black from La Rioja, a slave of the Bazán family. . . . One night he was on guard duty and he went to sleep forever when an enemy scout slit his throat. Well, before leaving we got the body and to save it from the vultures we put it in a huge cave in the hillside, and there we left it, without so much as a wooden cross. After all, the black left nothing on this earth besides his bones—who would ever remember him?

As it turned out, the teller of the story did. Four years later he happened to be campaigning in the same area when a thunderstorm broke and he took refuge in a nearby cave. Surprise of surprises, it proved to be the same one in which they had left the black man's body. "Would you believe that the bones of that poor guy served as fuel to make our fire and keep us dry that night? See what some people are destined for, eh? Some are useful even after they're dead, and others even when they're living are worthless."[36]

Other feature stories on the Afro-Argentines were less gruesome, but they all agree on the recurring theme of the blacks' being killed in the wars. As recently as 1976 a Buenos Aires newspaper article recalling the end of the slave trade went on to discuss how "the blacks fell to the last man in all the battles of the young nation, in the Army of the Andes, in the wars against the Indians, in the marshes of Paraguay."[37]

To what extent is this image of the Afro-Argentines' dying en masse in the country's wars an accurate one? It has more than a kernel of truth, of course, as can be seen from the marked sexual imbalance in the city's black population, documented by the census of 1827. The low death figures registered for the regiments described above should not obscure the fact that all it took was one disastrous battle for a unit to lose more men in an afternoon than it had lost in three years. Though black losses at such battles as Salta (eleven killed), Tucumán, and Chacabuco (eight killed) were minimal, clashes such as Ayohouma, Sipe-Sipe, Maipú, Pichincha, Ituzaingó, Caseros, and a host of others levied a hideous toll on the Afro-Argentines, as well as on the whites, Indians, and mestizos unfortunate enough to be drafted into the armed forces.

Even more destructive was the sickness endemic among nineteenth-century armies throughout the world, Argentina being no exception. When the Argentine army invaded Bolivia in 1813 the worst enemy it faced there was the *soroche*, a crippling condition produced by prolonged exposure to the altitude and the bitterly cold weather of the Bolivian *altiplano*.[38] Between December 1811 and July 1812, when the Battalion of Pardos and Morenos of Upper Peru was stationed in the Argentine province of Jujuy, bordering on Bolivia, an average of 22.2 percent of the battalion was sick each month, the majority of them with *soroche*.[39] When the integrated Río de la Plata Regiment left Lima in 1823 for the Campaign of the Ports, it left behind over 150 sick men in the city's hospitals; almost all of them died.[40] During the anti-Indian campaign of 1824, the Second Cazadores lost hundreds of men dead or permanently crippled by freezing and frostbite.[41]

Given the miserable conditions of army life, it is amazing that Argentine historians have consistently overlooked the single most important source of losses in the Afro-Argentine regiments. Perhaps attracted by the drama and pathos of the subject, historians have ascribed the losses suffered by those units to battlefield deaths, though a minority do mention the living conditions that caused so many deaths from illness. Only one study has pointed to desertion as a factor in the losses suffered by black regiments, and that study concluded that desertion was relatively infrequent among black troops.[42] This is completely untrue. Blacks and whites alike deserted in droves in all of Argentina's wars, especially the early ones. General Paz's memoirs recalled that during an 1815 march from Buenos Aires to Bolivia, an army of five thousand men was reduced to three thousand by desertions. A draft sent to northwestern Argentina three years later lost two thirds of its men in a matter of months as a result of desertions.[43]

Afro-Argentines did not hesitate to embrace discretion as the better part of valor, joining their white comrades in wholesale flight from the front. The debilitating effect that these desertions could have on a unit's manpower can be seen in the fact that while the roll calls of the Battalion of Pardos and Morenos of Upper Peru show it losing 47 men through death from 1810 to 1813, it lost 69 men through desertion. The Sixth Regiment lost 18 men dead between October 1814 and August 1815 but 98 men through desertion. Similar figures for the Seventh Battalion (March 1814 to August 1815) are 30 deaths, 189 desertions; the Ninth Regiment (September 1814 to August 1815), 27 deaths, 145 desertions; and the white Second Infantry Battalion of Peru (January through June 1813), 34 deaths, 64 desertions. An obviously discontented unit was the Afro-Argentine Fourth Cazadores, which between November 1827 and October 1829 lost 31 soldiers dead and an astonishing 802 in desertions, many of which must have been multiple, since the battalion at its largest numbered only 715 men. And the same military report that mentions that the Río de la Plata Regiment left 150 sick men behind in Lima when it departed the city in 1823 adds that it also had to leave behind some 350 deserters who had not been apprehended by the military police and who remained at large in the city.[44] Therefore, when one reads such accounts as Domingo Sarmiento's description of how he encountered the remnants of an Afro-Argentine regiment at the siege of Montevideo in 1851, reduced to thirty men and commanded by a sergeant,[45] one should not immediately draw the conclusion that Sarmiento implies—that the rest of the regiment was killed in fighting. It is entirely possible that they took the rational course of action and left for home rather than be killed or maimed in the grueling siege. . . .

By claiming an almost complete destruction of the black male population through military service, the nation's historians were able to ignore the fact that many of those soldiers returned alive from the wars to contribute to Buenos Aires's cultural, social, and demographic development. It is significant that the best-known Afro-Argentine military hero is not a historical figure like Colonels Domingo Sosa and José María Morales, who fought in a host of battles, served Buenos Aires heroically for forty or fifty years, and died quietly at home in bed, but rather the mythical Falucho, who, if in fact he ever existed, was killed while suicidally defending the flag of Argentina.[46] Emphasis on the heaps of white Afro-Argentine bones and the pools of red Afro-Argentine blood provides a convenient distraction from the continued presence of black Afro-Argentine skin in the nation's capital. This is not to belittle the disastrous effect that virtually continuous military service over six decades exerted on the city's black population. Many of those deserters clearly never made it back to Buenos Aires and thus were as effectively removed from the black community as they would have been if they had died. Several Argentines who visited Lima in the 1830s and 1840s reported encountering survivors of San Martín's expeditionary force there, and one of the more celebrated anecdotes of nineteenth-century Argentine literature concerns an old black deserter encountered living among the Ranquele Indians by the writer Lucio Mansilla.[47] And many more of the deserters who did make it back to Buenos Aires arrived broken in health, suffering from wounds or the rigors of campaigning. But it is clearly incorrect to say that the Afro-Argentines fell "to the last man" fighting for a country that consistently denied them the rights they were fighting for. To pretend that this was so is to deny them the most elementary common sense or instinct of self-preservation.

When one considers the meager rewards received by the black warriors for their services, the infrequent promotions, the miserable pay, the hardships, [and] the grudging and long-delayed granting of rights promised them during the revolution, one must be amazed at the heroism and endurance that Afro-Argentines consistently displayed. The only major Argentine commander who ever criticized the Afro-Argentines' military performance was Manuel Belgrano, who after presiding over a series of defeats in Paraguay, northeastern Argentina, and Bolivia, wrote to General San Martín that "I'm not at all pleased with the *libertos*; the blacks and mulattoes are a rabble who are as cowardly as they are bloodthirsty, and in the five actions we have been in, they have been the first to break ranks and hide behind walls of bodies."[48] General Paz, a subordinate of Belgrano's who later made brilliant use of black troops in the civil wars, disagreed sharply, once remarking that one black soldier was worth at least three Europeans.[49] Paz and San Martín both preferred *liberto* troops, whose experience as slaves made them more amenable to military discipline than the whites. When the Seventh Infantry arrived in northwestern Argentina in 1813, Paz was extremely pleased with the way they had mastered their drills: "Along with the Mounted Grenadiers the handsome Seventh Battalion arrived to enlarge the Army of Peru. They came already instructed in modern tactics with which we were unfamiliar, so that they served as a model to the rest of the infantry and cavalry."[50] Generals Rondeau, Viana, Miller, and Guido are also on record as lavishing special praise on Afro-Argentine troops.[51]

The devotion with which thousands of Afro-Argentines fought for their country is a puzzling phenomenon, when one considers the meager rewards they received in return. Perhaps they actually believed the appeals to defend God and country with which their officers fired them before battle, but it is more likely that their bravery and even ferocity in battle sprang from two sources. The first source included the resentments and frustrations they suffered due to their position in Buenos Aires's society. The discontent and rage that they had to repress in the city could be released on the battlefield without fear of punishment, and the occasional testimonials to the "bloodthirstiness" and "savagery" of the Afro-Argentine soldiers suggest that they did not hesitate to take advantage of this opportunity. The fury they displayed on the battlefield was truly above and beyond the call of duty and hints at some deeper motive than mere love of country. The second source was the hope for promotion: upward mobility in the army and perhaps even in the greater society.

The Officers

Historians writing on the Afro-Argentines have traditionally maintained that it was virtually unheard-of for black men to attain officer rank. José Ingenieros stated unequivocally that the soldiers of the independence wars were always mestizos or blacks, their officers always white.[52] Emiliano Endrek concurred, saying that a few Afro-Argentines may have reached officer level during the post-1820 civil wars, but that black units of the colonial and independence periods were commanded entirely by white officers.[53] José Ramos Mejía maintained that even during the Rosas period, when the government made a policy of courting Afro-Argentine support, it was almost impossible for black men to rise above the rank of sergeant or lieutenant.[54] José Luis Lanuza echoed this statement, and even the normally well-informed Leslie Rout flatly states that "no acknowledged Negroid" held officer rank in the Argentine or Uruguayan colonial militias, and that no black Argentine rose above the rank of captain until after 1820.[55]

The very authors who make these assertions include incidental information which strongly suggests, and in some cases conclusively demonstrates, that black men did in fact reach command positions. In the same essay in which Endrek claims that no blacks served as colonial- or independence-period officers, he includes the quotation in which General Belgrano excoriated his black troops as cowardly rabble, a quotation which terminates: "My only consolation is that white officers are coming [to command them], under whom perhaps they can be made of some use."[56] The implication is that at that point they were under the command of black officers. Later, Endrek refers specifically to the black officers of Córdoba's Afro-Argentine militia, who were displaced by white officers when the unit was sent off to fight in Bolivia.[57] Another case in point is a thesis written at the University of Córdoba in 1972, whose author asserts that blacks never became officers and then quotes an 1830 decree by General Paz that all *liberto* prisoners-of-war were to be returned to their owners, with the exception of "those slaves who have served as officers in the invading army"![58] And there is little question that the above-mentioned authors are familiar with Vicente Fidel López's *Manual de la historia argentina*, one of the most frequently quoted Argentine histories from the nineteenth century. Lanuza, for example, cites it frequently but inexplicably omits López's statement that every officer in Rosas's elite Fourth Battalion was black, with the sole exception of the colonel.[59]

Not only did black men serve as officers in Buenos Aires's army, but some rose to high levels of command. It seems to have been an unwritten rule that no Afro-Argentine could be allowed to reach the rank of general, but at least eleven rose to be full or lieutenant colonels; doubtless more such cases lie concealed in the documentation of the period, waiting to be discovered. Furthermore, Afro-Argentine colonels could hardly have existed in isolation from an even larger number of Afro-Argentines at lower levels in the hierarchy. In order to identify these men and arrive at a coherent representation of the evolution of the black officer corps, I examined the officer staffs of seven all-black battalions in existence between 1800 and 1860.[60] White and integrated units were not included in this study because black officers in those units appear to have been too few in number to justify the expenditure of time and energy involved in searching for them. All seven battalions were infantry; four were regular line units, two were militia, and one, the Restorer Battalion, was a mixed unit of militia and line companies, a common form of military organization under the Rosas administration.

In order to ensure comparability between militia and regular officers (who, as will be seen shortly, occupied very different positions in the military establishment), I relied wherever possible on the individual's regular line rank rather than his militia rank. Since almost all of the men in this study held line commissions at one or more points during their lives, it proved possible to compare careers over time using reasonably consistent data.

The names of every officer mentioned in the battalion rolls produced a universe of 186 men. Since roll calls never indicated an individual's race, it was necessary to verify race using other sources. These included military service records and evaluations, which occasionally mention race; enlistment records, which always do; censuses; birth, death, and marriage records; and newspaper articles. Using these data it was possible to establish the race of 104 of the 186 men, somewhat over half.

I tend to suspect that, due to a documentary bias in the data available, the majority of the unknown officers were black. The men for whom it was easiest to get information were those who had the most successful careers and were most prominent in the army and in the society as a whole. For obvious reasons, they tended strongly to be whites. Another complicating factor is the demonstrable tendency on the part of record keepers to cover up evidences of the black officers' African ancestry. Several instances may serve to illustrate this phenomenon. Sublieutenant Bernardo Pintos of the colonial Corps of Indians, Pardos, and Morenos was a successful musician and a rather well-known figure in the city. Histories of colonial Buenos Aires single him out as a renowned black organist, but in the municipal census of 1810 he was counted as white. When he married in 1828, his marriage certificate was filed in the book reserved for whites, despite the fact that the document specifically labeled him as a *pardo*.[61] Captain Gregorio Sanfines's 1761 baptism certificate described him as the son of a *moreno* father and a *parda* mother. By the time his son José María Sanfines married in 1813, however, the young Sanfines was eligible to be described in the marriage certificate as an *español*, a white. When Sanfines's other son, José Gregorio, married in 1816, no mention was made of his race, but when this son and his wife had a daughter in 1824 (the original captain's grandchild), her baptism record was inscribed in the book reserved for *españoles*.[62] Thus an Afro-Argentine militia captain produced a white Spanish son and granddaughter. Lieutenant Colonel Cabrera's entire family was labeled as *pardo* in the 1827 census, but by the time his daughter Agueda died in 1881 she had been transformed into a white woman, at least according to her death certificate.[63] Lieutenant Lorenzo Castro of the Restorer Battalion was labeled a *pardo* in the 1827 census, but the priest who officiated at his 1818 wedding made no mention of his race on the marriage certificate. Castro is described simply as a native of Caracas and a lieutenant in the regular army, though his *porteña* wife is described as a *parda*.[64]

One can hardly blame the Afro-Argentine officers, who had attained some measure of social standing in the city, for wishing to conceal documentary evidences of their blackness, a guarantee of inferior social status in nineteenth-century Buenos Aires. But coupled with the other documentary bias, this results in its being very difficult to reconstruct the genuine racial composition of the officer corps. This is undoubtedly another contributing factor behind the misconceptions concerning Buenos Aires's black officers.

Table 2 describes distribution of the sample by race and unit. Of the 104 officers whose race was verifiable, 39, over a third, were black, 61 were white, and 4 were Indian.[65] (The totals in Table 2 exceed these figures due to the fact that several officers in the sample served in more than one unit.) If one is willing to assume that the percentage of black officers

Table 2. Racial Composition of Officer Corps in Selected Battalions from Buenos Aires Province, 1800–1860

Unit	Indian	Black	White	Unknown	Total	Percent black[a]
Corps of Indians, Pardos, and Morenos (1808)[b]	4	17	2	7	30	74
Battalion of Pardos and Morenos of Upper Peru (1813)	0	3	5	8	16	38
Seventh Infantry Battalion of Libertos (1814–15)	0	0	25	14	39	0
Second Battalion of Cazadores (1817–1820)	0	1	11	7	19	8
Fourth Battalion of Cazadores (1829)	0	0	15	14	29	0
Restorer Battalion (1834–35)	0	6	4	8	18	60
Restorer Battalion (1852)	0	4	0	13	17	100
Fourth Battalion of the National Guard (1853)	0	10	2	12	24	83
Total[c]	4	41	64	83	192	38

Source: Data on the race of individual officers were taken from a variety of sources, including enlistment and service records; parish birth, death, and marriage registers; censuses; and newspaper articles. For citations of sources on each individual, see George Reid Andrews, "Forgotten but Not Gone: The Afro-Argentines of Buenos Aires, 1800–1900" (Ph.D. diss., University of Wisconsin, Madison, 1978), 396–410.

[a]Column calculated excluding unknowns from total.
[b]Dates in parentheses indicate years from which roll call records were taken.
[c]Totals exceed sample totals because several officers served in more than one unit.

among the unknowns was much higher than among the knowns, as seems reasonable, it is probable that black men made up at least half of the officer corps of the Afro-Argentine battalions.

The role of the black officers in Buenos Aires's army changed markedly between 1800 and 1860. The first unit considered, the colonial militia Corps of Indians, Pardos, and Morenos, was officered almost entirely by blacks and Indians, in complete contradiction of traditional claims that no black men achieved officer rank in the colony. Of 23 officers whose race is known, 17 were black, 4 were Indian, and only 2 were white. These free black officers went on to serve in two line units in the revolutionary army, the Sixth Infantry Regiment of Pardos and Morenos and the Battalion of Pardos and Morenos of Upper Peru. Only the latter was included in this study, and very little information could be obtained on its officers, half of whom remain of unknown race. Of the 8 officers whose race could be verified, 5 were white and 3 black. More useful for the purposes of this study would have been the Sixth Infantry, whose roll calls were unfortunately not discovered until after this research project had been completed, at which time it was not possible to subject each name on the rolls to the careful cross-checking in a variety of sources undergone by officers in other units. However, of 39 officers in its 1814–15 rolls, 9 were immediately recognizable as black men who had served at lower ranks in the colonial militia.[66]

Free black troops in the revolutionary army were therefore commanded in large part by black men. This was not the case in the *liberto* units, represented in this study by the Seventh Infantry Battalion and the Second Cazadores. Only one officer in these two units was verifiable as Afro-Argentine. There are several possible explanations for this dichotomy between the free black battalions and the *liberto* battalions. First, the government was under no political necessity to make black men the officers of these units. Since the free blacks were accustomed from their colonial experience to serving under black officers, and members of the free black militia had been led to expect that a certain percentage of their number would eventually acquire officer status, the revolutionary government would instantly have alienated free black support by failing to continue this practice. Among the slaves, on the other hand, no such precedent existed. The mere promise of freedom was sufficient to ensure their support for the new regime. Since there had never been slave officers, there was no need to elevate *libertos* into command positions.

Second, and perhaps more important, keeping the *liberto* regiments officered by whites prevented alliance of any sort between free black officers and the slaves, which the *liberto* troops in essence still were. In 1806 the town council had described the job of commandant of the Slave Corps (formed during the emergency of the English invasions and disbanded shortly thereafter) as "one of the most delicate positions imaginable."[67] The last thing the upper echelons of the military and the government wanted was to put recently freed black troops under the command of free black officers, producing a potentially explosive convergence of interests between the two.

The destruction of the free black battalions at the Battle of Sipe-Sipe therefore marked the end of a brief five-year period in which many Afro-Argentines enjoyed officerships in the regular army. As free black troops were displaced by *libertos*, the black officer corps in the regular army withered away and, by 1820, had disappeared almost completely. Regular army Afro-Argentine units from 1815 to 1830 were officered almost entirely by whites, as may be seen in the cases of the Second and Fourth Cazadores. Of 29 officers in the latter unit, 15 are of known race, and every one of them was white.

The color bar preventing Afro-Argentines from reaching officer status was dropped by the Rosas administration. Roll calls of the Restorer Battalion at the beginning and end of its existence (1834–35 and 1852) produce a list of 35 officers, of whom 14 are of known race. Four are white and 10 black. This pattern of black dominance was continued in the post-Rosas Fourth Battalion of the National Guard. Of 24 officers in the unit's 1853 roll calls, 12 are of unknown race. Two are white and 10 black, including the commander, Colonel Domingo Sosa.

How does one explain the resurrection of the Afro-Argentine officer corps in the 1830–1860 period, after its apparent demise between 1815 and 1830? One explanation must be Rosas's policy of courting Afro-Argentine support for his administration, a policy which did not allow the continued relegation of black men to the lowest ranks of the army. Just as the revolutionary government of 1810 bartered officerships for black political support, so Rosas did the same in the 1830s and 1840s.

Another reason for the return of the black officers may be found in the changing legal status of the black population. The municipal census of 1810 showed that 22.6 percent of the city's black population was free; by 1827 that proportion had risen to 54.8 percent. Following the policy adopted by the revolutionary government in 1810, the Rosas administration recognized that free black men could be impressed into service, but they would not fight well unless there were genuine opportunities for advancement. Since the need for manpower to fight the Indian and civil wars of the 1830s and 1840s was as great as it had been to fight the Spanish in 1810, the government was forced to cede black men the right to rise through the ranks.

When Governor Rosas came to power, he found a readily available supply of potential Afro-Argentine officers in the form of the militia officers. The dearth of black officers in the regular units from 1815 to 1830 can be deceiving, since it hides the fact that black men continued to exercise command in the city's militia units throughout that period. A cursory glance at the 1815 officer list of the Civic Regiment of Men of Color reveals a number of black men from the earlier colonial militia.[68] These officers, later joined by regulars returning from the campaigns in the northwest, continued in the unit well into the 1820s. Black officers who were later to achieve high rank in Buenos Aires's army all served in the black militia during this period in which their access to the regular army was barred. Young Domingo Sosa, after returning from service in the Sixth Infantry, was assigned to duty as a drill instructor in the slave militia, the Argentine Auxiliaries, and in 1828 was called up to serve in the all-black Fourth Militia Battalion.[69] Feliciano Mauriño, later to rise to major, served from 1826 to 1833 as an officer in the various black militia units of the city. He then made the unfortunate decision to be an anti-Rosista in the 1833 uprising, for which he was broken to common soldier in the Restorer Battalion.[70] Even the extraordinarily talented Lorenzo Barcala, Argentina's best-known black officer, saw service in the War with Brazil not in a regular unit but in the Fourth Militia Battalion.[71]

Being restricted to the militia set the Afro-Argentines several ranks lower in the military hierarchy than the white regulars. For one, regular officers assigned to mobilized militia units were always elevated one or two ranks above their customary rank. Thus, a regular lieutenant assigned to the militia became an acting captain or even major, with authority over all those officers below him. Black militia officers always came out on the short end of this arrangement. Also, periods of active service in the militia counted toward retirement and pension rights, but periods of inactivity did not. Such slack time did count for regular army officers, enabling them to collect the pensions that often eluded the Afro-Argentines. Finally, regular officers were subject at all times to the *fuero*, military legal jurisdiction, while militia officers were subject to such jurisdiction only when they were on active duty. Being subject to the *fuero* was considered to be one of the great privileges of military service, since it made one immune to the civilian courts and the police; officers found that their military peers tended to be more lenient in punishing civil offenses than were the civilian courts.[72]

Although the Afro-Argentine militia officers do not appear to have been disadvantaged in relation to white militia officers, their inability to acquire line commissions during the 1820s was clearly the result of a policy of racial exclusion. While not every white man could win a position in the regular officer corps, no black man could. It was therefore of concrete benefit to them that Governor Rosas allowed the Afro-Argentines back into the ranks of the regulars.

Once having entered the regular army, however, the Afro-Argentines' race continued to have an adverse effect on their possibilities for advancement. A tabulation of the highest known rank reached by each individual in the sample (Table 3) shows that the average black officer in service between 1800 and 1860 was most likely to end his career as a captain, while the average white officer was most likely to end his as a colonel. No black man achieved the rank of general, whereas 10 percent of the

Table 3. Highest Known Rank Achieved by Individuals of Known Race in Selected Buenos Aires Battalions, 1800–1860

	Indian	*Black*	*White*	*Total*
General	0	0	6	6
Colonel	0	2	16	18
Lieutenant colonel	0	5	12	17
Major	1	5	7	13
Captain	1	13	10	24
Lieutenant	0	9	7	16
Sublieutenant	2	5	3	10
Total	4	39	61	104

Source: See Table 2.

whites did. And the increasing difficulty that black men experienced in winning promotion past the rank of captain can be seen in the fact that there are fewer black majors and lieutenant colonels than captains, and fewer black colonels than lieutenant colonels. Among the whites, there were more lieutenant colonels than majors, and even more colonels than lieutenant colonels.

Military service could and did serve as an avenue of upward mobility for those men skilled and determined enough to make their way to the top. An Afro-Argentine male looking to rise as high in the society as possible was probably best advised to join the army and bend such talents as he had toward acquiring a colonelcy. But such a man would have been a fool not to realize that the odds against his reaching that goal were extremely long, that access to the topmost levels of the hierarchy would be forever closed to him because of his race, and that even if he were lucky enough to rise as high as a black man could go, his influence and prestige could be cut short at any moment by political reversals or violent death. Men seeking less spectacular but more secure advancement were better advised to master a more reliable and less hazardous trade than that of arms.

The twentieth-century reader may level the charge that the black soldiers and officers prostituted themselves to fight white men's wars. The charge is anachronistic, since it presupposes a political consciousness that simply did not exist in nineteenth-century Buenos Aires, nor in the United States. Many Afro-Argentines sincerely believed in love of country and the principles of heroism, loyalty, and valor, just as thousands of North Americans went to their deaths under similar banners in colonial wars in

Mexico and Cuba. Others capitalized on their military service to win the upward mobility denied them by the society at large. The Afro-Argentines lived in a white man's society; the alternatives were either to fight his wars or to suffer the consequences of refusing to do so. While fighting those wars they served not only as followers but also as leaders, and as soldiers and officers they compiled a record of achievement that has been too easily relegated to history's back drawers. Let the record stand corrected.[73]

Notes

1. See Jack D. Foner's excellent book, *Blacks and the Military in American History* (New York, 1974) for a discussion of how North Americans have consistently ignored and denied the extent of Afro-American participation in fighting the United States' wars in order to avoid making social, political, and legal concessions to the country's black population. The post-Civil War period was the only instance in which black people experienced an improvement in their situation as a result of black men's wartime services (pp. 50–51).

2. For descriptions and analyses of this militarization, see Tulio Halperin Donghi. *Hispanoamérica después de la independencia* (Buenos Aires, 1972), Chap. 1; and Halperin Donghi, *Revolución y guerra* (Buenos Aires, 1972), pp. 210–47, 395–400.

3. *Reseña histórica y orgánica del Ejército Argentino*, 3 vols. (Buenos Aires, 1972), 1:294–300. See AGN [Archivo General de la Nación], 10 26-2-6, for a series of sentences to military service handed down between 1842 and 1852.

4. *Reseña histórica*, 1:421–23.

5. AGN, Sucesiones 6917. Testamentaria de D. Federico Mendizábal.

6. AGN, 10 31-11-5.

7. José Torre Revello, *La sociedad colonial* (Buenos Aires, 1970), pp. 115–16; and *Reseña histórica*, 1:84–85, 97–99.

8. *Documentos para la historia argentina*, 23 vols. to date (Buenos Aires, 1913–), 12:324–25; and *Uniformes de la patria* (Buenos Aires, 1972), unnumbered pages. See also José Luis Molinari, "Los indios y negros durante las invasiones inglesas al Río de la Plata, en 1806 y 1807," *Boletín de la Academia Nacional de la Historia* 34 (1963): 663.

9. Felix Best, *Historia de las guerras argentinas*, 2 vols. (Buenos Aires, 1968), 1:218.

10. Marta B. Goldberg de Flichman and Laura Beatriz Jany, "Algunos problemas referentes a la situación del esclavo en el Río de la Plata," in *IV Congreso Internacional de Historia de América* (Buenos Aires, 1966), 6:65–66.

11. Emeric E. Vidal, *Picturesque Illustrations of Buenos Ayres and Montevideo* (London, 1820), p. 32.

12. Nuria Sales de Bohigas, *Sobre esclavos, reclutas, y mercaderes de quintas* (Barcelona, 1974), p. 78.

13. Goldberg and Jany, "Algunos problemas," p. 68.

14. Ibid., pp. 65–66.

15. For the roll calls of the Seventh Battalion, in which the notation "entregado a su amo," "handed over to his master," frequently appears, see AGN, 3 44-2-1.

16. Goldberg and Jany, "Algunos problemas," p. 68.

17. Manuel Alvarez Pereyra, *Historia del Regimiento 8 de Infantería de Linea* (La Plata, 1921), p. 22.

18. Gerónimo Espejo, *El paso de los Andes* (Buenos Aires, 1953), p. 344; and M. F. Mantilla. *Páginas históricas* (Buenos Aires, 1890), p. 368.

19. Espejo, *El paso*, pp. 400–401, 411; Alvarez Pereyra, *Regimiento 8*, p. 21; and Ramón Tristany, *Regimiento 8 de Infantería de Linea* (Buenos Aires, 1897), pp. 12–13.

20. José Luis Lanuza, *Morenada* (Buenos Aires, 1967), pp. 83–87; and AGN, 10 10-2-5.

21. AGN, 3 45-4-2, 45-2-9, 46-1-10; *Reseña histórica*, 1:396; and Jacinto R. Yaben, *Biografías argentinas y sudamericanas*, 5 vols. (Buenos Aires, 1938–1940), 5:293.

22. AGN, 3 5-1-3, 11-1-1; Yaben, *Biografías*, 4:727.

23. *Gaceta de Buenos Aires, 1810–21*, facs. ed., 6 vols. (Buenos Aires, 1910–1913), 3:289–90, 4:717–19, 5:592, 593, 742–43, 6:93, 154; *Reseña histórica*, 1:188, 189, 298–300, 412; and Yaben, *Biografías*, 1:249, 3:708, 4:727.

24. Bohigas, *Sobre esclavos*, p. 134. The practice of slaves substituting for their masters in the militia also occurred in Colombia. See Allan J. Kuethe, "The Status of the Free Pardo in the Disciplined Militia of New Granada," *Journal of Negro History* 56 (April 1971): 105–17.

25. See the petition of Sublieutenant Anastasio Sosa. AGN, 9 26-7-4, folios 173–74. See documents concerning Lieutenant Manuel Gutiérrez. AGN, 9 12-5-3, folios 338–39.

26. *Reseña histórica*, 1:151, 153.

27. AGN, 3 59-1-1, 59-1-6, 59-2-1, 59-2-4, 59-2-7. I am indebted to Colonel Ulises Muschietti for having suggested this method of studying integration in Buenos Aires's army.

28. See, for instance, AGN, 10 26-2-6, which contains many sentences of military service.

29. AGN, 10 17-8-1.

30. Bohigas, *Sobre esclavos*, pp. 93–94.

31. Yaben, *Biografías*, 2:400.

32. *Partes oficiales y documentos relativos a la Guerra de la Independencia Argentina*, 2 vols. (Buenos Aires, 1900), 2:186–87.

33. These statistics are taken from roll calls contained in the following volumes of documents: the Battalion of Pardos and Morenos of Upper Peru, the Second Battalion of Peru, and the Eighth Battalion of Peru (AGN, 3 44-2-7); the Ninth Infantry Regiment (AGN, 3 44-2-2); the Seventh Infantry Regiment (AGN, 3 44-2-1); and the Sixth Infantry Regiment (AGN, 3 44-1-15).

34. Alvaro Yunque, *Calfucura, la conquista de las pampas* (Buenos Aires, 1956), pp. 187–88. Florence Brooks supplied this citation.

35. This image of bones is also employed by León Pomer in his book *El soldado criollo* (Buenos Aires, 1971), p. 10.

36. "Un sargento de la independencia," *Caras y Caretas*, Feb. 25, 1899.

37. Andrés Avellaneda, "Prohibe la Junta el ingreso de esclavos," *La Opinión*, May 28, 1976, p. 8.

38. Bohigas, *Sobre esclavos*, pp. 67–68; and Carlos Monge, "Aclimatación en los Andes: Influencia biológica en las guerras de América," *Revista de la Historia de América* (1948), pp. 1–25.

39. AGN, 10 35-10-2.

40. Enrique Martínez, *Manifestación de la conducta observada por el jefe de la División de los Andes Aucsiliar del Perú* . . . (Lima, 1823), p. 20.

41. Lanuza, *Morenada*, pp. 86–87.

42. Goldberg and Jany, "Algunos problemas," p. 73.

43. Pomer, *El soldado criollo*, pp. 44–46.

44. Martínez, *Manifestación de la conducta*, p. 24.

45. Domingo F. Sarmiento, *Conflicto y armonía de las razas en Américas*, 2 vols. (Buenos Aires, 1900), 1:76.

46. Marcos Estrada, *El cabo segundo Antonio Ruiz (a.) "Falucho"* (Buenos Aires, 1964); and Mantilla, *Páginas históricas*, pp. 349–53.

47. Mantilla, *Páginas históricas*, pp. 349–53; Espejo, *El paso*, pp. 400–401; and Lanuza, *Morenada*, pp. 168–69.

48. Quoted in José Luis Masini Calderón, "La esclavitud negra en la República Argentina—Epoca independiente," *Revista de la Junta de Estudios Históricos de Mendoza*, Ser. 2, 1 (1961): 142–43.

49. Ibid., p. 148.

50. Mantilla, *Páginas históricas*, p. 367. See also Goldberg and Jany, "Algunos problemas," pp. 72–73.

51. Yaben, *Biografías*, 5:688–89; Estrada, *Antonio Ruiz*, p. 6; and Mantilla, *Páginas históricas*, pp. 371–72.

52. José Ingenieros, *La locura en la Argentina* (Buenos Aires, 1937), p. 30 n. 3.

53. Emiliano Endrek, *El mestizaje en Córdoba, siglo XVIII y principios del XIX* (Córdoba, 1966), p. 83.

54. José Maria Ramos Mejía, *Rosas y su tiempo*, 3 vols. (Buenos Aires, 1907), 3:209–10.

55. Lanuza, *Morenada*, p. 167; and Leslie B. Rout, *The African Experience in Spanish America* (Cambridge, 1976), pp. 151, 171.

56. Endrek, *El mestizaje en Córdoba*, p. 83.

57. Ibid., pp. 84–85.

58. Nelly Beatriz López, "La esclavitud en Córdoba, 1790–1853" (Thesis, Universidad Nacional de Córdoba, 1972), pp. 68–69.

59. Masini Calderón, "La esclavitud negra en la República," p. 149.

60. The units, the time periods for which the rolls were taken, and the location of the rolls are: Corps of Indians, Pardos, and Morenos (1808), AGN, 9 26-7-6, folios 436–37; Battalion of Pardos and Morenos of Upper Peru (1813), AGN, 10 35-10-2; Seventh Battalion of Libertos (1814–15), AGN, 3 44-2-1; Second Battalion of Cazadores (1817–1820), AGN, 10-2-5; Fourth Battalion of Cazadores (1829), AGN, 3 45-4-2; Restorer Battalion (1834–35), AGN, 3 5-1-3; Restorer Battalion (1852), AGN, 3 56-1-2; Fourth Battalion of the National Guard (1853), AGN, 3 56-1-12.

61. Francisco L. Romay, *El barrio de Monserrat* (Buenos Aires, 1971), p. 69; AGN, 9 10-7-1, ward 14; AGN, 9 8-4-2, folios 197, 255; and "Parish of Monserrat," Bk. 3, *Matrimonios*, folio 120.

62. "Parish of La Merced," Bk. 9, *Bautismos de Color*, folio 372v; "Parish of Monserrat," Bk. 2, *Matrimonios*, folio 369v, 414v, and Bk. 5, *Bautismos de Españoles*, folio 176v.

63. AGE [Archivo General del Ejército], Personal File 2338.

64. AGN, 10 23-5-6, ward 20, Calle Venezuela 258; and "Parish of Monserrat," Bk. 2, *Matrimonios*, folio 480v.

65. For a detailed listing of the documentation by which each officer's race was verified, see George Reid Andrews, "Forgotten But Not Gone: The Afro-Argentines of Buenos Aires, 1800–1900" (Ph.D. diss., University of Wisconsin, Madison, 1978), pp. 396–410.

66. The list [was] taken from AGN, 3 44-1-15. The black officers are Captains Juan Loy Taboada, José San Martín, Lorenzo Espinosa, Felipe Malaver, and Dionisio Gamboa; Lieutenants Domingo Sosa and Antonio Porobio; and Sublieutenants Santiago Sosa and Casimiro Mendoza.

67. *Acuerdos del Extinguido Cabildo de Buenos Aires*, 88 vols. (Buenos Aires, 1907–1934), Ser. 4, Vol. 2, Bk. 61, p. 476.

68. *Gaceta de Buenos Aires*, 4:338.

69. Yaben, *Biografías*, 5:727.

70. Ibid., 3:708.

71. Ibid., 1:468.

72. For a discussion of the *fuero*, see Lyle McAlister, *The "Fuero Militar" in New Spain, 1764–1800* (Gainesville, Fla., 1957).

73. Readers wishing to consult an expanded and more detailed version of this chapter are referred to Andrews, "Forgotten But Not Gone," Chaps. 6–7; and George Reid Andrews, "The Afro-Argentine Officers of Buenos Aires Province, 1800–1860," *Journal of Negro History* 64 (Spring 1979): 85–100.

5

Afro-Creoles on the Frontier: Conquering the Ecuadorian Pacific Lowlands

Norman E. Whitten, Jr.

Exploration and conquest of the frontier had an indelible impact on American history. According to Frederick Jackson Turner, the foremost spokesman of this interpretation, the existence of unexplored land and the advancement of Europeans into this region provided the key to U.S. history. Turner used the frontier experience (which he saw primarily as the breakdown of European culture under the demands of the American environment) to explain the distinctive nature of developments in North America. Although scholars criticize this thesis for its Eurocentrism and its tendency toward geographic determinism, Turner nevertheless laid the foundations for study of the frontier and of the relationship between the physical environment and cultural patterns. Most scholars agree that the dynamics of a frontier community created new opportunities for social mobility, and such settlements in North and South America tend to confirm this thesis. The frontier in Latin America continues to be a contemporary preoccupation. In Brazil, Peru, Ecuador, Colombia, and the Guianas, schemes for the colonization and settlement of the Amazon*

From *Black Frontiersmen* (Rochester, VT: Schenkman Publishing Company, 1974), 10–12, 50–51, 53, 56–62, 71, 74–77, 80–81, 86–93. Reprinted by permission of Schenkman Publishing Company.

*See his "The Significance of the Frontier in American History," originally published in 1893 and widely reprinted. David J. Weber and Jane M. Rausch, eds., include the essay in *Where Cultures Meet: Frontiers in Latin American History* (Wilmington, DE: SR Books, 1994). Their volume provides a valuable comparative examination of the frontier experience.

*basin have received great attention and much criticism for their damage
to the ecology of the rain forest.**

Little research has been conducted on the contributions of Africans
to the process of exploration, especially in Latin America. Perhaps these
people have been ignored because Europeans directed most of the expeditions. Moreover, in colonial times the African explorers generally were
runaway slaves, fleeing to new territories to avoid being recaptured. They
willingly faced the hostile frontier for their freedom, establishing communities called* palenques *in Spanish-speaking countries,* quilombos *in
Brazil, and maroons in the English-speaking Caribbean.*

*Traditionally, both government and private development agencies
have paid scant attention to South America's Pacific Coast, the lowlands
in particular. For this reason Norman Whitten calls these areas South
America's last frontiers. Whitten conducted research in a predominately
Afro-Creole community in northwest Ecuador. His discussion does not
examine the negative impact of modernization schemes on the frontier
lands. Rather, it focuses on the Afro-Creole pathfinders and pioneer settlers and their adaptability in new surroundings. These men and women
discovered that self-reliance was crucial for survival in the absence of
outside support. Although written two decades ago (1974), this remains
the only text in English that explores the role of Afro-Creoles on the Pacific lowlands frontier.*

B lack men and women today in the wet littoral are *mobile.* Scarcely
   can one ascend a river, move a few miles along the coast, follow the
estuary pathways of giant tidal swamps, or even slog along a trail without
meeting single men, groups of men, or whole families from three to a
dozen or more people traveling to some other place. Travel is extremely
hard, often necessitating great physical power to move a heavily loaded
canoe against a current by pole or paddle. Even when moving with a current, the action of waves, or river rapids, together with ubiquitous flot-
sam, keep people constantly alert. Sometimes, though, in the estuaries,
the tide and currents are favorable to easy movement, and then the rise of
work and travel songs resounds through the trees, or across the water.
The music itself may follow the lines and melody of national music, but
more often it takes on a leader-response pattern where one male or
female leader maintains continuity of expression, while others answer
and respond to the leader in stylized West African patterns. . . .

Men are a bit more spatially mobile than women. Consequently, every river and estuary has more men on the move than women, and every
town has more women who have recently been "left" than men without

---

*See Susan E. Place, ed., *Tropical Rainforests: Latin American Nature and
Society in Transition* (Wilmington, DE: SR Books, 1993).

women. Marriage, a Catholic rite, is regarded by most men as a bit too binding, and few take part in the ceremony. Women, on the other hand, are often a bit closer to the church and the advantages (economic and social) which the local or visiting priest may confer, and tend to favor a church ceremony, though again, few find time, opportunity, or the right man with whom to undertake "marriage." Some men travel to and from villages and towns, and may have two or more "common law" wives, who remain more or less sexually faithful and work within the framework of his enterprise. Some particularly strong and clever men are able to muster the sexual and economic wherewithal, together with the psychological powers of maneuver, to have two, and occasionally three, women as *mujeres* (wives), in the same town and occasionally in the same house. More often, the existence of two or more wives signals the attenuation of one consensual bond, and the intensification of another. For this reason, I use the term "serial polygyny" as a marriage pattern characteristic of Afro-Hispanic culture.

Men work together in pairs, and shun the lone endeavor more characteristic of mestizo colonists. The overlapping of pairs of men can define chains of individuals loosely united for some tasks (usually for cash gain) which can melt away in other situations. The ability of large numbers of men to cooperate with one another when there is cash gain, but to return to their basic work habits of pairs of cooperating men in the absence of such gain, is a particular characteristic of the wet littoral social system. Not infrequently, a large group of men clusters around one particular man. Such a man is the locus for many work parties and is regarded as an equal. But he is particularly *responsible* to someone from the outside, to a white or mestizo who will actually *pay* for work done. It also usually results that such a man takes most of the earnings of a cooperative endeavor, such as collecting lumber, but pays back each worker through time. . . .

Racial Succession

As white dominance spread insidiously into village after village, following the dispersal of black men and women into forests and swamps, black survival strategies themselves had a profound effect on aboriginal Indian cultures. As these Black South Americans expanded, native Indians became hemmed in. Intertribal contacts were everywhere buffered by expanding black settlements, and in some areas black households were built between aboriginal houses.

Colombia and Ecuador today have no "Black Indian" settlements analogous to the "Black Carib" of Central America. Nor have blacks acquired facility with aboriginal languages, in spite of their enduring and continuing contact. In the Chocó of Colombia, Cuna culture is nearly gone, and the inland Chocó, or Emperá, are to be found mainly in small settlements far from the rivers of trade, where their attempts to maintain subsistence life are of necessity supplemented with minor sales of baskets and sleeping mats in the larger towns. The money gained from such endeavor, however, is normally used to increase personal and group prestige through the purchase of silver ornaments such as nose rings and ear plugs. The coastal Chocó, or Noanamá, are also to be found near the headwaters of major streams, above the commercially valuable sector which is inhabited completely by blacks. The Yurimanguí, who may have spoken a Hokan-Siouan language, have not been seen for a century. But as late as the early 1930s they were still reputed to be sending little model boats downriver, and current tales of their existence far up the Yurimanguí River are carried today. The Coaiquer have maintained an ethnic awareness on the slopes of the western Cordillera of Colombia by keeping their overt identity obscure, by keeping their language and aboriginal customs "secret" from travelers, explorers, and the like. In Ecuador, the Cayapa dispersed settlements are filled in their interstices by black people who are ever-more encroaching on their territory.

In the context of purely subsistence life, i.e., back on the rivers where sizable numbers of Indians live, they are looked up to by the ordinarily dominant black people. But at the same time, the Indian, though proud of his ethnicity vis-à-vis blacks, is not unafraid of the louder, more sizable black aggregates forever spreading into his territory. Whether simply by upstream retreat, or by becoming surrounded, aggregates of Indians are dominated by aggregates of black settlers. But on a one-to-one basis the black man shows considerable deference to the Indian, provided that money does not enter the situation. Black men feel that they have achieved a most desirable marriage should they win an Indian woman's hand, though the black man moving to town might leave his Indian wife in the forest. Such unions are quite rare, and there is considerable antiblack sentiment among Indians in terms of black man-red women sexual relationships. Indian men, on the other hand, readily sleep with black women, and take them as wives now and then. The children of mixed black-Indian unions are called *zambo*; they always fall into a non-Indian category, from the Indians' standpoint. . . .

Black Frontiersmen

Early decimation of Indian populations through disease, warfare with the Spaniards, and slavery produced a need for the continuous importation of Black Africans. Afro-Americans in this zone actively expanded their territory and customary ways of doing things at the expense of surviving Indian groups. Both black and Indian aggregates developed survival strategies linked both to subsistence agriculture, hunting, and fishing, and to trade networks within the confines of a boom-bust economy. Black expansion at the expense of the Indians seems to lie in the *relative* black success within the wider political economy, supported by an expanding, mobile population.

The historical material and this mode of analysis suggest that both Indians and blacks in the wet littoral make up what Mary Helms (1969) calls a "purchase society."

> Members of purchase societies appear as rural participants within the wider *economic* network formed either by industrializing nations searching for raw materials for their growing industries, or by trade with agrarian states. Geographically, purchase societies can be found on economic frontiers of states, in territory that is beyond de facto state political control (although often falling within the official de jure boundaries claimed by the state), but lying within economic reach of state activities. From the point of view of the local society, the over-riding factor, the channel that directs and influences all other activities, is the need, small at first but constantly growing, for items of foreign manufacture. These goods quickly become cultural necessities, either because traditional crafts are forgotten, or because they become necessary for the psychological well-being of the group.

The idea of a purchase society suggests that black people in this zone are *frontiersmen*—veritable *pioneers*—men and women beyond the effective national boundaries (though within the formal confines of two nations) who cope with nature in a manner at least partly prescribed by the dictates of world demand for commercial products. Here, and subsequently, the term "frontiersmen" is used in the sense of people facing a particular type of cultural ecological experience. Self-reliance and the ability to sustain, and expand, a population and a culture in the absence of "outside" support is crucial to frontier life, even within the purchase society. We turn now to the material apparatus of the black frontiersman adaptation, and then set this in the political economy of the wet littoral frontier zone.

Exploiting Nature

Afro-Hispanic culture in the Pacific littoral contains considerable capacity for the exploitation of forest, river, swamp, and sea. Black frontiersmen regard the environment as theirs to exploit. They do not see themselves as merely "fitting into" the environment—they seek to conquer it. In all three environmental zones—riverine-forest, sea edge, and

mangrove swamp—the mobility necessary for survival must be comple-
mented by a flexible, but relatively durable, system of shelter. Shelter
does not merely refer to the houses themselves, which are the most obvious sign of human habitation. Shelter is a dynamic concept with an ideal
model which is not always realized. Let us consider the frontier shelter
system, and then turn our attention to exploitation of nature in the three
environmental zones.

Shelter in the Pacific littoral may be thought of in terms of a sequence
of increasingly permanent forms. At the start is the *rancho*—a hastily but
well-constructed sleeping structure made by bending limbs or stems of
small pliable bushes into an archform, and arranging thatch over them.
Binding by *lianas* completes the temporary shelter used in the forest (usually about ten to fifteen feet off the ground with a hurriedly constructed
platform underneath for sleeping). When a sleeping structure is attached
to the stern of a canoe, the canoe becomes known as a *canoa ranchera*.
The *canoa ranchera*, in turn, symbolizes long trips, or change of primary
residence. Some people who frequently make overnight canoe trips keep
one or two portable *ranchos* around home.

The first movement toward settlement is the construction of a *cocina*
(kitchen), which also serves as first sleeping room (*cuarto*). The kitchen
is like a lean-to on piles, with a low sloping roof about four to five feet
high in the back, and eight to ten feet high in front. The floor is split
bamboo, or split palm, and extends out beyond the lower side from five
to ten feet. The sides are made of split bamboo, and the roof consists of
cross poles, bound by *lianas*, and thatched.

A *fogón* (hearth) is built, consisting of a raised platform with split
palm or wood base, lined with clay and salted with rocks. Into this *fogón*
(and sometimes under it, on a bed of clay) charcoal is placed, and kept
burning if possible. Fire fans (*abanicos*) are woven from split reeds and
used to tease charcoal into a blaze when new charcoal, or even fresh wood,
is added. The charcoal is produced outdoors by starting a fire of wood
and mounding dirt over the fire. A broom made from a simple pole and
grassy fibers, calabash dishes (*calabazos*), shallow wooden bowls (*bateas*),
and hexagonal loose-weave baskets of various sizes make up the minimal
equipment used in the early *cocina*. Meat and fish may be hung over the
fogón to dry; other foods are stored in the *cocina*. At this stage of house
construction there is little or no surplus, and people may go without meals
to get the *cocina* built.

The platform extending out back is used by women as a work space.
Only the machete is absolutely essential for the construction of the *cocina*,
though an adze is needed for making *bateas* and in squaring the pilings.

Tin pots and pans are preferable to calabash shells, both for cooking and for providing a pot for children (and sometimes women) to eliminate into. Waste is normally thrown off the kitchen platform, as are the sweepings from the floor.

The *batea* is used to wash clothes and children, carry loads, shuck beans and cacao, and to wash gravel in placer gold mining. The *batea* and *fogón* are as basic to intrahousehold life as the canoe, paddle, and pole to life on the river and sea.

The *cocina* may or may not be elaborated upon. If housing is temporary, or to be sporadically used during occasional work in the forest, or near a small farm, additions will not be made. The next addition will only be made to a particular house if it becomes central to regular economic endeavor. We might note in passing that any house that is *regarded as temporary* is known by the term *rancho*. Hence, even a completed house, if provided by a mining company, might be called a *rancho* if the occupants did not expect to spend much time there. Indians frequently call the typical, completed black dwelling, *rancho*.

The second phase of settlement consists in extending the floor of the kitchen outward through the higher side from ten to fifty feet, with more or less equal breadth. The most difficult job during this process is the felling, hewing to shape, and insertion of heavy hardwood pilings, which are frequently the nearly indestructible *guayacán*, but may be mangrove. Boards are used for floors and sides, when available. Otherwise, a floor is built of split palm and bamboo, arranged over bamboo poles, themselves supported by cross beams. This construction is more time-consuming than the work going into the *cocina*, and in fact the work itself may be destructive of the particular *cocina* (though it usually is not). A notched log or bamboo ladder provides access to the platform. An axe and an adze are necessary, in addition to the machete, for building this part of the house. People continue to sleep in the *cocina*, but eat on the *sala* platform.

Step three, though entirely logical in sequence, may not take place for some time, for reasons discussed below. It consists of building sides of bamboo or wood, cutting windows, and a front door, erecting cross beams and bamboo supports. Onto these supports more supports are laced by *lianas* or rope woven from plant fibers to form a rectangular roof structure, which is thatched with palm fronds, and capped by a crown held in place by *burros*. Sometimes the *burros* are carved, and sometimes a plank over the front door is carved into curving forms. One partition may be built separating the sleeping quarters from the rest of the *sala*; the sleeping quarters then become known as the *cuarto*. But people use the word *cuarto* for wherever they sleep, and *sala* for whatever room (outside of the *cocina*) they gather in. Often, *cuarto* and *sala* are the same room.

Smoke from the kitchen passes up through the crest of the main roof, and on out through coarse areas in the thatch. Storage platforms may be built on the roof supports. Sleeping mats, musical instruments, fish spears, and other paraphernalia are hung from exposed beams. The front of the house may be on the far side from the *cocina*, or it may be on a side adjacent to the *cocina*.

Although one or two stools might have been fashioned prior to the completion of sides and a roof, little elaboration of material culture is evident in the houses in the first couple of phases. With the completion of the house, though, other apparatus such as stools, perhaps a table, more baskets, sleeping platforms in the *cuarto*, bark cloth called *damajagua* made into a sleeping mat by pounding it with a wooden mallet, and woven *petates* (sleeping mats) are added. Lighting consists of adding more beeswax candles, or purchased candles, kerosene lanterns, or even electic lights in some towns. The final step (in logical sequence) is totally dependent on the developmental sequence of the particular people coalescing in and around the household. This consists of adding sections to the house, either by building a second story, or adding more rooms onto the sides. Sometimes adjacent houses are built, and when this occurs the occupants may, with sufficient help from kinsmen and neighbors, forego the sequence just described, and go directly into construction of a stage three house; but, again, such building is a function of the coalescence of people engaged in economic activities through mutual cooperation.

It must never be thought that house building is the only labor expenditure which settlers have. Quite the contrary is the case. The *cocina* provides shelter and warmth, and the platform of the *sala-cuarto* assures an aggregating area in the household. Many things must be done before full attention can be turned to the construction of the desirable stage three and four house. Unless one is fortunate enough to be building adjacent to relatives who are already established, the house builders must turn their attention to a number of vital activities. People must always maintain a food supply, and this means farming, fishing, and hunting-gathering as a vital subsistence backdrop to the exploitation of cash opportunities. The carrying through of the latter activities is often predicated on successful understanding of the former basis and, for that reason, we continue to develop the concept of black exploitation of nature, prior to introduction of black exploitation of the capitalistic political economy. . . .

Exploiting Man

Black frontiersmen adapt not only through exploitation of their natural environment; they also adapt to shifting emphases in national and international demand for specific products. Until now I have used the word "exploit" in the first sense of *Webster's Third International Dictionary*: "to make use of: utilize; turn to account." To understand black adaptation to a money economy we must expand the usage to include a broader meaning, "to make a profit from the labor of others."

International demand for certain products periodically affects the wet littoral. The demand brings with it people who are not black, but rather associated with some variant of the nonblack world. By making use of resident labor such "outsiders" exploit the frontier through the frontiersmen. Whenever they see the frontiersmen as black they "color code" their labor force. It is necessary then to consider people making up such a labor force as "color coded" in relation to the "color coders," the outside exploiters who "make use" of black labor. At the same time, we should consider the ways by which black people in the wet littoral devise techniques to wrest an income *from* outsiders—the ways and means by which they "make use" of cash inputs. "Exploiting man," then, refers to the ways by which black people are used *for* profit, *and* to black people as exploiters—people who attempt to maximize the advantages and minimize the disadvantages coming into the littoral according to the resources available to them, and to their concepts of resources. We view black people in the wet littoral as pawns of external exploitation. But they are not passive pawns who play by imposed rules. They are active, organized people who move according to *their own* strategies and rules in response to inevitable external pressures. We shall begin to build a perspective of black adaptation to the boom-bust economy.

The Political Economy

The insatiable European demand for gold established, so to speak, the primary conditioning economic domain for black frontiersmen. Black Africans came in large numbers as slaves to mine placers; they revolted; and they adjusted to hemmed-in-freedom through a labor system represented by the slave and free *cuadrillas*. Today, *cuadrillas* still work various gravels, and small groups of women may pan gold nearly anywhere, selling by the ounce to resident buyers in various towns. In some places, platinum is found in with the gold. Large-scale mining financed by foreign concerns has taken place in the Chocó. Recently, large-scale dredging has been attempted here and there by foreign speculators.

Medicinal herbs, roots and barks such as sarsaparilla, ipecac, and quinine were historically purchased in various centers in the wet littoral, along with sandalwood, tagua, kapok from the ceiba tree, balsa, and furs. All were gathered by Indians and blacks and sold in centers established primarily to provide an outlet for gold. On the whole, men and women gathered the products in the forest, selling them individually in the respective centers.

Ivory nut (*tagua*) enjoyed a boom just prior to World War II. At one time this wild palm product, which looks sort of like a potato, was in demand because all of our buttons were made from it. The advent of plastics changed this, and tagua today is used primarily to carve "ivory" chess pieces, tops, and other toys. Gathering tagua involved individuals (both men and women), who spotted the trees in the forest, stripped them of their nuts, either by climbing them, or cutting the palm down, and delivered them to a center of distribution, or way station on a river. Tagua buyers were generally from Ecuador or Colombia and they sold to foreign buyers in other port cities. World demand for wild rubber caused booms from the mid-nineteenth century through World War II. Individuals gathered the latex and sold it to local buyers at stations on rivers, or bypassed the local buyers and went directly to the centralized towns, where they made contact with foreign buyers.

Right after World War II a banana boom hit the Province of Esmeraldas, Ecuador, and black people began to put in special crops of this fruit (which they despise as a food, regarding it only as pig fodder, or starvation fare). Plantations grew near large towns (such as Esmeraldas) run by highland and south-coast lowland whites and mestizos. The fruit was sold on various rivers to buyers who announced the day of purchase in advance. The banana boom affected the ecology in a new way, for the crop had to be planted in land which otherwise could have been used in the subsistence economy. It affected the agricultural round, as well as travel and work habits. The introduction of this cash crop encouraged expansion of the cultivation complex, and often forced sellers to turn around and pay cash for subsistence goods that otherwise could have been raised for home consumption or barter. Banana buyers came from within the nation, and were also foreign entrepreneurs. In parts of the Colombian Pacific lowlands, including the mouth of the Atrato which empties into the Atlantic, wet rice cultivation is now growing in commercial importance. In such areas the impact on subsistence crops is comparable to that discussed for bananas.

Timber exploitation of the soft- and hardwoods of the Pacific littoral has been going on since World War II. At first sawmills were established in distribution centers, or near a road or railroad. Timber was floated to the mill and sold there, the sellers often working to bring the timber in on credit relationships with buyers. More recently, new types of timber operations are creating an economic boom in some zones. Timber buyers are predominantly foreign middlemen—including North Americans, Europeans, and other Latin Americans.

Shellfish, notably the conchas, are in demand in Ecuador, and the demand is manifest in mangrove zones where the mussels live in symbiotic relationship with the mangrove trees. The conchas are purchased by the sack in distribution centers and either sent to the highlands by rail, or to coastal towns by ship. Buyers are national Ecuadorians, usually from the highlands or southern coast.

Mangrove bark contains about 50 to 60 percent tannic acid and so is in some demand in tanneries, in Ecuador, Colombia, and in the United States. Mangrove bark is purchased in bundles in distribution towns, and either freighted to the interior of the country by rail or truck, or shipped to other port towns for export or subsequent distribution. Buyers and sellers are usually highland nationals or hail from large coastal towns.

Dried fish and coconuts are in constant demand. Bales of dried fish and bundles of coconuts are purchased in distribution centers by middlemen in shellfish, mangrove bark, gold, and fur businesses, as well as by captains of ships or other shippers. They are often sold to small shops in poor areas, where they make up an important source of protein and minerals. Local people do their own trading of these items, sometimes traveling to a market to sell directly to buyers, but they more often sell to distributing middlemen in various towns. The cash value, however, is a function of the boom-bust economy because of the dependence on towns and money.

The means by which inputs of money are made are generally the same: (1) a center of operations is established where access to supply, and access to the shipping lanes, is advantageous; (2) white and mestizo outsiders take up residence at the center, and purchase the desired product which is gathered by blacks, *zambos*, mulattoes, and Indians. The same outsiders sell to shippers or manage the transference of the product to the outside world. As the demand for goods waxes and wanes, and as sources are discovered and depleted, sellers and shippers move, and the entire system arising in response to external demands is forced to readjust. The bases for such major readjustments lie in *spatial mobility* just as in the subsistence economy. In any area where the center is developing or expanding we can think in terms of an economic "boom"—a rapid influx of cash—and where centers are exiting, or declining, we may talk of a "bust"—a rapid decrease in money and consequent dependence on nature. The characteristic economic picture then is that of a "boom-bust" economy imposed on a subsistence economy.

In the purchase society, a creation of international capitalism, goods and labor have cash value. I shall give all figures in the Ecuadorian sucre, which was worth about five U.S. cents in 1965. The Colombian unit is the peso, worth about one and a half sucres in 1965. The normal day wage of a dock worker, sawmill worker, lumberjack, railroad worker, helper on a farm or in moving produce to market, and other comparable laboring jobs is from twelve to twenty sucres per day, either in cash, or in credit redeemable in the towns. Day labor for women is not yet possible in most of the littoral, although preparing and serving food and washing other people's clothes brings in seven to twelve sucres per day. For the most part, though, the only reliable paying jobs are concha gathering, and prostitution. In a previous work (1965) I argue that "averaged over a month, the daily net income of a lower-class family may amount to fifteen sucres. The significant point here is that by marketing essentially subsistence products, a lower-class household may earn as much money as it could by working regularly for wages."

I do not propose to recapitulate the calculations leading to this conclusion here. . . . I do think that this point is accurate: *people giving proportionately more time to wage labor make choices invariably costing them more money when they go to buy subsistence goods; while those choosing to produce subsistence crops, to fish, or to hunt may also make the same amount of money which allows them to purchase goods.* Wage labor in the Pacific littoral does not provide any measure of security for black frontiersmen. Money is a basic necessity but there is no institutionalized means within the purchase society to guarantee a worker a subsistence income. Even regular wage workers cannot *rely* on cash return for their labor; they must have other social and political supports, and these supports themselves demand outlays of money and time. The manner by which man exploits man in the Pacific littoral is in itself dependent on external exploitation strategies, and on the degree of penetration of national infrastructure which creates a series of niches within which adaptive strategies take place.

Black settlers in the wet littoral are in partial control of natural resources. But they are *not* in control of the money economy which so affects them. They must deal both with the impressors—outsiders who pay for goods—and with one another. Black people in this setting must deal in *social and political capital*—with human beings as potentially exchangeable tokens. To do this they generate a cultural code based on the concept of *reciprocity*. We will now examine the expanding infrastructure and niches of the environment, and then return to culture and adaptive strategy.

Expanding Infrastructure

An infrastructure is the network of transportation facilities enabling economic expansion, together with the administrative and educational apparatus which establishes a bureaucratic-information system facilitating the expansion based on transportation networks. The expanding infrastructure in the wet littoral consists of roads and rails, together with shipping systems—which include port construction and canoe tentacles to the interior. The expansion of infrastructure itself produces various booms in various places from time to time, sometimes in direct response to the international need for a particular product, and sometimes due to the internal need to "open" a given area.

Usually, infrastructure expansion brings a number of laborers from the interior of a nation (mestizos, highland Indians) together with a bevy of bosses, speculators, managers, engineers, politicians, and others, representing various economic class sectors of the respective nation. Completion of work frequently marks a "bust" in the local economy, even though natural resources should be more accessible to local exploitation for cash gain.

Niches

With the notion of an expanding infrastructure, conceived of as an environing feature, we can introduce the notion of *niche*, a concept establishing the local parameters for adaptive strategies. The concept of niche refers to not only where the particular human aggregate lives (its *environment*—sea edge, mangrove swamp, or forest) but what it *does* within this environment. It is convenient to classify human activity in the wet littoral by relating it to four settlement patterns: rural scattered dwellings, rural settlements, towns, and large urbanized towns. This suggests that human activity, and the organization of human activity into describable roles and statuses, is a function of residential advantage and population concentration. Residential advantage and the accompanying social demography in the wet littoral vary according to the demands imposed by international markets, and the expanding national infrastructure.

The crucial difference in behavior adjustments in the four niches are defined as follows.

Rural Scattered Dwellings

The activities defining this niche, in any of the three environmental zones, are oriented toward providing for household subsistence by clear division of labor by sex and age. The orientation of men's work is toward establishing a *rastrojo*, where possible, providing meat and/or fish by hunting, fishing, or barter, and finding some means of exploiting something of value to the money economy. Women and children work the *rastrojo*, gather foods, prepare foods, wash clothing, and engage in almost unending subsistence tasks. Only by freeing the men of the household for gathering, planting, harvesting, and marketing cash crops (e.g., bananas, pineapples), or fishing, mangrove stripping, *and* bundling and marketing the fish or bark, is there hope for more than a day-to-day, hand-to-mouth existence.

Households in this rural niche tend to be large, averaging eight to ten people. Within the household there tend to be interlaced kinship ties, such as we find when first cousins marry one another, and the subsequent children themselves marry their cousins and bring some into the household to live, work, and cooperate. As the household expands, through the natural processes of reproduction and mating, one of two things must occur: either the majority of children move on out of the immediate area, or they do not. If they stay, and continue the process of consolidation and physical expansion, we enter niche B, the rural settlement, and other activities define people's relationships to one another.

In niche A an *egalitarian* pattern of human interaction pertains. There are no *positions* of prestige beyond those of physical strength, mental wit, or particular conviviality. Differential interaction based on race or ethnic affiliation is nonexistent. People owe one another the same sorts of things: food for food, work time given for work time accepted, a tool (axe, adze) for a tool (machete, net), and so forth. Cooperation by people in other dispersed households is repaid in kind, and/or by festive exchange. For example, sometimes several people (usually "cousins") will come for a week to help a family build a house; when possible they are rewarded by large meals, aguardiente, music, and a general festive spirit. But more often the sheer expense involved in festive exchange demands the more common agreement to simply reciprocate the same sort of task, and dispense with the festive repayment. Such reciprocity is "symmetrical." Sometimes a group of people aligned by repeated requests and answers for aid move into the vicinity of one another, or elect to move to a sector of a town as a group. But again, such behavior generates niche B.

Niche A is a lonesome place for the inhabitants. Life is grim, hard, and oriented toward settlement activity—toward creating niche B. But the general adaptive strategy of the littoral—balance subsistence-based survival activities with those bringing in a cash gain—necessitates such movement ever outward from the growing settlements where money is more available to the upwardly mobile, but where it is also necessary to buy more subsistence goods.

Rural Settlements

Activities in this niche allow for hamlet or village specialization in addition to the patterns described for niche A. For example, a group of men may fish daily together, and cooperate in drying and transporting bales of fish to a market, while others in the settlement carry on the intrahousehold cooperative activities making for subsistence. Also, family specialization is possible, as occurs when one family builds a little sugar mill (*trapiche*), and specializes in making *guarapo* which others buy or trade goods to obtain. The settlement itself is usually definable in terms of its particular mode of articulation to the money economy.

Households tend to remain about the same size, though some expansion by mating causes a few splinter families to begin building their own homes. Cousin marriages are common, and the notion that one ought to marry a cousin, or kinsman, is prevalent. Within the household individuals have acknowledged obligations to close family and kinsmen in other local households (often adjacent), and these obligations serve to unite people through chains of reciprocities. The clever man or woman who can become central to a series of obligations may occasionally "pull" these ties together, and get a number of people to help him in some activity. A man known to be able to so manipulate his kinsmen and neighbors for economic gain gets the label *jefe* (chief) attached to him. The *jefe de la minga* (cooperative group head) or *jefe de la madera* (lumber chief), for example, is a man who is known to be able to mobilize people for short-run gain—such as the cutting and transporting of timber to a sawmill or export center. The jefe has high *rank*, but his obligations in return to all those who help him *drain him of differential wealth*.

The rural settlement, then, has the *criterion of ranking* built into its structure. Some positions within this community are regarded as carrying higher prestige than other positions, but the prestige position itself does not ensure the holder of differential economic power over his neighbors, kinsmen, and friends. Rather, higher rank confers greater responsibility to reciprocate, and thereby serves as a leveling, egalitarian mechanism.

Relationships between people in the rural settlement are symmetrical, as in the rural dispersed dwelling niche, and they are also asymmetrical. In the latter type of reciprocity, partners owe one another different sorts of things. For example, the *jefe de la minga* owes all who help him aid in *cash* or *goods* when *they are in need*, while those who make up his party owe him *labor*.

Nonblack visitors to the rural settlement are not treated as equals, for whatever the potential exchange may eventually come to be, the partners in that exchange will come to owe different sorts of things. The white or mestizo outsider entering the rural settlement should not expect deference, though. People in the rural settlement are aware that asymmetric contracts with absentee whites are useless, and in this sense are far more demanding for hard cash for services rendered than townsmen, who may opt for long-term patronage relationships with resident whites.

Black visitors are not treated as whites, but rather as potential future resources, as well as potential dangers. As a future resource, a visiting black man or woman may later be called on for comparable service. As a potential danger, the visitor may steal with impunity since he is not as yet bound by residence or kinship to settlement members.

Ritual life is rich in the settlement, in striking contrast to the rural scattered dwellings. Special days to saints are observed by women, weekly marimba dances, *currulaos*, are held in the *casa de la marimba* (almost all settlements are characterized by *one* such house), and, it seems, the demons and frightening spirits, as well as the various protective and supportive saints, find the settlement and bedevil or help inhabitants. Black frontiersmen in the settlements fight back, booming the child-snatching ghost *Tunda* away with the *bombo* (bass drum), setting candles to ward off *El Riviel*, a ghostly cannibal, soliciting the help of saints in their struggle with human and nonhuman adversaries.

Sorcery and witchcraft too are prevalent in the settlement. Fears of soul theft while dreaming and fear of those who walk trails in other worlds and visit ancestors best long forgotten lead to defensive personal ritual, to the wearing of amulets, and to the burying of roots in strategic places where those walking mystic and real trails will step over them, and be injured in their malign activities.

Because the rural settlements are dependent on the vicissitudes of the money economy for their structure, growth, and continued vitality, and because they are nonetheless removed from the town niche, where money defines most human relationships, they are often loci for fugitives. People who have stolen money or goods flee to settlement niches. One might think that the dispersed rural dwelling would be safer, but this is only true when one carries goods necessary for survival. The settlement can provide enough surplus for refuge, particularly in exchange for needed cash or goods, and the cash and goods support the growth of the settlement. Perhaps because of this refuge function the settlement is also the locus of powerful diviners, called *brujos*, who are able to "find" lost money, or a motor, or supply of goods.

Niche B is a vibrant place, precariously balanced between subsistence and cash pursuits. Its social relationships are symmetrical and asymmetrical, with ranking defining high prestige-obligation roles for big men. The settlement, qua niche B, lacks formal administration apparatus, lacks differential access to cash except as discussed, and is usually built on a foundation of kinship and affinity. Introduction of stratification and administrative apparatus moves us into niche C, the town.

The Town

Today the littoral town falls in the path of the expanding national infrastructure. In earlier times the town occurred as a center for the outward dispersal of some goods demanded by world markets. Activities defining this niche revolve around what black people in the United States refer to as "the man." Administrators with legitimate authority and external power over black townsmen, together with capitalists with economic advantage and differential access to goods and services, impose new organizational imperatives. People must adjust their activities not only to the egalitarian and ranked behavior of fellow men and women, but also to the activity and organizational patterns of people with differential administrative, political, and economic power. The town is *stratified*. Those of high rank hold differential power over their life chances due to their differential purchasing power. Most people holding differential advantages are called *blanco* (white). The concept of "whiteness" in the town niche becomes a "categorical," or "stereotypic" social relationship, through which access to money is channeled. The town then is defined by white over black asymmetry, whether or not there are people of color standing in the category "white."

Formal town offices include that of *teniente político* (political lieutenant), or his secretary or designee (depending on the size and national importance of the town—in large administrative canton seats a *jefe político* coordinates the *tenientes*). In the larger towns there is a *comisario nacional de policía*, appointee of the supreme and regional courts of justice, who oversees the *policía rural*. Police live in the town niche, and very seldom visit the settlements, unless murder has taken place. Political parties oriented toward influencing public policy are also here, including those with international as well as national affiliation.

There are also Catholic clergy and nuns, and sometimes Protestant missionaries, and occasionally local fundamental Protestants. Schoolteachers (government and mission) provide instruction through about the fifth grade, and public-health officials administer campaigns against malaria and yaws. There is normally a physician and perhaps a dentist when the town passes three thousand in population. Saloons, cantinas, shops, hotels, and small "restaurants" exist as permanent edifices. Carpentry and masonry workshops have sporadic business, and *motoristas* working the various rivers and estuaries have permanent bases in the towns. Sawmills provide boards and planks so that the frontier dwellings can evolve into western houses.

A town is not specialized. Sawmills, resident buyers and shippers, and owners of cash-crop farms all provide some employment on a wage-labor basis. They also buy products from people organizing their own labor force to make money from forest and sea products. Resources provided by legal-juridical and political office are used by people to advance themselves and to compete with others also seeking advancement in this niche. The paperwork necessary to the carrying through of any economic activity gives the literate manipulator in the jural political domain asymmetrical control over economic activity.

Activities in the town niche are oriented toward the acquisition of money, or toward alliances with people known to have access to the goods and services which money can buy. Role positions that I label "rural contact," and "ethnic-cultural broker" are important. The rural contact is a man or woman able to mobilize people outside of the town for gainful economic activity (farming, logging). He is the town analog to the settlement jefe. A cultural or ethnic broker is a man or woman able to translate demands and needs of controlling outsiders into activity patterns of black frontiersmen. It is through brokerage roles that black people have transformed their activity patterns from settlement to town, from subsistent peasant adaptation to proletarian participation during boom periods. The broker himself may best be regarded as an entrepreneurial role finding new goals to which to apply Afro-Hispanic organizational patterns.

Division of labor within households (which vary greatly in size from one to two individuals to more than twenty persons) is frequently in terms of balanced activity in many different economic pursuits. Because national and regional politics impinge on so many activities in the town niche some men in every household, or kinship grouping, must maintain awareness of events affecting the town economy, and must also maintain some viable contact with those who are able to manipulate the political economy to personal advantage.

In the town niche the household is not the basic economic unit, and first-cousin marriage is not favored, and rarely found. The basic economic unit is somewhat larger and may be termed a "kindred." It includes all those consanguineal and affinal relatives upon which a given person can depend, for a particular purpose, at a particular time, under particular conditions. Some of the small rural settlements in the wet littoral consist of one kindred (usually focused on the first settlers, or their resident children); some include many. In similar manner, some town *barrios* (neighborhoods or sections) contain one or two kindreds, again focused on the resident children of successful settlers.

Since the town is a place where people compete with one another for economic advantage and since such competition may involve either success (upward mobility) or failure, individuals' affiliations to kinsmen also involve the factor of economic advantage-disadvantage. The manners by which successful individuals maintain a network of cooperating kinsmen, without owing so much that success levels their economic gain through expected obligation fulfillment, defines a particular kind of social organization. The adaptive strategies within the town niche affect people in the settlements and scattered dwellings, too, as we shall see later on.

All of the activities described for niches A and B go on in the town niche, *among those who fall into the lower economic class*. But these activities themselves are caught up by the various organizations and alliances defined by mobility processes *out of* the lower class. Hence a class-oriented frame of reference helps us understand even subsistence activities.

Saints, spirits, and attendant ritual behavior to solicit help and exorcise evil go on in the town niche, side by side with scoffing saloon-goers and damning clergy. From town to town the particular mix varies, but careful observers find no difficulty in perceiving the basic complex of settlement life intertwined with the ritual life prescribed for town. As towns become larger than five hundred to one thousand people, barrio formation tends to take on increased ritual significance and sacred rituals are performed in relative secrecy. It is within the barrio that particular spirits tend to visit, or particular demons tend to haunt. As the town grows, and the center of administrative activity becomes lighter and lighter, barrios get their own marimba houses, their own specialists, and characterize their lifeways as increasingly "traditional." Town sections resemble rural settlements as the town grows larger. As this process expands and barrios spread from the center, the secrecy of sacred rituals declines.

The town is a wild, exciting place when a boom is on—when there is actually cash to sustain the mobility strategies of black frontiersmen. It is a place where ethnicity sharpens, but also where interethnic relationships become intertwined in class-defined interests which would seem at first to negate the ethnic categories.

When the demand for a product declines, or the nation is unable to sustain its infrastructure in a particular area, the town becomes a terribly depressing place. The shell of activity rapidly decays, leaving precariously wobbling docks, green mold-covered foundations of older frame houses, and some remnants of previous size and importance. Most such towns become settlements again. Many maintain some national facade of previous importance: a priest visits occasionally, a schoolteacher comes for a few months every few years, a political appointment is made; but without anything to exploit, administration is at best nominal. The bust town is common in the wet littoral, and all too often travelers see life in the bust town as slow and "lazy," and blame local inhabitants for letting "their" town go. The concept of the purchase society teaches us that we cannot blame those caught up in international capitalism for the effect of decreasing product demand on the expansion of administrative units, the towns.

Large Towns: Consequences of Urbanism

Buenaventura and Tumaco in Colombia, and Esmeraldas, Ecuador, range from over one hundred thousand down to forty to fifty thousand people. I shall call these "large towns," though the reader might prefer "small cities." However we label them, we refer to changes which occur with demographic growth due to increased cash opportunities, and greater stratification and division of labor—these are the processes of urbanization. The attendant culture of cities, or large towns, is called "urbanism."

Urbanism, of course, extends throughout a region, far beyond the city or large town, but an expanding infrastructure is necessary to realize goals of urbanization.

All the activities sketched in niche C continue in niche D. I would not even bother discussing niche D as separate, were it not for three interrelated phenomena: (1) the appearance of labor unions as a political and economic organization; (2) increased ethnicity separating "white" from "black" with a concomitant *expanding* set of middle-range concepts (mulatto, *zambo*, *claro*, etc.); and (3) concentration of black people in outlying barrios which resemble in activity pattern the rural settlement.

As a result of these three patterns there is a tendency to identify black behavior with country-bumpkin life, and lighter behavior with union-political (urban-national) orientation. De facto exclusion of black people —a sort of social circumscription of black frontiersmen—forces them back into a settlement niche, though the settlement itself now is in, or on the edge of, a large town rather than swamp or jungle. The relevant environment for black frontiersmen in *this* settlement niche becomes the large town, rather than the natural environmental zone.

All three of these larger towns are ports. Through these ports pass products of the respective nations. There are markets, stores, hotels, restaurants, bars, houses for amusement and sexual outlet, and movie theaters. All three are connected by road and air to the national centers, and all three are totally immersed in the money economy. Political apparatus is that of the national urban type, with elected mayor, resident governor in the case of Esmeraldas, urban police (as opposed to rural police), courts, public-health centers, Protestant and Catholic churches. Strangers are constantly in the large towns, and the number of goods to buy (watches, souvenirs, jewelry, etc.) reflect this. Each of the three large towns also has a nationally known tourist resort nearby.

Yet much of Afro-Hispanic culture is as settlement-oriented as back on the rivers, or in the mangrove delta. Black people play their marimbas, beat the drums, light candles to saints, and perform rituals of death and veneration as they do in the rural areas. In fact, in the large towns one finds a rural-areal focus of the majority of poor black people. Such people name their barrio after the river or area of the founder, and discuss interbarrio differences in terms of differences reputed to exist between people of various zones in the hinterland.

In fact, many rural people, including tribal Indians, bypass the smaller towns and head directly for the three large towns. Such people give two reasons for this: (1) there is more likely to be a ready, immediate market for their products in the largest towns; (2) they are more comfortable in the larger towns for *they are more likely to have relatives there.* . . .

But before we close this chapter, a word of caution is perhaps warranted. Niches refer to activity patterns of definable aggregates within particular environments. Actual people come and go from the different niches, and the different environments. We are not classifying people, but activity patterns. The activity patterns are contextual, subject to the immediate environing features, as well as a product of the specific cultural styles and adaptive strategies which have evolved through past generations. In fact, people must maintain series of complementary strategies played in the various niches, if they are to find ways to survive in the total environment of the wet littoral purchase society.

6

Kongo in Haiti: A New Approach to Religious Syncretism

Luc de Heusch

Although Iberians brought the dominant culture to the western side of the Atlantic, Africans carried their mores, whole or in part, with them. This African component cannot be reduced to a single set of customs because the transatlantic slave trade brought people from all the major regions of Africa to the Americas. The majority came from West Africa, especially from Dahomey, today the Republic of Benin, and the Yoruba Empire, now encompassed by modern Nigeria, and they had the most pronounced influence.

Latin American religions, another product of mestizaje or syncretism (the fusion of forms, beliefs, or practices to create a distinct faith), reveal the most apparent effect of West African cultures. As practices and cults survived the Middle Passage in various degrees, different ethnic groups embedded practices and beliefs in the dominant, required religion in the Western Hemisphere. The Yoruba religion, for example, was transformed into candomblé in Brazil, shangó in Trinidad, and Santería in Cuba, Puerto Rico, and Panama.

In Haiti a new religious form called vodun or voodoo appeared in the eighteenth century. It is usually described as the fusion of the Dahomey religion with Roman Catholicism after the 1685 Code Noir that ordered masters to convert their slaves. Forced into Roman Catholic practices, the slaves freely associated Dahomey deities with Catholic saints, holidays, and liturgy. Slaves, adapting their customs to new circumstances and environments, used Afro-Creole religion as an integral form of their resistance to European domination. These Afro-Latin American religions

From *Man* 24, no. 2 (1989): 290–303, trans. Noal Mellott. Reprinted by permission of the Royal Anthropological Institute of Great Britain and Ireland.

became a source of inner strength and an affirmation of identity that con-
tributed to the slaves' survival.[*]

    Luc de Heusch, a Belgian anthropologist from Université Libre de
Bruxelles (Brussels), reevaluates generalizations about syncretism as he
examines the origins and complexities of Haitian voodoo. He concludes
that the outward forms have been mistaken for syncretism. Roman Ca-
tholicism provided only superficial patterns, he argues, while the actual
syncretism of faith and practices fused Dahomey's rada *cult with a sec-*
ond African influence, the petro *cult of the Kongo culture (present-day*
Angola). His essay argues persuasively for a reevaluation of the religious
syncretism that for many years has been described as the result of the
asymmetrical relationship between dominant and subordinate cultures.

S teadfast faith in the ancestral divinities enabled the slaves of the French
  colony of Saint-Domingue to survive in the most dreadful conditions,
and it inspired them to take up arms under the leadership of Toussaint
Louverture in the first successful revolt of non-European peoples against
the colonial powers. The complex syncretic religious system known as
voodoo is still one of the strongest factors of social cohesion among the
Haitian peasantry. The many temples (*houmfort*) with their priests and
priestesses (*houngan* and *mambo*, respectively) have provided the only
sanctuary that a people living in utter poverty could find. This religion is
not an opium of the people, cynically administered by sorcerers in league
with the *tontons macoutes* thugs of the Duvalier period, even though such
a version of events is murmured—when it is not loudly proclaimed—by
the Catholic and Baptist Churches, thus fueling yet one more religious
war on our planet.

    In Haiti, a deep cleavage separates the culture of the urban, Western-
ized elite—most of whom are mulattoes and Roman Catholics—from that
of the illiterate black peasantry. François Duvalier knew how to take advantage of this long-standing social, economic, and cultural antagonism,
the foundation of the Haitian tragedy. A simple country doctor, Duvalier
presented himself as the representative of the black petite bourgeoisie
that had been kept out of political and economic power. While laying
claim to Western models, he proclaimed himself the spiritual father, even
the messiah, of the traditional peasantry. He skillfully played a double,
social and religious, role. On the one hand, he partly controlled voodoo
priests through secret societies and claimed to be able to use witchcraft.
On the other, he ingratiated himself with the Catholic clergy by appointing black bishops who proved to be as hostile to voodoo as the whites had

---

    [*]Voodoo also has produced an intriguing and popular folk art. See Sal Scalora,
"A Salute to the Spirits: Vodun Flag Artists Pay Tribute to the Traditional Gods
of Haiti," *Americas* 45, no. 2 (March 1993): 26–33.

been. He thus looked like a hero who had decolonized the Church, which had been dominated by foreign priests since the hundred-year-old Concordat. Duvalier's involvement with black magic has, unfortunately, resulted in the discrediting of a folk religion that is in itself a peaceful possession cult.

When Jean-Claude Duvalier lost the backing of these two antagonistic spiritual forces, his power collapsed. After a long period during which it had been compromised by association with the government, the Catholic Church began using its radio network to oppose the regime. By contrast, the opposition of voodoo priests took place in the shadow of secret societies. One of them was active in the incidents at Gonaïves, which were crucial to the fall of the dictator. During my trip to Haiti in the summer of 1985, the Catholic Church had already entered into political opposition. When the dictator was overthrown in February 1986, and the *tontons macoutes* were pursued, the Catholic Church profited from its apparent victory and relaunched its merciless, century-old campaign—which had been suspended under Duvalier—against a religion that it still judges to be satanic. By also applying the term "satanic" to the abolished but not yet extirpated regime, some preachers confused listeners by associating the former political system with the folk religion. The revolutionary language of the more radical sections of the Church, regardless of the latter's real intentions, has thus become a call for religious persecution. This conflict has cost the lives of hundreds of priests and priestesses (*houngan* and *mambo*) during the recent political turmoil. The ancestral gods have come under attack.

But who are these divinities (*loa*), these forces which have sustained the Haitian peasantry over the centuries? Historians and ethnologists quite rightly take Dahomey to be the first of the many places of origin from which these gods and goddesses have come. Practiced in secret during the era of bondage, this cult of possession—which bears a Fon name (*vodun*)—has indeed kept alive the memory of many Dahomean divinities. However, this fact should not prevent us from exploring the meanders of ritual and ceremonies, from searching through the profusion of divinities in the voodoo pantheon, from discovering the stream of religious thought that, as we travel back through history, might lead us to other sources. Our question is how do contributions from two major African sources coexist within a single religion, voodoo? What relations of opposition and complementarity bring them together?

But at the outset, we must do away with the fake problem of Christian syncretism in voodoo. Throughout Haiti, the temples are decorated with color reproductions of Catholic saints that evoke the *loa* through what Michel Leiris (1953: 207) has referred to as a pun based upon objects instead of words (*un calembour d'objets*). For example, Ogun, the Yoruba war god, is likened to St. James portrayed as a victorious knight wielding a sword. Ogun belongs to the *nago* family of gods, the Fon term for their Yoruba enemies. An especially well-qualified informant stated that the *nago* spend their time making war on horseback. Hence, Ogun, whenever he enters the bodies of his followers, is like a knight on horseback wielding a sword. Thus is explained the iconographic equivalence between the African god and the Catholic saint. In such a case, the saint is but a front, a mask that hides the god, and we cannot rightly talk about syncretism, since African signs and emblems prevail. Believers in voodoo are baptized and participate without any contradiction in Catholic masses. Métraux (1958: 287) notes a peasant's comment: "You have to be Catholic to serve the *loa*." Two distinct religions coexist without merging. Catholic influences are superficial in voodoo, whose reality is African. For voodoo worshippers, Catholicism is a parallel, complementary religion. Major voodoo ceremonies open with the *Guinin* prayer, a long litany that is punctuated by the ringing of bells and calls on the saints before calling up the *loa*. But only the *loa* come to possess participants. In ritual terms, these two categories—*loa* and saints—are not at all mixed up; they are juxtaposed. According to Métraux (1958: 291), praying and kneeling are acts inspired by Christianity that precede the voodoo service and "make the *loa* begin to move."

This movement is the dance of possession, the perfect identification of initiates (*hounsi*) with the *loa*, the direct communication between human beings and divinities. The latter ride their human mounts who become passive objects, having lost their own personality. Introducing the saints into the voodoo pantheon was structurally impossible, for Catholicism has radically refused any such dealings because possession comes from the devil (Lucifer has become a *loa* in certain black magic ceremonies!). The religions of masters and of their slaves could not syncretize. In fact, the masters strove, in vain, to forbid this folk religion: the last violent campaign against voodoo was led by the Catholic Church with the government's help in 1942.

I have elsewhere proposed the term "adorcism" to refer to the ritual attitude in the voodoo trance. In this, possession is a means of calling up the gods. From a structural viewpoint, I contrasted this attitude with "exorcism" whereby some religions, in various ways and to varying degrees, consider the possessing force to be an evil that must be driven out of the victim's body. The latter attitude is typical in the Catholic Church, as well as among the Thonga in South Africa (de Heusch 1981: 158). I now admit, however, that this contrast is too stark since there are dangerous *loa* who must be warded off. My aim here is to situate these *loa* within the pantheon and to show that syncretism is itself a structural process. Let us pursue this aim with the cavalry of the *nago* gods.

Any religion, including Christianity, is ultimately a syncretic phenomenon. Historical and structural interpretations have to be brought together within the scope of the anthropology of religion. Instead of choosing between two opposed explanations, we need to show how both work together. The challenge of research into Haitian voodoo is to do just this.

Meeting this challenge is particularly difficult since there are so many regional variations. Voodoo is by no means a unified religion; there is no central authority, and the *houngan* and *mambo* are very individualistic. Some of them claim to be guardians of a purer tradition. It would be necessary to draw an ethnographic atlas of ceremonies and beliefs in order to shed light upon the relationships between the teachings of various priests.

In 1937, Melville Herskovits, who carried out fieldwork in the Mirebalais Valley, noticed that the classification of the gods varied from one informant to another. This holds true for other areas of the country too. Nonetheless, a single, constant concern runs through these various classifications: the gods are grouped into families or "nations" as a function of their geographical or tribal origins. Two major groupings are discernible: the *rada*, a kind of dominant aristocracy, are the major cosmic gods of the Fon of ancient Dahomey, whereas the worship of the *petro* has always been said to be of Creole origin.

Referring to the works of Moreau de Saint-Méry (1797: 1, 210–11), a late eighteenth-century Haitian historian, Métraux, like Herskovits, believed that the *petro* cult was introduced in 1768 by Don Pedro, a black man who came from the Spanish part of the island and settled in Petit Goave, in southern Haiti. For Herskovits (1937: 150), the *petro loa* are mighty ancestors who were divinized after death. Métraux's opinion (1958: 31–32) is more nuanced: the name Don Pedro was put "for obscure reasons in place of some African *nanchon* (nation) whose ceremonies he promoted." He added that the many spirits belonging to minority nations such as the Ibo and the Kongo fit, to varying degrees, within two major groupings, *rada* and *petro*. Herskovits noticed that some temples had a distinct room reserved for the Kongo *loa*.

During my first field trip to the Port-au-Prince area in 1970, I was surprised to find many *loa* of Kongo origin in the supposedly Creole *petro* pantheon. *Simbi*, *Nkita*, and *Mbumba* are well known in the Kongo religion of lower Zaire. The *Simbi* and *Nkita* are nature spirits, aquatic or terrestrial depending on the region. Among the Mpangu, a Kongo tribe south of the Congo River, the *Nkita* are the protective spirits and forefathers of clans—forefathers who experienced violent deaths. They dwell in streams and forests whereas the *Simbi*, pure nature spirits, like to stay near water (Van Wing 1938: 18–19). This Kongo contribution to voodoo has been recognized by a new generation of researchers (Janzen 1982; Thompson 1981).

Nonetheless, two major problems have been overlooked. How can we explain the coexistence of so many spirits with Haitian names alongside the Kongo spirits in the *petro* pantheon? And the fact that the Kongo spirits have managed to keep their identity in spite of the dominant *rada* cult? Why have these Kongo and Fon divinities not been syncretized? This question is all the more important in that the possession cults in Africa welcome new divinities.

This is the crux of the historical and structural problem. Let us begin by looking at Don Pedro himself. Far from being a Spaniard as has been believed, his eponym brings to mind the name of the four kings (Pedro I, II, III, and IV) who reigned over the Kongo Kingdom from the mid-sixteenth to the late eighteenth centuries (Cuvelier 1946). Don and Dona were honorary titles used by the Kongo in imitation of the Portuguese. Furthermore, several apparently Creole *petro loa* can be likened to major symbolic figures among the Kongo. For example, the chief of the Congo Savannah (or Zandor) *loa*, an awesome nation to which the *kita* belong (Menesson-Rigaud & Denis 1947: 13), is Ti Jean Pié Sèche (Little John with the Dry Foot—he was maimed or lame), a dangerous spirit who violently possesses people. In this respect, he can be compared to the *baka*, the *loa* who are dreaded witches. In the traditional Kongo religion, *mbaka* refers to dwarfs. Herskovits (1937: 241) described the voodoo *baka* as small, bearded men who can change themselves into animals; and according to Métraux (1958: 76), Ti Jean Petro is sometimes said to be a one-legged dwarf. What is amazing is that dwarfs and the maimed have the important ritual role of nature spirits in the *kimpasi* initiation ceremony, which the Mpangu observed till recently in an attenuated form (Makenda 1971: 30). This observance goes back far in time: in 1690, Cavazzi (French translation by Labat 1732: 1, 296, quoted by Van Wing 1938: 229) wrote, "The *ndembola*, those born with crooked feet, have an appreciable rank among the *nquiti* (*nkita* spirits) as do pygmies or dwarfs, who are called *mbaka* (or *ngudi a mbaka*)." Dwarfs and the lame, the family of Ti Jean Petro and the *baka*, are thus symbolically equivalent.

Among the Mpangu, young people (both male and female) from several lineages used to be initiated into the *nkita* cult during the *kimpasi* ceremony. An old woman, as hideous as possible, presided over this ceremony; she had been possessed by an *nkita* spirit; her only child, who was misshapen, had died very young (Van Wing 1938: 183). We may ask whether the awesome Marinette in the *petro* pantheon is not based on a memory of this woman. In Haiti, Marinette is the wife of Ti Jean Pié

Sèche. During trances, she appears with upturned eyes and a twisted mouth (Menesson-Rigaud & Denis 1947: 14), features that bring to mind the legendary ugliness of the *kimpasi* mother. Marinette is believed to carry out murders for the *kita* spirits. During the *kimpasi*, the *nkita* were said to devour novices, whose corpses were laid before the initiatory mother (Van Wing 1938: 195–96). A famous priest reluctantly admitted that the Savannah Congo *loa* demand human sacrifices; this can be taken to be a transformation of the Kongo belief that novices died, albeit symbolically, at the hands of the *nkita*. Marinette's color is red (Menesson-Rigaud & Denis 1947: 16). The mother of the *kimpasi*, who gave birth to initiates as *nkita* spirits after their ritual death, was called Ngwa Ndundu (albino mother) and said to be *bwaka* (red) (Van Wing 1938: 183). Her head was covered with a red scarf (Makenda 1971: 14), like that of Marinette whose element is fire (Menesson-Rigaud & Denis 1947: 14). Inside the *kimpasi* lodge in Kongoland, a ritual fire—in fact, a funeral pyre—was kept burning by dwarfs, the maimed, and young girls or old women. After the novices' symbolic death, this fire was fed with a ritual wood that was normally used to smoke corpses and was handled only by the ugly albino mother and female twins (Makenda 1971: 6, 30). Dwarfs and the maimed, albinos and twins, are associated with nature spirits in Kongo traditional beliefs. Let us leave aside this triangle of sacred monsters after having remarked that in Haiti the *marassa* name of a special category of twin *loa* comes from Kongo *mapasa* or *mahasa* (Swartenbroeckx 1973: 303).

Let us look at another aspect of the Kongo *nkita* cult. These spirits possess their followers during healing ceremonies (Mata Makala 1973: 72–109) held around a fireplace. The ancestors speak through the possessed men and women whom they have chosen. These intermediaries lead the sick person and the crowd to the river where, still in trance, they look for stones to be used as props for the *nkita* water spirits. Some of them will learn the art of healing through dreams and trances, whereas others will serve only as mounts for these spirits. Only the first become full-fledged priests and priestesses to the *nkita*; their duty is to combat sorcery directed against their lineages.

Thus the traditional Kongo religion, south of the Congo River, practices trance as does the Fon religion of Dahomey. But healing services under the auspices of the *kita* are not held in Haiti, for these spirits are too dreadful. Far from combatting sorcery *kita*, the Haitian *nkita* are thought to be sorcerers. After the epoch of slavery and the consequent collapse of all familial ties, these protective lineage spirits have, it seems, deliberately changed roles by entering the realm of magic and/or sorcery like the other *petro loa*. It is worth noting that north of the Congo River, among the Yombe, the *nkita*, dangerous and aggressive, are not associated with benevolent ancestors as among the Mpangu, but are taken to be earth spirits who cause paralysis in the legs and blindness (Bittremieux 1936: 55). They thus stand opposite the kindly *simbi* water spirits who heal the one-eyed, the lame, the misshapen (Doutreloux 1967: 217). Clearly, Yombe myths are a structural transformation of the aforementioned Mpangu system. For the time being, let us be satisfied with the conclusion that Ti Jean Petro the Lame, a Creole spirit, bears the marks of the *nkita* of lower Zaire, as does his wife Marinette.

Before turning to the ambiguous role of the *simbi* spirits in Haitian voodoo, let us consider the structural position of the *bumba loa* in the *petro* pantheon. They too are of Kongo origin. They play an important role at the end of the principal *petro* ceremony held at Christmas. In order to understand this ceremony better, we must recall that, among the Yombe in Zaire, Mbumba is the major earth spirit: the rainbow serpent who presides over many rites of passage (Doutreloux 1967: 217; Bittremieux 1936: 244–65). He is the master of the *khimba*, the Yombe equivalent of the Mpangu *kimpasi*. For Haitians, the many *bumba loa* belong, like the *kita*, to the vast, powerful, and dreadful family of Savannah Congo *loa*.

Although there is no doubt about the Kongo origin of *simbi*, *kita*, and *bumba*, their incorporation in voodoo raises a major problem. In central Africa, the aquatic aspect of these nature spirits is clearly marked whereas, in Haiti, they are associated with fire in the *petro* ritual. Among the Mpangu, the favorite abode of both the *simbi* and *nkita* is water, even though they are all associated with the forest or savannah. Mbumba, the Yombe earth spirit who has given his name to the Haitian family, is also a water being according to a myth (Bittremieux 1936: 244–65). We have seen that the fire burning in the *kimpasi* hut during *nkita* initiation was associated with death. During the healing ceremony, the *nkita* spirits indwell the stones fetched from the river. Sand from the river, after being placed in boiling water, is poured out onto the ground, and initiates lie down there to die symbolically. They are then placed in a large ditch, and their fathers make payments so that they can come back to life. The initiates are likened to catfish (Mata Makala 1973: 107). During the *kimpasi* ceremony too, the same association exists between this fish and the *nkita* water spirits (Van Wing 1938: 216).

What is the explanation for almost all the Haitian *petro loa* and, in particular, the so-called Congo Savannah gods, being said to be hot and associated with fire? This crucial question has to do with the structural nature of syncretism. Indeed, the *petro* pantheon and rites contrast with the *rada* ones, which, of Dahomean origin, are mainly associated with water. In most *rada* temples, there is a cement basin in honor of Damballah-Wedo, the principal freshwater divinity (as opposed to Agoue, who rules the sea). The *kita* and *bumba* figure only in *petro* rituals associated with fire like the *simbi*. But there are *simbi* in the *rada* pantheon who have kept their original attributes as water beings. Hymns clearly relate the *rada simbi* to springs. According to Métraux (1958: 2), a woman "mounted" by Simbi-Yan-Kita "never stopped repeating 'Water! Water!'; then opening and closing her mouth like a fish out of water, she would now and then jump fully clothed into a fountain."

During fieldwork, I noticed that believers do not agree on the names of these aquatic *rada simbi*. Even Simbi-Yan-Kita is sometimes classified among the *petro simbi*. The same happens to Simbi Dlo (Simbi of the Water), the aquatic *rada simbi* par excellence. I was told that, in the Léogane area, Simbi Dlo is the only *petro simbi* who likes to abide in water. This authentically aquatic *simbi* figured in a *petro* ceremony organized at Christmastide and described by Menesson-Rigaud (1951: 49). When he made his presence known, the chorus sang "Simbi, ask for water to bathe in; Simbi, call for water in water." However, this water *simbi* belongs to the category of "mystery leaves," associated with the heat of magic and the power of "medicine," namely the powders made by pounding plants in a mortar, that were set ablaze with rum. "The *loa* rush up, take fire in their hands and ecstatically pass it over their faces, arms and bodies, and also over the *houngan* and the men holding the pestles" (Menesson-Rigaud 1951: 50). Along with the author of these lines, I saw such a ceremony in the Léogane area some twenty years later. I saw a *simbi* brandishing a burning faggot alongside Bumba and Grand Bois, the master of medicine leaves. The name of Bumba Maza, who was invoked by the *houngan*, bears the marks of this spirit's water origins: *maza* or *masa* means water in Kikongo (Swartenbroeckx 1973: 303), but participants no longer understand the meaning of the word. At the end of the ceremony, *bumba*, who were dressed like corpses (Bumba Cimetière), rolled in the bonfire lit in the courtyard. In 1951, O. Menesson-Rigaud (54) described a water *simbi* "using pieces of burning wood like steps" to climb up a huge pyre.

Fire is the favorite element of both the *simbi petro* and the *bumba*. Obviously we may wonder why Simbi Dlo (Simbi of the Water) is still aquatic within the *petro* pantheon. History has undoubtedly left deep marks here. This *loa* is in a mediating position between the *rada* and *petro* rituals. Owing to his name, he could be transferred into the *rada* pantheon where he takes an almost natural place. In the *petro* pantheon, however, he is a drunk, the husband of fearsome Red-Eyed Erzilie (Herskovits 1937: 316). Another *simbi petro* is qualified as *makaya*, a term meaning leaves in Kikongo (Swartenbroeckx 1973: 291). These *simbi*, far from being gentle like the *rada* ones, are sometimes thought to be criminals, for the borderline between magic and sorcery is not very clear. Simbi en Deux Zo is the god of poisons (Davis 1985: 152). Some of Herskovits's informants (1937: 241) simply placed the *petro simbi* in the *baka* squad of bad *loa* with whom sorcerers make deals (Herskovits 1937: 240). Nonetheless, it would be misleading to make a major distinction between the *petro* and *rada* divinities on this ethical basis, for there are also "white" (beneficial) *petro loa*: the *don pedro* proper (Menesson-Rigaud & Denis 1947: 13). In the *petro* pantheon, the *simbi* hold a middle position between the good and bad uses of leaves and powders. Unaware of the Kongo origin of the *simbi*, Métraux (1958: 78) mistakenly wrote that they belong "by their very nature" to the *rada* and are served during *petro* ceremonies, only whenever "neglected by their followers and cramped with hunger pangs, they tend to be cruel."

Haitian syncretism also tolerates a symmetrical, reverse phenomenon: some *rada loa* who are beneficial and peaceful have fiery, violent counterparts in the *petro* pantheon. Damballah, for instance, is often called the "Torch" (*flambeau*) in *petro* ceremonies. Opposite the voluptuous Erzilie Freda Dahomey, the paragon of a woman in love, is the brutal Erzilie Mapyang who, appearing in the *petro* cult with a very bad reputation (Métraux 1958: 78), is sometimes called Erzilie Zyeux Rouge (Red-Eyed Erzilie), an attribute that likens her to Marinette.

We would be mistaken to suppose that all the *rada loa* are water gods opposite the *petro loa* who are fire gods. However, the former are "soft" and "gentle" whereas the latter are "bitter," "salty," or "harsh" (Métraux 1958: 77). A *petro* service may consist of "fencing in," "binding" to a piece of wood (*bornez*) or even "chaining" certain dreaded *loa* every seven, fourteen, or twenty-one years. I witnessed such a ceremony in the garden of a temple not far from Pétionville during the summer of 1970. Nails were pounded into four roughly squared-off pieces of wood, which were then wrapped with knotted strings. The *petro* divinities were firmly fastened to these knots by coiling a wire around them "so that the other *loa* can eat and work in peace," as my informant said. This defensive magic was interpreted in military terms; these knots "were fixed in order to arrest the *petro* escort." The two priests who performed this rite next stuck the four pieces of wood and two wooden crosses into a hole around which were placed bottles of rum, a vial of perfume, and four plates with food offerings. The four "bound" divinities were Ti Jean Petro, Bumba, Simbi en Deux Zo, and Erzilie Dantor, who is also called Queen Petro. A nearby fire was fueled with gasoline and salt. Several animals were sacrificed. The sacrificer, who organized the ceremony in order to "feed" his own *petro loa*, was possessed by Ti Jean. His behavior was especially brutal.

During this ceremony, the *petro loa* were warded off (in contrast to the *rada loa* whose benediction is sought). But some *petro loa* are welcomed within the sanctuaries, just like the *rada loa* (Menesson-Rigaud 1953). In this case, offerings and sacrifices take place near the altar dedicated to the *petro loa* in the *houmfort.* The inside of the home contrasts with the outside where the *loa*, thought to be dangerous or hostile, are deliberately kept at a distance after having been appeased by offerings and sacrifices. In the Léogane area where much of my fieldwork has been carried out, the most awesome *petro* divinities—the Savannah Congo or Zandor nation—are worshipped in the woods, at a wild spot far from the domestic realm. They are *bornés* (bound to a piece of wood) or "chained" there. Herskovits (1937: ch. 9) described a *petro* ceremony in the Mirebalais area during which Lemba and Simbi Nan Dlo (in the Water) were bound whereas Ti Kita, Ti Jean Pié Sèche, and two other *petro loa* (Red-Eyed Erzilie and Three-Horned Bossou) were "sent back."

The *petro* are treated differently depending on how fearsome they are. Dangerous *loa* cannot be eliminated from the pantheon for they are usually, like friendly ones, part of a family's heritage, which generally comprises both *petro* and *rada* divinities. When an initiate dies, as when a *houngan* or *mambo* dies, a family member inherits his ritual duties; the person selected by the divinities cannot avoid these duties lest he fall seriously ill or become mad.

In all the temples where the *petro* and *rada loa* are served together, as is usually done, the altars of these two pantheons are located in two distinct rooms that do not communicate with each other or even in two separate buildings (*cailles*). Certain divinities may, like Erzilie, have their own private rooms.

Drums and other ritual objects are different in *rada* and *petro* ceremonies. During *rada* services, the *houngan* or *mambo* shakes a calabash (*Lagnaria vulgaris*) covered with snake vertebrae or with a net of glass beads whereas, during *petro* services, he or she shakes a calabash of a different variety (*Crescentia linearifolio*) containing small seeds or pebbles (Menesson-Rigaud 1953: 236). The sound is produced from things on the outside or, alternatively, on the inside of the calabash. During *petro* services, at least one pig has to be sacrificed. Métraux (1958: 75) noticed other signs of the *loa petro*, signs that manifest their violence: they are welcomed to the crack of whips, and small quantities of gunpowder are fired in their honor.

Voodoo should be taken to be a bicephalous religion; the structural arrangement of its components has to do with history. There are, however, linkages between the two pantheons. The *nago* nation—in fact of

Yoruba origin—and especially the Ogun family of war gods have an intermediate position that is the reverse of the Simbi's, these originally water spirits of Kongo origin. The *nago* are the only gods of fire who are tolerated as such among the *rada loa* while being incorporated into the *petro* pantheon. Of course, when Ogun possesses an initiate during *petro* ceremonies, he manifests himself more violently than during *rada* ceremonies. Even his name changes: he is qualified as being "red-eyed" like Marinette.

Fire is not missing from the *rada* ritual. During the *boulin zin* (burning the pots) ceremony, which is held on various occasions, different foodstuffs are prepared in pots (*zin*). These pots are then emptied and filled with olive oil. Once their outsides are greased, they are set on fire. There is much excitement, and many people are possessed. The fire warms up the *loa* and increases their power (Métraux 1958: 181–87). All ritual objects are passed through the fire in order to recharge them with force. . . .

In 1973, Odette Menesson-Rigaud, a remarkable French ethnographer to whom Métraux was much beholden, told me that at Nansoukry near Gonaïves in northern Haiti there was a temple where the Kongo *loa* were fully independent, related to neither the *rada* nor the *petro* pantheon. I went to Nansoukry ten years later. A famous *houngan* sent me to see the "Emperor" of the Kongo society, Simon Hérard, a fascinating person whose temperament ranges from sudden bursts of gusty laughter to a sense of reserve and authority. He was wary of "intellectuals" of my sort who write books and think they know everything. Nonetheless, he welcomed me warmly and told me surprising things that largely confirmed unpublished observations recorded by Menesson-Rigaud twenty or thirty years earlier. Hérard heads the small committee that is charged with the administration of the cult. He is not its priest. The religious leader is not called *houngan* (priest) but simply "servant." He is the chamberlain of an invisible royal court over which a *loa* called Bazou reigns. This king undoubtedly came from Angola since he is also called "King Wangol" or "Kongo chief." With Mambo Inan, his wife, said to be a Kongo queen, Bazou begat 101 children, grouped in "escorts" that are part of an army specialized in magically warding off misfortunes of all sorts.

Nansoukry is an unassuming village isolated in the countryside. This high place of the Kongo gods is laid out like a fort. At the entrance to the village is an arch. The *bumba* and *lemba* escorts—who form the vanguard of the army of *loa*—are stationed near the big *mapou* tree along the path. The *bumba loa* are great warriors whom people in dire straits call upon; I might add that, among the Yombe of lower Zaire, Mbumba not only presided over initiation rites but also protected warriors (Doutreloux 1967: 217). The phrase *Escalier Bumba* (Bumba staircase) means that these mighty *loa* help overcome hardships. A few years ago, a large temple in masonry was built not far from the arch. Dances, trances, prayers, and sacrifices take place in this temple. Toward the south, a rather steep slope leads to a hilltop where the rearguard, the *ganga loa*, are posted. This term brings to mind *nganga*, a word that still denotes the masters of ceremonies and especially medicine men among the Kongo of lower Zaire. The *ganga* escort is accompanied by many and various *simbi*.

The vanguard and rearguard demarcate a ritual territory with its center at the foot of the *ganga* hill. The center is the preferred abode of Jatibwa, a son to whom King Bazou entrusted all the secrets of magic. Bazou himself dwells in a dry well located to the west, toward the road leading to the stream where his wife, Mambo Inan, likes to abide. People bathe in this stream on her feast day, August 15. The actual ruler is Bazou's elder brother, Nounk Lufiatu Ganga, whom all the other *loa* call "my uncle" (*nonk*). He is a discreet chief who has chosen as his exclusive human vehicle a small, silent old woman, whom he makes fall into trance from time to time. Though lacking authority, this woman may lay hold of whatever she wants in the village.

The full genealogy of the Kongo *loa* cannot be analyzed herein. According to Empress Hélène Hérard, Simon's wife, it covers four generations. I would like to point out only that Grandmother (*Gran*) Nkenge, Bazou's mother, is called Gran Matundu Tedi during ceremonies. Matundu was the name of the first person to be initiated during a *nkimba* or *kimpasi* session in Zaire; *tedi* is a Kikongo verb meaning "has said" (Swartenbroeckx 1973: 662, 624). Nkenge is, by the way, the name of a heroine carried off by water spirits in a well-known Kongo legend (Struyf 1936). Grandmother Nkenge never appears through possession, for she stayed back—in the sea—when the Kongo *loa* migrated to Haiti.

In the realm of myth, Bazou and his wife represent the divine kingship of the Kongo. Simon Hérard declared, "Nansoukry is a kingdom from father to son." Bazou, King Wangol, is likened to Gaspard, the Negro king among the three Wise Men; and for this reason, his feast day is January 6, whereas that of Mambo Inan, the Kongo queen, is Assumption Day, the feast of the Holy Virgin, the celestial queen. Bazou and Mambo Inan bore triplets, Jatibwa, Laoka, and Ganga, three brothers.

Laoka slept with his sister, Madam Lawé (who, according to Simon Hérard, acts like a whore during possession). A baby was born whom Madam Lawé abandoned in the woods. Jatibwa found and baptized him. Named Zinga Bwa after his godfather (*bwa* means forest), this child was raised by his second uncle, Ganga, for whom he picked the leaves necessary for making medicine. Zinga Bwa is said to be a perpetual child. Capricious and mischievous like a naughty boy, he makes faces at people.

Born of an incestuous couple and abandoned in the woods, he belongs to nature. This *loa* personifies disorder and assumes an important role in magic, whose elements come from wild nature.

Ganga was a great magician who, according to Simon Hérard, also practiced sorcery; his father, Bazou, had to chain him. I might add that Ganga Doki is a member of the *ganga* escort and that, in Kikongo, *ndoki* denotes the evil sorcerer in opposition to *nganga*, the good medicine man. Jatibwa is the only spirit whom Bazou has authorized to free Ganga so that he may appear through trances. When he thus appears, he is violent, for he is a hard *loa*. Recall that Jatibwa holds a central place—between the entrance and Mount Ganga—in this mystical territory; he mediates between his brother's unchained magic and Bazou's royal magic. Simon Hérard, who is "mounted" by a *ganga* spirit during ceremonies, summed up the situation by saying that all the Kongo divinities are great magicians.

Among Bazou's other sons, Lemba—sometimes said to be one of the triplets instead of Laoka—stole part of Ganga's magical knowledge (which is incomplete). For this reason, these two brothers do not get along well. In fact, *lemba* was the name of a major magic-religious institution of the Yombe from the seventeenth to the early twentieth centuries (Janzen 1982). *Lemba* ceremonies, like *nkimba* initiation, took place under the auspices of the earth spirit, Mbumba (Doutreloux 1967: 217). Thus it is no surprise to find the *lemba* and *bumba* escorts guarding together the entrance of Nansoukry.

In some areas of Haiti, the term *lemba* is used to refer to *petro* rites, and Simon Hérard stated that these are derived directly from Kongo ones. To my surprise, he corroborated the argument that I had been striving to prove for over ten years! He is deeply convinced that "people from the south"—as he calls them with a hint of scorn in his voice—laid hold of the Kongo gods who were worshipped at Nansoukry, changed their names and attributes, and made them into *loa maluk*—wicked *loa*. Whether this explanation holds or not, we may presume that the Kongo spirits arrived by various means in Saint-Domingue. Nansoukry is the high place of the Kongo cult, but it may not be the only source of *petro* rites. For instance, the *kita*, though commonly placed among the *petro loa*, are unknown in Nansoukry. But we must not forget that the religion of the Kikongo-speaking peoples—from the realm of Loango in the north to the kingdom of Kongo in the south—was not unified. Nowadays, the Woyo of the former Ngoyo kingdom, who had close ties with Loango, know nothing about the *nkita* (Mulinda 1986). In contrast, the *simbi* are worshipped as nature spirits throughout the Kikongo-speaking zone, and we are not surprised to find that they play a major role in the Kongo ritual at Nansoukry as well as in all *petro* ceremonies.

This mythology seems to be a *bricolage* of old Kongo elements; spirits (Simbi, Bumba), along with magicians (Ganga), are part of a mythical army. This army is at the service of a king whose name does not figure in the historical chronicles of the Kongo kingdom. This original restructuring was carried out following a warlike scheme, visibly inspired by the long resistance of escaped slaves (*marrons*) living in hiding. The role of these *marrons* in the making of voodoo has, no doubt, been underestimated by historians. Oral tradition relates that a fugitive slave named Figaro founded the first sanctuary at Nansoukry.

Figaro Pangodin Bazou ménin lukwenda. This esoteric formula is a serious explanation of the origin of the Kongo cult. Simon Hérard commented upon it as follows. Figaro Pangodin came from Africa and brought Bazou with him. *Ménin* is a Creole word derived from the French *mener*, "to lead." In Kikongo, the verb *kwenda* means "to leave for" (Swartenbroeckx 1973: 225). It is redundant, given the Creole term. Figaro [Pangodin] was a fugitive slave from Limbé in the north. He had run away from a sugar plantation and, after passing through Pangodin near Gonaïves, founded the sanctuary in Nansoukry which, at that time, was a wild place surrounded by forests and swamps. He is often called simply Figaro or even Gao. Recall that this name was coined by Beaumarchais for the hero of *The Barber of Seville* (1775) and of [*The*] *Marriage* [*of Figaro*] (1784), two plays which, after Paris, were performed several times at Cap-Haïtien, the capital of the French colony (Fouchard 1955). An owner probably named one of his slaves Figaro. If so, he would not have been the only one to do so, for this name figures on a list of slaves dating from 1796 (Debien & Houdaille 1964: 200).

We may conclude that the Kongo cult was brought to Nansoukry before the end of the colonial period. During the second half of the eighteenth century, more and more "Congo" slaves were being imported. Moreau de Saint-Méry (quoted by Debien 1961: 370) wrote at the time: "The most common Negros and those who are much appreciated are those from the coast of the Congo and Angola in the colony, they go under the generic name 'Congos.' " According to the books of an indigo plantation factory from 1777, the "Congos" are, after Creoles, the largest ethnic group (Debien 1961: 369). In any case, the priest called Don Pedro would have introduced the *petro* cult in 1768, apparently before Figaro settled in Nansoukry. But Don Pedro and Figaro were not the only persons who diffused the Kongo *loa*. According to the tradition of the Celixte family in the Léogane area, Tony Congo introduced these *loa*. Tony (the diminutive of Antoine) was the name of a Kongo king who lived during the second half of the seventeenth century, and there were many Antoines called Tony on eighteenth-century slave lists (Debien & Houdaille 1964: 192).

What is amazing is that the place where Figaro chose to install a purely Kongo but thoroughly original cult is located a few kilometers from the important temple of Souvenance, which is dedicated to the purest Dahomean cult on the island! Not far from there, in Nanbadjo, another temple has been built for the *nago* divinities alone. Side by side but at distinct sites in this area are the three fundamental components of voodoo. The triangle delimited by these three temples in the Gonaïves countryside covers three cultural zones, each of which, in spite of syncretism, has kept its identity. This fact should prompt us to bring historical and structural approaches together rather than to set them at odds.

Syncretism is a dynamic social phenomenon. In Haiti, as in African possession cults, new divinities, often with strange names, appear. But syncretism is also a structural process. I have tried to show that it can be approached by adopting two different but complementary perspectives: the one synchronic, the other diachronic. As I have endeavored to show here, all aspects of anthropology cannot be reduced to meaningless, historical phenomena.

References

Bittremieux, L. 1936. *La société secrète des Bakhimba au Zaïre* (Mém. Inst. R. col. Belge). Brussels: Institut Royal Colonial Belge.
Cuvelier, J. 1946. *L'ancien royaume de Congo*. Brussels-Bruges-Paris: Desclée de Brouwer.
Davis, W. 1985. *The Serpent and the Rainbow*. Toronto: Collins Willow.
Debien, G. 1961. "Les origines des esclaves des Antilles." *Bull. Inst. franç. Afr. noire* B23: 3/4, 363–87.
——— & J. Houdaille. 1964. "Les origines des esclaves aux Antilles." *Bull. Inst. franç. Afr. noire* B26: 1/2, 166–211.
Doutreloux, A. 1967. *L'ombre des fétiches: Société et culture yombe*. Louvain & Paris: Nawelaerts.
Fouchard, J. 1955. *Artistes et répertoire des scènes de Saint-Domingue*. Port-au-Prince.
Herskovits, M. 1937. *Life in a Haitian Valley*. New York: Reyerson Press.
Heusch, L. de. 1981. *Rois nés d'un coeur de vache*. Paris: Gallimard.
———. 1986. *Sacrifice in Africa: A Structuralist Approach*. Manchester: Univ. Press.
Janzen, J. M. 1982. *Lemba, 1650–1930: A Drum of Affliction in Africa and the New World*. New York & London: Garland.

Labat, J. B. 1732. *Relation historique de l'Ethiopie occidentale* (5 vols). Paris: C. J. B. Delespine (Italian text by Cavazzi, translated by Labat).

Leiris, M. 1953. "Note sur l'usage de chromolithographies par les vodouisents d'Haiti." In *Les Afro-Américains* (Mém. Inst. Franç. Afr. Noire 27). Dakar.

Makenda, A. 1971. "L'initiation au kimpasi et les rites nkita chez les Kongo." Thesis, University of Brussels.

Mata Makala ma Mpasi. 1973. "L'initiation Nkita en sociéte Ntandu." Thesis, University of Lubumbashi, Zaire.

Menesson-Rigaud, O. 1951. "Noël vodou en Haïti." In *Haïti: Poètes noirs* (Prés. Afr. 12). Paris.

————. 1953. "Service pour Simbi (sur rite petro)." In Rigaud 1953.

———— & L. Denis. 1947. "Cérémonie en l'honneur de Marinette." In *Bulletin de Bureau d'Ethnologie* 11–3, Port-au-Prince, 13–21.

Métraux, A. 1958. *Le vaudou haïtien*. Paris: Gallimard.

Moreau de Saint-Méry, L. E. 1797. *Description topographique, physique, civile, politique et historique de la partie française de l'ile de Saint-Domingue (avec des observations générales sur sa population, sur le caractère et les moeurs de ses divers habitants; sur son climat, sa culture, ses productions, son administration, etc.* (2 vols). Philadelphia.

Mulinda Habi Buganza. 1986. "La société Woyo: Structures sociales et religieuses." Thesis, University of Brussels.

Rigaud, M. 1953. *La tradition vaudoo et le vaudoo haïtien*. Paris: Niclaus.

Struyf, Y. 1936. *Les Bakongo dans leurs légendes* (Mém. Inst. R. col. Belge). Brussels: Institut Royal Colonial Belge.

Swartenbroeckx, P. 1973. *Dictionnaire Kikongo et Kituba-Français*. Bandundu, Zaïre: CEEBA.

Thompson, R. F. 1981. *Flash of the Spirit: African and Afro-American Art and Philosophy*. New York: Random House.

Van Wing, R. P. J. 1938. *Etudes Bakongo, 11, Religion et magie* (Mém. Inst. R. col. Belge). Brussels: Institut Royal Colonial Belge.

7

Black Music and Cultural Syncretism in Colombia

Peter Wade

Religion represents only a part of the broader fusion of cultures, often called mestizaje *or syncretism, in Latin America. Men and women of African descent, both slave and free, influenced the creation of unique Latin American cultural expressions, especially in art and music. The roots of this music come from the European, the African, and the native American peoples who make up the population. The region's modern music represents a hybrid inheritance, but at the same time the distinct rhythms of all three groups remain separate from the fused forms.*

This vibrant tradition emerged from the popular classes, where musicians had creative freedom unlimited by the standards imposed by upper-class mores. Afro-Creoles and Africans figure prominently in these popular classes and as originators of the musical forms. Moreover, music has wide-ranging roles, as it enhances social interaction, provides an escape mechanism from daily drudgery, and conveys political opinions. As a deep psychological and aesthetic expression of the human spirit, music has preserved the African element in daily life from the beginnings of slavery to the present. The Afro-Latin American musical tradition in the nineteenth century became widely known for the Cuban habanera. *It inspired Georges Bizet, for example, to write his own variation in 1875 and incorporate it into* Carmen. *Today, several Afro-Latin American forms exist: the merengue, the national music of the Dominican Republic, whose rhythmic base came with slaves from Puerto Rico, Haiti, or Cuba; the samba, associated worldwide with the merriment of Rio de Janeiro's Carnival (although many other forms exist); the* mariñera, *which became a*

Reprinted by permission of the author.

wartime expression of nationalism in Peru; the* cumbia, *the Colombian dance music whose name has African origins; and the tango, the national dance of Argentina. In the wake of racial consciousness movements beginning in the 1930s, Latin Americans have begun to classify musical forms with strongly audible African instrumentation and rhythm under the umbrella term "Afro-Latin Music."*

In this chapter, Peter Wade, a member of Liverpool University's Department of Geography and the author of Blackness and Race Mixture: The Dynamics of Racial Identity in Colombia *(1993), examines what he calls the "black music" of the Caribbean coast of Colombia. His essay contributes to the research on the African influence in the Americas by illustrating the connection between music and the identity of a population often dismissed in the official censuses. Moreover, he also challenges the commonplace explanations of syncretism in this music. Rather than a fusion of African and European forms, the music, which is already syncretic, is given a "black" character by Afro-Colombians.*

Syncretism and Black Culture

Syncretism may appear to be a self-evident word. Derived from the Greek word meaning to unify, it generally refers to the fusion of different forms, often linguistic or religious, into one. However, it has sometimes been used with pejorative implications, applied to the notion of a degenerate hybrid, and a loss of purity and authenticity. Diana Brown, for example, found that the study of "Macumba" and Umbanda in Brazil was scarce due partly to the perception, scholarly and popular, of it as an inauthentic mishmash of other religious traditions (1986: 5–6, 25–26). This highlights the important role played in processes of "syncretism" by power relations which can, for instance, define some traditions as authentic but folkloric (and hence controllable), others as authentic and orthodox (and hence hegemonic), and yet others as impure and debased (and hence to be suppressed or ignored). Power is, then, a crucial issue, and I believe that to talk of syncretism without talking of the social relations, including those of power, within which it occurs is misguided. As the case of Macumba shows, anthropologists can themselves be tied up in those social relations, since they may make judgments about the "authenticity" of a cultural complex and its value as an object of analysis.

---

*This dance and music, which probably developed in Lima, was first known as the *Cueca chilena* because of its immense popularity in Chile. When Peruvians and Chileans fought each other in the War of the Pacific (1879–1883), patriots changed the name of the music to the *mariñera* to recognize the Peruvian marines who were battling the Chileans.

The problem is related to the classic anthropological distinction between emic and etic perspectives. On the one hand, deciphering "syncretic" cultural complexes can rely for identifications of what is "authentic" or "syncretic," that is, for identifications of provenance, similarity, and difference, on the actors' point of view, which will of course be varied and will contest each other; issues of power difference clearly arise in this context. On the other, the decoding can aspire to an etic or "objective" genealogy of cultural forms, tracing the development of certain beliefs and social practices to chronologically and/or geographically removed antecedents which are independently documented. Here, judgments of identity, that is, similarity of and difference between given cultural forms, are based on the scholars' (supposedly objective) criteria. This type of "archaeology" can be of immense interest in itself, although it may become what Edmund Leach termed "butterfly collecting." However, it may also have a political purpose, challenging fondly held notions of cultural and national identity, unmasking the invention of tradition. The real African roots of Colombian culture may be revealed by these means, just as the disparate and "foreign" origins of a mythically traditional and homogeneous "English" culture can be adduced: both disturb ethnocentric notions of national identity. Here, scholarly "objectivity" feeds back into political concerns, drawing its power from its very claims to objectivity.

The emic approach attempts to make sense of culture in its own right. Here, preoccupations about where such-and-such a cultural element "really" comes from are subordinated to how such elements are used to convey meaning in a given social context. A classic example of this type of perspective is the Barthian, formalist approach to ethnicity and ethnic boundary maintenance. Reifications of "cultures" and "nationalities" are eschewed for a study of how boundaries are constructed through social practice, how people use cultural signs in the process of reproducing identity through interaction. This can lead to the position, held somewhat ambiguously by Barth (1969: 14–16), and more unequivocally by, for example, Leach, that the cultural "content" of the ethnic "vessel" is rather insignificant. Leach states that culture provides the "form" of the social situation, a "dress" which is "a product and an accident of history" (1954: 16). Such an apparently structuralist emphasis on signifiers does not mean ignoring questions of politics and economics; on the contrary, in this view, ethnicity is frequently simply an idiom which clothes economic and political forces (Barth 1969; Cohen 1974). Rather, the nature of the cultural signs involved is pushed aside in the analysis (Eriksen 1991).

In this paper, using "black music" as a focus, I wish to argue that the study of black culture and black community in Colombia seems to be best suited to an emic analysis. While the etic unearthing of real African contributions to Colombian culture is a vital part of an attempt to disrupt the apparently natural order of Colombia which consigns blacks to "invisibility" (Friedemann 1984), the fairly Hispanicized nature of "black culture" in Colombia (especially when compared to, say, Brazil or perhaps Cuba) seems to demand an emic approach able to cope with cultural transformations in which actors' definitions of identity are paramount. Black culture in Colombia often has clear European roots, in many cases predominating over traceable African heritage; yet it may retain its identity as "black culture," not because of its origins as revealed in historical analysis, but because of where actors think it comes from and what they think it is, conceptions strongly influenced by the identity of those who practice it, and where and how they practice it. In this sense, black culture is defined in processes of interaction between people making claims and ascriptions of "racial" identity.

However, I also wish to argue, again with reference to music, that black culture is not an arbitrary system of signs; that the cultural "content" is significant and that there are important continuities over time within black culture, despite its ambiguous boundaries and its changeability. These continuities have formed within the cultural context of Colombia, especially the power relations in which blacks have been involved, relations which, although varied, do have an important element of continuity. In brief, those classified by others as "blacks" (not, it should be noted, a straightforward category of people) have tended to be subordinate and dependent, a position reinforced by racist ideologies. In this situation, what blacks do has often been categorized by others (nonblacks) as black culture and seen as inferior. In response, black culture may take on, whatever its origins, a certain autonomy and independence which derives in part from its role in marking blacks' separateness from their oppressors. In this sense, then, the nonarbitrariness of the signifiers in black culture derives from continuing interactions within contexts of persistently unequal power relations. What black culture is held to be is not established simply in a series of interactions, but in historically persistent patterns of inequality.

However, I think that there is more to it than that. Continuities in meaning are also arguably related to Africanness, or, more accurately, certain "principles" of West African culture (Mintz and Price 1976: 5). It is important here to avoid reifying black culture and attributing to it certain specific cultural attributes which remain unchanging, but there is good evidence to assert some continuity between West African music and music as practiced by blacks in certain areas of Colombia (Abadía Morales 1973; Ocampo López 1988; Friedemann 1978; List 1980, 1983; Ortiz

1965). Lomax (1970), for example, argues for an underlying continuity of style, if not form and content, between music of the Pacific Coastal region and West African music. Thus what constitutes black culture, despite the heterogeneity of its origins, often owes something to Africa. This may seem banal, but there are contexts in Colombia where blacks are practicing traditions derived almost purely from archaic European contexts; and yet there is something particular about the style in which they practice them and indeed about the very importance of music as a cultural focus.

It is not just a question of Africanness, however: this is not a straightforward category, and it has to be located in relation to European understandings of Africanness. These of course have changed over time and cannot be easily summed up (Banton 1987), but there is strong evidence that from before the discovery of the New World, Europeans saw Africans as inferior and also as immoral and lascivious.[1] The interesting thing is that throughout the colonial and republican periods and right up to the present day, ideas about "black culture," while obviously varied and changing, have also had significant continuities which play on themes of black culture and particularly black music and dance as primitive, but also as physical, sensuous, erotic, and lascivious (and hence possibly attractive). Nonblack categorizations of black culture are therefore obviously not made from scratch in any interactional context, but build on ideas already extant and which have considerable antiquity.[2]

In sum, then, the study of syncretism as a simple archaeology of culture may be a powerful challenge to entrenched ideas of "national identity," but it is inadequate as a way of understanding a cultural complex. On the other hand, neither can it be dismissed: the specificities of cultural difference are important elements in the analysis since, although they are historically established [and] they are not, therefore, "accidental," and although "one cannot predict from first principles which [cultural] features will be emphasised and made relevant by the actors" (Barth 1969: 14), this does not mean that they are randomly distributed (Eriksen 1991). Rather, in the social context of interaction, claims and ascriptions of identity establish certain realms and types of behavior as "black" (and nonblack), but these claims categorize behaviors which are already invested with possible meanings derived from previous interactions.[3] Clearly, this does not imply that those possible meanings can be constructed outside of actors' memories and understandings of the past, but an historical grasp of the continuities involved is needed to fully grasp the present.

In the following sections, I want to explore these general considerations in relation to "black" music in Colombia, and then specifically to look at the role music plays among black migrants from the Chocó department of the Pacific Coast to the nonblack city of Medellín in the interior of the country.[4] My aim is to show certain continuities in the nature and cultural location of music classified as "black," continuities that derive partly from the context of power relations in which "blackness" is interactionally defined, but which also derive from a certain black tradition.

Black Music in Colombia

In Colombia, as in other Latin countries with significant black populations, the culture of black people seems the same in many respects as that of nonblacks. Especially in Colombia, black culture is highly Hispanicized. This is to miss, however, the subtle ways in which black people, living in black regions, have molded their own cultural forms out of Hispanic cultural traditions, often with traceable African influences at work in the process.[5] As with the category "black" itself, there are certain regional contexts in which the cultural patterns of black populations are distinctive. In the Pacific Coast region, an area traditionally inhabited predominantly by blacks—descendants of black slaves used for mining—family structures, while similar to those of nonblacks in other areas, are rather different: for example, polygyny is not only present but quite overt, informal unions are more frequent, and so on. Patron saints' festivals, again very similar to those of the interior, are distinctive: the Church is a more muted presence and music and dance have a more central place.[6] Music and dance are themselves distinctive, as we shall see. Ultimately, there is no easily demarcated national "black culture," but rather localized cultures, with more or less African influences, practiced by people who are more or less "black." Hence, at its boundaries black culture is in a constant state of negotiation, and black and nonblack Colombians themselves use these cultural differences to help establish ethnic distinctions in specific contexts. In this sense, "black culture" is contextually defined. But this does not mean that within Latin American culture, black cultural forms do not have a specific and distinctive pattern which has an historical continuity.

Musically, Colombia can be seen as part of the Caribbean basin.[7] Bilby (1985) traces for this region a process of creolization which gave rise to a musical spectrum, ranging from neo-African styles, through Euro-African hybrids, to mostly European styles. The spectrum is analogous to a linguistic continuum (cf. Drummond's [1980] idea of a cultural continuum) in that individuals can operate with several different styles within it, according to the appropriate context—although Bilby fails to explore the idea of hierarchy which is fundamental to these continua. Frequently the most neo-African styles are associated with African-derived religious complexes, although this is not always the case. The Euro-African hybrids were often descendants of European dances, military band styles (and sometimes religious music) which became creolized in the hands of black and mulatto musicians. But there were also new creations, rooted of course in African and European forms, but essentially original developments. Finally, there are European forms with little black influence.

Crosscutting this continuum are different musical contexts: religion (African-derived sects, wakes, European-derived sects); diversion (whether everyday dances, or centered on the great carnivals or saints' days); labor (for example, work songs). In all these contexts, blacks made their musical presence felt to a greater or lesser degree.

In Colombia, many of these styles and contexts are to be found, although African-derived religions and their associated music are more or less absent: most black music fits into the Euro-African hybrid segment of the continuum (see, however, Escalante 1954; and Friedemann and Patiño 1983). The syncretic development of music, with individual musicians inventively weaving together elements inherited from an increasingly varied musical milieu, is complex in the extreme, but it is not divorced from its overall context. In contrast, music is embedded in the social relations that connect individuals and populations that classify each other in terms of different racial identities.

I see three themes as characteristic of black music in Colombia, and I argue that certain processes can be observed in the historical development of black music in Colombia which are paralleled in a transfigured form in the recent history of music in Medellín. The first theme is that the blacks establish a musical independence of some kind which is a symbol of their identity as a black group and of their separateness. The second is that they may do this using elements that come from a variety of sources and that are already a product of cultural syncretism and do not necessarily come from their own autochthonous tradition. That is, what is classified as black music is not *dependent* on Africanisms, although there are important continuities of style. Third, the music they create or use is frequently looked down upon as inferior and crude, noisy and licentious, and again this forms a significant continuity in the relations between blacks and nonblacks in which musical forms are embedded. However, "black" music may also be taken up again by the dominant nonblack society and reincorporated into their world, perhaps because it seems to embody some dionysian impulse that is particularly attractive.

Black Musical Traditions

In the past, blacks have established independent traditions using elements that are at hand and that are copied to a large extent from the dominant culture, but infused with a specifically black, often African, style or feel. Marulanda (1979: 6) says of Pacific Coastal dances: "The choreographic rhythms learnt by [the blacks, slave and free] could not be reproduced by them with the soft and well-studied European cadences. . . . The movements were copied by the slaves with the ardor of African rhythm, with the freedom conferred by erotic gestures and the force transmitted by a mode of being and feeling that was very different from the tastes of the Old Continent. Although some schemes [of movement] were conserved . . . the rhythmic content was profoundly altered." Of the *contradanza* of the Chocó, a traditional dance derived originally from the Scottish country dance and taken to the New World by several European powers, Marulanda says, "The apprenticeship of the mining slaves in the *fiestas* of their masters . . . established a type of black style which took possession of the refined gallantries and coquetries of the country style." The blacks substituted for the dance square "a complex circle, whose accelerated rhythm dissolves the traditional waltz-like 6/8 and creates its own syncopation more in tune with the tastes of mulatto-ization" (Marulanda 1979: 13). Equally, the *danza*, a derivation from the *contradanza*, underwent in the Chocó "an acclimatization which allowed it to acquire a different structure . . . the gallant and evocative feel conferred on it by stringed instruments was eliminated and its content became varnished over with the virility and pagan nuances of the blacks" (Marulanda 1979: 10). Marulanda's use of words like ardor, freedom, erotic, force, virility, and pagan tells us as much about how nonblacks see black music as about black music itself, but that is, of course, germane to my argument about how music classified as "black" has been viewed over a long period of time. In any event, his commentary serves to establish that, although the *chirimía* bands of the Chocó are derived in instrumentation from the colonial military bands and they play mazurkas, polkas, *jugas* (from fugues), and *contradanzas*, all these are stamped with their own particularly black feel—a feel arguably derived from an African background and perceived by nonblacks as rather erotic.[8]

The principal rhythm and dance genre of the Pacific Coast south of the San Juan River of the southern Chocó is the *currulao*, which in its various forms is one of the most undiluted and independent black genres. The origin of the word itself is unclear, but it was used to describe a "slave dance" in seventeenth-century Cartagena (Marulanda 1979: 8), and both Cordovez Moure (1957: 484) and [José María] Samper (quoted in

Ocampo López 1988: 220) in their late nineteenth-century writings use the word to describe the dance of the *bogas* or black boatmen of the Magdalena River. Nowadays, the term refers exclusively to the Pacific Coast genre and its Africanness is quite apparent. Marulanda (1979: 8) refers to it as "the rhythm which best synthesizes the survival of Africanness," and Whitten (1974: 111) remarks that it has an African rhythm completely distinct from that of Afro-Caribbean musical styles (see also Whitten 1968; Lomax 1970; Abadía Morales 1983: 212). The *currulao* involves the *marimba*, a type of xylophone of African origin, two *cununos* or conical drums designated male and female, one or two *bombos* or double-headed drums, *guasás* or bamboo-tube rattles, and a lead male singer with several female vocalists who sing in a call-response fashion.

It is harder for the case of the Atlantic Coast region to pinpoint an independent black musical tradition due to the advanced cultural and racial mixture that has occurred there, and most *costeño*[9] music is clearly of mixed origins. Nevertheless, it is clear that the blacks created their own musical forms and were the main driving force in the creation of the Euro-African hybrids which form the basis of later developments. José Cassiani, a Jesuit commentator on the life of San Pedro Claver of seventeenth-century Cartagena, noted that the blacks were trying to introduce dancing, that drums were publicly on sale, and that one black woman had opened up a "public dance house and tavern" (quoted in Valtierra 1980: II, 217). In 1769, the king requested a report on dances known as *bundes* in Cartagena. *Bunde*, according to Marulanda (1979: 9), was a general term for black dances, although now it refers to funerary songs in the Pacific region (Abadía Morales 1983: 220). The 1770 report stated that the *bundes* were "very old" and widespread and took the form of a circle of men and women in the center of which pairs danced in turn to the sound of drums and singing (quoted in Valtierra 1980: II, 219). In another case, there are reports from Cartagena between 1777 and 1780 of a cabildo of Carabalís which was the object of a complaint from another cabildo protesting that the noise of the Carabalís in their reunion was too loud—"as if they did not also create their own *guachafita* [hubbub, din]" (Raúl Porto del Portillo, quoted in Escalante 1964: 153).

Later, around 1830, Joaquín Posada Gutiérrez (1920: 334–349) describes the great annual festival to venerate the Virgin of La Candelaria in Cartagena which he witnessed as a youth. Each day different guilds had their festivities until the last day, Carnival Sunday, which was for the slaves, African and creole. Each cabildo then had a formal procession with a king and queen holding umbrellas as a signal of their rank, and with male dancers with faces, legs, and chests painted red, holding wooden swords and wearing leopard-skin aprons and paper crowns with bright feathers, "imitating the customs and costumes of their native lands"; the women wore jewels lent by their mistresses. They danced along "singing, leaping and making contortions to the sound of drums and tambourines, and beating cymbals and copper mortars [i.e., bells]." They proceeded to La Popa, a church set on a hill overlooking the city, and here they heard a mass before descending back into the town. They were then "completely free to enjoy themselves in their *cabildos*" for three days. During the evenings leading up to this final day, dances were held. These were for the various social classes of the city nominally organized around socioracial distinctions, and including a first class of *blancas de Castilla*,[10] whites from Spain, a second class of *pardas*, mixed-blood women, and a third class of free blacks. These people who, whatever their color, "occupied a certain social position," danced to the military bands of racially segregated regiments which played minuets, *contradanzas*, waltzes, and some *bailes de la tierra* or local dances; these bands were based on brass and percussion instruments (Triana 1987: 84). In addition to these groups, there were the *blancas de la tierra*, locally born whites, and the *cuarteronas* or light-skinned mixed-bloods.

Below all these groups, and out in the streets, were the poor people and slaves, blacks for the most part, but also mulattoes and other mixed-bloods, who, "to the thundering sound of African drums," danced in a large circle which rotated around a group of male drummers accompanied by female singers who kept rhythm with handclaps "enough to swell within ten minutes the hands of any other than they." Men and women danced barefoot in pairs, without touching, and the woman held aloft in her hand two or three candles wrapped in a cheap muslin cloth which she threw outside the circle when they had burned down. The basic circular structure of the dance with the use of candles and the accompaniment of drums, handclapping, and singing is typical of the period, although it receives different names from different observers. Posada calls it a *currulao* and later remarks that by the time of writing in 1865 it was called *mapalé*. The observers of the *bogas* also called it *currulao*. Nowadays, such a dance with only drums, singing, and handclapping might be termed a *bullerengue*.

The current *costeño* repertoire of traditional folkloric genres is very diverse and includes a wide variety of forms, which are often somewhat inaccurately grouped under the vague umbrella term of *cumbia*. Principal genres include *cumbia*, *bullerengue*, *mapalé*, *gaita*, *porro*, and merengue, and these are played by a variety of instrumental lineups such as *cañamilleros*, *gaiteros*, and *tamboras* which use different types of flutes, drums, rattles, and scrapers. My purpose is not to describe these (see Triana

1987; Abadía Morales 1983; Delia Zapata Olivella 1962), but rather to highlight how the blacks laid the basis for a series of musical and dance forms which, although they received Indian and European influences, and became more and more syncretized over time, remained heavily identified with the blacks. Names like *mapalé, cumbia* (in its folkloric form), and *bullerengue* were and still are seen as essentially black dances. The Indian influence, whatever its real impact, is generally taken to be via the *gaita*, a long vertical flute occasionally mistaken for an arabesque import akin to the oboe (Chamorro 1982), but which has no vibrating reed and is of well-documented indigenous origin (Abadía Morales 1983: 234; Triana 1987: 72). The black tradition today retains its purest form in the *tambora* lineup of conical drums, *tablitas* (small wooden spatulas beaten together), and responsorial singing (Triana 1987: 75), a lineup which harks back to the eighteenth- and nineteenth-century descriptions of black *costeño* dances. In the Atlantic Coast region, then, it is clear that the blacks early on established their own kind of music, based in large part on the drum, and this was influenced by and influenced in its turn white and to a lesser extent Indian music to produce a series of syncretic forms.

In the north of the department of Cauca, blacks celebrate various festivals, including the Adoration of the Child. The blacks there say that these are *fiestas de negros* which date from colonial times and, according to one black informant, have their roots in "pagan ceremonies" from Africa (Atencio and Castellanos 1982: 36). A local historian is quoted as saying that all the fiestas in honor of St. John, St. Peter, St. Paul, the Immaculate Conception, the Child Jesus, the Virgin Mary, and so on, "had their syndicates, some from the city, others from the countryside, [which] all included the contracting of a band of musicians which enlivened the evening preceding [the fiesta]." Almost certainly in colonial times these syndicates were the cabildos, lay brotherhoods which blacks were also allowed to organize. Again, then, the blacks took an essentially Spanish tradition—this time the fiesta itself as well as the music—and made it into something that expressed their own sense of identity, even imputing to it African origins: here is a good example of how the context of interaction, over time, defines actors' ideas about provenance and identity of cultural elements. Today there are still fundamental black features: "the presence of dance in sacred ceremonies, the rhythmic structure of the music . . . the interaction between soloist and the chorus in the religious songs" (Atencio and Castellanos 1982: 38). The basic musical form is the *fuga*, played by a band that is essentially like a *chirimía* and sung by a female chorus and the general public. The *fuga* is clearly a European derivation, and the lyrics are Catholic in reference, but Atencio and Castellanos emphasize the particularity of the *fuga* in these black fiestas and attribute the call-response pattern to an African past (1982: 118).[11] Another important form in the fiestas, overlapping with the recitations of the *fuga*, is the *copla* or rhyming verse. This, Atencio and Castellanos trace to old Spanish ballad forms and quote an authority on the Colombian ballad tradition to the effect that "the black population represents the most important exponent of traditional Spanish music and oral poetic forms" (1982: 110). In the Atlantic Coast region, too, the black presence was important in the development of oral poetic musical forms, manifested in a variety of work songs which became the basis for the more modern *vallenato* forms (see below; Triana 1987: 66).

Persecution, Attraction, and Syncretism

To talk of syncretism in this whole process is inadequate if it implies a neutral mixing: we look at the end result and see the disparate elements—syncretism is the answer, and we can unravel its origin with a careful archaeology of culture. But the process by which this mixture is created is not neutral at all. Musical syncretism involves the whole relationship between blacks and nonblacks, including whites—and, to complicate matters, Indians—as it happens to manifest itself through music, so these contexts of relations and their power differences need to be looked at, as well [as] the way the origin of given elements influenced the meanings attached to them. Hierarchy was fundamental to this process, as indeed was the ambivalent fascination of the nonblack world with black music.

The persecution of black music was a direct expression of this hierarchy. San Pedro Claver, the great seventeenth-century healer and evangelist of the Cartagena slaves, who licked clean their ulcerous sores in an apotheosis of self-abnegation, also repressed their dances and confiscated their drums: "He would walk along the public streets where these dances used to take place, and finding one he would disperse the blacks and take away their drum [. . .]; at first, the bewildered blacks obeyed him, but later it appeared to them too great a submission, and they resisted him; [. . .] when he encountered resistance . . . he would take out his scourge, instrument of his penitence, and . . . with lashes disperse that cloud which blinded modesty" (Cassiani, quoted in Valtierra 1980: II, 217). The bishop of Popayán decreed in 1763 that "since there have been introduced several dances called *zaraza, el castillar, zamo de cabro, bundes,* and others of the same class and type, with actions and movements both dishonest and provocative . . . we order, under pain of excommunication, that under no pretext, neither in public nor in private, should these prejudicial dances be played or sung" (Perdomo Escobar 1963: 54). The bishop of Cartagena prohibited *bundes* and fandangos in the early 1730s "recognizing the inconveniences and sins which originate in such dishonest diversions" (Perdomo Escobar 1963: 318). Friedemann and Arocha (1986: 418) recount a campaign directed against the "diabolical" *marimba* dances of the blacks of the southern Pacific Coastal region by one Father Manuel Mera in 1908.

As these comments suggest, dances associated with blacks were deemed immoral; and white observers of the dances of the *bogas*, the black boatmen of the Magdalena, were also impressed by their "lubricity." Cordovez Moure, writing in the late nineteenth century, described how the boatmen performed the *currulao*, "durante el cual los negros ejecutan sin rubor ante sus parejas movimientos eróticos, saturados de palabras obscenas, que arrancan mayores aplausos cuanto más impúdicos son" (1957: 484). Equally, José María Samper, a parliamentarian and essayist of the same period, thought that the *currulao* had movements full of "voluptuosidad" and "lubricidad cínica." However, "todo el mundo quiso contemplar la escena," precisely because it revealed "toda la energía brutal del negro y el zambo de las costas septentrionales de la Nueva Granada" (quoted in Ocampo López 1988: 220).

A good deal of dancing and celebration was organized through the cabildos, and these were subject to constant suspicion and persecution. Roberto Arrázola (1970: 129) reports on the interrogation in Cartagena in 1693 of blacks from *palenques* and cabildos who were allegedly plotting a rebellion together. One Francisco Arará (a slave in the Santa Clara convent; Borrego Pla 1973: 102) testified that "the Arará are a people who today have no *cabildo*, that he had been named governor [of the cabildo], and that when they have the *fiesta de la Popa* [i.e., of La Candelaria], they collect in the house of Manuel Arará, slave of the Company of Jesus, who is the king [of the cabildo], and there they give alms and go to enjoy themselves, and that he only takes care [of the burial] when a relative dies, because since the *Provisor* removed the drum and took it to his house there is no *lloro*." *Lloro*, literally a crying or wailing, was the name given to the funerary ceremonies and dances of the blacks. Jaramillo Uribe also reports on a 1785 court case against blacks accused of conspiring to form a *palenque* in the Cauca region: they had a cabildo with mayors, governors, and viceroys, and those elected to such posts "paid for the necessary refreshments at their dances and celebrations" (1968: 70). The conflict between the Carabalí cabildo and its neighbor in Cartagena in 1777 led the governor of the city to try to shut down the cabildos, apparently to little effect since they were still there and active in 1830.[12]

Persecution existed, and yet the nonblacks' attitude to black music, or more accurately black musicians, was not so simple. While in Cuba, for example, they might recoil at a "savage" and "rowdy" *merienda de negros* (*merienda* signifies tranquil picnic; when it is *de negros* it means bedlam), the blacks, parallel or as an alternative to immersing themselves in their *bailes*, also conquered the minuet, the waltz, the *contradanza*, and, "taking over the orchestra, adapted it to their tastes." The black plays "white music in the drawing rooms, the churches, and the theaters; but . . . he infiltrates into this . . . African elements; dance music, above all, would have its African imprint" (Díaz Ayala 1981: 28, 39). Carpentier notes that blacks and mulattoes predominated in musical production in late nineteenth-century Cuba and notes that "certain *contradanzas* were better liked when played by *pardos* [mulattoes]. Blacks and whites played the same popular pieces. But the blacks added an accent, a vitality, an unwritten 'something' which 'picked you up' " (1946: 112). They added, for example, a "simple ligature" to the *contradanza* to create the conga, and *Tu madre es conga* was the rage among "the most aristocratic society" of Santiago in 1856. Díaz Ayala (1981: 39) writes that the Cuban *contradanza* bore the mark of black participation, as did its later derivative, the *danzón*, "the first genuinely Cuban creation" and a principal musical genre from the 1870s until quite recently. African roots also showed in the Cuban *son*, a major genre on the basis of which salsa later emerged (see also Urfé 1977; Bilby 1985). The Euro-African hybrids which arose from the creolization of European forms in the hands of the blacks and mulattoes had an "irrepressible vitality" (Bilby 1985: 195) which was very attractive. Clearly, the perceived connection of black music with sexuality was a potent force here.

In Colombia, too, whites found black-influenced music attractive. Posada Gutiérrez (1920: 341) observes that in the smart *bailes de salón*, the younger people of all three classes "yawned and dozed" during the minuets, but gave shouts of joy when the *contradanza* and the waltz were played, music which though of European origin had become "Hispanicized" and "adapted to our fiery climate." The *bailes de la tierra* had their place from midnight onward and were "happy and vivacious," although not, he notes prudently, indecent. Since the military bands were of blacks and mulattoes for the third-class dance, it is likely that the *contradanzas*, the waltzes, and even more probably the *bailes de la tierra* had by that time picked up some of that "unwritten something" which the blacks had given the salon dances in Cuba. Interestingly, the men of the higher-class dances deserted their own women to dance in the lower-class ones: perhaps it was not only the women there which they found attractive.

In more recent periods, this process is also obvious. The *cumbia* and associated *costeño* genres received much of their creative impulse from black traditions and, although they are still practiced by the traditional *conjuntos* (groups), as from the nineteenth century they also began to be played by the brass bands which were playing the minuets, *contradanzas*, waltzes, and so on of the higher social classes; the music played by these *bandas* is generically known as *porro*. In this century, *costeño* genres also evolved into more commercial music which, under the generic title *cumbia*, spread across the nation. From the 1930s onward, people in the interior of the country listened and danced to *cumbias* from the Atlantic Coast region alongside Caribbean musical genres from Cuba (see Ulloa 1992 for data on Cali). Later, in the 1960s, *cumbia* also formed a major element in the repertoire of *costeño* bands such as Los Corraleros de Majagual which made use of more brass instrumentation and the accordion and helped popularize *costeño* music on a nationwide basis. The *cumbia* has eventually become rather far removed from the traditional folkloric genres or even the music played by Los Corraleros, although confusingly the term is still applied to all three variants of music since they are basically developments of the same tradition. *Cumbia* in its most modern form is now a highly commercial product, popular not only in the interior of Colombia, but as far afield as Peru and Mexico, where it is subsumed under generic titles like *música tropical* which include many Caribbean styles. It is a classic instance of a black-inspired tradition which has been steadily "whitened" over time, persecuted in the past when practiced independently by blacks, but becoming more and more acceptable as it spreads into the nonblack world, losing both its Africanness and its main association with black people, and yet retaining its attractive "hot" quality. It is no coincidence that *música tropical* is also known as *música caliente*, hot music. It may be hard to recognize in the slick pop music which is now commercialized as *cumbia*, the "noisy African singing" of Cartagena's nineteenth-century blacks, but the continuity is a real one and I would argue that its generative force lies partly in the taste of the nonblack world for black rhythms.

Perdomo Escobar, for example, says in his history of music in Colombia [that] "the music of the littoral heats the blood of the highland man, invades him with irresponsible happiness, and shakes him out of the spiritual and geographical prison in which he lives" (1963: 227). Ocampo López, talking of the festivals and folklore of the Atlantic Coast region, says that "el costeño colombiano es amante de las diversiones; expansivo y explosivo en el hablar y en el reír; en el amor fulminante y fugaz; por ello su gran atracción por la música y la danza" (1988: 182). Very telling here is the phrase, *por ello*: a natural connection is made between music/dance and emotional and erotic expression. More explicitly, when talking of the dances of the Atlantic Coast, Ocampo López says that black dance channels the emotional conflicts of individuals and "exteriorizes joy, sadness, anger, sexual stimulation, etc." (1988: 188). Turning to the *currulao* of the Pacific Coast, he quotes Enrique Pérez Arbeláez on how the dance partners manifest "el bajeo, esa suerte de emisión corporal magnética que se esconde en muchas prácticas de tipo africano" which links the man with the woman (1988: 220). Clearly, then, black music and dance are still perceived as particularly erotic and emotional by nonblack observers, a perception which I think owes as much to nonblack ideas about blacks as it does to whatever eroticism blacks themselves find in their dances.

The cultural dynamic involved is a complex one because Colombia cannot be represented as a simple opposition between black and white. Although at an early stage it was a matter of the blacks creating their own tradition with different rhythms and musical forms, in places like the Atlantic Coast region musical and dance genres soon arose that were intermediate between black music and white music, giving rise to the nineteenth-century hierarchy which ranged from a minuet to an "Hispanicized" waltz, to the *bailes de la tierra*, and from there to *cumbias* and other music which had soon spread beyond the confines of black cabildos and became traditional *costeño* folk music played and danced to by the very mixed-blood population of the Atlantic Coast region.

The point remains, however, that in certain contexts, blacks managed to establish relatively independent musical forms, which were subject to transformation in much the same way as the category "black" itself in a Latin American context, but which also formed part of the hierarchical relations in which black and nonblack relations were established. These musical styles varied greatly with respect to "Africanness," yet they all had a specific style which was arguably derived from generalized African origins. And many nonblack observers concurred in seeing at least the secular contexts of this music as lewd and lascivious.[13] This very fact, however, also implied that such music was attractive and desirable and this was one force behind its penetration into the nonblack world, albeit in an altered form.

In this sense, the cultural content of the ethnic relations pertaining between "black" and "nonblack" in certain contexts cannot be seen as an arbitrary set of signifiers which simply established ethnic boundaries. The nature of these symbols was historically influenced by the African origin of the blacks which gave the music they played an important role in their cultural repertoire, and also particular stylistic traits, such as, for example, the centrality of the drum in certain genres. Just as important was the way black music was perceived by the nonblacks as lascivious and improper. Clearly a perception that was related to power relations, it also made a material difference to the way some aspects of these relations developed, since alongside "lasciviousness" went "hotness" and music that "picked you up," or "heated the blood." Thus, alongside persecution went attraction, and this influenced patterns of cultural change.

Blacks and Music in Medellín

Blacks migrate from the Pacific Coast to various cities of the interior of the country, including Cali, Medellín, and Bogotá. Between 1986 and 1987, I did fieldwork among black migrants to Medellín who are in the vast majority from the Chocó department of the Pacific littoral.[14] I found that they mostly concentrated in domestic service, construction, and the sale of items (generally cooked food) on the street. I also found that, although most Chocoanos lived in a dispersed fashion around the city (inevitably so in the case of the domestic servants), there were some notable concentrations of blacks, both occasional and more permanent. And I found that music, and dance, were an important aspect of the way in which these concentrations were established and of the relations they maintained with the nonblack Antioqueño[15] city dwellers.

In brief, I found the patterns outlined on a more general level above also operated in Medellín. Although, as in much of Latin America, there was no easy black-white opposition, nevertheless the Chocoanos were an identifiable minority and, especially when they concentrated together, established a definite identity as a black community; music formed part of that identity. This music was predominantly salsa and *vallenato* which are by no means easily identifiable as "black" music, nor straightforwardly derivable from an "African" heritage, although both have clearly been heavily influenced by black musical traditions within the New World.[16] But, as I have argued, black culture is to a large extent contextually defined. Although the behavior of the Chocoanos in Medellín is in many respects different from that in the Chocó, it may continue to be defined as black culture, both by the Chocoanos and the Antioqueños, chiefly because it is being practiced by Chocoanos in a context in which blackness is, even if only temporarily, the normal state of affairs. Equally, assimilation of urban Antioqueño culture is not simply a matter of altering specific patterns of behavior, but of altering the social context of behavior by associating more with Antioqueños and cutting links with the Chocoano ethnic network. In short, it is not only the actual cultural elements which define "black culture," but also the context in which they appear and from which they derive their meaning. This context is essentially formed by the ethnic relations and interactions existing between the Chocoanos and the Antioqueños, relations in this case partly manifested in spatial arrangements: the constitution of a black space through the concentration of blacks itself tends to define what happens in it as black culture, for the purposes of Medellín and its people.

But there are also some important continuities. First of all, it is noticeable that music itself formed an important element in defining localized Chocoano identity. Second, it is no accident that the genres involved, although not straightforwardly "black," have been heavily influenced by black musical traditions rooted in an African past and, more important, are recognized by blacks and nonblacks as being associated with blacks and with regions seen as tropical and dark-skinned such as the Atlantic Coast region, or the Caribbean basin. Third, Chocoano concentrations and specifically their manifestations of music and dance were, and still are, perceived by local Antioqueños as intrusive and alien, and as rather immoral and improper. As such they have been persecuted. At the same time, however, I would argue that the presence of the blacks in the city has fomented the widespread adoption of salsa and *vallenato* by the local youths, even though these genres were becoming nationally popular anyway.

The first notable concentration of Chocoanos in Medellín seems to have been in Barrio Antioquia, near the old Medellín airport. Displaced from the city center by urban improvement programs, many people moved to this area, among them many blacks. In 1963 a Chocoano society founded its headquarters there as a social, mutual-aid, and educational organization. Dances were held which attracted large numbers of black domestic servants and other blacks. Shortly afterward, other Chocoanos started up dance halls[17] and the whole neighborhood became a focus for Chocoanos from all over the city. Many of them rented rooms in the tenement buildings there. The Antioqueño reaction was not entirely friendly. The local youths harassed the young black women; and in the late 1960s, the civic leaders of the barrio started a campaign among the owners of the tenements to prevent the settlement of more blacks. The women especially were considered to be loud, foul-mouthed, and bad-mannered. This, along with other urban processes of relocation and residential dispersal, represented the end of Barrio Antioquia as a Chocoano focus.

Also in the 1960s, a few Chocoanos settled in a more peripheral area, called Zafra, on the outskirts of the city. In 1968, the first residents also started a Sunday *bailadero* which became a mecca for other Chocoanos. Another family took over in 1978. Again the local Antioqueño reaction was hostile. The young men would pick fights and create trouble, and the Chocoanos would retaliate. Both Chocoanos and Antioqueño informants identified Antioqueños as the instigators of the trouble. Antioqueño informants also told me that the Chocoanos *velorios* (funeral wakes) had caused some expression of concern among the local Antioqueños who saw them as improper and impious.[18] Over time the Chocoano dance halls stopped functioning, partly due to the problems encountered and also because some of the Chocoanos moved away.

La Iguaná is an invasion settlement near the city center to which many of the Zafra Chocoanos moved, although the first Chocoano had arrived in 1966. It was he who started a small weekend *bailadero* which again provoked some indignation among the Antioqueños who thought the place encouraged drunkenness and licentiousness among the young. The major influx of Chocoanos occurred around 1978, making them a total of about 14 percent of the area's population when I was there in 1986–87. Several blacks opened *bailaderos* in their houses and these again became the focus of ethnic tension during the late seventies. As in Zafra, attacks occurred, and the dance halls were stoned; some of the Chocoanos would retaliate. Over time, conflict quieted down and by 1986 there was no overt hostility, even though there were still functioning Chocoano *bailaderos* which attracted large numbers of blacks from within and outside the barrio at the weekends. However, the dance halls located in the more central part of the zone had closed down, and the only ones still operating at that time were in the least consolidated and most recent part of the barrio where blacks, although they did not quite form a majority, were certainly a powerful presence. In this sense a certain degree of segregation had occurred.

More transient concentrations of Chocoanos occur in the city center over the weekends, especially on Sundays, when the domestic servants have a day off. At the beginning of the sixties, a couple of bars were started by Antioqueños which became centers for Chocoanos and which, as time went on, increasingly concentrated their musical repertoire almost exclusively on *vallenato*. These bars did not attract attacks, partly no doubt because they were owned and run by Antioqueños, and because they were on much more public territory, but they certainly established ethnic barriers: as one bar owner told me, if Antioqueños happen to step in, "they leave straight away when they realize it's not their atmosphere." The atmosphere is established partly by the simple presence of blackness; but [it] is also established by music. Nothing but *vallenato* is played, and although this genre can be heard in many places in Medellín, it is the exclusiveness of the repertoire that serves to establish the difference.

Salsa has a less segregated history. Although the salsa bars were all originally concentrated along city center streets near the *vallenato* bars (in the "bad area" of town), and although they were also focal points for blacks, they were never as predominantly black: salsa from the start had a wider appeal to the Antioqueño youth. Accordingly it has spread more widely around the city.

These various examples document the role of music in the establishment of a specific black identity in Medellín, even bearing in mind that such an identity is by no means unambiguous at a citywide level. They also suggest that when [the] black community makes its presence felt, partly through music and dance, it often attracts a hostile reaction from nonblacks who feel their cultural authority threatened by what they see as impropriety and alien intrusion. What is interesting here is that the kind of reactions to black music and identity evident in Medellín are not dissimilar to those illustrated earlier in an historical context: persecution and charges of impropriety, but at the same time the acceptance of some of that music into the nonblack world. "Hot" music from the Caribbean and from the Atlantic Coast region has long been attractive in the interior of the country, and in the 1950s people were dancing mambos, and *cumbias*, and, more generally, genres identified as *música tropical* in Bogotá and Medellín. Equally, younger people all over Medellín will now put on salsa and some *vallenato* at their parties or dance to them in discotheques and bars. But that music is still heavily identified with the blacks, with "black" regions and with tropicality and eroticism. And it is typically accepted in a conditional form: watered down with other genres in the evening's repertoire.

Conclusion

In sum, then, the use of music to establish black identity in Medellín and reactions to that music are not simple symbols in a process of ethnic interaction which is based on economics and politics, but are cultural processes with a long history in Colombia (and elsewhere) which have their own dynamic. It is not sufficient either to analyze the interactive process on its own or to unearth the genealogy of the cultural elements involved. It is necessary to examine the historical interaction of both aspects together. In this endeavor, the aim is to analyze how people build on past meanings and transform them. For this, more information is necessary than I have available for the case of music in Colombia on people's sense of history and memory and how they understand the past, and it is clear that this is an avenue for future research.

The significance of this approach to syncretism and black culture is twofold. First, both academics and, more often, official spokespeople engaged in the representation of national culture and identity make recourse to notions of "syncretism" as the reality underlying "Colombianness." It is important to set the context of power relations within which cultural transformations have taken and continue to take place, rather than appropriating them as a simple force of democratization and homogenization, which levels inequality by absorbing difference. Second, there is a politicization of ethnic identities currently under way in Colombia, although "Indians" are favored over "blacks" as the objects of the state's discourse of pluralism. In this conjuncture, the objectification of ethnic traditions frequently makes recourse to simplistic attributions of "Africanness" to Colombian black culture, seeing the persistence of Africanisms as a symbol of the generic quality of resistance which is said to pervade black culture. The analysis of cultural transformations does not aim to deny either Africanisms or resistance: it does aim to put them both in their historical context and reveal the true nature of the continuities and resistances at work. It is vital to see that "black culture," and its representation for political purposes, do not depend on ideas about Africanisms, just as it is important to see that modern resistance by blacks to grossly uneven development and cultural discrimination does not rest solely upon a simplified idea of heroic black resistance, however much the real historical instances of black heroism can act as a banner for political mobilization. Not only has resistance been more subtle than violent confrontation but it can be created anew in the conjunctures of modern nation building.

Notes

1. See, for example, Curtin (1965: 3–57); Barker (1978: 100–141); Jordan (1977: 3–43). These works refer mostly to English attitudes, but in the sixteenth century some of the major texts influential throughout Europe were written in Spanish (e.g., those by Leo Africanus and Luis del Marmol Carvajal). See also Rout (1976: 3–21).

2. The role of phenotypical markers as signifiers for cultural difference is important here, as their obvious heritability (although subject to transformation, like culture, through processes of *mestizaje*) gave a good basis for building ideas about continuity.

3. In Colombia, as in other Latin American countries, these contexts of interaction are complex in that there is often not a straightforward opposition between "black" and "nonblack." These identities are ambiguous and contestable in many situations, and this simply serves to multiply the possibilities for syncretism and the transformation of identities.

4. Research in Medellín was financed by a Research Fellowship at Queen's College, Cambridge, and by grants from the Social Science Research Council (USA) and the British Academy.

5. For a review of much of the literature relating to blacks and black culture in Colombia, see Friedemann (1984) and Friedemann and Arocha (1986).

6. See Villa (1985) and Velásquez (1960) for comments on festivals in the region. See also Friedemann (1966–1969).

7. See Béhague (1985) and the works cited in the text for references on music in Colombia; see also Abadía Morales (1973, 1983); Escalante (1964); Velásquez (1961b); List (1980, 1983).

8. The *chirimías* of the Andean region not only have a different instrumentation, but have a very different style to them.

9. I use the word *costeño* to refer to the Atlantic Coastal region.

10. Posada tells us that the dances were organized around the women of each category, as if the females were the symbol or bearers of each stratum's socioracial status.

11. It is hard to believe that call and response is classed as characteristic of black music, especially in a religious context, when precisely this format is so common in Western religious contexts (see Tagg [1989]).

12. This type of repression has parallels in other New World contexts. Aretz (1977) gives many examples of the repression of cabildos all over Latin America. For Cuba, Díaz (1981: 84) reproduces a 1922 resolution which orders the suppression of dances, "especially that known by the name of *Bembé*," carried out under the auspices of the Societies of Mutual Aid and Recreation, which were nothing less than the old cabildos under a new name and which worshipped African deities. These dances allegedly led to the murder of white children as sacrifices to their gods and were "prejudicial to public security and contrary to morals and good customs." Ortiz (1917: 400) also recommends the surveillance of the "African dances" in Cuba which harbored witchcraft practices that led to delinquency, fraud, and even the murder of white children. In a much later work, Ortiz observes that in Cuba "there was a time when the music of the blacks was looked down upon. . . . It was not even music; it was said to be merely 'noise' " (1965: 146). Words of African origin meaning dance or music came to be synonymous with disorderliness or rowdiness (1965: 150), and he states that "the slave-owners in their eagerness to justify subjugation by the supposed 'racial inferiority' of the slave, saw in the musical fervor of the blacks not only banal and infantile entertainment . . . but also a blemish characteristic of 'races' classified as deficient and destined always to domination by others" (1965: 153). Not surprisingly, the same repression occurred in the United States. Walton (1972: 20) produces as an example an 1811 decree of Georgia in which it was thought that "it is absolutely necessary to the safety of the province that all due care be taken to restrain negroes from using or keeping drums."

13. More sacred ritual contexts have not escaped censure either. For Chocoano *velorios*, Velásquez quotes Church observations which characterize these as "ridiculous *fiesta*" (1961a: 35). The funeral banquet on the last day of the wake seems to the Church especially irreverent: "Only in the Chocó could this abomination of the *ninth day* exist in which people of all ages and conditions congregate, festive and gay[. . . .] They play cards, draughts, dominoes; they sing absurd verses, they tell obscene stories which cause laughter, they smoke, they drink *aguardiente* and they eat in abundance [. . .] as if with cups of liquor they would win indulgences" (Velásquez 1961a: 56). The cabildos in the colonial era were also clearly involved in the reproduction of black-influenced religious practices, and these too were hounded by the authorities.

14. See Wade (1990, 1988, 1993) for details.

15. Medellín is the capital of Antioquia, a comparatively well-developed region with important industrial and coffee-growing wealth. The Antioqueños have quite a powerful sense of regional identity, one aspect of which is the ideology of *la raza antioqueña*, a racial strain supposedly little "contaminated" by black heritage. See Twinam (1980); Wade (1990, 1993).

16. Salsa made an explosive appearance in New York in the late sixties. There, Puerto Rican, Cuban, Panamanian, and other Latin American immigrants were creating a "new" sound out of what was essentially Cuban and to a lesser extent Puerto Rican music, a sound that was also an expression of their Latin identity in a North American city (see Díaz [1981: 335]; Roberts [1979]; Gerhard and Sheller [1989]; Duany [1984]; Singer [1983]). Salsa grew out of Cuban genres like the *son* which emerged from the blacks' role in adapting, and adapting to, earlier European forms. It was created in New York, and as many whites as blacks have been and are its star figures. Nevertheless, the black influence is an historical fact, and it is evident partly in the almost uncanny predominance of blacks and mulattoes in the drumming and percussion sections of the salsa bands (a feature also noticeable in the *vallenato* groups). Also some salsa lyrics—although they may be sung by whites in later cover versions—make explicit reference to this in lines like: "I'm black because I was born of the rumba, and the *sabor* I inherited from the *guaguancó*." Rumba and *guaguancó* are both Cuban genres associated principally with blacks (Crook [1982]); *sabor* literally means flavor and is commonly used to denote the "hot," danceable quality of music. Another song declares, "Sure, I'm black, I'm of the race. . . . Where there are no blacks, there is no salsa." Artists like Alfredo de la Fe and Monguito, among others, make references to Africa in songs like *Vamos pa' Dakar* and *Guaguancó*.

Vallenato only emerged as a specific genre in the 1940s, but it derived from traditional *costeño* genres based not on the drum and dance, but rather on sung verses, work songs, picaresque songs, and so on, which also formed part of the *costeño* and the black Colombian musical traditions, as the material on the Cauca valley showed (Atencio and Castellanos [1982]; see also Triana [1987: 66, 68]; Llerena [1985]; Quiroz [1982]; Araújo [1973]). *Vallenato* has recently become a heavily commercialized genre which enjoys national popularity.

Although black musical traditions were fundamental to both salsa and *vallenato*, these two genres actually have very mixed origins and are not "black music" in an unambiguous sense. Nevertheless, they are strongly associated with blacks, and blacks are seen as the ambassadors of this kind of music in Colombia. It is only in places like Quibdó and Cartagena that salsa is pervasive and ubiquitous; it is the blacks of Cali who have the reputation as *the* dancers of salsa, and Ulloa cites the black cultural heritage of Cali as one reason why salsa became so popular there (1992). Equally, *vallenato* is a nationally commercialized type of pop music, but it only forms an integral part of popular culture in places like the Atlantic Coast region and the Chocó and in black nuclei in the interior: its identity is essentially *costeño* and, to that extent, black.

17. One of these, for reasons I was not able to clarify from the ex-owner, was named El Congo.

18. See note thirteen, above.

References

Abadía Morales, Guillermo. 1973. *La música folklórica colombiana*. Bogotá: Dirección de Divulgación Cultural, Universidad Nacional.
———. 1983. *Compendio general del folklore colombiano*. Bogotá: Fondo de Promoción de la Cultura del Banco Popular.

Araújo Molina, Consuelo. 1973. *Vallenatología: orígenes y fundamentos de la música vallenata*. Bogotá: Ediciones Tercer Mundo.

Aretz, Isabel. 1977. "Música y danza en América Latina continental (excepto Brazil)." In *Africa en América Latina*. Edited by Manuel Moreno Fraginals. México and Paris: Siglo XXI and UNESCO.

Arrázola, Roberto. 1970. *Palenque, primer pueblo libre de América*. Cartagena: Ediciones Hernández.

Atencio Babilonia, Jaime, and Isabel Castellanos Córdova. 1982. *Fiestas del negro en el norte del Cauca: las adoraciones del Niño Dios*. Cali: Universidad del Valle.

Banton, Michael. 1987. *Racial Theories*. New York: Cambridge University Press.

Barker, Anthony. 1978. *The African Link: British Attitudes to the Negro in the Era of the Atlantic Slave Trade*. London: Frank Cass.

Barth, Frederick. 1969. *Ethnic Groups and Boundaries*. London: George Allen and Unwin.

Béhague, Gerard. 1985. "Popular Music." In *The Handbook of Latin American Popular Culture*. Edited by Harold Hinds and Charles Tatum. Westport: Greenwood.

Bilby, Kenneth. 1985. "The Caribbean as a Musical Region." In *Caribbean Contours*. Edited by Sidney Mintz and Sally Price. Baltimore: Johns Hopkins University Press.

Borrego Pla, María del Carmen. 1973. *Palenques de negros en Cartagena de Indias a fines del siglo 17*. Sevilla: Escuela de Estudios Hispanoamericanos.

Brown, Diana. 1986. *Umbanda: Religion and Politics in Brazil*. Ann Arbor: UMI Research Press.

Carpentier, Alejo. 1946. *La música en Cuba*. México: Fondo de Cultura Económica.

Chamorro, Arturo. 1982. "Chirimías, sondeo histórico de un modelo islámico en América Latina." In *Latin American Music Review* 3 (2): 165–187.

Cohen, Abner (ed.). 1974. *Urban Ethnicity*. London: Tavistock.

Cordovez Moure, José María. 1957 [1983]. *Reminiscencias de Santa Fe y Bogotá*. Madrid: Aguilar.

Crook, Larry. 1982. "A Musical Analysis of the Cuban Rumba." In *Latin American Music Review* 3 (1): 92–123.

Curtin, Phillip. 1965. *The Image of Africa: British Ideas and Action, 1780–1850*. London: Macmillan.

Díaz Ayala, Cristobal. 1981. *Música cubana: del Areyto a la nueva trova*. San Juan, Puerto Rico: Ediciones Cubanacan.

Drummond, Lee. 1980. "The Cultural Continuum: The Theory of Intersystems." In *Man* 15: 352–374.

Duany, Jorge. 1984. "Popular Music in Puerto Rico: Toward an Anthropology of *Salsa*." In *Latin American Music Review* 5 (2): 186–216.

Eriksen, Thomas Hylland. 1991. "The Cultural Contexts of Ethnic Differences." In *Man* 26 (1): 127–144.

Escalante, Aquiles. 1954. "Notas sobre el Palenque de San Basilio, una comunidad negra de Colombia." In *Divulgaciones Etnológicas* 3 (5).

———. 1964. *El negro en Colombia*. Monografías Sociológicas, no. 18. Bogotá: Facultad de Sociología, Universidad Nacional.

Friedemann, Nina de. 1966–1969. "Contextos religiosos en un área negra de Barbacoas (Nariño)." In *Revista Colombiana de Folclor* 4(10): 63–83.

————. 1978. *The Study of Culture on the Caribbean Coast of Colombia*. Paris. UNESCO.

————. 1984. "Estudios de negros en la antropología colombiana." In *Un siglo de investigación social: antropología en Colombia*. Edited by Jaime Arocha and Nina de Friedemann. Bogotá: Etno.

Friedemann, Nina de, and Jaime Arocha. 1986. *De sol a sol: génesis, transformación y presencia de los negros en Colombia*. Bogotá: Planeta.

Friedemann, Nina de, and Carlos Patiño Rosselli. 1983. *Lengua y sociedad en el Palenque de San Basilio*. Bogotá: Instituto de Caro y Cuervo.

Gerhard, Charley, and Marty Sheller. 1989. *Salsa! The Rhythm of Latin Music*. Crown Point, IN: White Cliffs Media Co.

Jaramillo Uribe, Jaime. 1968. *Ensayos sobre historia social colombiana*. Bogotá: Universidad Nacional.

Jordan, Winthrop. 1977. *White Over Black: American Attitudes Toward the Negro, 1550–1812*. New York: Norton.

Leach, Edmund. 1954. *Political Systems of Highland Burma*. London: Athlone.

List, George. 1980. "Colombia: Folk Music." In *New Grove Dictionary of Music and Musicians*. Vol. 4: 570–581. Edited by Stanley Sadie. London: Macmillan.

————. 1983. *Music and Poetry in a Colombian Village*. Bloomington: Indiana University Press.

Llerena Villalobos, Rito. 1985. *Memoria cultural en el vallenato*. Medellín: Centro de Investigaciones, Universidad de Antioquia.

Lomax, Alan. 1970. "The Homogeneity of African-Afro-American Musical Style." In *Afro-American Anthropology*. Edited by Norman Whitten and John Szwed. New York: Free Press.

Marulanda, Octavio. 1979. *Colección música folclórica*. Vol. 1, *Costa Pacífica de Colombia*. (Sleeve notes.) Bogotá: Instituto Colombiano de Cultura.

Mintz, Sidney, and Richard Price. 1976. *An Anthropological Approach to the Afro-American Past: A Caribbean Perspective*. Philadelphia: Institute for the Study of Human Issues.

Ocampo López, Javier. 1988. *Las fiestas y el folclor en Colombia*. Bogotá: El Ancora Editores.

Ortiz, Fernando. 1917. *Hampa afro-cubana: los negros brujos*. Madrid: Ed. América.

————. 1965 [1950]. *La africanía de la música folklórica cubana*. La Habana: Editorial Universitaria.

Perdomo Escobar, José Ignacio. 1963. *La historia de la música en Colombia*. 3rd edition. Bogotá: Editorial ABC.

Posada Gutiérrez, Joaquín. 1920. *Ultimos días de la Gran Colombia y del libertador*. Madrid: Editorial América.

Quiroz Otero, Ciro. 1982. *Vallenato: hombre y canto*. Bogotá: Editorial Icaro.

Roberts, John Storm. 1979. *The Latin Tinge: The Impact of Latin American Music on the United States*. New York: Oxford University Press.

Rout, Leslie. 1976. *The African Experience in Spanish America: 1502 to the Present Day*. New York: Cambridge University Press.

Singer, Roberta. 1983. "Tradition and Innovation in Contemporary Latin Music in New York City." In *Latin American Music Review* 4(2): 183–202.

Tagg, Philip. 1989. " 'Black Music,' 'Afro-American Music,' and 'European Music.' " *Popular Music* 8(3): 285–298.

Triana, Gloria. 1987. *Música tradicional y popular colombiana.* Vols. 5–7, *El litoral Caribe.* Bogotá: Procultura.

Twinam, Ann. 1980. "From Jew to Basque: Ethnic Myths and Antioqueño Entrepreneurship." In *Journal of Inter-American Studies* 22: 81–107.

Ulloa Sanmiguel, Alejandro. 1992. *La salsa en Cali.* Cali: Universidad del Valle.

Urfé, Odilio. 1977. "La música y la danza en Cuba." In *Africa en América Latina.* Edited by Manuel Moreno Fraginals. México and Paris: Siglo XXI and UNESCO.

Valtierra, Angel. 1980. *Pedro Claver: el santo redentor de los negros.* 2 vols. Bogotá: Banco de la República.

Velásquez, Rogerio. 1960. "Fiestas de San Francisco." In *Revista Colombiana de Folclor* 2(4): 15–37.

———. 1961a. "Ritos de la muerte." In *Revista Colombiana de Folclor* 2(6): 9–74.

———. 1961b. "Instrumentos musicales del alto y bajo Chocó." In *Revista Colombiana de Folclor* 2(6): 77–114.

Villa R., William. 1985. "Carnaval, política y religión: fiestas en el Chocó." Unpublished fieldwork report. Departamento de Antropología, Universidad Nacional, Bogotá.

Wade, Peter. 1988. "The Cultural Dynamics of Blackness in Colombia: Black Migrants to a 'White' City." In *Afro-Hispanic Review* 7(1, 2, 3): 53–59.

———. 1990. "Black Culture and Social Inequality in Colombia." In *Cultural Encounters.* Edited by Robin Cecil and David Wade. London: Octagon Press, for the Institute of Cultural Research.

———. 1993. *Blackness and Race Mixture: The Dynamics of Racial Identity in Colombia.* Baltimore: Johns Hopkins University Press.

Walton, Ortiz. 1972. *Music, Black, White, and Blue: A Sociological Survey of the Use and Misuse of Afro-American Music.* New York: Morrow and Co.

Whitten, Norman. 1968. "Personal Networks and Musical Contexts in the Pacific Lowlands of Colombia and Ecuador." In *Man* 3(1): 50–63.

———. 1974. *Black Frontiersmen: A South American Case.* New York: John Wiley and Sons.

Zapata Olivella, Delia. 1962. "La cumbia: síntesis musical de la nación colombiana; reseña histórica y coreográfica." In *Revista Colombiana de Folclor* 3(7): 189–204.

8

Afro-West Indians on the Central American Isthmus: The Case of Panama

Michael L. Conniff

The most spectacular engineering feat of the twentieth century remains the joining of the Atlantic and Pacific Oceans with the Panama Canal. This magnificent project began only after the United States arranged the independence of Panama from Colombia and, in turn, Panama authorized the United States to dig the canal. The 1903 treaty assigned the portion of Panama intended for the canal to U.S. territorial administration. Once construction began, digging the big ditch demanded massive numbers of laborers. American bosses sought workers who spoke English, had been acclimated to the tropics, and could be cheaply relocated. Laborers from the English-speaking Caribbean islands met these criteria, and the discussion in this chapter focuses on the West Indian migration within Latin America and the transformation of Central America's east coast by people of African descent from the West Indies.

These new West Indian immigrants were by no means the first of African descent to arrive in Central America. The isthmus (with the exception of Panama, administered from Spanish Colombia) was once part of the Spanish colony called the Captaincy-General of Guatemala. The Spanish introduced slaves throughout the region, although the African peoples numbered in smaller percentages here than in Mexico, the Caribbean islands, or Portuguese Brazil. Virtually all of the Central American nations received migrants from the Caribbean islands. Not only did this migration change the demographics, but it also spawned a new and vibrant, predominantly black, West Indian culture in the region that had

From *Black Labor on a White Canal: Panama, 1904–1981* (Pittsburgh: University of Pittsburgh Press, 1985), 24–44. © 1985 by the University of Pittsburgh Press. Reprinted by permission of the University of Pittsburgh Press.

once been dominated by mestizo or indigenous peoples. Today, blacks constitute a large percentage—in some cases the majority—of the population in the coastal zones of Belize, Costa Rica, Honduras, Guatemala, Nicaragua, and Panama.

The migration of blacks to the region at the end of the nineteenth century had a different character. The English-speaking West Indians went to all of the Central American nations, but the majority went to Panama, lured first by the need for labor for the construction of the transisthmian railroad and then by the call for workers for the digging of the canal. Initially, the West Indian population settled in the Canal Zone, especially Colón City, but the 1930s many had relocated to Panama City. Michael Conniff, in his Black Labor on a White Canal: Panama, 1904–1981, *looks at the West Indian people, especially the Afro-Creole canal workers, and their contribution to Panamanian culture. He explores the demand for laborers and the political negotiations among officials from Panama, the United States, and West Indian governments—Barbados and Jamaica, in particular—that resulted in this great wave of Afro-Creole workers. In this chapter, he examines labor and race relations in Panama during the construction of the canal. Conniff, professor of history at Auburn University, has continued his research on the African experience in the Americas. His latest work, coauthored with Thomas J. Davis, is* Africans in the Americas *(1994).*

O ld-timers white and black considered the construction years on the canal as the heroic era, one of vast accomplishments, sacrifices, great men, camaraderie, and history-in-the-making. Dozens of books described the canal even before it was finished, and the final success helped rank the United States among the great nations. Yet canal officials made mistakes and poor decisions, and inefficiency dogged the works. From the standpoint of U.S. relations with Panama, the worst errors were the exclusion of Panamanians from managerial positions and the decision to segregate the workforce by color and nationality. The Panamanian government, for its part, paid little attention to the massive influx of laborers who, once they decided to stay, would transform sections of the terminal cities into West Indian townships. With regard to labor relations, construction-era leaders avoided some hard decisions and made others that were to become original sins in the eyes of later generations.

Recruitment and Early Living Conditions

No one doubted the need to recruit large numbers of workers for the American canal project—Panama's tiny population simply could not supply them. Moreover, most outsiders regarded Latin Americans as inferior laborers. Consensus ended here, however. Engineers and supervisors argued over which laborers to bring.

A natural choice was more West Indians, since seven hundred of them formed the bulk of the railroad and canal force inherited from the French. Panama Railroad manager Jackson Smith, on orders from the ICC [Isthmian Canal Commission] chief engineer, began the importation of thousands more to start necessary construction. Jamaicans were excellent artisans and could be found in sufficient numbers due to chronic unemployment at home. Yet the railroad's agent met with undisguised obstructionism in Kingston, for the governor simply refused to authorize recruitment. He feared another debacle like the French bankruptcy. In addition, he seemed to be under pressure from planters and the United Fruit Company not to allow emigration. Over the next five years, officials from President Roosevelt down to Smith tried unsuccessfully to change the governor's mind. Perhaps twenty thousand Jamaicans emigrated on their own, but without contracts and only after paying their passage and a five-dollar repatriation deposit. On the whole, the Jamaicans came from the skilled artisan class and were said to be more enterprising than recruits from other islands.[1]

Faced with problems in Jamaica, Smith sent his recruiter to Barbados in early 1905, where he found the government cooperative. Officials on the tiny island had long faced the emigration-or-starvation dilemma and welcomed the chance to send off more workers. Canal officials liked the Barbadians, who went to do pick-and-shovel work and harbored none of the pretensions that some Jamaicans had. Most of the twenty thousand eventually recruited were under contract and received free passage to Panama. In addition, another recruiter went to Curaçao and Martinique to find workers, and over the years several thousand signed on for canal service. However, French subjects were not held to be as robust or productive as those from the British islands.

Chief Engineer John Stevens, meanwhile, became pessimistic about the quality of the West Indian laborers. He complained that they quit to take better-paying jobs, would not work unless forced to, and took unauthorized time for holidays and trips home. He wrote the British minister, "I have no hesitancy in saying that the West Indian Negro is about the poorest excuse for a laborer I have ever been up against in thirty-five years of experience." Another engineer told Congress that West Indian blacks were half as productive as U.S. blacks and a quarter as good as northern white labor.[2] Enough complaints arrived to force Washington to consider alternative sources of labor.

Stevens pushed hard to import Chinese workers, because they had performed well for him building railroads in the United States. President

Theodore Roosevelt was willing to try anyone who could "make the dirt fly." But Secretary of War William H. Taft, under whose supervision the canal was being built, decided not to use Chinese labor because he thought it smacked of slavery: "Peonage or coolieism, which shortly stated is slavery by debt, is as much in conflict with the thirteenth amendment of the constitution as the usual form of slavery." Panamanian exclusion laws (inspired by those in the United States) presented yet another obstacle, and Stevens abandoned the idea of Chinese laborers in late 1906.[3]

Southern Europe offered a third source of labor. In February 1906 an agent brought five hundred Spaniards, and Stevens claimed they did three times the work the West Indians did. Colonel Robert E. Wood, who became the specialist in labor relations, urged Stevens to view "our Gallego and other white labor [as] our dependable nucleus, and the Negro our floating supply." Some also hoped Europeans would be a buffer between the blacks and North Americans, who from the beginning did not get along well. A recruiter stationed in Europe from 1906 to 1908 sent twelve thousand men to join the canal force, at double the wages of the West Indians.[4]

Soon after arrival, however, many Spaniards drifted into Panama in search of better opportunities or shipped out for places offering higher wages. Those who stayed demanded quarters and mess halls separate from the West Indians' and often got into fights with them. Spanish anarchist organizers tried to stir up trouble and started a few strikes. In all, the Europeans cost at least twice as much as West Indians in wages and accommodations but accomplished about the same amount of work. By mid-1907, Wood recommended discontinuing European recruitment, which was done the following year.[5]

The canal also recruited white U.S. workers, who signed up at the New York offices of the railroad. White Americans were expected to supervise the unskilled blacks and Europeans and perform the highly skilled crafts and mechanical services needed. They would quickly grasp the complexities of the entire job and fit into the bureaucracy. Although they did these things eventually, the Americans disappointed canal officials in the construction era. The complaints were many. First, this demand for tradesmen coincided with an expansive economic cycle in the United States. The mediocre or adventurous men who applied still demanded high wages and exceptional fringe benefits. And despite these advantages, turnover remained high—the average American stayed in Panama only a year.[6]

Second, U.S. workers quickly formed trade unions that bargained locally, occasionally struck or slowed down work, and used lobbyists in Washington to pressure the administration. Congress extended civil service status to the white-collar staff, but the blue-collar sector remained independent and unruly. Partisanship exacerbated labor trouble because the unions allied with Democratic leaders in the industrial states while management associated with the Republicans.

Finally, the Americans soon adopted a southern-style division of labor where whites supervised and blacks did the heavy, dirty, disagreeable, yet increasingly skilled work. Union procedures prevented blacks from becoming journeymen, even after years as canal apprentices, because they were excluded from union membership. Nevertheless, blacks sometimes became more proficient than their supervisors, and observers noted the inequity of the situation. Officials refused to change it, however.[7]

The recruitment process on the islands foreshadowed the West Indians' second-class treatment as canal laborers. Recruiters paid local agents several dollars for each able-bodied man delivered to the docks. Agents sent runners to the countryside to spread the news, and they published announcements in newspapers. When workers arrived at the docks on appointed days, they received medical exams and vaccinations against smallpox. Chief Sanitary Officer William C. Gorgas told recruiters to accept only men between eighteen and forty-five years, of sound mental and physical condition. He recommended a cursory check of eyes, lungs, heart, digestive tract, joints, and skin. They automatically rejected those with venereal disease. Since the doctor in Barbados received only thirty cents per man and twenty cents per vaccination, the exams must have been brief. In 1906 rejections ran between 20 and 25 percent, mostly for VD, poor physical condition, youth, and hernia.[8]

Once passed, the men took their baggage to the docks for the trip to Colón. Because they traveled topside with no protection or comforts except meals, they were known as deckers. Sailing time ranged from five to thirteen days, depending upon weather and port of embarkation. When they arrived in Panama they received yellow fever inoculations. The entire package—recruitment, exam, and passage—cost the canal about ten dollars per person.[9]

Between 1904 and 1909 most recruits signed contracts that were notarized by colonial officials (see table). The contracts stipulated minimum wages and benefits and included free repatriation. Until 1909 recruiters paid the fare to Colón. Afterward, sufficient numbers migrated voluntarily to discontinue contracts altogether. Men often hoarded their papers for years only to find them unnecessary for repatriation, which the canal provided almost automatically.[10]

At first, recruiters had tried to take into account the various emigrant protection laws in the islands, but they soon desisted. Oral contracts

Sample Contracts for West Indian Laborers, 1904–1908

	1904	1906	1907	1907	1907	1908
Where issued	Barbados	Barbados	Barbados	Trinidad	Barbados	Barbados
Length of service	500 days	500 days	4,500 hrs.	4,500 hrs.	500 days	500 days
Minimum wage (in U.S. dollars)	$.75/day	$.80/day	$.10/hr.	$.10/hr.	$1.00/day	$.75/day
Work week (days x hours)	6 x 10	6 x 8	6 x 10	6 x 10	6 x 10	6 x 10
Overtime	1.5	1.5	1.5	1.5	1.5	1.5
Medical care	free	free	free	free	free	free
Unfurnished quarters	free	free	free	free	free	free
Trip over	deducted from wages	free	free	free	free	deducted from wages
Return trip	free	free	free	free	free	free

Sources: For 1904, PCC 2-E-1, ca. December 1904; for 1906, Lancelot S. Lewis, *The West Indian in Panama: Black Labor in Panama, 1850–1914* (Washington, DC: University Press of America, 1980), appendix 2; for 1907–08, Mallet to FO, 2 September 1907, 18 January 1908, in FO 371/300/31889 and 493/4644.

sufficed in the various French islands, because authorities could not agree on which language was official for written documents. Besides, places like Bridgetown and Fort-de-France were collection points for people from smaller islands, so colonial officials had little leverage over recruiters. For the most part, they worked together closely.

In order to encourage voluntary migration from Jamaica, canal officials hired men on the docks in Colón, and by 1907 two or three independents showed up for every contract man. Canal officials took advantage of this labor surplus to lower the minimum wage 25 percent, eliminate overtime, and deduct passage over from wages. In 1909 they also stopped recruiting in the West Indies, which produced more savings. In 1912 recruiters returned to Barbados because too few local workers signed up at ten cents an hour. The colonial government at first refused but then allowed about one thousand men to go. That ended formal labor recruitment in the West Indies until World War II.[11]

Officially, canal authorities brought over 31,000 West Indian men and a few women. But in fact, between 150,000 and 200,000 men and women must have migrated during the construction era, for in most years some 20,000 West Indians were on the canal payroll, and turnover was high. Contemporaries estimated that only about a third of the West Indian community worked for the canal at any moment. The rest were dependents or had jobs and businesses in Panama's terminal cities. These figures are staggering when we recall that in 1896 Panama City had only twenty-four thousand inhabitants and the country as a whole four hundred thousand. The West Indian migrations to Panama constitued a demographic tidal wave, the largest yet in Caribbean history.[12]

Tens of thousands of West Indian women migrated to Panama, and eventually the sex ratio in the immigrant community balanced out. Canal managers early recognized the need for women and brought over 150 Martinican women in late 1905. The incident led to charges of prostitution and the practice was ended.[13] Still, much of the auxiliary work could best be performed by women, and a good market arose for their services. At first, many women simply paid their own passage and went to look for jobs in the construction camps and terminal cities. Others were sent for by husbands or boyfriends. Often the men returned home after completing contracts and, sporting new clothes and savings of "Panama money," married former sweethearts. Then, when the money ran out, the new families went back to Panama. Most West Indians chose mates from their own islands.

Immigrant women performed a variety of essential tasks for the canal workforce. They cooked for men in camps established along the construction line. They also washed and mended clothes, nursed the sick, and maintained boardinghouses. Only a small proportion of the women engaged in these chores were on the canal payroll; most were self-employed or worked for others. As a result, very little information about women is available in canal records, making it difficult to trace their experience in Panama. Two things are certain, though. Canal construction would have taken longer and been more unbearable without women, and women worked as hard as men yet earned less and had less job stability.

Working and living conditions for the West Indians ranged from difficult to appalling. Those employed by the canal had the right to unfurnished quarters in the Zone, but only a small proportion occupied them. Most of the barracks, dating from the French period, were cramped and accommodated only bachelors; the average space in 1906 was twenty square feet per person. Some of the men built shacks near the work sites, which allowed them to keep families and to plant vegetable gardens. Most rented rooms in the tenement districts of Panama [City] and Colón, where they could catch the labor trains into the Zone. These tenements were death traps, but many men preferred the bustle of life in the city to living in the jungle. Only in 1913 did canal officials begin building permanent quarters for the silver employees [per the classification scheme explained below] who would stay on after the canal was completed.[14]

Canal authorities encouraged men to bring their families, on the grounds that this would make them more stable and productive. Immigration officers objected that such a policy would open the doors to all kinds of undesirables, since it would be difficult to test kinship and means of support. Eventually they and the Panamanians worked out a system by which employed West Indians could request family entry. In addition, independents with fifteen dollars in cash could disembark. As it turned out, consuls approved virtually all requests, since the immigration fees were their principal income. During most of this time, the Panamanian elite permitted free immigration, because newcomers generated more business. Only after the wave receded did leaders seriously consider the consequences of these policies, or their responsibility toward the vast numbers of West Indians who chose to remain in Panama. By that time, the immigrant community had produced its first generation of children born on the isthmus, about two thousand youngsters.[15]

Feeding the armies of workmen proved a major challenge. At first, the men simply bought food from grocers or ate in West Indian diners. In 1905 the canal created silver commissaries for noncitizen employees, after Panamanian merchants had begun charging exorbitant prices. Then, between 1906 and 1912, the canal operated a series of messes serving basic nutritious food. Since the cost of meals was deducted from the men's pay, most felt obliged to eat there, but the fare was hardly appealing to the West Indians. One old-timer described it as "cooked rice which was hard enough to shoot deer; sauce spread all over the rice; and a slab of meat which many men either spent an hour trying to chew or eventually threw away." Authorities reported improvement in the men's stamina due to the meals, but it could also have resulted from daily doses of quinine, an increase in family living, better health service, and a more regular supply of groceries. At any rate, American institutional cuisine was one of the many features of Zone life that the West Indians had to adjust to during construction years. Today, West Indian cooking is rare enough to be a specialty food in Panama.[16]

Accidents and disease took a heavy toll among the West Indians in Panama. William C. Gorgas became famous for eliminating yellow fever and controlling malaria. But little could be done about industrial accidents, which cast a shadow over the works. Virtually all the old-timers had vivid memories of accidents—train derailments, dynamite explosions, landslides, boat sinkings—that took multiple lives. In 1913 alone, thirty-eight blacks perished in railroad accidents, twenty-three drowned, and fifteen died in explosions. Many suffered falls from scaffolding during construction of the locks and gates.

In addition, diseases dogged the men. Pneumonia and tuberculosis killed the most, amounting to 110 deaths in 1913. Malaria, even though it did not kill, brought down most people at some point in their stay in Panama. Official figures of 1904–1914 show 4,500 deaths among black employees from all causes during the period.[17] Since a larger number of West Indians lived outside the Zone, where sanitation and medical treatment were inferior, the total number of deaths in the West Indian community probably approached fifteen thousand, or one out of every ten immigrants. No wonder so many of the old-timers gave thanks for surviving the dangers of construction days.

Wages for non-U.S. employees remained fairly stable throughout the construction era. Jobs changed rapidly, however, due to shifting demand, rising skill levels, and chance opportunities. Accounts by West Indian old-timers gave the impression of constant turnover. Arriving recruits would be assigned to available jobs according to their preparation. Young unskilled men became water or messenger boys, starting at between five and seven cents an hour. The robust unskilled workers started as pick-and-shovel men at ten cents. Artisans such as carpenters and plumbers earned from thirteen to sixteen cents. Especially able West Indians could become subforemen or machine operators, making twenty-five cents or more an hour. Machinists and boilermakers in the railroad yards could make between thirty-five and fifty cents an hour. Finally, about 10 percent of the West Indians had white-collar jobs as clerks, stenographers, typists, and so forth. Their monthly rates ranged up to seventy-five dollars a month (about twenty-seven cents an hour).

After the labor glut of 1908, officials put a fifty-cent ceiling on West Indian wages and reduced the number of grades of silver classifications. They secretly urged other employers to join them in lowering wages to ten cents for West Indian common labor, thirteen for Spanish-American common labor, sixteen for noncontract Europeans and U.S. blacks, and twenty for contract Europeans. Another round of reductions came in 1913–14, when the construction neared completion. Many lost their jobs through reductions-in-force, and most suffered wage cuts.

The base of ten cents an hour for West Indian common labor remained quite stable throughout the construction era. Inequities due to race and national origin also persisted. Two other disturbing trends from the West Indian point of view were wage ceilings and compression of grades, both of which prevented West Indians from advancing very far. Occasionally supervisors themselves complained that private firms hired away their best men because the canal wage ceiling was too low. This policy discouraged workers from acquiring additional training and undoubtedly drove off some of the most talented. The main reason for the policy was to preserve a gap between silver and gold wage rates.

The Gold and Silver Rolls

Within months after beginning construction, canal administrators established the system of racial distinctions which was to grow enormously complex over the years. It began in 1904 when they adopted the railroad's policy of different payrolls, gold for American citizens (somewhat higher than pay rates in the United States) and silver for noncitizens (somewhat higher than rates prevailing in the Caribbean basin). Silver rates were always lower than gold, a disparity heightened by the fact that until 1909 silver currency had only half the nominal value of gold. In addition, benefits such as spacious furnished housing, sick leave, and paid home leave were tied to the gold roll. Just as in the French era, the two rolls also connoted skilled and unskilled, and supervisors used the gold roll as a reward for especially deserving blacks because of the status it conferred. The dividing line between the rolls had been intentionally ambiguous, and in 1906 over one hundred skilled blacks, both West Indian and American, were on the gold roll.

In September 1905, however, canal authorities prohibited transfers from silver to gold, on the grounds that they complicated bookkeeping and violated the color line. Some supervisors objected that this set up pay inequities and eliminated a key incentive for outstanding blacks, but the rule stood. One official wrote, "I believe . . . the original intention [was] that the Gold rolls would indicate the number of white men working and the Silver rolls would indicate the number of colored employees." By the end of 1906 they went a step further, putting gold roll blacks who were not U.S. citizens on the silver roll at the same pay. Some men objected to the lower prestige and benefits, and a few exceptional black machinists and administrators remained on gold. In addition, black teachers, post-masters, and policemen stayed on the gold roll, because they required a higher status to exercise authority in the West Indian community.[18]

By 1908 color became the leading, though not the sole, criterion used to assign men to gold or silver rolls, as revealed in an exchange of memos between two executives:

> I have been endeavoring to transfer all Negroes from the Gold to the Silver roll. Under the former operations of the Panama Railroad this question was not given very much attention. . . . Some of these people resent this transfer. . . . The situation, however, is getting to be some-what awkward, as we have divided the Gold from the Silver employees in our commissary.
>
> It is the policy of the Commission to keep employees who are un-doubtedly black or belong to mixed races on the Silver rolls.

Gold and silver distinctions applied to public facilities as well, consoli-dating a system of Jim Crow segregation. It became one of the most ob-jectionable and tenacious features of Canal Zone life.[19]

After 1908 the gold-silver distinction took another twist, when a na-tionality test was applied. In February, Taft issued an executive order that henceforth only American citizens would be appointed to the gold roll. Taft had begun to campaign for the presidency, and his action seemed designed to win the support of the American unions. Union workers in the Zone faced increasing competition from Europeans and West Indians who came with or learned skilled occupations, and a nationality restric-tion would prevent this. The Panamanian government protested that the order violated Taft's 1905 assurances that natives would enjoy the ben-efits of the canal and equal employment opportunities. It also had the effect of declaring Panamanians aliens in the Zone, even though Panama retained residual sovereignty there.[20]

Taft modified the order to allow appointment of citizens of the United States *and* Panama to the gold roll. The administration did not apply the rule retroactively, but they did fire aliens first. After 1908 the gold roll increasingly became an exclusive white American club to which a few Panamanian and West Indian trusties might be admitted.

In late 1909 canal managers attempted to define for themselves just what constituted the two rolls. No one had ever laid down coherent rules, and the assumed guidelines were riddled with exceptions. One valiant attempt produced this:

> *Gold*: 1. white Americans receiving over seventy-five dollars a month.
>   2. white Americans holding Gold jobs at less than seventy-five dollars a month.
>   3. Panamanians holding Gold jobs at over seventy-five dollars a month.
>   4. other whites not native to the tropics holding special positions for which Americans are not available and who earn over seventy-five dollars a month.

Silver: all other persons not covered above.

They decided against publishing the results of their exercise, probably because race figured in most of the criteria.[21]

Following the 1908 gold citizenship decision, labor unions began campaigning to remove West Indians and Europeans from managerial or skilled positions. In 1909 they achieved an important victory: President Taft himself agreed with union leaders that no more blacks should be hired as railroad engineers. He wished to protect the older black employees from dismissal, but he nevertheless signaled the start of a decades-long vendetta in which white Americans identified blacks or Europeans in skilled positions and had them demoted or fired.

Colonel George W. Goethals, who became chief engineer and chairman of the Isthmian Canal Commission in 1907, went along with instituting racial segregation under the guise of the gold and silver distinction. He later registered the customary disclaimer about race: "I think the real point at issue is probably the question of citizenship more than color. We cannot very well draw a color line, but we can limit the employment of engineers to American citizens."[22] Unions obtained a series of guild regulations that restricted to journeymen the use of metal-edged and air-powered tools and the operation of any major pieces of equipment. Over the objections of many department heads who valued the work and seniority of their black men, the unions succeeded in demoting railroad engineers of all sorts, yardmasters, hostlers, boat pilots, machinists, carpenters, wiremen, and other skilled workmen. It was one of the most vicious episodes in canal history, remembered and resented deeply by the West Indians for years afterward.[23] The effect was to widen the gap between gold and silver workers and to subordinate the latter to the former.

The Americans-only rule and the subsequent purge of West Indians from skilled positions might have resulted from a desire by Taft and Republican leaders to win over a segment of organized labor from the Democrats. During and after the Taft administration, Goethals kept his political ear to the ground and was mentioned for the presidential nomination in 1916.[24] If this was the motive, it failed. After 1913 organized labor found a better sponsor in the Democrats, under President Woodrow Wilson.

Who instituted Jim Crow segregation in the Canal Zone? At the highest level of responsibility were the Republican administrations of Roosevelt and Taft. Both men followed canal affairs closely and concurred in segregation decisions. They could not publicly admit to Jim Crow practices, however, because the Republicans regularly denounced the southern Democrats for the same thing and enjoyed the support of most American blacks. Moreover, the Constitution did not permit segregation by the federal government. But the early twentieth century saw a great rise in racism among all Americans, and Roosevelt and Taft had little power to prevent it from becoming associated with imperialist expansion. The Wilson administration likewise did nothing to disturb the gold-silver system.

Some canal executives favored using southern whites as labor foremen, on the grounds that they knew how to manage blacks. Yet the American workforce was mostly northern, from top to bottom. Chief Engineers Stevens and Goethals were from Maine and New York, for example. But more to the point, many of the top executives were officers in the army (segregated until the 1950s), had worked in a variety of regions, and were familiar with racism. Therefore, whether or not they were brought up as racists, they had lived in a segregated society. Stevens, for example, frequently compared the low productivity of West Indian and southern blacks and saw labor problems in the Zone and the U.S. South as analogous.[25] At any rate, their job, as Stevens and the others saw it, was to dig a canal, not reduce racism in American society.

The rank and file of American employees came mostly from the North and Midwest. Only about a third came from the South in the early days. The oft-repeated view that the Canal Zone was racist due to southern influence is simply a myth. No doubt many arrived without racist ideas or experience with blacks, but when confronted with the need to supervise British colonial subjects, they adopted bigoted behavior. Harry Franck remarks, "Any northerner can say 'nigger' as glibly as a Carolinian, and growl if one of them steps on his shadow."[26]

In 1921 the Zone governor observed, "Our supervisors, of a class above the ordinary bias of race and nationality, are almost unanimous in the opinion that only the most routine mechanical and clerical work can be trusted to the West Indians." In other words, imperialism (the assertion of white superiority over "backward" peoples) reinforced racism

(white superiority over nonwhites). The system remained rigid until the
1940s, by which time it compared unfavorably with race relations in Louisiana and Mississippi.[27]

Black West Indians and white Americans formed the poles of the
silver-gold system, but three subgroups fit into it at intermediate points:
U.S. blacks, Europeans, and white West Indians. The way they fit and
interacted with the nodal groups reveals much about the system itself.

Black Americans signing on for canal work in the first few years
received appointments to the gold roll. When West Indians were demoted
to silver in 1906, U.S. blacks remained on gold. However, officials instructed recruiters in the United States not to give U.S. blacks gold contracts. Instead, canal officials devised for them a special silver category
which provided sick and home leave privileges but not access to gold
housing, commissaries, or clubhouses. American blacks continued to earn
more than West Indians, due to skills and nationality, but most on the
gold roll were reclassified as silver. In 1912 a White House aide, preparing election materials, inquired about the treatment of blacks on the canal. Goethal's perfunctory answer was that sixty-nine U.S. blacks received
average annual wages of $820. He failed to mention that whites earned
double that. Because black Americans did not fit well into the gold-silver
system, canal authorities hired them only for a few sensitive positions
overseeing West Indians. By 1928 only twenty-three U.S. blacks remained,
all but a few on the silver roll.[28]

Europeans also posed awkward classificatory problems for canal administrators, especially when gold and silver came to mean white and
black. Spaniards, Italians, and Greeks were judged semiwhite, but they
ended up on a special rung of the silver roll because they did not deserve
home leave or wages as high as those of white Americans.[29] They had
separate quarters and mess halls. Recruitment of Europeans ended in 1908
and their numbers diminished rapidly thereafter.

A final intermediate group was made up of whites and light mulattoes from the islands who could "pass," a group I call the white West
Indians. Recruiters avoided sending such people from the islands because
they found that this group disliked heavy labor and was sensitive about
racial treatment. However, many migrated from Jamaica on their own.
They posed as British supervisors who, because of experience in handling Negroes at home, could coax more work out of them. In 1907 about
eight hundred white West Indians worked for the canal. Classic cultural
brokers, they used their color and familiarity with two cultures to become
intermediaries. Americans and West Indian blacks both trusted them, but
neither group could count on their loyalty. White West Indians, hired on
both gold and silver rolls at first, suffered status anxiety when demoted to

silver and resented their poor treatment at the hands of the Americans. They occasionally played a malevolent role in Canal Zone race and labor relations.[30]

Social Control

Colonel Wood once compared gold and silver workers to officers and soldiers in the army, an analogy that probably revealed more domination of one group by another than he intended. The two rolls, with their racial and national distinctions, served as a powerful brake on laborers' aspirations and were a divisive element. Throwing Panamanians and West Indians together in the same class spurred the desires of each to be different, better than the other. Panamanians resented being classified with blacks, while West Indians disliked being labeled inferior laborers. The competition undermined potential labor solidarity and increased management's power. In effect, being on the silver roll induced Panamanians and West Indians to fight over the scraps that fell from the master's table.

Canal officials established more specific devices for social control in the early days. The police obviously kept order so that the construction could proceed. Three different police units existed, in fact. The hundred or so white American policemen formed the elite. Their duties included coordinating security services, supervising black officers, gathering intelligence through plainclothesmen, maintaining liaison with other agencies, and operating the jails. About an equal number of West Indian police patrolled streets and labor camps, their job being to control their own people, potentially the most volatile element. Finally, Americans sporadically tried to supervise the Panamanian police. From all accounts, the Canal Zone police system was intimidating and effectively kept the Zone peaceful. Virtually all contemporaries remarked on the peaceful behavior of the West Indians, and white Americans left no record of fearing violence from the blacks.[31]

The vast majority of persons arrested received fines or short jail sentences. Peak activity came in 1912, when seven thousand arrests occurred: Barbadians made up 24 percent of the total, Jamaicans 19 percent, Panamanians and Americans 9 percent each, and Martinicans 4 percent. The most frequent crimes were disorderly conduct, loitering, petty larceny, and vagrancy.[32] The canal deducted fines from employees' wages. Those convicted of serious crimes went to the army-administered penitentiary for longer sentences. The highest number of convicts there was 133 in 1913, a number never again matched. West Indians, Americans, and Panamanians composed the bulk of the inmates and lived in separate cell blocks. Prison population steadily declined after the end of construction.

The effectiveness of the police forces in the Zone and low levels of serious crime have several explanations. First, the British claimed to have taught their subjects respect for law and order. Second, the work regime of sixty hours a week kept the men under close watch during their working hours and left little time or energy for getting into trouble afterward. Third, the summary justice meted out by U.S. and Panamanian courts was so harsh as to be a positive restraint. British Minister Claude Mallet wrote, "Much of my time is taken up in receiving complaints," a fact borne out in his reports. Even though the West Indian was said to "dearly love lawsuits" and to have "the habit of writing directly to his king about his many grievances," in fact he must have done all he could to avoid contact with the police and courts.[33]

The Canal Zone police spent much of their time averting or solving labor troubles. A 1904 planning document foresaw that "the enforcement of contracts for services made with these ignorant people will be a very difficult matter, unless the power exists somewhere of arbitrarily controlling imported contract labor." The police served that function. They used spies, deportation, strike-breaking, intimidation, and diplomatic intervention. The latter consisted of bringing in representatives of the country whose nationals were involved in a dispute. A final technique was to have the Panamanian police arrest unemployed men and threaten them with jail or deportation if they did not sign up for work on the canal.[34]

Panama's police worked closely with their canal counterparts. In 1904 the Panamanian government disbanded its army altogether to prevent its meddling in politics, and the police force remained weak, especially in view of the explosion of population during construction days. Police relied to a great extent on the good behavior of the West Indians and, failing that, on the intervention rights of the United States.[35] This police relationship had resulted partly from a 1905 incident in which Panamanian police attacked protesting Jamaican laborers in Panama City. The episode embarrassed U.S. officials and further reduced hopes of recruiting Jamaicans.[36]

Panama's police adopted a rather predatory attitude toward West Indians living under their jurisdiction. At best, they tolerated the foreigners as a temporary inconvenience caused by canal construction and employed normal tricks of the trade to extort money from them. At worst, they harassed and intimidated the outsiders to demonstrate their own intermediate position in the pecking order. The British minister finally prevailed upon Panama to hire West Indians to police their own neighborhoods, which apparently proved successful.[37]

Physical and verbal abuse of blacks by whites constituted another form of social control in the Canal Zone. In 1906 the police chief listed nine cases ("a small percentage") in which white Americans were fined for accosting blacks. The U.S. government had decided not to use juries in Zone courts because of their ineffectiveness in handling racial violence in the South. Whites still managed to intimidate witnesses. An observer noted in a letter written in 1907, "Race feeling . . . is at a fever heat and is liable to develop seriously at any moment. Every man who resorts to the courts, or is a witness in any case, is immediately discharged."[38] In 1908 jury trials were introduced, and in several scandalous cases whites were acquitted after murdering blacks. But the everyday verbal abuse by whites never made headlines and was only recorded by scattered observers. Most of the black old-timers, however, recalled the intimidating treatment they received as "niggers." One remembered, "Life was some sort of semislavery."[39]

Not all forms of social control required force. Zone officials encouraged other institutions designed to preserve harmony. Male immigrants could bring their families, and eventually they got better quarters in the Zone. Taft and Roosevelt recommended offering small salaries to priests and ministers, in order to prevent "dissipation and dissolute habits" among the workmen. However, Stevens did "not regard it as practicable . . . to use the same church for both blacks and whites . . . the color line should be drawn." Nondenominational churches for whites were built at several construction sites. Blacks at first used school buildings for worship, but soon they erected chapels with the help of the canal. By 1908 authorities had expended $100,000 to build churches or remodel other structures. They paid about a dozen priests and ministers as chaplains under the hospital budget, and they granted them housing and other privileges as well.[40]

The Anglican-turned-Episcopalian Church proved the most popular West Indian sect, with some fifteen thousand members, followed by the Baptist and the Catholic. Religion served to reassure the West Indians, and perhaps the very dangers of construction made them more religious. One chaplain wrote at the time: "Religion means very much to the West Indian. He prefers his Church to everything else." It certainly became a stabilizing force in the community.[41]

A final method of social control, at least in the long term, was the educational system for West Indian children. With the frenetic work of construction going on, children playing near work sites could cause accidents. Moreover, schooling and child rearing at home could distract the West Indians from the primary job. So from the very beginning, municipalities in the Zone operated schools for the workers' dependents. At first, five schools accommodated 140 white children and over 1,000 blacks in racially mixed schools with segregated classrooms. Most children rode the train to school. As part of an administrative centralization in 1906, the municipalities were extinguished and the schools put under a superintendent from Nebraska, David O'Connor. Chief Engineer Stevens's main goal in appointing O'Connor was to reduce discontent among U.S. workers by providing as many support facilities for families as possible. By mid-1906 four schools had entirely white student bodies, while the other twenty-three were mixed but predominantly black.

The Zone schools followed an American curriculum. In the words of Superintendent O'Connor, "The present public school system . . . is essentially American, conducted by Americans, supplied with American textbooks, and in large and increasing measure with American teachers using American methods, with American songs and literature, which should in a short time affect the pupils with American ideals and American patriotism." From the very beginning, the black schools were a nether appendage of the white system, and the color line was rigid.[42]

In order to improve morale among American parents, O'Connor expanded the number of white schools to twenty-eight by 1908, so that few white children had to ride the trains. Black schools dropped to only nineteen, even though they had five times the white enrollment. Jamaicans predominated among teachers in the black schools, because of Jamaica's reputation for educational excellence. Those with three years or more of high or normal school earned sixty dollars a month on the gold roll, compared to ninety to a hundred dollars a month earned by U.S. teachers. No matter how good the Jamaicans were, though, they could hardly have taught much with an average class size of 115 students in 1909. In 1910 and 1911 the schools recruited teachers in Kingston, and by 1915 they lowered the average class size for blacks to 65. Even at that, they did not make attendance compulsory because they could only take in about half the black children of school age.[43]

White children attended schools designed to provide an education at least as good as they would receive in the United States, and teachers aimed for college preparation. Black children marked time in overcrowded rooms using cast-off supplies from the white schools. West Indian teachers emphasized rote memory, discipline, oration, and manners—a curriculum tailored for social control. Administrators assumed that black children were intellectually deficient, so they put black schools on a twelve-month schedule. This also kept the children under year-round adult supervision.

Toward the end of the construction period, officials set up vocational studies for the blacks, so they could move onto the lowest rungs of the employment ladder. Alda Harper had concluded that "the educational policy for colored schools . . . became one of preserving the status quo . . . of keeping the West Indian and his progeny in positions of common labor."[44]

Few people at the time realized that West Indians and Panamanians, but not Americans, paid the taxes that sustained all of the Zone schools. In other words, the nonwhites paid for the whites' quality education while their own children got inferior schooling. One could never point to the early Canal Zone schools as an example of the civilizing influence of American imperialism. They were merely an instrument of social control paid for by the controlled.[45]

Early Relations between the United States and Panama

The United States exercised a protectorate over Panama during the construction era. Although the canal was built for the benefit of both countries, Panamanians had little to say about how it was done. They viewed the worker army of West Indians as a necessary element but also as an opportunity to make some profits. Property owners and entrepreneurs immediately threw up stores and rooming houses to cater to the immigrants. They fought unsuccessfully against the 1905 decision by canal officials to operate commissaries for silver roll employees. Thereafter, Panama's chief benefit from construction was rents, so even more tenements went up in Colón and Panama [City]. An early study on immigration urged continued exclusion of Chinese (who controlled a major share of retail commerce) but did not mention West Indians. Well-to-do Panamanians hoped to live comfortably from commerce and real estate investments.[46]

Many Panamanians also sought access to better-paying jobs, and in the early days canal authorities appointed about a hundred members of the local elite to the gold roll for public relations purposes. That had also been the policy of the railroad. Roosevelt assured Panama of "full and complete and generous equality between the two republics," confirming Taft's agreement of two years before.[47]

When Taft issued the executive order in early 1908 to appoint only Americans to the gold roll, Panamanians objected and Taft amended it in December. This appeared to be a victory for the State Department, which forwarded the Panamanian protest with a favorable recommendation. Goethals and other executives, however, gave the order the most narrow construction possible. They *could* hire Panamanians for gold roll positions when they had the best qualifications, but they were not obligated to appoint equal numbers. Moreover, U.S. employees still enjoyed preference over Panamanians in promotion and retention.[48]

Internal rules since 1905 provided paid home leave for U.S. citizens but only one or two months' unpaid leave (schedules permitting) and two weeks' paid vacation for noncitizens on the gold roll. The reasons for this policy derived from the third-country national system. Panamanians competed with West Indians, not Americans, and needed an edge over the aliens to maintain parity. Zonians never dreamed of giving Panamanians opportunities or treatment equal to those they themselves enjoyed.[49]

In 1914, as part of the transition from construction to permanent operation of the canal, Zone officials got an executive order renewing that of 1908 and extending access to gold roll employment to Panamanians.[50] Again, Panamanians saw it as giving them an edge over aliens, but aliens could become Panamanian citizens quickly by bribing a few bureaucrats. A number of Europeans and immigrants from elsewhere in Latin America did so after 1908, but Goethals discouraged the practice by refusing to recognize Panamanian naturalization certificates issued after 1 January 1914. He assumed that anyone receiving papers afterward did so for the purpose of qualifying for the gold roll and was not a genuine citizen of Panama. Nobody seemed to realize that in several years West Indian children born in the Canal Zone would also qualify for the gold roll if Panama extended them citizenship.[51]

A final aspect of early U.S.-Panamanian relations requires mention, because it elucidates how North American racial attitudes affected diplomacy. From 1903 on, the Roosevelt administration had preferred the Conservative Party, which had close ties to the railroad and had led Panama's independence movement against Colombia. As a rule, the U.S. government favored Conservatives in Latin America throughout the imperialist era.

In Panama, racial preferences reinforced the tilt toward Conservatives, because the Liberal Party drew upon the black lower class in the cities and was led by a mixture of whites, mulattoes, and mestizos. U.S. Minister Squiers, for example, made no secret of his partisanship. In 1906 he backed a measure to disfranchise many of the blacks: "There is no question that a limited suffrage will guarantee a better and more conservative government. The voting population is said to be seventy-five percent blacks, of whom only ten percent can read or write."[52] Most observers reported that the Liberals enjoyed majorities in the cities and rural areas.

Several times in the early years the United States became embroiled in Panamanian politics without wishing to, and in 1908 Taft decided to back a moderate Liberal for the presidency, apparently hoping he could govern more successfully than the Conservatives. Taft forced the Conservative candidate to desist and the Liberal won unopposed.[53]

In 1910 another complication arose and nearly brought U.S. military occupation. The president and vice president of Panama both died, and a Liberal, Carlos Mendoza, succeeded to the highest office. Mendoza, a mulatto, enjoyed great popularity and now commanded the Liberal Party.

He had participated in the 1903 revolution against Colombia and had written Panama's declaration of independence. The constitution stipulated that if (as in this case) more than two years of the presidential term remained, the National Assembly would select an interim president. Since the Liberals controlled the Assembly and Mendoza controlled the Liberals, his selection appeared to be guaranteed.

Conservatives approached the U.S. chargé d'affaires, R. O. Marsh, and requested American pressure to prevent Mendoza from remaining in office. Goethals and Marsh disliked the prospect of dealing with a black president for two years, and they cited a no-reelection clause in the constitution as a reason for opposing Mendoza. This rule did not seem to apply to Mendoza, and the Assembly had the power to interpret such questions. The opposition, therefore, stood on soft ground. In June the British minister judged Mendoza's chances a toss-up.[54]

Marsh, with Goethals's approval, tried to convince Washington of the need to bar Mendoza's succession. His argument rested principally on race: "I believe him to [be] an able, clever and comparatively high-minded politician, but I consider the unfortunate circumstance of his race will produce more harm . . . than his able qualities will produce good." Nonwhites in Panama and Central America would become unmanageable, while the United States would lose the respect of the white elements. He also objected to a timber contract with an American firm, rumored to be favored by Mendoza. Summing up, Marsh wrote, "Mendoza's election will strengthen the hold of the Liberal party, which includes the Negro and ignorant elements and is most apt to be anti-American."[55]

Over the coming weeks Marsh and Goethals met several times to coordinate activities, taking care to avoid scandal due to the congressional election under way at home. Mendoza soon agreed to desist if he could be finance minister, so all that remained for the Assembly was to choose another Liberal as interim president. By this time, Goethals had grown fearful that Marsh's high-handed dealings with the Panamanians would strain relations to the point of jeopardizing work on the canal. He warned him not to meddle in the presidential selection. Marsh, however, continued to do so without authorization from Washington—or worse, from Goethals. As his frustration rose, so did his audacity. The climax came when Marsh threatened occupation or annexation should the Assembly not follow his suggestions regarding the presidency. Goethals counteracted Marsh, who eventually went home in disgrace.[56]

The 1910 crisis would not have occurred had U.S. officials not objected to Mendoza's color, because he was among the abler politicians available. Marsh, of course, committed gross errors and deserved censure. But behind his action was Goethals's desire not to deal with a black president. And Goethals made U.S. policy for Panama. Sir Claude Mallet, Britain's ranking diplomat in Panama, a thirty-year resident married to a Panamanian, wrote, "I am in a position to state positively that the attitude in Washington was taken entirely on the initiative and recommendation of Colonel Goethals, who is prejudiced against señor Mendoza on account of his colour."[57]

Important results flowed from this episode. White Panamanians, who had been aware of American racism from the start, learned how to manipulate it for their own benefit. In doing so, however, they surrendered a measure of sovereignty. An informal alliance of sorts emerged between Panama's white elite of *both* parties and the canal executives, whereby racially mixed persons were kept in subordinate positions. Since Panamanian prejudices were milder than American ones, the net effect was less disadvantageous to the native mestizos and blacks than to the West Indians, who had to contend with racism in the Canal Zone and chauvinism in Panama. Panamanians rarely admitted to racial prejudice, and when they did, they could blame the Americans for having introduced it.

In this way American racial practices during the construction era left a deep imprint on formal and informal relations between the United States and Panama. The West Indians who came to build the canal and then settled as immigrants found themselves in double jeopardy, caught between two hostile forces.

By 1912, Goethals could make plans for the permanent organization of the canal. He foresaw a small civilian force composed of about 1,500 Americans and 2,500 West Indians. In addition, the army would station about eight thousand troops there for defense. Such a small population compared to the sixty thousand at peak construction must have appealed to Goethals, and he asked foreign consuls to discourage laborers from coming and to prepare for repatriation of tens of thousands to the islands. At one point his architect, designing a permanent commissary, asked if he could dispense with divided gold and silver areas and assume that the two rolls would use the same premises at different hours. Goethals responded, "This arrangement has worked very well so far and I do not know of any good reason why the present plan should be discontinued." He already envisioned a permanent canal force of whites and blacks (and a few intermediaries), separated by the color line.[58]

A few years later Goethals was asked about the gold-silver system. He explained that it was "customary in these tropical countries for white men to direct the work and for Negroes to do the harder parts of the manual and semiskilled labor. The relative proportion of the white and black races in these countries fixes to a large extent the division of labor. . . . It is not compatible with the white man's pride of race to do the work which it is traditional for the Negroes to do."[59] This statement reveals how officials sought to hide the imperialist and racist character of their actions. The canal caused some 150,000 West Indians to migrate to Panama, greatly disrupting the "relative proportion of the white and black races." In order to keep costs down and to control vast numbers of laborers, authorities devised a sui generis system of segregation based upon race and nationality. It began as a simple color line, but soon took on more complexity, with gradations for American blacks, Europeans, whites, West Indians, and Panamanians. The gold and silver system distributed rewards—wealth, power, and status—in a unique and castelike fashion. In addition, U.S. officials interfered openly in Panamanian affairs, controlling presidential successions and imparting a racist hue to subsequent relations between the two countries.

To say that segregated payrolls were the custom in tropical countries would be false. The British and French governments did not treat their Caribbean subjects in this manner, nor did major employers like the banana and petroleum companies. The Panama Canal Zone was a unique American creation for a unique enterprise. Had it occurred in another country, gold and silver might have faded away after the decline of imperialism in the 1940s. As it happened, the system became even more complicated and entrenched in the decades after construction.

Notes

1. Robert E. Wood, "The Working Force of the Panama Canal," in *The Panama Canal: An Engineering Treatise*, ed. George W. Goethals (New York: McGraw-Hill, 1916), 2: 195–98; 1904–1912, *passim*, in PCC [Panama Canal Commission] 2-E-2/Jamaica, and PCC 2-E-1; Velma Eudora Newton, "British West Indian Emigration to the Isthmus of Panama, 1850–1914," M.A. thesis, University of the West Indies, 1973, 148–55; *Canal Record*, 28 October 1914, 91–92; Raymond Allan Davis, "West Indian Workers on the Panama Canal: A Split Labor Market Interpretation," Ph.D. diss., Stanford University, 1981, 81–99.

2. Mallet to FO [Foreign Office], 12 September 1906, in FO [Foreign Office] 371/101/34896; U.S. Congress, Senate, *Hearings before the Committee on Interoceanic Canals . . . An Investigation of Matters Relating to the Panama Canal* (Washington, DC: Government Printing Office, 1906–07), 680–81. Cf. ICC [Isthmian Canal Commission], *Annual Report*, 1905, 9–11, and 1906, 5. For a representative description of the West Indians, see Frederick J. Haskin, *The Panama Canal* (Garden City, NY: Doubleday, Page, 1913), ch. 13. Willis Fletcher Johnson, *Four Centuries of the Panama Canal* (New York: Henry Holt, 1907), 354–59, discusses the labor question.

3. Taft to ICC Chairman Shonts, 13 April 1905, Moody to Taft, 5 June 1905, Shonts to Stevens, 29 November 1905, in PCC 2-E-1; U.S. Congress, Senate, *Hearings . . . Panama Canal*, 2575; Roosevelt to Taft, 27 July 1906, and Executive Order of 15 March 1907, in Taft papers, series 4A, LCMC [Library of Congress Manuscript Collection (Washington, DC)]; Magoon to Taft, 15 July 1904, in Taft papers, series 3, LCMC.

4. Stevens to Shonts, 4 May 1906 and 16 January 1907, Wood to Stevens, 22 October 1906, in PCC 2-E-1.

5. April and May 1907, *passim*, Gaillard to Stevens, 12 July 1907, Wood to Goethals, 20 May 1907 and 1 October 1913, in PCC 2-E-1.

6. U.S. Congress, House Committee on Appropriations, *Panama Canal—Skilled Labor, Extracts from Hearings, 1906–1914* (Washington, DC: Government Printing Office, 1915), 107–10; U.S. Congress, Senate, *Hearings . . . Panama Canal*, 2498–99.

7. Gerstle Mack, *The Land Divided* (New York: Knopf, 1944), ch. 44; Wood, "The Working Force," 191–92.

8. Karner to Smith, 24 May and 3 July 1906, in PCC 2-E-2/Barbados; Gorgas circular, 11 April 1906, in PCC 2-E-1.

9. U.S. Congress, House Committee, *Panama Canal*, 90–99; March 1906, *passim*, in PCC 2-E-2/Barbados.

10. JKB memo, accounting department, 13 August 1908, in PCC 2-D-40.

11. U.S. Congress, House Committee, *Panama Canal*, 109; 1908–09, *passim*, in PCC 2-D-40; 1912–13, *passim*, in PCC 2-E-2/Barbados.

12. Newton, "British West Indian Emigration," 165; Mallet to FO, 30 October 1912, in FO371/1417/50353.

13. Magoon to Stevens, 14 November 1905, Belle Flanagan to Franklin Bell, 13 September 1908, in PCC 2-E-1; U.S. Congress, Senate, *Hearings . . . Panama Canal*, 931–81.

14. H. S. Reed to Stevens, 16 March 1906, in PCC 11-E-6; Newton, "British West Indian Emigration," 213–15; ICC, *Annual Report*, 1913, 373.

15. Sullivan to Magoon, 2 January 1906 and 1909 *passim*, in PCC 79-F-5; Mallet to FO, 9 November 1912, in FO371/1417/52667.

16. Newton, "British West Indian Emigration," 208–12; Smith to Karner, 23 March 1906, in PCC 2-E-2/Barbados; Stevens to Shonts, 16 February 1907, in PCC 2-E-1; quote from John Oswald Butcher, "Reminiscences of Life and Work during the Construction of the Panama Canal," unpublished, IHS [Isthmian Historical Society]. Cf. U.S. Congress, Senate, *Hearings . . . Panama Canal*, 2500–03, 2758–60; ICC, *Annual Report*, 1905, 8.

17. See Gorgas's report in ICC, *Annual Report*, 1913, 526–29, and testimony in U.S. Congress, House Committee, *Panama Canal*, 90–99, 107–10, 139–41, 221–25.

18. Tucker to Shannon, 1 September 1906, and Shannon to Williams, 10 April 1907, in PCC 2-F-14; Burnett to Stevens and Stevens to Burnett, 15 and 16 February 1907, in PCC 2-C-55; George Westerman, "Fifty Years of West Indian Life in Panama, 1904–1954," unpublished, Westerman papers [private collection, Panama City], ch. 3.

19. Slifer to Gaillard, 12 and 15 February 1908, in PCC 2-F-14; "Privileges of Americans on Silver Roll," ca. 1916, in PCC 2-C-55; Davis, "West Indian Workers," 4–9.

20. See 1908–10, *passim*, in PCC 2-E-11; and note 48 below.

21. October–December 1909, *passim*, in PCC 2-F-14.

22. Goethals to Smith, 25 September 1912, in PCC 2-P-49.

23. 1909–14, in PCC C/2-E-11/A; 1913–14, in PCC 2-E-11/P; 1909–13, in PCC 2-P-49/P; PCWIEA [a section of the Panama Canal Collection that includes information about West Indian economic activities], *Annual Report*, 1936, 13–17.

24. Goethals to secretary of war, 13 September 1910, Judson to Goethals, 22 October 1913, Goethals to Judson, 12 June 1912, in Goethals papers, LCMC.

25. Harry A. Franck, *Zone Policeman 88: A Close Range Study of the Panama Canal and Its Workers*, 2d ed. (New York: Arno, 1970), 119; U.S. Congress, Senate, *Hearings . . . Panama Canal*, 52–53.

26. Schoolchildren in 1909 were 35 percent southern, and in 1932 employees were 28 percent southern: see George Ninas report, 16 July 1913, in PCC 91-A-37; Alberto Wilson to Evans, 30 April 1932, in PCC 2-C-124; Wood, "The Working Force," 194; John Biesanz, "Cultural and Economic Factors in Panamanian Race Relations," *American Sociological Review* 14 (1949): 23; Franck, *Zone Policeman*, 225–26.

27. Morrow to Connor, 19 July 1921, in PCC 28-B-5; *Panama Tribune*, 23 October 1955; Lewis interview, 8 August 1981.

28. Gaillard to Jackson Smith, 11 February 1907, Wood to Henry Smith, 24 July 1907, McIlvaine to Washington office, 18 July 1928, and 1907–12, *passim*, in PCC 2-C-55; Franck, *Zone Policeman*, 119.

29. Sullivan to Bolich, 4 August 1906, in PCC 2-F-14.

30. Burnett to Thomas O'Connell, 9 November 1905, in PCC 2-E-2/Jamaica; Burnett to Karner, 23 March 1906, in PCC 2-E-2/Barbados; Mallet to FO, 2 September 1907, in FO371/300/31889; Mallet to FO, 9 November 1912, in FO371/1417/52667.

31. Franck, *Zone Policeman*, 145; Slosson and Richardson, "Two Panama Life Stories," *Independent*, 19 April 1906, 922.

32. ICC, *Annual Report*, 1913, 486, and 1915, 446–47.

33. Mallet to FO, 12 June 1911 and 2 May 1916, in FO371/1176/27051 and FO368/1086/175925, Bennett to FO, 1 March 1920, in FO371/4536/A986; U.S. Congress, Senate, *Hearings . . . Panama Canal*, 2766.

34. See 1905–13, *passim*, in PCC 2-P-59; unidentified to Walker, 4 October 1904, in PCC 2-D-40; Rousseau to Thatcher, 7 January 1913, in PCC 2-E-11; U.S. Congress, Senate, *Hearings . . . Panama Canal*, 2265–67, 2730–34.

35. William D. McCain, *The United States and the Republic of Panama* (Durham, NC: Duke University Press, 1937), chs. 3–4; Gustavo Adolfo Mellander, *The United States in Panamanian Politics: The Intriguing Formative Years* (Dansville, IL: Interstate Printers and Publishers, 1971), 66–67.

36. "Affray between Jamaican Laborers and Panama Police," in C0137/645/19405 and C0137/646/29539, *Foreign Relations of the United States*, 1905, 709–12.

37. Mallet to FO, 12 June 1911 and 14 March 1919, in FO371/1176/27051 and FO371/3857/17158; Franck, *Zone Policeman*, 231.

38. Police chief to John Carr, reporter for *Outlook Magazine*, 17 April 1906, in PCC C/28-B-233; Newton, "British West Indian Emigrants," 206; Skinner to Shannon, 8 April 1907, in PCC 2-P-59.

39. Mallet to FO, 4 April 1914, in FO371/2058/18805; William Archer, *Through Afro-America: An English Reading of the Race Problem* (Westport, CT: Negro Universities Press, 1970), 284; Wayne Bray, *The Common Law Zone in Panama: A Case Study in Reception* (San Juan, Puerto Rico: Inter-American University Press, 1977), 104; A. Beeby Thompson, "The Labour Problem of the Panama Canal," *Engineering*, 3 May 1907, 590; U.S. Congress, Senate, *Hearings . . . Panama Canal*, 81; quotation from Harrigan Austin, "Reminiscences of Life and Work," unpublished, IHS.

40. Stevens to Shonts, 19 April 1906, Belding to Rousseau, 17 January 1907, and 1904–11, *passim*, in PCC 28-A-31; *Canal Record*, 4 December 1907, 107, and 1 January 1908, 139.

41. Lancelot S. Lewis, *The West Indian in Panama: Black Labor in Panama, 1850–1914* (Washington, DC: University Press of America, 1980), 73; 1906–14, *passim*, in PCC 28-A-32/Alpha.

42. Rufus Lane to Magoon, 8 August 1906, and 1904–13, *passim*, in PCC 91-A-39; 1904–13, *passim*, in PCC 91-A-37; annual school reports, 1905–13, Webster papers [private collection]; George W. Westerman, "School Segregation in the Panama Canal Zone," *Phylon* 3 (1954): 276; "Press Comments on the CZ Schools' Changes, 1954," Westerman papers.

43. *Panama Journal*, 12 October 1908, and Moore to Chief of Record Bureau, 13 May 1943, in PCC 91-A-39; Alda Harper, *Tracing the Course of Growth and Development in Educational Policy for the Canal Zone Colored Schools, 1905–1955* (Ann Arbor: University of Michigan School of Education, 1979), ch. 2; Osborne biographical sketches in George W. Westerman, *Pioneers in Canal Zone Education* (Panama Canal Zone: n.p., 1949), 13–20; Lowell C. Wilson et al., *Schooling in the Panama Canal Zone, 1904–1979* (Panama Canal Area: Phi Delta Kappa, 1980), 106–10.

44. Harper, *Tracing the Course of Growth*, 59.

45. MCL memo, 20 July 1911, Thatcher to Goethals, 4 August 1911, O'Connor to Reed, 1 May 1907, in PCC 91-A-39.

46. Walter LaFeber, *The Panama Canal: The Crisis in Historical Perspective*, rev. ed. (New York: Oxford University Press, 1979), ch. 2; Mellander, *The United States in Panamanian Politics*, chs. 5–12, *passim*; 1904–15, *passim*, in PCC 80-F-9, PCC 79-F-5, PCC 58-A-1, PCC 94-A-3/T, and PCC 58-A-6; Mallet to FO, 1 February 1909, in FO368/315/9133; *Canal Record*, 18 December 1907, 121–22; Antonio Burgos, *Panamá y su immigración* (Panamá: Imprenta Nacional, 1913), 104–07.

47. *Foreign Relations of the United States*, 1906, 2:1196.

48. Taft to Roosevelt, 16 May 1908, in Taft papers, semiofficial, LCMC; Collins, "Relative Rights of Citizens," 5 March 1919, U.S. chargé to Jackson Smith, 6 June 1919, and State Dept. to War Dept., 19 June 1919, in PCC 2-E-12.

49. See 1919, *passim*, in PCC 2-E-12.

50. Executive order 1888 (2 February 1914), in PCC 2-D-4.

51. HR 27250, *Congressional Record*, 9 February 1909, 2168, remitted in FO371/785/7443; Mallet to FO, 19 June 1913, in FO371/1703/33655; 1909–14, *passim*, in PCC 80-F-9.

52. Roosevelt to Taft, 19 December 1904 and 13 April 1905, in Taft papers, semiofficial, LCMC; Squiers, quoted in Mellander, *The United States in Panamanian Politics*, 124.

53. Mellander, *The United States in Panamanian Politics*, 134–35.

54. Chalkley to FO, 14 March 1910, and Mallet to FO, 15 June 1910, in FO371/944/11516 and 25146; Thatcher to Goethals, 29 June 1910, in Goethals papers, LCMC.

55. Marsh to State Dept., 28 July 1910, Goethals to secretary of war, 13 September 1910, in Goethals papers, LCMC.

56. See State Dept. files 847 and 819.00 for 1910, RG 59, National Archives.

57. Mallet to FO, 22 August 1910, in FO371/944/33140.

58. Goethals to Wilson, 4 December 1912, in PCC 2-C-124; Goethals to Witlock, 2 August 1912, in PCC 58-A-13.

59. Goethals to Boggs, 20 March 1915, in PCC 2-E-11.

9

The Four-Storeyed House: Africans in the Forging of Puerto Rico's National Identity

José Luis González

An intimate relationship may exist between race and national identity, and many Latin Americans have sought to define nationality in racial terms or to interpret the region along cultural—that is, racial and ethnic—lines. Cuban patriot José Martí, for example, attempted to distinguish the Creole nature of Latin American societies in Our America.[*] *Mexican nationalist José Vasconcelos referred to the people of Latin America as the "cosmic race," while the Peruvian Raul Haya de la Torre argued that the Andean region should be called Indo-America because the indigenous population provided the cultural and demographic base.[†] Other writers, from Brazil's Gilberto Freyre to Cuba's Nicolás Guillén, have created positive national images of* mestizaje *and melting-pot cultures.*

Defining nationality often requires the construction of some symbol or metaphor that will reflect the contribution of its people. Symbols such as the melting pot or the cosmic race recognize multiple ethnic and racial contributions, including those of Africans, to the creation of national identity. Richard Jackson has examined how Latin Americans treat the African dimension in national discourse and criticizes the way many

From *Puerto Rico: The Four-Storeyed Country* (Maplewood, NJ: Waterfront Press, 1990), 1–29. Reprinted by permission of Waterfront Press.

[*]See his *Obras completas*, vol. 6 (Havana: Editorial Lex, 1946).
[†]See José Vasconcelos, *La raza cósmica* (Mexico City: Agencia Mundial de Librería, 1920); Victor Raul Haya de la Torre, *Adónde va Indoamérica?* (Santiago, Chile: Editorial Ercilla, 1936).

intellectuals discuss the African experience in a stereotypical, folkloris-tic, and often condescending fashion. Although this is valuable criticism of the African images, these historical and literary interpretations never-theless must be considered in context. Writers in the 1930s, for example, included popular and marginal social groups in their discussion of national identity. Their contribution came not in the images that they pre-sented but rather in the fact that for the first time they inserted popular groups, such as blacks, into the official history.*

In this chapter José Luis González traces the formation of Puerto Rican identity, emphasizing the contribution of the African, who formed the base of this nationhood. While arguing in favor of independence, he discusses the various stages in the construction of the Puerto Rican cul-tural character as symbolized by a four-storeyed nation. Although this image perpetuates the notion of a static culture, it forges an identity based on the recognition of contributions from all members of Puerto Rican society. This essay by Gonzalez serves as an example for discussion of the role of the African in other Latin American national images.

> History was political propaganda, it was used to create the national unity, in other words the nation itself, from without and in despite of tradition, laying its foundations on literature and saying "I *want* things to be this way," not "This is the way they *should* be, given existing conditions." The intellectu-als, because they shared this position, had to distance themselves from the masses, stand aside, create or strengthen among themselves the spirit of caste, so that they came to *distrust* the masses, feel them as alien, be fearful of them—because for the intellectuals the masses were an unknown quantity, a mysterious hydra of innumerable heads. . . . By contrast . . . many intellec-tual movements aimed at modernizing and at de-rhetoricizing culture and bringing it closer to the masses, nationalizing it, one might say. ("Nation-masses" and "nation-rhetoric" might serve as approximate labels for these two tendencies.)
>
> —Antonio Gramsci, *Letters from Prison* (III, 82)

In September 1979 I was conducting a seminar in Latin American stud-ies at the University of Puerto Rico. A group of Puerto Rican students in this seminar, enrolled in the social science faculty of the university but mostly graduates of various schools at the National Autonomous Univer-sity of Mexico, put the following question to me in the course of our discussions: *How, as you see it, has American colonial intervention affected Puerto Rican culture and what do you think about the present state of that culture?* The essay that follows is my attempt to provide an answer to this question. I have subtitled it "Notes toward a Definition of Puerto Rican Culture" because all I aim to do in this essay is suggest the

---

*See *The Black Image in Latin American Literature* (Albuquerque: Univer-sity of New Mexico Press, 1976) and *The Afro-Spanish American Author: An Annotated Bibliography of Criticism* (New York: Garland, 1980).

nucleus for an interpretive study of the historical and cultural realities of Puerto Rico, something that I am sure requires a more sustained analysis and more carefully reasoned conclusions than anything I can provide here. Still, I hope that this essay, in spite of its limited scope, may prove useful for the members of the Latin American studies seminar and for any other readers who may decide to honor it with their critical attention.

As we all know, the question you students asked me raises an enormously important issue that has preoccupied and continues to preoccupy those many Puerto Ricans who are involved, from a variety of ideological standpoints, in the Puerto Rican situation and who are naturally concerned with how that situation will develop. But before attempting an answer I asked myself (as I am sure you asked yourselves before passing the question on to me) what you really meant by the phrase "Puerto Rican culture." It struck me that you might not mean exactly what I mean by it, and so I thought it wise to tackle that difficulty first since I suspect that everything I shall go on to say is the rough sketch of a thesis in direct contradiction to what most Puerto Rican intellectuals have for many decades taken to represent established truths, and even, sometimes, articles of patriotic faith. I shall therefore try to be as explicit as possible within the brief space that a reply of this nature allows—which, let me again stress, makes no claim to being definitive but aims only at providing a starting point for a dialogue that I feel sure will remain cordial in spite of any valid and productive differences of opinion between us.

Let me begin, then, by agreeing wholeheartedly with the idea, held by many sociologists, that there coexist two separate cultures at the heart of any society divided into classes, a culture of the oppressors and another culture of the oppressed. Now it is clear that these two cultures, precisely because they *co*-exist, aren't to be seen as watertight compartments; in fact they are most like intercommunicating vessels between which there is a constant reciprocal flow. The dialectical nature of that flow usually gives the impression of homogeneity, but in fact no such homogeneity really exists—indeed it could only exist in a society *without* classes, and only then after a long process of consolidation. By contrast, in any society *with* classes the true relation between the two cultures in that society is one of dominance, with the culture of the oppressors dominating and the culture of the oppressed being dominated. It follows that what is often passed off as "the general culture," even as "the national culture," is, naturally enough, merely a description of but one of these cultures—the dominant culture of the oppressors. So I really cannot begin to answer the question you put to me without first trying to determine precisely what that "national culture" was really like at the time of the American arrival in Puerto Rico, although here too, if we are to treat this issue with the seriousness it merits, we first have to make sure we know the answer to another question: Just what sort of a "nation" *was* Puerto Rico in 1898?

Needless to say, many Puerto Ricans have asked that question before and their answers to it have been various and sometimes contradictory. (I am speaking, of course, of those Puerto Ricans who have conceived of Puerto Rico as a nation; those who have denied the existence of such a nation, last century and this, pose a problem that should also be analyzed, although for the moment I intend to leave it to one side.) To make a start, then, let us consider two important figures who both *did* conceive of Puerto Rico as a nation: Eugenio María de Hostos and Pedro Albizu Campos.

For Hostos in 1898, what the Spanish colonial regime had left in Puerto Rico was a society "where life was lived under the sway of barbarity"; barely three decades later, Albizu Campos defined the social reality of that same regime as "the old collective happiness." How is one to explain the extreme contradiction between such statements by two honorable and intelligent men, both of whom struggled to achieve the same political goal, the independence of Puerto Rico? If we recognize, as I believe we must, that it was Hostos who stuck close to the historical truth and Albizu who distorted it, and if we don't wish to fall into subjective interpretations which apart from possibly turning out to be wrong would be unjust, then we should look for explanations of this contradiction in the historical processes that caused it rather than in the personalities who gave it expression. In other words, it is not so much a matter of Hostos versus Albizu as of one historical vision versus another historical vision.

Let us begin by asking ourselves about the state of affairs that prompted Hostos to stick to the historical truth in his opinion about the condition of Puerto Rico at the time of the American invasion. In other words, what permitted Hostos to recognize, without thereby betraying his belief in Puerto Rican independence, that in 1898 "the social and individual weakness one sees on every hand seems to render our people incapable of helping themselves"? What permitted such critical frankness was without a doubt his vision of the stage Puerto Rico had then reached in the course of its political evolution. It was the vision of a society only just beginning its journey toward nationhood and then wracked by enormous collective ills (the ills Manuel Zeno Gandía denounced in his novels dealing with "a sick world" and that Salvador Brau analyzed in his "sociological disquisitions"). If the nineteenth-century Puerto Rican separatists with Ramón Emeterio Betances at their head believed in and fought for national independence, it was because they understood that independence was necessary to carry forward to completion the forging of a national identity, not because any of them believed that such a national identity already existed. Not confusing politics with sociology, the separatists knew that with Puerto Rico, as with Latin America as a whole, the creation of a national state was intended not so much to express an already fully formed national identity as to provide the most potent and effective means of stimulating and completing the creation of that identity. In fact, *no* Latin American country that century had arrived at independence as the culmination of a process of creating a national identity, but only by previously having forged political and judicial institutions to foster and encourage that same process.

Be that as it may, the fact remains that the Puerto Rican separatists never achieved any such independence and still today many supporters of Puerto Rican independence wonder why. Some continue to think it was because somebody or other betrayed the rebellion at Lares, or that the five hundred rifles that Betances had loaded on a boat in Saint Thomas didn't reach Puerto Rico in time. Others think it was because twenty years afterward Puerto Rican separatists were fighting in Cuba rather than in their own country, or . . . who knows how many other "reasons," all equally foreign to any truly scientific conception of history? But in fact the only *real* reason the separatists never achieved independence in the nineteenth century is the reason that was offered on more than one occasion by that revolutionary hero who, after his first defeat, acquired the wise habit of never pulling the wool over his own eyes: Ramón Emeterio Betances himself. The reason (and this is a direct quotation from this father of the separatist cause) is that "Puerto Ricans don't want [their] independence." But what do such words mean when spoken or written by a man like Betances, a man who insisted that independence was the only just and reasonable destiny for his country and who viewed that independence as Puerto Rico's necessary first step toward her incorporation into the great Antillean federation? Who exactly were those "Puerto Ricans" Betances was talking about—and what did he mean by saying they "don't want [their] independence"?

Betances himself explained what he meant soon after the uprising at Lares in a letter from Port-au-Prince in which he attributed the failure of this uprising to the fact that "the rich Puerto Ricans have abandoned us." Betances didn't have to be a Marxist to know that in his day and age a revolution against the colonial powers was doomed to failure without the support of the creole ruling class. In Puerto Rico it was precisely the members of *this* class who "didn't want [their] independence." They didn't want it because they *couldn't* want it, because their weakness as a class, determined fundamentally though not exclusively by Puerto Rico's weak economic substructure, didn't allow the ruling class to go beyond the reformist yearnings which had always characterized it. The relative development of the economy between 1868 and 1887 and consequently of the ideology of the landowning and professional class—what then most closely resembled an incipient national bourgeoisie—is what determined the shift from assimilationism to autonomism in the political attitudes of that class. But these landowners and professionals never went as far as to believe, not even by 1898, that Puerto Rico had become a nation capable, as an independent state, of guiding its own destinies. In the case of Hostos, then, the desire for independence was never at odds with a realistic appraisal of the historical situation he lived through. And it was this appraisal that led Hostos to declare in 1898, when after an exile of several decades he came face-to-face with Puerto Rican reality, that the Puerto Rican people were incapable of governing themselves and so to propose, to overcome this incapacity, a program of moral and physical regeneration which he believed could be completed in twenty years, if the time were well employed.

By contrast, the time Albizu had to live through some thirty years later was characterized not only by the political immaturity of the creole ruling class (whose members Albizu had hoped to mobilize in the struggle for independence) but by an even more disheartening feature—the cooption, disenfranchisement, and subsequent crippling of that class by the irruption of imperialist American capitalism into Puerto Rico. Angel Quintero Rivera has admirably explained the political and economic aspects of this process by showing clearly how the ever-growing economic weakness of the creole ruling class rendered it incapable of countering American imperialism with a plan of its own for the historical development of Puerto Rico and in fact finally led it to abandon the liberalism that characterized it in the last century, for the conservatism that has so far characterized it in this. The idealization—or rather, the misrepresentation—of the historical past has always been one of the typical traits of the ideology of this ruling class. Pedro Albizu Campos was without a doubt the most coherent and consistent spokesman for that conservative ideology—conservative in content, that is, but in Albizu's case radical in expression, since he spoke on especial behalf of the most desperate members of that class (and I owe that very precise adjective "desperate" to the distinguished nationalist poet Juan Antonio Corretjer). That historical desperation, so understandable that there is no reason why it should come as a surprise to anyone, was what forced Albizu to distort the truth by calling the Spanish colonial regime in Puerto Rico "the old collective happiness."

Now we can turn to the relevance all this has to the problem of the Puerto Rican "national culture" today. If Puerto Rican society has always been a society divided into classes, and if, as we maintained earlier, there are in every class-divided society two cultures, the culture of the oppressors and the culture of the oppressed, [and,] moreover, if what is known as "national culture" is generally the oppressing culture—then it is necessary to recognize that what in Puerto Rico we have always called "the national culture" is in fact nothing more than the culture of that class of landowners and professional men to which I have already referred. One should, however, make one thing clear about our use of the term "oppressors" and "oppressed" in the Puerto Rican context, which is that there is no denying the fact that the creole oppressors at home have at the same time been subject to oppression from abroad. It is precisely this that explains the cultural achievements of this class last century. These achievements, insofar as they expressed a resistance to Spanish domination, were essentially progressive, given the totally reactionary nature in all respects of that domination. But the same class that was oppressed by the imperial power was in turn oppressing one other social class in Puerto Rico, the class made up of slaves, until their emancipation in 1873, of landless laborers, and of small craftsmen. (As for industrial workers, strictly speaking, there were very few of them in nineteenth-century Puerto Rico, given the country's almost total lack of what could be called modern industries.) The "culture of the oppressed" in Puerto Rico has been and is the culture produced by this "other social class" I have just mentioned. (As a matter of fact, it is a culture that has been studied by the ruling class intellectuals only as *folklore*, that invention of the European bourgeoisie which has served so well to spirit away the true significance of popular culture.) And from now on, so as to avoid misunderstandings, let us refer to these two cultures, of oppressors and oppressed, as respectively "élite culture" and "popular culture."

To answer your question we must first examine, even if it has to be in a somewhat schematic form due to lack of space, how each of these cultures came into being and how it subsequently developed. The obvious thing would be to start with the popular culture, for the simple reason that of the two it was born first. It is by now a commonplace to assert that this culture has three historical roots: the Taino Indian, the African, and the Spanish. What isn't however a commonplace—in fact just the opposite—is to say that of these three roots the one that is most important, for economic and social—and hence cultural—reasons, is the African. As is well known, the indigenous population of Puerto Rico was wiped out in a matter of mere decades by the genocidal brutality of the Spanish Conquest. (Well known *as a piece of information*, though without a doubt poorly assimilated both morally and intellectually, to judge by the fact that the principal avenue of our capital city still bears the name of that greedy adventurer and enslaver of Indians, Juan Ponce de León.)

The extermination of the Indian population couldn't of course keep aboriginal elements from figuring in our definition as a people, but it seems clear to me that their contribution to our Puerto Rican identity was achieved primarily by cultural exchange between the Indians and the other two ethnic groups, in particular the blacks, because Indians and blacks had been trapped in the most oppressed stratum of the social pyramid during the early period of colonization and therefore had more contact with one another than either had with the dominant Spanish group. It is also well known, because it has been documented, that the composition of the Spanish group was exceptionally unstable throughout the first two centuries of colonial life. For example, it is worth remembering that in 1534 the governor of the colony gave an account of his efforts to stop the Spanish population's mass exodus to the mainland in search of riches. The island, he wrote, was "so depopulated that one sees hardly any people of Spanish descent, but only Negroes." The Spanish ingredient, then, in the formation of a popular Puerto Rican culture must have taken the form of agricultural laborers, mostly from the Canary Islands, imported to the island when the descendants of the first African slaves *had already become black Puerto Ricans.* It is because of this that I believe, as I have said on various occasions to the embarrassment and irritation of some, that the first Puerto Ricans were in fact *black* Puerto Ricans. I am not claiming, needless to say, that these first Puerto Ricans had any idea of a "national homeland," for in fact *no one* at that time in Puerto Rico entertained, or could have entertained, such an idea. What I *am* claiming is that it was the blacks, the people bound most closely to the territory which they inhabited (they were after all slaves), who had the greatest difficulty in imagining any other place to live. Of course, it might be argued against this line of reasoning that the goal of several of the slave conspiracies that took place in Puerto Rico in the nineteenth century—at least according to the statements of official documents—was to escape to Santo Domingo, where slavery had been abolished. But it shouldn't be forgotten that many of these conspiracies were led either by slaves born in Africa, the so-called *bozales,* or by slaves imported from other Caribbean islands, *not* by *negros criollos* or creole blacks, the name given to blacks born on the island before it became customary to recognize them as *Puerto Ricans.*

As for the white campesinos or countrymen of those early times, in other words the first *jíbaros,* the truth is that this was a poor peasantry that found itself obliged to adopt many of the life habits of those other poor people already living in the country, namely the slaves. In this connection, it is not irrelevant to point out that when people today speak for example of "*jíbaro* food," what they really mean is "black food": plantains, rice, codfish, *funche*, etc. If the "national cuisine" of all the Caribbean islands and the bordering mainland territories is virtually the same in using certain basic ingredients albeit with slight though often imaginative variants, even though the territories were colonized by European nations of such widely differing culinary traditions as the Spanish, French, English, and Dutch, then I think this can be explained by the fact that all we Caribbeans eat and drink today more like blacks than like Europeans. The same thing, or something quite similar, can be said of the Puerto Rican "national dress," the characteristics of which, to my knowledge, the folklorists haven't yet accurately defined. The truth is that the white campesinos for strictly economic reasons had to wear the same simple, comfortable, cheap clothing that the blacks wore. The upper-class creole tended to dress as a European as soon as that was feasible, and, as any Puerto Rican of my own generation with a good memory can confirm, the popular *guayabera* or embroidered shirt of our own day arrived on the island only three decades ago from Cuba, where it had been created as a garment for casual use among country landowners.

Throughout the first three centuries of our post-Columbian history Puerto Rican popular culture, which was essentially Afro-Antillean in character, defined us as just another Caribbean population. And the social majority which produced that culture also produced the first great historical figure in Puerto Rico, Miguel Henríquez, a mulatto shoemaker who became the richest man on the island during the second half of the eighteenth century thanks to his extraordinary energies as smuggler and pirate. (Richest, that is, until the Spanish authorities became alarmed at his power and decided to remove him, first from the island and then from this world.) Our first important artist also came from this same class: José Campeche, the mulatto son of an *esclavo "coartado"* or "limited" slave, i.e., a slave purchasing his liberty in installments. And if after that Puerto Rican society had gone on evolving in the same way other Caribbean islands did, then our current "national culture" would be like theirs, a popular mestizo culture of a predominantly Afro-Antillean type.

But Puerto Rican society didn't in fact evolve this way in the course of the eighteenth and nineteenth centuries. At the beginning of the nineteenth century, when no one in Puerto Rico was thinking about a "national culture," what one might call a *second storey*—in social, economic, cultural, and, as a result of all these factors, ultimately political, terms—was being added on to our national culture. A wave of immigrants fleeing from Spanish colonies then fighting for independence in South America began building and furnishing this second storey, joined almost immediately afterward, under the aegis of the *Real Cédula de Gracias* of 1815, by numerous foreigners (English, French, Dutch, Irish, etc.) and with a second wave, composed mainly of Corsicans, Majorcans, and Catalans, following them about the middle of the century.

This second wave of immigrants created virtually a second colonization, this time in the mountainous central area of the island. The institution of the *libreta* or passbook contributed to this colonization by creating a workforce at once stable and, needless to say, servile. The world of the coffee plantations, in this century mythicized as the epitome of "Puerto Ricanness," was in reality a world dominated by foreigners, whose wealth was founded on the expropriation of the old creole landlords and on the ruthless exploitation of a native campesino class then existing on a subsistence level. (A splendid portrayal of this world is to be found in Fernando Picó's book *Libertad y servidumbre en el Puerto Rico del siglo XIX*, Ediciones Huracán, Río Piedras, 1979).

These new Spanish, Corsican, and Majorcan coffee plantation owners were inevitably among the main props of the Spanish colonial regime and the culture they produced was, for equally natural reasons, a seignorial culture that looked abroad for its cultural norms. Even at the end of the century the Majorcan coffee growers spoke Majorcan among themselves and only used Spanish when they wanted to be understood by their Puerto Rican workers. And until well into the twentieth century, as many literary and historical sources attest, the Corsicans were perceived as foreigners, often as "Frenchmen," by the native Puerto Ricans. As for the Majorcans, it's enough to point to a historical fact which merits a good deal of sociohistorical examination: many of these emigrants were what in Majorca are known as *chuetas*, i.e., the descendants of converted Jews. What I am getting at is this: What social attitudes would result when a minority discriminated against in its country of origin became, as the result of emigration, a *privileged* minority in its new home? We could, of course, ask the same question about the Corsican immigrants, who were either semi- or wholly illiterate peasants in their native country and who became gentlemen landowners after a few years in Puerto Rico. The poverty of the culture which this landlord class on the coffee plantations produced throughout the second half of the nineteenth century, when compared to the culture produced by the social élite in the coastal areas, reveals a class, in social and human terms, that was basically uncultured, arrogant, and conservative, and that despised and oppressed the native poor, and were, in turn, hated by them. It is this hatred, among other things, that explains the "seditious bands" that in 1898 attacked coffee plantations in the mountainous "uplands" of the island.

I have just mentioned 1898—and this brings us, after our necessary historical excursion, to the gist of the question you asked me earlier. I began to answer by saying that in order to describe Puerto Rico's "national culture" at the time of the American invasion, it would first be necessary to ask what kind of a nation Puerto Rico was at that time. Well then, in the light of everything I have just said it seems no exaggeration to state that Puerto Rico was a country so divided racially, socially, economically, and culturally, that it should rather be described as *two* countries than as one. Or more precisely, perhaps, as two distinct societies that hadn't yet had time to fuse into a true national synthesis. But then this shouldn't surprise anyone, since such a phenomenon is not at all exclusive to Puerto Rico but is typical of Latin America as a whole. Mexico and Peru, for example, are still debating the problem of the "different countries": that of the Indians, that of the creoles, and that of the mestizos. In Argentina there is a long-standing conflict between the "old creoles" and the more recent immigrants and their descendants. In Haiti there is a notorious rivalry between blacks and mulattos. And so on.

What sets the Puerto Rican case apart is that for more than half a century we have been peddled the myth of social, racial, and cultural homogeneity which it is now high time that we began to dismantle, not so as to "divide" the country—a prospect that some people contemplate with terror—but rather so as to gain a true perspective on the country's real and objective diversity. Were we to imagine two contrasting Puerto Rican types as for example a (white) poet from Lares and a (black or mulatto) stevedore from Puerta de Tierra, we would immediately have to admit that there is a great difference between them, and I submit that it is a difference of a historically determined *cultural tradition*, which must in no way be underestimated. (None of this implies, let me state bluntly to avoid any misunderstanding, that the one is necessarily "more Puerto Rican" than the other.) The difference I have referred to ultimately derives from two visions of the world, two *Weltanschauungen*, that are diametrically opposed in many important respects. All thinking Puerto Ricans, and more especially independentists, are distressed, and rightly so, by our people's persistent inability to agree on the final political organization of the country—in other words, the so-called issue of status. In this sense at least we are responding to the reality of a "divided people." But what we haven't yet been able to recognize are the profound causes, the profound *historical* causes, of that division.

The traditional independence movement has maintained that this division only came into being because of the American invasion, and that what characterized Puerto Rican society during the Spanish colonial period was, in the words of Albizu Campos, "a homogeneity among all the components and a highly developed social sense dedicated to mutual aid for the perpetuation and preservation of our nation, in other words a deeply rooted and unanimous sense of fatherland." Only the obfuscating power of a profoundly conservative ideology could have produced a view of things so essentially at variance with historical reality. All mythologizing apart, the Puerto Rico of 1898 can only, in fact, be described as a country *on the way to nationhood*. So Hostos saw it and Hostos was right. And if during the nineteenth century this process of nation-building suffered profound setbacks because of the two great waves of immigrants who, to repeat my metaphor, built a second storey on Puerto Rican society, then what happened in 1898 was that the American invasion began to add a *third* storey to a second which was still not entirely habitable.

To repeat: in this nation-in-the-making, divided as we know, or should know, not only into classes but also into distinct ethnic groups which were true castes, the two cultures of which I speak always coexisted. But precisely because we are dealing with a nation-in-the-making, these two cultures were not in themselves homogeneous. To start with, the social élite was divided into two clearly distinguishable groups: plantation owners and professional men. Quintero Rivera has explained with great clarity how these two groups of the élite were ideologically distinct, with the landowners inclining more to conservatism and the professionals to liberalism. And when we come to culture, what must be stressed is that the culture of the landowners was above all a *way of life*, seignorial and conservative. The landowners themselves weren't capable of creating a literature that would describe or extol that way of life, and so this task fell, well into the present century, upon their descendants, members of a class in decline (but in decline *as a class* let it be understood, because individually the grandchildren of the "ruined" landowners, now become for the most part professionals, managers, or bureaucrats, enjoyed a standard of living much higher than any known to their grandparents). Only by seeing things in such a light can one understand, for example, the ideological content of a literary work such as René Marqués's *Los soles truncos*.

By contrast, the culture produced by the nineteenth-century professional men consisted of *creative works* and of *institutions*: virtually all our literature of this period, the Atheneum, and so on. And in these creative works and institutions it was the liberal ideology of their creators that predominated, with the result that "the culture of the dominant class" in nineteenth-century Puerto Rican colonial society isn't necessarily synonymous with "a reactionary culture." (It is very important to get this last point clear so as to avoid the simplifications and confusions peculiar to a certain type of underdeveloped "Marxism.") There certainly *were* reactionaries among cultivated Puerto Ricans at this time, but they neither formed a majority nor were they typical. Those who *did* form a majority and those who *were* typical were both liberal and progressive: Alonso, Tapia, Hostos, Brau, Zeno. . . .

Then, too, there were of course some revolutionaries, but these were in the minority and, characteristically and revealingly, often mestizos: one has only to think of Betances, of Pachín Marín, and of an artisan like Sotero Figueroa who mixed culturally with the élite. The most radical of the autonomists—and who will dare say it was by chance?—were also mestizos; just recall Baldorioty and Barbosa, whom conservative independentists have so misunderstood and slighted this century, the former as a "reformer" and the latter as a "Yankophile." (As though at least half of the separatists in the nineteenth century hadn't wanted to break with Spain so as to become part of the United States, in those days a shining symbol of republican democracy for most of the enlightened world!) There is the revealing history, for those who don't insist on ignoring the truth, of the Puerto Rican section of the Cuban Revolutionary Party in New York, where until 1898 separatist-independentists like Sotero Figueroa made common cause with separatist-annexionists (perhaps a grammatical but not a political contradiction) like Todd and Henna. (And don't these very names clearly speak to us of that "second storey" added by immigrants to Puerto Rican society in the early and middle years of the century?)

All this might seem, but in fact isn't, a digression, for Puerto Rican "national culture" at about the time of the 1898 invasion consisted of all these elements. That is to say, in its strengths, weaknesses, and contradictions it was an exact reflection of that social class which gave it life. And if that class, as we have argued, can be characterized by its historical weakness and immaturity, could the culture that resulted possibly have been strong and mature? What gave the culture a *relative* strength and maturity was, first, the fact that it had its roots in an old, rich European culture, namely the Spanish; and second, that it had already begun to put its own creole stamp, in an Hispano-Antillean sense, on whatever it produced. This last fact is undeniable and for that reason those who maintain, or at any rate maintained two or three decades ago, that there is no such thing as a "national culture" in Puerto Rico are obviously wrong. But wrong, too, are those who ignored and continue to ignore the class basis of such a culture and describe it as the *only* culture of the Puerto Rican people, identifying its decline under the American colonial regime with a presumed decline in national identity. Seeing things in this way not only confuses the part with the whole, because that culture has in fact only been *part* of what in an all-inclusive sense might be called the "Puerto

Rican national culture"—it certainly can't claim to represent *all* the
island's culture—but it also fails to recognize the existence of the *other*
Puerto Rican culture which under the American colonial regime has undergone not so much a deterioration as a development, an uneven development no doubt and one that has been full of vicissitudes but a
development nonetheless. And to say this is not, as certain conservative
patriots insist, to make a leftist apology for American colonialism, but
merely to recognize a historical fact: the progressive dismantling of the
culture of the Puerto Rican élite under the impact of the transformations
in Puerto Rican society resulting from the American colonial presence
has resulted less in the "Americanization" of Puerto Rican society than in
a transformation of cultural values *from within*. The vacuum created by
the dismantling of the culture of the Puerto Rican élite hasn't been filled
(far from it) by intrusions of American culture; on the contrary, what *has*
filled that vacuum has been the ever more perceptible rise to prominence
of the culture of the Puerto Rican lower classes.

We must now ask how and why such a thing came about. I see no way
of giving a valid answer to this question except by putting it in the context of the class struggle which lies at the heart of Puerto Rican society. It
is high time we began to understand, in the light of a scientific theory of
history, just what the change of colonial regime in 1898 really meant for
Puerto Rico. And by "what it really meant" I want to emphasize—what
the change meant for the different social classes that composed Puerto
Rican society. We can easily see, because it is abundantly documented,
that the Puerto Rican propertied class welcomed the American invasion
when it occurred with open arms. Every political spokesman of that class
saw that invasion as bringing to Puerto Rico liberty, democracy, and
progress, and as the prelude to the annexation of Puerto Rico by the richest and most powerful, and, we should remember, most "democratic,"
nation on earth. The subsequent disenchantment only occurred when the
new imperial master made it clear that the invasion did not necessarily
imply annexation, or the participation of the propertied class in the sump-
tuous banquet of the expanding American capitalist economy, but instead
their colonial subordination to that economy.

It was then and only then that the "nationalism" of this class came
into being. (Or rather to put it more exactly, the "nationalism" of the
members of that class whose economic weakness made it impossible for
them to profit from the new situation.) The well-known opposition of
José de Diego, which is to say the opposition of the social class that he
represented as president of the Chamber of Delegates, to the extending of
American citizenship to Puerto Ricans, was founded on the categorical
declaration by President Taft that citizenship did not necessarily pave the

way for annexation or even the promise of annexation, as De Diego himself explained in a speech that all Puerto Rican independentists should read or reread. And when in addition it became clear that the new economic order, which is to say an economy based on cultivating sugarcane instead of one based on coffee, meant the ruin of the island's propertied class and the beginning of the independent participation of the working class in the political life of the country, the "patriotic" rhetoric of the property owners reached such heights of demagoguery that not even the liberal professionals hesitated to ridicule and condemn it. Only in this context can we explain the virulent attacks by Rosendo Matienzo Cintrón, Nemesio Canales, and Luis Lloréns Torres on the "anti-imperialist" tirades of José de Diego, the wealthy lawyer of the Guánica sugar mill turned thundering "*Caballero de la Raza*" ("Knight-Errant of his People").

(And directly related to this last point, let me here add a long parenthesis on a subject so relevant that I find I cannot leave it out. Criticism of the political behavior of an historical figure of José de Diego's importance—and "to criticize is not to censure but rather to exercise the critical faculty," as José Martí used to say—should be interpreted as an effort, in the spirit of devotion to historical accuracy, to understand and pin down the reasons which determined the behavior of a whole sector of Puerto Rican society at a given moment. This behavior has been subject for half a century to the myth-making propensities of that sector's social and ideological heirs, and those of us who reply, or seek to reply, on behalf of the historical interests of the *other* Puerto Rican social class, the working class, shouldn't try to combat those earlier myths by inventing new myths. And *that*, unfortunately, as it seems to me, is what those two admirable researchers into Puerto Rican social history, Juan Flores and Ricardo Campos, have done in their essay entitled "Migración y cultura nacional puertorriqueños: perspectivas proletarias."* What Flores and Campos do in this essay is to contrast the mythical figure of the reactionary leader José de Diego with another mythical figure, the distinguished agitator and proletarian ideologue Ramón Romero Rosa. But had Flores and Campos borne in mind the fact that saints belong to religion and not to politics they would not have suppressed the fact that Romero Rosa, after giving great service to the Puerto Rican working class, wound up by joining the Unionist Party, which as we all know was the party of the opposing class. Flores and Campos obviously have no lack of pertinent information to explain all this and it is precisely for that reason that their essay, very

---

*Included in *Puerto Rico: Identidad nacional y classes sociales (Coloquio de Princeton)*, Ediciones Huracán, Río Piedras, 1979.

much worth attending to in every other respect, falls into a certain Manichaeism which is at odds with the essential justice of their argument. But to return to my subject . . .)

The Puerto Rican working class for its part also warmly welcomed the American invasion, but for very different reasons than those that had at the same time encouraged the property owners. For what the workers saw in the arrival of the Americans was an opportunity for an all-out *settling of scores* with the property-owning class on all fronts, and on the cultural front, which is the one that now immediately concerns us, this settling of scores has been the motive force for all the cultural changes in Puerto Rican society from 1898 until our own day. The often-denounced American cultural penetration of Puerto Rico has of course been a fact and I should be the last to deny it. But I refuse to agree that this penetration amounts to a "transculturation," which is to say to an "Americanization" understood as a "de-Puerto Ricanization," in the whole of our society. Furthermore, I am convinced that the causes and consequences of this penetration can only be fully understood in the context of the struggle, which in fact is only one aspect of the class struggle at the heart of our national society, between the "two cultures" of Puerto Rico.

The so-called Americanization of Puerto Rico has had two dialectically linked aspects. On the one hand it has obeyed *from without* an imperialist policy aimed at integrating Puerto Rican society into the American capitalist system as a dependent; but on the other hand it has corresponded *from within* to the struggle of the Puerto Rican masses against the hegemony of the property-owning class. The cultural achievements of this latter class under the Spanish colonial regime had, for reasons we have already explained, a liberal-bourgeois cast; but the new relation between social classes under the American regime obliged the property-owning class, marginated and expropriated by American capitalism, to abandon the liberalism of the professionals in that same class and to struggle for the conservation of its own cultural values. The cult of the land characteristic of the literature that the Puerto Rican élite has produced in this century no longer expresses, as is generally taught in literature courses in our university, a disinterested and lyrical sensibility moved by the beauties of our tropical landscape; what in fact it expresses is a very specific and historically determined nostalgic longing for a lost land—and not land in either a symbolic or a metaphorical but in a literal sense, as the medium for material production now in the hands of foreigners. In other words, those who could no longer continue "doing the rounds of the farm" astride the traditional horse now devoted themselves to "doing the rounds" astride a *décima*, short story, or novel. And, stretching the metaphor only a little, with the same patriarchal spirit as in "the good old days," they substituted for the work force of peons and sharecroppers a work force consisting of—their own readers!

What nonetheless complicates matters is the fact that at the time of the American invasion a very important part of the landowning class in Puerto Rico consisted not so much of Puerto Ricans as of Spaniards, Corsicans, Majorcans, Catalans, and so on. All these landowners were seen by the Puerto Rican masses for what they were: foreigners and exploiters. It was precisely this social world that the three protagonists of *Los soles truncos* longed for, idealizing that world to the point of mythification. And to pass off this world as the world of "Puerto Ricanness," at grips with "American adulteration," not only constitutes a flagrant misrepresentation of the historical truth but also (and this is truly serious) an aggression against the Puerto Ricanness of the popular masses, whose ancestors, in many cases within living memory, lived in that world as slaves, squatters, or peons. Hence, just as the cultural values of the property-owning class helped them to resist "Americanization," so that same "Americanization" has helped the masses to oppose and supplant the cultural values of the property-owning class. But it helped not only the popular masses (and I think this should be emphasized) but also certain very important elements of that same property-owning class oppressed from within their own class, particularly women. For who can deny that the women's liberation movement in Puerto Rico, essentially progressive and just, in spite of any limitations that can be alleged against it, has been in very great measure the result of the "Americanization" of Puerto Rican society?

The prevailing ignorance or underestimation of these realities has had a baleful consequence: the idea put forward and spread by the traditional independence movement, that independence is necessary to protect and shore up a national cultural identity that the Puerto Rican masses have never felt as *their* true identity. Why have these advocates of independence been accused again and again of wanting to "return to the Spanish era"? Why have poor Puerto Ricans and black Puerto Ricans been conspicuous by their absence from the ranks of the traditional independence movement, whereas they have flocked into the populist annexationist movement? The traditional independence movement has usually answered the last question by saying that black Puerto Ricans who support annexation have become "alienated" as a result of colonialism. And their reasoning runs as follows: if black Puerto Ricans wish to become part of a racist society like that of the United States, then such an "aberration" can only be explained as a symptom of alienation.

However, those who reason thus either don't know or have forgotten an elementary historical truth: the experience of racism of Puerto Rican blacks came not from American, but from Puerto Rican society. In other words, those who have discriminated against blacks *in Puerto Rico* haven't been Americans, but white Puerto Ricans, many of whom moreover have always taken conspicuous pride in their foreign ancestry (Spanish, Catalan, Majorcan, etc.). What a Puerto Rican black, or for that matter what any poor Puerto Rican, even a white (and everyone knows that there has always been a much higher proportion of poor people among the blacks than whites) understands by "returning to the Spanish era" is this: returning to a society in which the white and property-owning part of the population has always oppressed and despised the nonwhite and non-property-owning part. For in fact how many black or poor Puerto Ricans could ever participate, even as simple voters, in Puerto Rican political life throughout the Spanish era? To be a voter in those days one had to be a property owner or a taxpayer as well as knowing how to read and write, and how many black Puerto Ricans, or poor Puerto Ricans of any sort, could meet those requirements?

And we won't even mention what it cost a black man to become a political *leader*. There is Barbosa, of course—but who else? And then it wasn't just plain Barbosa, it was *Doctor* Barbosa. And where did Barbosa study medicine? Not in Puerto Rico, where Spain never permitted the founding of a university, nor in Spain itself, where Puerto Rican students were invariably the sons of landowners or white professionals, but in the United States, more specifically in Michigan, a northern state with an old abolitionist tradition—all of which easily explains many of the things that the traditional supporters of independence may never have been able to understand about Barbosa and his annexationism. So that, in short, if the traditional Puerto Rican independence movement this century has been—in political, social, and cultural terms—a conservative ideology, engaged in the defense of the values of the old propertied class, then why on earth blame "alienation" for the failure of the masses to support that independence movement? Who have been and really still are the "alienated" in a true historical sense?

But when we turn to popular culture we have to admit that this culture, too, has in the course of its historical development seldom been homogeneous. For the first and much of the second hundred years of colonial life the mass of laborers, both in the countryside and in the towns, was concentrated near the coasts, most of them being black or mulatto and with a preponderance of slaves over free men. Later this proportion became inverted and freed blacks and mulattos outnumbered slaves until the abolition of slavery in 1873 formally put an end to the latter's inferior status. The earliest popular culture in Puerto Rico was therefore basically Afro-Antillean. The white *campesinado*, which came into being at a later

date and then mainly in the mountainous central region of the island, produced a variant of the popular culture which developed in a relatively
autonomous way, until the decline in coffee production in the mountains
coinciding with the boom in sugar production in the coastal plains caused
a major population shift from the "uplands" to the "lowlands." From that
point on, the two currents of the popular culture flowed into one channel,
but with a clear predominance of the Afro-Antillean current, for demographic, social, and economic reasons.

The conservative marginated landowners, however, misrepresented
these new social realities in their own literary production, proclaiming
that the popular culture of the white peasantry was *the* popular culture
par excellence. The literary "*jíbarismo*" of the élite has been nothing else
at bottom than that class's statement of its own racial and social prejudice. And so in the Puerto Rico of our own day, where the *jíbaro* has
virtually ceased to have any demographic, economic, or cultural significance, the myth of the Puerto Rican as essentially a *jíbaro* stubbornly
survives—whenever the old conservative élite, whether openly or covertly
racist, sets pen to paper. And this at a time when it is really the proletarian Puerto Rican of mixed race who increasingly typifies popular
society!

In short, each time the ideological spokesmen for the old conservative élite accuse the Puerto Rican popular masses of "alienation," "un-
awareness," or "loss of identity," all they are doing is to betray their own
lack of confidence and their own alienation from those who, little though
some people like having to admit it, constitute the immense majority of
Puerto Ricans. What is more, those ideological spokesmen have done
something equally negative and counterproductive: they have convinced
many foreigners of good will, who are sympathetic to our independence,
that the Puerto Rican people are the object of "cultural genocide." A particularly sad victim of this "anti-imperialist" propaganda, which is really
nothing but the swan song of a dying social class, has been the outstanding Cuban revolutionary poet Nicolás Guillén, whose "Canción
puertorriqueña," as ill informed as it is well intentioned, has spread around
the world the image of a culturally hybrid people capable of expressing
themselves only in a ridiculous stutter of English and Spanish. All Puerto
Ricans, whether supporters of independence or not, know that this vision
of the cultural situation in Puerto Rico bears no relation whatsoever to
the truth. And there are so many good reasons to justify Puerto Rico's
independence that one cannot forgive an attempt to justify it by a reason
that is patently false.

In my view, the good cultural reason for supporting independence is
that independence is absolutely necessary to protect, orient, and secure

the full development of Puerto Rico's true national identity, the identity that has its roots in that popular culture which the independence move-ment—if it *really* aspires to represent the authentic national will in this country—must understand and espouse without conditions or scruples born of distrust or prejudice. What is really happening in Puerto Rico today is the spectacular and irrevocable disintegration of that *fourth storey* which an advanced American capitalism and an opportunistic Puerto Rican popu-lism began to build onto the island's social structure from the 1940s on. The patent collapse of the idea of the *Estado Libre Asociado*, or Com-monwealth, clearly demonstrates, if we view it from what seems to me the right historical perspective, that American colonialism, after sponsor-ing widespread economic transformations fundamentally in order to sat-isfy the needs of an expansionist imperialist economy at home, thereby creating a very real modernization-within-dependency in Puerto Rican society, can now only lead this society into a dead-end street and into a generalized malaise, whose rightly alarming symptoms are everywhere to be seen: massive unemployment and margination; a demoralizing de-pendence on a false generosity from abroad; an uncontrollable upsurge in delinquency and criminality, to a great extent of foreign provenance; a disenchantment with politics and civic irresponsibility resulting from in-stitutionalized demagoguery; and a whole Pandora's box of social ills that you know better than I, since you must live with them every day.

But to speak of the *present* bankruptcy of the colonial regime in no way implies that such a regime was a "good" regime until recently and only now becomes "bad." What I am trying to say—and it matters a great deal to me not to be misunderstood—is that the eighty years of American domination in Puerto Rico represent the history of a political and eco-nomic undertaking whose immediate stages were viable *as they occurred*, but which were inevitably doomed, as indeed is any historical undertak-ing based on colonial dependency, to founder *in the long run* into the state of *un*viability in which we are now living. This unviability of the colonial regime is precisely what for the first time in our history makes national independence viable. And not merely viable, but also, as I have just argued, absolutely necessary.

Those of us both from within and without our country committed to a socialist future for Puerto Rico have before us the daunting task of nei-ther more nor less than the total reconstruction of Puerto Rican society. (And when I speak of "a socialist future for Puerto Rico" I speak, as you should already know, of a *democratic* socialism, pluralist and indepen-dent, which is the only socialism worthy of the name, and not of that other "socialism" which is bureaucratic, monolithic, and authoritarian, and instituted *in the name* only of the working class by a new ruling class one can only call a state bourgeoisie, since it is the real proprietor of the means of production, held by virtue of the at-once immovable and all-powerful "apparatus" of the state.) My well-known disagreement with the traditional independence movement in this respect is a disagreement between two conceptions of the historical aims of such a reconstruction of Puerto Rican society. I do not believe in reconstructing backward, to a past bequeathed us by Spanish colonialism and an old élite irrevocably condemned by history. I believe instead in reconstructing forward, toward a future as defined by the best proletarian socialists in Puerto Rico early in this century when they advocated a national independence capable of organizing the country into "an industrial democracy governed by the workers"; toward a future which, basing itself on the cultural tradition of the popular masses, will rediscover and redeem the essentially *Caribbean* nature of our collective identity and thereby acknowledge, once and for all, that the natural destiny of Puerto Rico is identical to that of all the other Caribbean peoples, whether they hail from the islands or from the mainland.

In this sense I conceive the national independence of all these peoples as merely a prerequisite—albeit the indispensable prerequisite—for achieving a great confederation that will definitively unite us in a just, effective, joint organization at the economic, political, and cultural levels. Only by means of such an organization may we take our rightful place within the greater communities of Latin America and the world. In economic matters, far from being merely an utopian wish, such unity is an objective necessity. In political matters, it answers to a manifest historical imperative, which is the liquidation of our common colonial past by establishing popular and noncapitalist regimes. And in cultural matters, which is what now specifically concerns us, it is essential for us so that we may recognize and *assume* a reality that even the most concerned among us have consistently ignored.

10

Afro-Creole Social
Consciousness Movements

Consciousness-raising, according to the well-known Trinidadian author V. S. Naipaul, protects a persecuted social group from extermination.* Afro-Creoles, in spite of discrimination, prejudice, and the lack of economic and political power, have continuously asserted their rights. Their heritage began with slaves, runaways, free blacks, and mulattoes who resisted in whatever ways they could. After abolition, they turned to movements for racial consciousness, cultural rejuvenation, civil rights, and social justice that reached one culmination in the 1920s-era of black power and consciousness-raising. Hemispheric leaders, such as the Jamaican-born Marcus Garvey, called on Africans to return home to Africa. Other activists, such as the Cuban Nicolás Guillén and the Martinican Aimé Césaire, demanded respect for and appreciation of the African cultural inheritance. The Pan-African movements identified Latin America as an integral part of the struggle for the rights of Afro-Creoles.

Cultural reaffirmation and civil rights movements led by peoples of African descent emerged in the French-, Spanish-, and English-speaking Caribbean, Hispanic America, and Brazil. This chapter includes four selections that represent distinctive civil rights movements, although they share a common defiance and call to action.

The Negritude movement championed the African race throughout the world. In one of the most important cultural revolutions of the twentieth century, black intellectuals became intent on exposing the racist attitudes that excluded black people from mainstream society, and they were determined to educate society about the African contributions to American civilization. Further encouragement for this black movement came from Oswald Spengler's prediction of the collapse of the West.† Writers

---

*See *India: A Wounded Civilization* (New York: Alfred A. Knopf, 1977), 168.

†See *The Decline of the West* (New York: Alfred A. Knopf, 1926). Spengler, who believed in cyclical patterns of civilization, predicted the imminent fall of European culture.

from the French Caribbean anticipated the renaissance of those cultures, especially African ones, that had been suppressed by Western civilization. They found confirmation of their forecasts in New York City's Harlem Renaissance, but they could not shed their dependence on Paris as their artistic center. In 1932, Césaire, from Paris, helped establish the journal Légitime Défense, *which demanded recognition of African traditions and praised writers such as Langston Hughes as worthy models. This appreciation of black culture, combined with a passionate attack on white European culture, became known as the Negritude movement.*

In the Spanish-speaking Caribbean, the Afro-Creole consciousness movements began to appear in the 1930s. Advocates such as Guillén chose to emphasize the mulatto nature of the Caribbean and called for cooperation rather than confrontation with whites. By the 1980s more defiant and well-organized Afro-Creole consciousness movements emerged in Venezuela, Colombia, Ecuador, and throughout Central America, calling for an end to discrimination. Many Afro-Creole activists argued that mestizaje, *or race mixing, had made it difficult to forge a consciousness among the Afro-Creole communities since individuals preferred to identify with the dominant mestizo or white society.*

Guillén achieved a balance between mestizaje *and black power. He recognized Cuba's mulatto nature while condemning its discrimination against blacks. A Communist Party member for most of his life, he saw the Afro-Cuban struggle as part of the international proletarian movement. His party affiliation resulted in a brief jail term and his decision to spend most of the 1950s in exile; he returned to Cuba only after the success of Fidel Castro's revolution in 1959. Ultimately, Castro honored him as Cuba's National Poet. Describing his work as mulatto poetry, Guillén wrote about the contributions of both Europeans and blacks to Cuba's culture. But, perhaps because of his friendship with Haiti's Jacques Roumain and other Negritude writers, his poetry increasingly portrayed the suffering of Cuban blacks and emphasized their part in building the national culture. He dedicated poems to Roumain, the Cuban labor organizer Jesús Menéndez Larrondo, and the U.S. lynching victim Emett Till.* *
Although he believed in the Cuban Revolution, he wanted to represent the aspirations of all blacks and mulattoes.

Artists such as Guillén and Césaire tried to create a "black art" that would serve as the instrument of liberation. These Negritude writers, even when they romanticized the soul of Africa as a dialectic force that would

---

*See Guillén's *Elegía a Jacques Roumain en el cielo de Haiti* (Havana: Imp. Ayon, 1948); *Elegía a Jesús Menéndez* (Havana: Editorial Págines, 1951). The poem to Emett Till is found in Guillén's *Las grandes elegías y otros poemas* (Caracas: Biblioteca Ayacucho, 1984), pp. 21–22. The 1955 lynching of fourteen-year-old Till is the subject of Steve Whitfield's historical study, *A Death in the Delta* (New York: The Free Press, 1988), and Lewis Nordan's novel, *Wolf Whistle* (Chapel Hill, NC: Algonquin Books, 1993).

replace the white man's preoccupation with reason, nevertheless provided an abrupt awakening for the West to the African contribution to world culture. Césaire, the outstanding author in this movement, expressed the feelings of Afro-Creoles in the Spanish- and French-speaking Caribbean. The selection that follows demonstrates his passionate commitment to the "colonized" peoples.

In the English- and Spanish-speaking Caribbean, Jamaican-born Marcus Garvey emerged in the 1920s as the best-known spokesman for Pan-African consciousness and black civil rights. Garvey, who emigrated to the United States, had previously traveled extensively in Central America. He founded two Afro-Creole publications, La Nacionale *in Costa Rica and* La Prensa *in Panama, to promote decolonization by urging the return to Africa. He campaigned on behalf of the African diaspora throughout the world, and his ideas inspired the Jamaican-African consciousness and religious organization, Rastafarianism. He is profiled here by Kenneth Ramchand, who offers excerpts from Garvey's writings.*

Garvey constantly urged Africans in the Americas to look to their homeland for a new king. When Ras Tafari was crowned King Haile Selassie of Ethiopia in 1930, black Jamaican intellectuals and activists such as Joseph Nathaniel Hilbert praised Garvey as a prophet and declared themselves Rastafarians. Jamaica at the time remained a colony of Great Britain, and the Rastafarians initiated a five-part campaign that affirmed: 1) the anticolonialist movement; 2) African culture; 3) the divinity of Haile Selassie as a direct descendant of King Solomon; 4) the music of revelation; and 5) the ceremonial use of marijuana. When the island gained its independence in 1962, Rastafarianism became synonymous with national freedom. The evolution of the music into modern reggae and the rise in popularity of its musicians, especially Bob Marley,* created an international movement of Rastafarians throughout the Caribbean and in Brazil and Central, South, and North America. Leonard Barrett provides a brief historical account of the Rastafarians in Jamaica.

In Brazil, black movements influenced by Garvey and other outspoken Afro-Creoles emerged during the era of Getúlio Vargas (1930–1954). The 1930s and 1940s, a period of intense nationalism, witnessed the rise of popular black social movements that began to challenge seriously the status quo. Founded on September 16, 1931, the Frente Negra Brasileira, the first major mobilization of blacks, called for the right to work and freedom from discrimination. By 1936 it had attained enough support to register as a political party. When President Vargas created the Estado Novo in 1937, a dictatorship that lasted until 1945, he shackled all social movements and abolished all political parties.

---

*For more information on Bob Marley's role in promoting Rastafarianism, contact the Bob Marley Museum, 56 Hope Road, Kingston, Jamaica. The museum's curator is Marley's sister.

The Afro-Brazilian social campaign reemerged after the demise of the Estado Novo. In the late 1940s, under the banner of the Teatro Experimental do Negro (T.E.N.), Afro-Brazilians made a determined effort to raise consciousness among all Brazilians by condemning racism and prejudice as well as by stressing the African contributions to Brazilian culture. T.E.N. attempted to forge an Afrocentric aesthetic through art, poetry, and beauty competitions. The movement endured until the military seized power in 1964, and even then many of its members continued to speak out in the 1970s and 1980s.

Today, a new generation of Afro-Brazilians continues the campaign. Racially conscious movements are especially strong in the Bahia region, where Afro-Creole women have played a significant role in these organizations. Moreover, Brazil's black-consciousness movements maintain close connections with the Pan-African struggle for human rights. At the First Congress on Black Culture in the Americas, held in 1977 in Cali, Colombia, Brazilian Abdias do Nascimento spoke on the need for continued efforts to raise black consciousness and for cooperation among all Afro-Creoles; his address is reprinted here.

Aimé Césaire ◆ Discourse on Colonialism

Born in Martinique in 1913, Aimé Césaire is one of the most eloquent writers of the French language. He, along with Sedar Sengor of Senegal, founded the Negritude movement in Paris in the 1930s. Césaire went on to become a deputy for Martinique in the French National Assembly. He is an essayist, dramatist, and poet and has continued to write on the African presence in and contribution to the Americas.

A civilization that proves incapable of solving the problems it creates is a decadent civilization.

A civilization that chooses to close its eyes to its most crucial problems is a stricken civilization.

A civilization that uses its principles for trickery and deceit is a dying civilization.

The fact is that the so-called European civilization—"Western" civilization—as it has been shaped by two centuries of bourgeois rule, is incapable of solving the two major problems to which its existence has given rise: the problem of the proletariat and the colonial problem; that Europe is unable to justify itself either before the bar of "reason" or before the bar of "conscience"; and that, increasingly, it takes refuge in a hypocrisy which is all the more odious because it is less and less likely to deceive.

Europe is indefensible.

Apparently that is what the American strategists are whispering to each other.

That in itself is not serious.

What is serious is that "Europe" is morally, spiritually indefensible.

And today the indictment is brought against it not by the European masses alone, but on a world scale, by tens and tens of millions of men who, from the depths of slavery, set themselves up as judges.

The colonialists may kill in Indochina, torture in Madagascar, imprison in Black Africa, crack down in the West Indies. Henceforth the colonized know that they have an advantage over them. They know that their temporary "masters" are lying.

Therefore [they know] that their masters are weak.

And since I have been asked to speak about colonization and civilization, let us go straight to the principal lie which is the source of all the others.

From *Discourse on Colonialism* (New York: Monthly Review Press, 1972), 9–25. © 1972 by Monthly Review Press. Reprinted by permission of Monthly Review Foundation.

Colonization and civilization?

In dealing with this subject, the commonest curse is to be the dupe in good faith of a collective hypocrisy that cleverly misrepresents problems, the better to legitimize the hateful solutions provided for them.

In other words, the essential thing here is to see clearly, to think clearly—that is, dangerously—and to answer clearly the innocent first question: what, fundamentally, is colonization? To agree on what it is not: neither evangelization, nor a philanthropic enterprise, nor a desire to push back the frontiers of ignorance, disease, and tyranny, nor a project undertaken for the greater glory of God, nor an attempt to extend the rule of law. To admit once [and] for all, without flinching at the consequences, that the decisive actors here are the adventurer and the pirate, the whole-sale grocer and the shipowner, the gold digger and the merchant, appetite and force, and behind them, the baleful projected shadow of a form of civilization which, at a certain point in its history, finds itself obliged, for internal reasons, to extend to a world scale the competition of its antago-nistic economies.

Pursuing my analysis, I find that hypocrisy is of recent date; that neither Cortez discovering Mexico from the top of the great teocalli, nor Pizarro before Cuzco (much less Marco Polo before Cambaluc), claims that he is the harbinger of a superior order; that they kill; that they plun-der; that they have helmets, lances, cupidities; that the slavering apolo-gists came later; that the chief culprit in this domain is Christian pedantry, which laid down the dishonest equations *Christianity = civilization, pa-ganism = savagery*, from which there could not but ensue abominable colonialist and racist consequences, whose victims were to be the Indi-ans, the yellow peoples, and the Negroes.

That being settled, I admit that it is a good thing to place different civilizations in contact with each other; that it is an excellent thing to blend different worlds; that whatever its own particular genius may be, a civilization that withdraws into itself atrophies; that for civilizations, ex-change is oxygen; that the great good fortune of Europe is to have been a crossroads, and that because it was the locus of all ideas, the receptacle of all philosophies, the meeting place of all sentiments, it was the best center for the redistribution of energy.

But then I ask the following question: has colonization really *placed civilizations in contact*? Or, if you prefer, of all the ways of *establishing contact*, was it the best?

I answer *no*.

And I say that between *colonization* and *civilization* there is an infi-nite distance; that out of all the colonial expeditions that have been un-dertaken, out of all the colonial statutes that have been drawn up, out of

all the memoranda that have been despatched by all the ministries, there
could not come a single human value.

First, we must study how colonization works to *decivilize* the colonizer, to *brutalize* him in the true sense of the word, to degrade him, to
awaken him to buried instincts, to covetousness, violence, race hatred,
and moral relativism; and we must show that each time a head is cut off
or an eye put out in Vietnam and in France they accept the fact, each time
a little girl is raped and in France they accept the fact, each time a
Madagascan is tortured and in France they accept the fact, civilization
acquires another dead weight, a universal regression takes place, a gan-
grene sets in, a center of infection begins to spread; and that at the end of
all these treaties that have been violated, all these lies that have been
propagated, all these punitive expeditions that have been tolerated, all
these prisoners who have been tied up and "interrogated," all these patriots who have been tortured, at the end of all the racial pride that has been
encouraged, all the boastfulness that has been displayed, a poison has
been instilled into the veins of Europe and, slowly but surely, the continent proceeds toward *savagery*.

And then one fine day the bourgeoisie is awakened by a terrific reverse shock: the gestapos are busy, the prisons fill up, the torturers around
the racks invent, refine, discuss.

People are surprised, they become indignant. They say: "How strange!
But never mind—it's Nazism, it will pass!" And they wait, and they hope;
and they hide the truth from themselves, that it is barbarism, but the supreme barbarism, the crowning barbarism that sums up all the daily bar-
barisms; that it is Nazism, yes, but that before they were its victims, they
were its accomplices; that they tolerated that Nazism before it was inflicted on them, that they absolved it, shut their eyes to it, legitimized it,
because, until then, it had been applied only to non-European peoples;
that they have cultivated that Nazism, that they are responsible for it, and
that before engulfing the whole of Western, Christian civilization in its
reddened waters, it oozes, seeps, and trickles from every crack.

Yes, it would be worthwhile to study clinically, in detail, the steps
taken by Hitler and Hitlerism and to reveal to the very distinguished, very
humanistic, very Christian bourgeois of the twentieth century that without his being aware of it, he has a Hitler inside him, that Hitler *inhabits*
him, that Hitler is his *demon*, that if he rails against him, he is being
inconsistent and that, at bottom, what he cannot forgive Hitler for is not
crime in itself, *the crime against man*, it is not *the humiliation of man as
such*, it is the crime against the white man, the humiliation of the white

man, and the fact that he applied to Europe colonialist procedures which until then had been reserved exclusively for the Arabs of Algeria, the coolies of India, and the blacks of Africa.

And that is the great thing I hold against pseudo-humanism: that for too long it has diminished the rights of man, that its concept of those rights has been—and still is—narrow and fragmentary, incomplete and biased, and, all things considered, sordidly racist.

I have talked a good deal about Hitler. Because he deserves it: he makes it possible to see things on a large scale and to grasp the fact that capitalist society, at its present stage, is incapable of establishing a concept of the rights of all men, just as it has proved incapable of establishing a system of individual ethics. Whether one likes it or not, at the end of the blind alley that is Europe, I mean the Europe of Adenauer, Schuman, Bidault, and a few others, there is Hitler. At the end of capitalism, which is eager to outlive its day, there is Hitler. At the end of formal humanism and philosophic renunciation, there is Hitler.

And this being so, I cannot help thinking of one of his statements: "We aspire not to equality but to domination. The country of a foreign race must become once again a country of serfs, of agricultural laborers, or industrial workers. It is not a question of eliminating the inequalities among men but of widening them and making them into a law."

That rings clear, haughty, and brutal and plants us squarely in the middle of howling savagery. But let us come down a step.

Who is speaking? I am ashamed to say it: it is the Western *humanist*, the "idealist" philosopher. That his name is [Joseph Ernest] Renan is an accident. That the passage is taken from a book entitled *La Réforme intellectuelle et morale* [(1872)], that it was written in France just after a war which France had represented as a war of right against might, tells us a great deal about bourgeois morals.

> The regeneration of the inferior or degenerate races by the superior races is part of the providential order of things for humanity. With us, the common man is nearly always a déclassé nobleman, his heavy hand is better suited to handling the sword than the menial tool. Rather than work, he chooses to fight, that is, he returns to his first estate. *Regere imperio populos*, that is our vocation. Pour forth this all-consuming activity onto countries which, like China, are crying aloud for foreign conquest. Turn the adventurers who disturb European society into a *ver sacrum*, a horde like those of the Franks, the Lombards, or the Normans, and every man will be in his right role. Nature has made a race of workers, the Chinese race, who have wonderful manual dexterity and almost no sense of honor; govern them with justice, levying from them, in return for the blessing of such a government, an ample allowance for the

conquering race, and they will be satisfied; a race of tillers of the soil, the Negro; treat him with kindness and humanity, and all will be as it should; a race of masters and soldiers, the European race. Reduce this noble race to working in the *ergastulum* like Negroes and Chinese, and they rebel. In Europe, every rebel is, more or less, a soldier who has missed his calling, a creature made for the heroic life, before whom you are setting *a task that is contrary to his race*—a poor worker, too good a soldier. But the life at which our workers rebel would make a Chinese or a fellah happy, as they are not military creatures in the least. *Let each one do what he is made for, and all will be well.*

Hitler? Rosenberg? No, Renan.

But let us come down one step further. And it is the long-winded politician. Who protests? No one, so far as I know, when M. Albert Sarraut, the former governor-general of Indochina, holding forth to the students at the Ecole Coloniale, teaches them that it would be puerile to object to the European colonial enterprises in the name of "an alleged right to possess the land one occupies, and some sort of right to remain in fierce isolation, which would leave unutilized resources to lie forever idle in the hands of incompetents."

And who is roused to indignation when a certain Rev. Barde assures us that if the goods of this world "remained divided up indefinitely, as they would be without colonization, they would answer neither the purposes of God nor the just demands of the human collectivity"?

Since, as his fellow Christian, the Rev. Muller, declares: "Humanity must not, cannot allow the incompetence, negligence, and laziness of the uncivilized peoples to leave idle indefinitely the wealth which God has confided to them, charging them to make it serve the good of all."

No one.

I mean not one established writer, not one academician, not one preacher, not one crusader for the right and for religion, not one "defender of the human person."

And yet, through the mouths of the Sarrauts and the Bardes, the Mullers and the Renans, through the mouths of all those who considered—and consider—it lawful to apply to non-European peoples "a kind of expropriation for public purposes" for the benefit of nations that were stronger and better equipped, it was already Hitler speaking!

What am I driving at? At this idea: that no one colonizes innocently, that no one colonizes with impunity, either; that a nation which colonizes, that a civilization which justifies colonization—and therefore force—is already a sick civilization, a civilization that is morally diseased, that irresistibly, progressing from one consequence to another, one repudiation to another, calls for its Hitler, I mean its punishment.

Colonization: bridgehead in a campaign to civilize barbarism, from which there may emerge at any moment the negation of civilization, pure and simple.

Elsewhere I have cited at length a few incidents culled from the history of colonial expeditions.

Unfortunately, this did not find favor with everyone. It seems that I was pulling old skeletons out of the closet. Indeed!

Was there no point in quoting Colonel de Montagnac, one of the conquerors of Algeria: "In order to banish the thoughts that sometimes besiege me, I have some heads cut off, not the heads of artichokes but the heads of men"?

Would it have been more advisable to refuse the floor to Count d'Hérisson: "It is true that we are bringing back a whole barrelful of ears collected, pair by pair, from prisoners, friendly or enemy"?

Should I have refused Saint-Arnaud the right to profess his barbarous faith: "We lay waste, we burn, we plunder, we destroy the houses and the trees"?

Should I have prevented Marshal Bugeaud from systematizing all that in a daring theory and invoking the precedent of famous ancestors: "We must have a great invasion of Africa, like the invasions of the Franks and the Goths"?

Lastly, should I have cast back into the shadows of oblivion the memorable feat of arms of General Gérard and kept silent about the capture of Ambike, a city which, to tell the truth, had never dreamed of defending itself: "The native riflemen had orders to kill only the men, but no one restrained them; intoxicated by the smell of blood, they spared not one woman, not one child. . . . At the end of the afternoon, the heat caused a light mist to arise: it was the blood of the five thousand victims, the ghost of the city, evaporating in the setting sun"?

Yes or no, are these things true? And the sadistic pleasures, the nameless delights that send voluptuous shivers and quivers through Loti's carcass when he focuses his field glasses on a good massacre of the Annamese? True or not true?* And if these things are true, as no one can

---

*This is a reference to the account of the taking of Thuan-An [in Indochina] which appeared in *Le Figaro* in September 1883 and is quoted in N. Serban's book, *Loti, sa vie, son oeuvre*. "Then the great slaughter had begun. They had fired in double-salvos! and it was a pleasure to see these sprays of bullets, that were so easy to aim, come down on them twice a minute, surely and methodically, on command. . . . We saw some who were quite mad and stood up seized with a dizzy desire to run. . . . They zigzagged, running every which way in this race with death, holding their garments up around their waists in a comical way . . . and then we amused ourselves counting the dead, etc."

deny, will it be said, in order to minimize them, that these corpses don't prove anything?

For my part, if I have recalled a few details of these hideous butcheries, it is by no means because I take a morbid delight in them, but because I think that these heads of men, these collections of ears, these burned houses, these Gothic invasions, this steaming blood, these cities that evaporate at the edge of the sword, are not to be so easily disposed of. They prove that colonization, I repeat, dehumanizes even the most civilized man; that colonial activity, colonial enterprise, colonial conquest, which is based on contempt for the native and justified by that contempt, inevitably tends to change him who undertakes it; that the colonizer, who in order to ease his conscience gets into the habit of seeing the other man as *an animal*, accustoms himself to treating him like an animal, and tends objectively to transform *himself* into an animal. It is the result, this boomerang effect of colonization, that I wanted to point out.

Unfair? No. There was a time when these same facts were a source of pride, and when, sure of the morrow, people did not mince words. One last quotation: it is from a certain Carl Siger, author of an *Essai sur la colonisation* (Paris, 1907):

> The new countries offer a vast field for individual, violent activities which, in the metropolitan countries, would run up against certain prejudices, against a sober and orderly conception of life, and which, in the colonies, have greater freedom to develop and, consequently, to affirm their worth. Thus to a certain extent the colonies can serve as a safety valve for modern society. Even if this were their only value, it would be immense.

Truly, there are stains that it is beyond the power of man to wipe out and that can never be fully expiated.

But let us speak about the colonized.

I see clearly what colonization has destroyed: the wonderful Indian civilizations—and neither Deterding nor Royal Dutch nor Standard Oil will ever console me for the Aztecs and the Incas.

I see clearly the civilizations, condemned to perish at a future date, into which it has introduced a principle of ruin: the South Sea islands, Nigeria, Nyasaland. I see less clearly the contributions it has made.

Security? Culture? The rule of law? In the meantime, I look around and wherever there are colonizers and colonized face to face, I see force, brutality, cruelty, sadism, conflict, and, in a parody of education, the hasty manufacture of a few thousand subordinate functionaries, "boys," artisans, office clerks, and interpreters necessary for the smooth operation of business.

I spoke of contact.

Between colonizer and colonized there is room only for forced labor, intimidation, pressure, the police, taxation, theft, rape, compulsory crops, contempt, mistrust, arrogance, self-complacency, swinishness, brainless élites, degraded masses.

No human contact, but relations of domination and submission which turn the colonizing man into a classroom monitor, an army sergeant, a prison guard, a slave driver, and the indigenous man into an instrument of production.

My turn to state an equation: colonization = "thingification."

I hear the storm. They talk to me about progress, about "achievements," diseases cured, improved standards of living.

I am talking about societies drained of their essence, cultures trampled underfoot, institutions undermined, lands confiscated, religions smashed, magnificent artistic creations destroyed, extraordinary *possibilities* wiped out.

They throw facts at my head, statistics, mileages of roads, canals, and railroad tracks.

I am talking about thousands of men sacrificed to the Congo-Océan.* I am talking about those who, as I write this, are digging the harbor of Abidjan by hand. I am talking about millions of men torn from their gods, their land, their habits, their life—from life, from the dance, from wisdom.

I am talking about millions of men in whom fear has been cunningly instilled, who have been taught to have an inferiority complex, to tremble, kneel, despair, and behave like flunkeys.

They dazzle me with the tonnage of cotton or cocoa that has been exported, the acreage that has been planted with olive trees or grapevines.

I am talking about natural *economies* that have been disrupted— harmonious and viable *economies* adapted to the indigenous population— about food crops destroyed, malnutrition permanently introduced, agricultural development oriented solely toward the benefit of the metropolitan countries, about the looting of products, the looting of raw materials.

They pride themselves on abuses eliminated.

I too talk about abuses, but what I say is that on the old ones—very real—they have superimposed others—very detestable. They talk to me about local tyrants brought to reason; but I note that in general the old tyrants get on very well with the new ones, and that there has been established between them, to the detriment of the people, a circuit of mutual services and complicity.

---

*A railroad line connecting Brazzaville with the port of Pointe-Noire (trans.).

They talk to me about civilization. I talk about proletarianization and mystification.

For my part, I make a systematic defense of the non-European civilizations.

Every day that passes, every denial of justice, every beating by the police, every demand of the workers that is drowned in blood, every scandal that is hushed up, every punitive expedition, every police van, every gendarme and every militiaman, brings home to us the value of our old societies.

They were communal societies, never societies of the many for the few.

They were societies that were not only ante-capitalist, as has been said, but also *anti-capitalist.*

They were democratic societies, always.

They were cooperative societies, fraternal societies.

I make a systematic defense of the societies destroyed by imperialism.

They were the fact, they did not pretend to be the idea; despite their faults, they were neither to be hated nor condemned. They were content to be. In them, neither the word *failure* nor the word *avatar* had any meaning. They kept hope intact.

Whereas those are the only words that can, in all honesty, be applied to the European enterprises outside Europe. My only consolation is that periods of colonization pass, that nations sleep only for a time, and that peoples remain.

This being said, it seems that in certain circles they pretend to have discovered in me an "enemy of Europe" and a prophet of the return to the ante-European past.

For my part, I search in vain for the place where I could have expressed such views; where I ever underestimated the importance of Europe in the history of human thought; where I ever preached a *return* of any kind; where I ever claimed that there could be a *return.*

The truth is that I have said something very different: to wit, that the great historical tragedy of Africa has been not so much that it was too late in making contact with the rest of the world, as the manner in which that contact was brought about; that Europe began to "propagate" at a time when it had fallen into the hands of the most unscrupulous financiers and captains of industry; that it was our misfortune to encounter that particular Europe on our path; and that Europe is responsible before the human community for the highest heap of corpses in history.

In another connection, in judging colonization, I have added that Europe has gotten on very well indeed with all the local feudal lords who agreed to serve, woven a villainous complicity with them, rendered their tyranny more effective and more efficient, and that it has actually tended to prolong artificially the survival of local pasts in their most pernicious aspects.

I have said—and this is something very different—that colonialist Europe has grafted modern abuse onto ancient injustice, hateful racism onto old inequality.

That if I am attacked on the grounds of intent, I maintain that colonialist Europe is dishonest in trying to justify its colonizing activity *a posteriori* by the obvious material progress that has been achieved in certain fields under the colonial regime—since *sudden change* is always possible, in history as elsewhere; since no one knows at what stage of material development these same countries would have been if Europe had not intervened; since the technical outfitting of Africa and Asia, their administrative reorganization, in a word, their "Europeanization," was (as is proved by the example of Japan) in no way tied to the European *occupation*; since the Europeanization of the non-European continents could have been accomplished otherwise than under the heel of Europe; since this movement of Europeanization *was in progress*; since it was even slowed down; since in any case it was distorted by the European takeover.

The proof is that at present it is the indigenous peoples of Africa and Asia who are demanding schools, and colonialist Europe which refuses them; that it is the African who is asking for ports and roads, and colonialist Europe which is niggardly on this score; that it is the colonized man who wants to move forward, and the colonizer who holds things back.

Kenneth Ramchand ◆ Marcus Garvey and the African Dream

A scholar from Trinidad and Tobago, Kenneth Ramchand is a lecturer on West Indian literature at the University of the West Indies. He has published a number of works on the literature and society of the region, including his acclaimed An Introduction to the Study of West Indian Literature (1976).

In the first half of the twentieth century there sprang up in the Caribbean and in North America a number of movements in which people of African origin turned for support to that heritage and root. Their labor had sustained economies, and the right to belong had been dearly bought, but New World Negroes were not at ease in the Western societies to which their ancestors had been shipped. Emancipation, they were told, had come; but for the mass of Negroes it seemed long gone. The conditions under which they lived as supposedly free men were at least as demoralizing, especially after the First World War, as those their chained ancestors had endured.

> At no time in the history of the world, for the last five hundred years, was there ever a serious attempt made to free Negroes. We have been camouflaged into believing that we were made free by Abraham Lincoln, that we were made free by Victoria of England, but up to now we are still slaves, we are industrial slaves, we are social slaves, we are political slaves, and the New Negro desires a freedom that has no boundary, no limit.
> —*The Philosophy and Opinions of Marcus Garvey*

Of the movements that arose to bring emotional sustainment and practical support to the victims of this depressing scene, the most spectacular was that surrounding the Jamaican Marcus Mosiah Garvey, founder of the Universal Negro Improvement Association. Born a colonial on August 17, 1877, Garvey died an obscure exile in the British metropolis in 1940. Between these two dates, Garvey rose to fantastic eminence among Negroes in America. He was the Black Moses, the spiritual leader sent to lead his people out of bondage; he was also the maker of the political kingdom, His Excellency the Provisional President of Africa.

> I asked: "Where is the black man's Government? Where is his King and his kingdom? Where is his President, his country, and his ambassador, his army, his navy, his men of big affairs?" I could not find them, and then I declared: "I will help to make them. . . ." I saw before me then, even as I do now, a

From the *UNESCO Courier* 34 (December 1981): 42.

new world of black men, not peons, serfs, dogs and slaves, but a nation of sturdy men, making their impress upon civilization and causing a new light to dawn upon the human race.

—The Philosophy and Opinions of Marcus Garvey

At its height in the mid-1920s, Garvey's Association is estimated to have numbered between four and six million, with branches, members, or supporters in all the countries where there were people of African origin.

Garvey envisaged a day in the future when all Negroes would have returned to a united and independent Africa. In the meantime, however, New World Negroes could contribute to the creation of a free Africa to which they could look for protection as they journeyed in the world, and to which they could return if necessary: "a nation of our own, strong enough to lend protection to the members of our race scattered all over the world, and to compel the respect of the nations and races of the earth." In their adopted countries, at the same time, they could organize themselves "for the absolute purpose of bettering our condition, industrially, commercially, socially, religiously, and politically."

However, as a result of mismanagement, incompetence, greed, and corruption among his lieutenants, most of Garvey's economic projects foundered like the broken-down ships he was sold by white owners at black-market prices for his Black Star Shipping Line, which he intended to be the foundation of Negro trade and the symbol of repatriation.

His educational aims were more nearly successful, but not as he originally intended. After founding the Universal Negro Improvement Association in Jamaica in 1914, Garvey proposed the establishment of colleges for Jamaican Negroes on the model of Booker T. Washington's Tuskegee Institute. It was in order to consult with Washington himself on this project that Garvey planned the 1916 visit to America which led to the shifting of the base of his operations to the United States. His enduring educational enterprise, however, was the founding of the weekly *The Negro World*, which ran from 1918 to 1933. In its pages, Garveyism was expounded in detail, and readers were educated in the glories of African history and the heroism of Negro revolts, and the comparative savagery of European peoples.

When Europe was inhabited by a race of cannibals, a race of savages, hated men, heathens and pagans, Africa was peopled with a race of cultured black men, who were masters in art, science and literature; men who were cultured and refined; men who, it was said, were like the gods.

—The Philosophy and Opinions of Marcus Garvey

There were inconsistencies and confusions in Garvey's thinking and in his actions, and it would be easy to use these to condemn him as an extremist and a crackpot, as many Negro intellectuals did at the time. His island antagonism toward the brown and light-skinned class of Jamaica was transferred to the Negro intelligentsia, whom he invariably saw as lackeys of white America.

He cooperated for a time with the Ku Klux Klan because he shared with them the wish for racial purity and the emigration of the Negro from the United States. Always rash and undiplomatic, Garvey skirmished with authority many times until at last they did for him, convicting him on a flimsy and put-up charge of using the U.S. mail to defraud investors in the Black Star Shipping Line. Garvey was deported from the United States in 1928 and returned to Jamaica where his brown and light-skinned antagonists were waiting. Humiliated at home, the failing prophet went into exile in England where he died a beaten and disillusioned man.

In 1964, Garvey's body was disinterred from its London tomb and returned to Jamaican soil. Several years later he was officially proclaimed a National Hero. Even before this, both his contemporaries and those who never experienced his movement had begun to separate the follies and foibles of this vain, egotistical, and insecure man from his enduring achievements.

Those elements in his philosophy or opinions that were sound were not new, many of them having been put forward by Negro intellectuals or men of letters of some of whom Garvey had probably never heard. Yet this skillful orator, showman, and propagandist *extraordinaire* communicated with ordinary Negroes and touched their hurts as no one had done before. Nobody before Garvey had been able to organize a mass movement of such size and enthusiasm from the vast Negro proletariat. Nobody had so stirred their imagination. "I shall teach the black man to see beauty in himself." Nobody had given them such self-esteem.

Leonard E. Barrett, Sr. ◆
Understanding the Rastafarians

Jamaican-born Leonard Barrett has produced the classic work on the history of the Rastafarians in Jamaica. Barrett, a professor of religion at Trinity College, Hartford, CT, has written a number of works on African religions in the Americas.

Who Are the Rastafarians?

The Rastafarian cult is a messianic movement unique to Jamaica. Its members believe that Haile Selassie, former emperor of Ethiopia, is the Black Messiah who appeared in the flesh for the redemption of all blacks exiled in the world of white oppressors. The movement views Ethiopia as the promised land, the place where black people will be repatriated through a wholesale exodus from all Western countries where they have been in exile (slavery). Repatriation is inevitable, and the time awaits only the decision of Haile Selassie. Known only to the true believers, the details of the actual departure are secret. In the past some fantasies called for planes to the United States, and then ships from there to Africa. Some envision the operation being launched from the shores of Jamaica by at least ten British ships at a time, while others see the operation being undertaken in Ethiopian vessels at Jamaican expense.

The destination of this great migration is also vague in the minds of some speculators. The majority see Ethiopia as their homeland; others view Africa as the true homeland. There is no unanimity about the destination. To many, Ethiopia means Africa, while to others, Ethiopia is the promised land, though they will settle for any part of the continent.

The author, who has observed the Rastafarians since 1946 and has carried out systematic research among them from 1963 to 1966 (on which his first monograph was based), later returned to Jamaica to study their development from 1966 to the deaths of Haile Selassie and Bob Marley. An up-to-date assessment of the movement may be stated as follows:

The present membership of the Rastafarian movement, including sympathizers, may number three hundred thousand. No census has yet given an accurate account of the membership, but a knowledgeable Rasta leader states that six out of every ten Jamaicans are either Rastas or sympathizers.

From *The Rastafarians* (Boston: Beacon Press, 1977), 1–28. © 1977, 1987 by Leonard Barrett. Reprinted by permission of Beacon Press. Footnotes omitted.

The membership is young and has no individual leadership. Up to 80 percent of those seen in the camps and on the streets are between the ages of seventeen and thirty-five. The leading brethren are mostly men from thirty-five to fifty-five years of age. The older members are either ex-Garveyites or sympathizers of his movement.

Most members are male. Women play an important role in Rastafarianism at present, but the majority are followers of their husbands. In special meetings women act as mistresses of songs or as secretaries, but these roles are changing rapidly. The male assumes most of the responsibilities of the movement, though at present, a large segment of Rastafarian women now sell their products such as knitted clothing, baskets, mats, brooms, art works, and other sundries.

Until 1965 the membership was essentially lower class, but this is no longer the case. Once considered "products of the slum," the Rastas have now penetrated the middle class. They are found among civil servants and the elite; some are students at the prestigious University of the West Indies; some are in the medical and legal professions and other upper-class occupations.

Based on the earlier research, the members were almost all of African stock. At present, the overwhelming majority of members still are, but there are also Chinese, East Indians, Afro-Chinese, Afro-East Indians or Afro-Jews, mulattoes, and a few whites. Every ethnic minority is now represented in the Rastafarian camps.

The members are predominantly ex-Christians. About 90 percent of the members interviewed were from Protestant or Catholic churches or Pentecostal sects. The minority who said they had no church connection did acknowledge that they came from Christian homes.

As a group the Rastafarians see Jamaica as a land of oppression—Babylon. Their only avenue of escape is by supernatural means or by seizing the power and creating a utopia for the oppressed.

The Place, People, and Language

The island of Jamaica is the third largest in size of the West Indian islands after Cuba and Haiti. Jamaica is 150 miles long and 52 miles wide, subtropical, a land of warm weather without the extremes of climate common to the mainland of the United States. Jamaican harbors are among the world's finest, and Jamaican rivers add beauty and economic value to the island. Hills and mountains form the center of the island, ranging from the gentle Cockpit Mountains of the west to the high John Crow and Blue Mountains of the east, with altitudes exceeding seven thousand feet.

These high mountains and the broad, easily drained plains below provide diversity of climate and agriculture.

The population of Jamaica is presently estimated at a little less than two million people, of which nearly a half-million now reside in Kingston, the capital and largest city.

The distribution of people by racial origin can be summarized as follows: those of African origin, 90 percent; Caucasians, about 1 percent; descendants of East Indians, 3 percent; those of Chinese descent, about 2 percent. Of the remaining 4 percent, the Jews and Lebanese are the largest identifiable groups. Thus the vast majority of Jamaicans are currently of African or Afro-European descent. By contrast, the original inhabitants of the island (when Columbus discovered it in 1494) were the Arawak Indians, a homogeneous people completely different from any group living there now. Columbus's arrival introduced the natives to the Europeans, a meeting which proved catastrophic for the Arawak Indians: by the time the British conquered Jamaica in 1655, the Arawaks were extinct.

English is the formal language of the island. The greater part of the masses, however, speak a Jamaican dialect. Cassidy's *Jamaica Talk* (the first scientific work to deal with the dialect) portrays Jamaica as a place where "a pepperpot of language is concocted." He observes that "Jamaica-talk" is not the same for every Jamaican because of the vast spectrum of dialects. "Jamaica-talk" exists in two main forms which Cassidy illustrates as lying at opposite ends of a scale. At one extreme is the type of "Jamaica-talk" that emulates the "London standard" or educated model spoken among many of the elite. At the other extreme is the inherited talk of peasant and laborer who remain largely unaffected by education and its standards. Their speech is what linguists call "creolized" English; that is, fragmented English speech and syntax assimilated during the days of slavery and mixed with African influences. This Anglo-African admixture continues to be spoken in much the same form today.

There is, though, a third dialectical element in Jamaica located in the middle of the language scale where one discovers an increasing inclusion of local elements of Jamaican rhythm and intonation of words that the Londoner would have no need to know. These characteristics of the language evolved within an island population, which Cassidy calls "Jamaicanism." He defines this term by citing five main divisions:

1. Retention, which includes English words now rare or poetic that are still in common use in Jamaica.
2. New formations, which are in turn subdivided into alterations, compositions, and creations.

3. Borrowings, which are French and Portuguese words which came into English as early as the eighteenth century.
4. Onomatopoeic echoisms.
5. Usage of words which, though not exclusively Jamaican, are the preferred terms on the island.

Speaking of the greatest influence on "Jamaica-talk," Cassidy concludes:

> Of non-British influences it is obvious that the African is the largest and most profound; it appears not only in the vocabulary, but has powerfully affected both pronunciation and grammar. We may feel fairly certain about two hundred and thirty loan-words from various African languages; and if the numerous compounds and derivatives were added, and the large number of untraced terms which are at least quasi-African in form, the total would easily be more than four hundred. Even at its most [*sic*], the African element in the vocabulary is larger than all the other non-English ones together.

Cassidy's studies, which were carried out in the 1950s, made no mention of the influence of the Rastafarian movement on "Jamaica-talk." Since the 1950s a new linguistic change has taken place in Jamaica. This is what we may call a "Rasta dialect"—highly symbolic and radically revolutionary. . . .

Education in Jamaica has generally followed the British pattern. Though understandable from a historical perspective, the system has created much confusion in the social patterns of the Jamaican people. During the colonial period (and to a great extent to the present day), children were taught about the English culture without attempting to relate it to the environment in which they lived. Madeline Kerr, in her analysis of five schools, points out that the subject matter was basically meaningless to the children. Central to the curriculum was the Bible, taught from a strictly fundamentalist point of view. Children memorized enormous passages of prose and poetry and learned to read by chanting passages from books. Discipline in the schools was often harsh, and although some teachers restricted the amount of lashing, beating was the rule, not the exception.

Prior to independence (and even today), children attended elementary school up to the age of eleven when they were expected to pass a common entrance examination. The completion of this test entitled the child to enter an approved school until he or she passed the General Certificate of Education. This certificate admitted the child, in some cases, to a university.

One of the great problems of education in Jamaica is the lack of proper training of teachers, the majority of whom, until recently, reached a standard scarcely higher than the American high school.

With the coming of self-government there has been a remarkable increase in educational facilities. In 1944 primary schoolteachers numbered less than three thousand; by 1960 the figure had grown to over five thousand. School attendance figures are even more revealing. Whereas in 1944 there were only 171,455 elementary-school pupils, by 1960 the figure had grown to 315,000. Great emphasis was also placed on secondary education. While there were only twenty-three secondary schools in 1944, by 1960 the number had reached forty-one. Recently, compulsory education has been instituted by the government. But the future of Jamaican education is in a deplorable state. Teachers are poorly paid, and with the economic downturn due to the closing of the bauxite companies and the weakness of the Jamaican dollar, high inflation has caused the closing of elementary and secondary schools, and even of one teachers' college.

The University College of the West Indies (now the University of the West Indies) was founded in 1948 at Mona, near Kingston, with an enrollment of thirty-three students. Current enrollment exceeds five thousand. A number of vocational and technical schools have been constructed on the island to encourage and meet the demand for mechanical and technical skills in a developing nation. These upper-level educational institutions provide an excellent education but their number and capacity to meet the needs of an exploding population are grossly inadequate.

Jamaica's economy is basically agricultural, employing over 40 percent of the island's labor force. Before the Second World War, agriculture accounted for 36 percent of the island's total exports in the form of sugar, bananas, and rum and comprised four fifths of the island's export revenue. By 1961, however, agriculture provided only 13 percent of the total income. In the past ten years, rapid developments have taken place in mining, manufacturing, and tourism. All three industries presently are experiencing the uncertainties of worldwide inflation and recession. Thus the future of the Jamaican economy will demand courageous leadership and sound fiscal planning.

A striking characteristic of Jamaica's agriculture is the large number of small farmers. There are 159,000 small farmers, of whom 113,000 work less than five acres. A recent report states that the agricultural pattern of Jamaican farmers has not changed in the last one hundred years, largely due to lack of land and primitive techniques. The former government was dedicated to rectifying this imbalance, and new laws have been instituted to make unused lands available to the small farmers. At present, efforts are being focused on increasing agricultural exports.

One of the largest known deposits of bauxite in the world was discovered in Jamaica in the early 1950s. This discovery promoted the establishment of a mining industry and boosted the general economy. Bauxite and aluminum accounted for 50 percent of the island's earnings in 1982. The Manley government moved to nationalize the bauxite industry, which created a mini-international upheaval among the ranks of multinational cartels. However, because of world inflation, the bauxite companies experienced a decline in profits and decided to cease mining bauxite in Jamaica. All three companies have now left the island or are about to leave. This has left Jamaica with a staggering deficit.

Industry has become a serious concern for the government. Its industrial development program has been implemented by the Industrial Development Corporation and included incentive legislation as well as promotional activities in the United States, the United Kingdom, and Canada. As a result, the island now has a wider variety of manufactured products using both local and imported raw materials. Among these new products are clothing, footwear, textiles, paints, and building materials, including cement. Some of these are used locally, but most are exported.

This economic picture greatly affects the lives of Rastafarians. It is in response to this cultural and economic condition that the Rastafarians have emerged as a movement. The competence of most Rastas lies in the semiskilled or the marginally skilled occupations. They are mostly prepared to do farm labor, but possess no land. Some have taken up painting, masonry, or carpentry; others have become domestic servants, janitors, woodworkers, or small shopkeepers. Wages for these occupations, when work is available, does not exceed twenty dollars per week. The labor problem in Jamaica is such that the number of unskilled laborers far exceeds the demand, and the population of unskilled laborers grows in geometric proportion yearly. Unemployment has created a large body of criminals who prey on both rich and poor. It has also caused mass emigration to North America and a deterioration of the human spirit.

Living Conditions

The city of Kingston and its environs are a study in contrasts; beautiful suburban communities in the highlands overlook miles of slum dwellings in various stages of blight and decay as they swelter in the hot, putrid air which varies only a degree or two each night year-round. The ten-mile bus route from Tower Street to Cross Roads—or any of the many arteries leading north—is a jungle of dilapidated housing projects interspersed with new government office buildings which tower over what was once a thriving community of commercial and cultural enterprises. Now these areas seem deserted by the exodus of the more affluent population to the suburbs with new shopping malls in the greener pastures of St. Andrew.

Leaving the city and going north, one comes to an abrupt divide known as Cross Roads. This is indeed the crossroads between poverty and ostentation displayed by the middle- and upper-class Jamaicans who flaunt their manicured gardens and mansion-like houses, complete with quarters for the servants who attend them. Cross Roads was once a charming village town, containing one of Jamaica's most beautiful movie theaters, and pride of the city—Carib. Today, the theater stands blushing at the Jamaican omnibus terminal which spreads like an ulcer just past the Carib's entrance. As many as twenty-five buses filled with sweating passengers converge on this spot hourly.

The line of demarcation seen at Cross Roads typifies the division of wealth between the Jamaican upper class and the masses from which the Rastafarian population is drawn. Slum conditions in Jamaican cities are probably the worst in the Caribbean, except for Haiti. The Rastafarian poet Sam Brown, in his unpublished poem "Slum Conditions," depicts the existing situation in Kingston more eloquently than any other. The first verse describes the appearance of the slums of Jones Town and Trench Town where most cultists live:

> Tin-can houses, old and young, mangey dogs, rats, inhuman stench,
> Unthinkable conditions that cause the stoutest heart to wrench.
> Tracks and little lanes like human veins, emaciated people,
> Many giving up the ghost, their spirits broken, their gloom deepens.
> Precocious boys and girls, yet adults, police, thieves, conglomerates,
> Generally disjointed, sexually abandoned masters of their fate.

The next verse portrays what it is like to exist under these conditions:

> Tribal warfares, rapings, inhumanity, police brutality, daily occurence,
> Yet, they are diamonds in the rough, who bites with this abhorence.
> Like Alice, slums without pity, lacking love, each grim and screws,
> Some ailing ones weaker than the rest, don't know what to do.

Sam Brown then shows that the cultists are aware of the causes of their oppression:

> Some young desperates look to the hills, see the seat of their distress,
> They see the dwellers of the hills as them that do oppress.
> Churches wedged in among the hovels, squealing pigs, juke-boxes blaring,
> Small land space, old cars and bars, Jesus could not get a hearing.

In the following lines he shows the callous attitude of the elite to the poor:

> Men, women and children stark naked, lunatics of wants, reformatory,
> Milk powder, polio victims, rickety, medical infirmary.

> Executives in horseless chariots sometimes pass through, hold their noses,
> Hapless poor look with vengeful eyes, for them no bed of roses.

Finally, the results of years of oppression—the gunmen who now make life unbearable:

> Better wanted, not worse, for him it can't be worse,
> Conscience of man, humanity, civilization in reverse.
> People in fear, bulldozer mashing, smashing, cannot save the situation,
> Lift the ban, free the food, for peace reassemble the nation.
> Corruption to achieve material, graft, bribes, high and low,
> Official-mantled crooks, gunmen equal, the innocent have no place to go.

The author of this poem has lived his entire life in the slums of Jamaica. He was an occupant of the tin-can houses in that part of the city known as "Back-O-Wall," before the government destroyed it with a fleet of bulldozers. Since then, the Rastafarians have moved into other tin-can houses in the heart of the city, or on the edges of it. The poem touches on all of the sights, sounds, and smells of Kingston: the churches in the hovels, the blaring juke-boxes, the gunmen and their victims, and the ever-present police. The attitudes of the slum dwellers are clearly shown in the lines, "Some young desperates look to the hills, see the seat of their distress," and "Hapless poor look with vengeful eyes, for them no bed of roses." Around 1975 the ratio of the haves to the have-nots in Jamaica was put at twenty to one. The narrowing of this gap is the declared goal of the present government. But for now, the result of the disparity in living conditions is hatred, fear, distrust, and anxiety among the wealthy, while the life of the poor grows only more unbearable.

The Rural Areas

Although great strides toward better living conditions have been made in the rural areas in the last decade, this has not changed the pitiful state of housing, cultivable lands, and economic wage differentials. In fact, the majority of rural Jamaican housing remains the same as that described by Martha Beckwith in her study of 1929. Typical of these areas are the "wattle and daub" dwellings, houses built with sticks, covered with wattle, plastered with clay and a little cement, and then whitened with lime. Thatch palms cover the roof, though sheets of zinc are used by the more affluent. The average house is occasionally floored with boards, but more usually has only an earthen floor. Three of every four of these houses have no electricity or running water and most have only an outside pit-latrine. Cooking is done outside the house in a separate kitchen with wood or coal. One out of four rural houses that has an inside kitchen has a kerosene stove for cooking. About half of the rural dwellers rent their houses or lease their lands from large estate owners. It is not unheard of for families who have lived on a piece of land for generations to suddenly find themselves dispossessed by a neighboring landowner who, by fact or by fraud, can show that the land belongs to him.

In the last decade much attention has been given to the plight of the rural poor by the Jamaican government. One of the most grievous problems in the countryside is the access to cultivable lands. Prior to independence, about 60 percent of the land was held by 1 percent of the population—largely cane farmers who acted as absentee landowners. The rural farmers had but a small piece of land, mostly on the hilly slopes, on which to eke out a living. A large proportion of the cultivable lands were either kept as grazing lands for the very rich or left idle as private holdings. Since independence, the government, under a very unpopular Land Acquisition Act, has been laying claim to these lands and returning them under a lease-hold arrangement to small farmers, hoping to improve the conditions of the rural poor and to encourage able-bodied persons in the city to return to the country.

The wage differential in Jamaica is probably the most alarming in the world. The few people who have a profession or some skill receive as much as thirty times more than the unskilled. In instituting the Minimum Wage Law of 1975, the prime minister, the Honorable Michael Manley, startled the House of Parliament with the following revelations: 28,000 or more Jamaicans earn less than ten dollars per week; 64,000 earn less than fifteen dollars per week; and 101,000 earn less than twenty dollars per week. The author is convinced that about one half of all Jamaicans would fall under the category of twenty-five dollars per week per capita.

Unemployment and Crime

The legacy of colonialism now seen in the maldistribution of land and wealth represents a growing problem which must be remedied quickly if Jamaica is to survive. Eighty percent of the common laborers who are unskilled earn twenty-five dollars per week when they do get work. Add to this the permanently underemployed and the unemployables, and the situation is a sociopolitical headache for a new nation. The Seaga government, which since 1981 has adhered to a platform of capitalism and private initiative, has rejected the socialist enterprise of the previous government and has adopted the American model, which has had a detrimental effect on Jamaica's poor.

In the meantime, the people who have no concept of the enormous difficulties facing the government are impatient. This impatience is mirrored in the rapid growth of crime on the island. Easy access to guns and their indiscriminate use have turned living conditions into a nightmare. The situation, though frightening, is understandable. The history of Jamaica is one long tale of exploitation by a few rich families whose privileges were never questioned. But with independence, Jamaica was thrust into the arena of the underdeveloped nations with little or no aid from those who benefited from the island. Many of these rich families continued to profit from their investments, spending little or nothing on the island. They were on the island but not of it. Most investors did not even keep their wealth in Jamaican banks, but stashed it in foreign banks. With the announcement of democratic socialism in the seventies and the sudden awakening of social and cultural consciousness under the Manley government, the people of wealth migrated from Jamaica, leaving the government and its people to simmer in a "stew" not of their own making.

With the passing of the old order, the oppressed masses have become bewildered by the rapid change which allows little time to learn the new symbols, which were in various stages of formulation. The result was a mild chaos, mirrored in an ambivalent longing for the old, oppressive society, while groping uncertainly toward an untried future. The birth pangs of unrest shook the body. The criminal element, which emerged from the people who have been consistently denied a share in the wealth of their homeland, is now determined to get a piece of the pie by any possible means. The means now utilized is violence against the black and white society. No one is excluded in this "war." The Jamaican gunman is a cold and systematic killer executing what he believes to be his duty. Gun crimes have become so pervasive that the former government originated an internationally unique institution (probably the first in any democratic country)—the Gun Court—which is both a court of law and a detention camp.

The term is a pseudonym for a process of incarcerating apprehended gunmen and later trying them under the Jamaica Gun Court Act of 1974. Under this act, if a person is found guilty of possessing an unlicensed firearm, or even a few bullets, he receives a mandatory sentence of "detention for life with hard labor." A gunman can be released from this sentence only when deemed fit to live a wholesome life in the community, and that at the discretion of the governor-general of Jamaica.

In 1978 this social modification technique was designed to control the crime wave that drove Jamaicans to the brink of despair. The island was flooded with illegal firearms of largely unknown origin. As a crime-control technique, the Gun Court was so unique in the Americas that it became a feature story on "Sixty Minutes" (CBS) in 1975. Despite the urgent need for the control of crime in Jamaica, some of the island's legal experts were convinced that a court set up outside the judicial provisions of the Jamaican constitution was illegal. As a consequence, in April of

1974, four men sentenced to indefinite detention for possession of firearms were encouraged to appeal their cases with the intention of testing the constitutionality of the Gun Court Act of 1974. The case was ultimately brought before the Privy Council Judicial Committee of Great Britain, which still operates as the court of last resort for Jamaican citizens. The Privy Council heard the case for six days; the final decision was that the Gun Court is constitutional, but a sentence of "indefinite detention is unlawful." Emboldened by this ruling, the gunmen opened a new campaign of violence. Shooting, burning, and other violent crimes spurred the government to rewrite the Gun Court Law of 1976. It demands a life term for firearm crimes, with no appeal; but under special privileges granted by the Jamaican Appeals Council, the act has also been widened to deal with violence of a political nature, which many observers believe to be at the heart of the Jamaican crime wave.

Early in 1976 violent crimes in Jamaica necessitated the government's call for a "national emergency," which temporarily suspended certain freedoms of its citizens in order to deal with the criminal outbursts. Since 1982 the police have begun the practice of shooting anyone found with a gun. The number shot by police each year is staggering. Meanwhile, the Gun Court still exists on South Camp Road.

At the extreme end of Jamaican society stands another group who disagree with the tactics of the gunmen, but whose philosophy suggests that the remedy for Jamaicans' woes is total revolution similar to that of Cuba. Supported by the gunmen, this philosophy is advocated by intellectuals who are avid students of Marx and Lenin. Although this group sympathized greatly with the declared democratic socialism of the former government, it felt that this halfway measure was not drastic enough to cure the ills of Jamaica. It might placate a few, but it could not cure the disease. To them, socialism was a step in the right direction. But anything short of scientific socialism and a social revolution which will dislodge the privileged and destroy the stranglehold of multinational corporations will be but salve on a deep wound.

The present government has reversed the socialist policies of the past and has instituted the American free-enterprise system, under which goods and services are brought in at exorbitant prices and profits. These businesses are staffed by a middle class who depend on their monied masters for their existence. On the bottom are the hungry masses, effectively kept at a distance by the arm of the law, whose duty it is to protect capital. With independence and the awakening consciousness of the masses—a climate which now pervades all Third World nations—there has emerged a militant avant-garde that opposes this reversal by the present government. The group feels that it is its duty to bring about the millennium by forcible means. The middle-class intellectuals, although sympathetic to socialism, feel that the problems demand revolution now. In the meantime, the once-beautiful island of paradise now exists with an overgrown serpent coiled around its center. The frustration of this situation was expressed by the columnist of the *Sunday Gleaner* on June 29, 1975, who wrote under the heading "Paradise Lost":

> More and more criminals appear to possess guns and to use them on victims with or without provocations; people's houses are being broken into and the inmates killed, wounded, or raped; residents are being chased away and their houses burned or broken down; shops, betting places, and payrolls are being robbed right and left; complainants and witnesses are disappearing so that [the] accused have to be let off for lack of evidences, and physical evidences have been destroyed, by bombing a police station; criminals are escaping after conviction; courthouses have been invaded and the police attacked to free prisoners; organized gangs of young thugs have taken over meetings; praedial larceny is more prevalent than ever.

The government has been trying to rectify these problems, but its success has been limited at best.

Religion

To enter into a discussion of Jamaican religiosity, one must first deal with a short historical background of the island's inhabitants, the earliest being the Arawak Indians, who were finally destroyed under Spanish rule between 1502 and 1655. When the British conquered the Spanish in 1655, not a trace of these Arawak people could be found. As a result, the Spanish substituted African slaves in small numbers until, under the British, thousands of West African slaves were brought to Jamaica.

The West Africans brought to the island were mostly from the Gold Coast and Nigeria. The British planters insisted on these people above all others because of their sturdiness. It was the Ashanti, however, that left the greatest cultural imprint on Jamaica, noticeable to this day. Consequently, the language of the Jamaican peasants still carries hundreds of words that need no translation from the original Ashanti tongue—Twi. But the area most dominated by Ashanti influence was the folk religion, still practiced today under the name of *Kumina*. The word comes from two Twi words: *Akom*—"to be possessed," and *Ana*—"by an ancestor." This ancestor-possession cult became the medium of religious expression for all Africans during the slave period. Throughout most of the Caribbean, this kind of African religious syncretism seems to have taken place. Examples can be found in Haiti where all tribes taken there seem to have fused their religious rituals under the Dahomean rubric known as *Vodun*.

The same thing happened in Trinidad where the Nigerian influence dominated, fusing the disparate elements into a cult known as *Shango*. A similar process also occurred in Cuba under the name *Santería*.

Slave Religion in Jamaica

Unlike Haiti, where the slaves were commanded if not forced to be members of the Catholic faith, the English planters in Jamaica adamantly refused to share their religion with the slave population. The Church of England and its high liturgy was considered too sophisticated for people of "lesser breed" and, further, the masters feared that the preachers—in their unguarded inspirational moments—would stretch the equality of humanity before God a little too far. The slaves, left to themselves, developed elements of the remembered religious systems from their homeland. This was not difficult to do because among the slave population were African religious functionaries who had been indiscriminately carried to the island. According to Herbert DeLisser, one of Jamaica's historians on slavery, "both witches and wizards, priests and priestesses, were brought to Jamaica in the days of the slave trade, and the slaves recognized the distinction between the former and the latter. Even the masters saw that the two classes were not identical, and they called the latter 'myal-men and myal women' . . . [these were] the people who cured."

DeLisser goes on to say that the legitimate slave priests and priestesses of African religion were unable to function in their customary roles and therefore turned to sorcery—practicing witchcraft as ritual aggression against the slave system. They became what is known in Jamaica as *obeah*-men and *obeah*-women. The word *obeah* is known throughout the English slave regions, and is derived from two Ashanti words: *oba*—"a child," and *yi*—"to take." The idea of taking a child was the final test of a sorcerer, a deed giving the status of Ph.D. in witchcraft. *Obeah*, then, became the most dreadful form of Caribbean witchcraft, plaguing both black and white in the days of slavery and continuing to haunt Jamaicans today.

Although the legitimate priests and priestesses were unable to do their work under slavery, they did not wholly forget their roles. They remained capable of casting and exorcising spells. Exorcism became the function by which they were best known and in this role became known as *myal*-men and *myal*-women. The word *myal* has come to mean "being in a state of possession," and the ritual which accompanied it was a rigorous dance now known as *Kumina*. *Kumina* soon caught on among the slaves and later became the slave religion.

The earliest eyewitness of this cult behavior was the Moravian missionary, J. H. Buchner, who was in Jamaica in the late eighteenth century:

> As soon as darkness of evening set in, they assembled in crowds in open pastures, most frequently under large cotton trees, which they worship, and counted holy; after sacrificing some fowls, the leader began an extempore song, in a wild strain, which was answered in chorus; the dance followed, grew wilder and wilder, until they were in a state of excitement bordering on madness. Some would perform incredible revolutions while in this state, until, nearly exhausted, they fell senseless to the ground, when every word they uttered was received as divine revelation. At other times *obeah* was discovered or a *shadow* was caught a little coffin being prepared in which it was enclosed and buried.

Buchner's observations were very accurate. The details hold true even today. A *Kumina* is called on special occasions, especially for ceremonies surrounding the rites of passage (birth, puberty, marriage, and death). But other calamities, such as sickness and other natural or unnatural occasions, may necessitate a *Kumina* service. This service is accompanied by drumming and dancing. A sacrifice is always necessary; alcoholic spirits are always present; and the dancing continues until spirit possession is achieved. These spirits are always the ancestors of the dancers or of the person who calls the *Kumina*. Under spirit possession a revelation is given by the ancestors concerning the occasion for which the *Kumina* is called. This revelation is considered very important and is heeded in every detail. It may consist of the reason for the sickness or the death, suggest the cure for the illness, or warn of coming calamities. Under possession, the evil spirit that may have caused the person's illness may be captured. It might be a ghost sent by an *obeah*-man or woman to haunt the house. Under *Kumina* possession, the revelation is sometimes given in an unknown tongue, very often in an African language, now forgotten, but known to the possessed.

Missionary Religions

Brief mention must be made of the entrance of missionary religions into the island. The Spaniards brought Roman Catholicism to Jamaica in 1509; few documents survive to describe the Spanish slaves. When we meet the remnants of these Africans, known as Maroons, who served the Spanish in the mountains, they were still worshipping their Ashanti God—*Nyankopong*. The Spanish Catholics seem to have evangelized the Arawak Indians found on the island before the arrival of the blacks. When the

British finally drove out the Spaniards in 1655, the Arawaks were extinct. Their number was estimated to have been sixty thousand.

When the English came, the Church of England followed, but they paid no attention to the African population. One hundred and sixty-one years after England took over Jamaica and established the slave trade, no attempt had been made to Christianize the slaves. All this time the slaves continued to serve their African deities. It was not until 1816 that the Jamaica House of Assembly passed an act to "consider the state of religion among the slaves, and to carefully investigate the means of diffusing the light of genuine Christianity among them." This act was not heeded. The resistance of the planters to teaching Christianity to the slaves was so strong that no clergyman would dare risk his benefits to do so. According to historian Edward Long, however, the Anglican ministers of that period were so deficient in morals that they were incapable of preaching the Gospel to anybody; as he said, "Some were better qualified to be retailers of salt-fish or boatswains to privateers than ministers of the Gospel."

The urge to consider the state of religion among the slaves was brought about by the entrance of the Moravians in 1734, the Methodists in 1736, the Baptists in 1783, and the Presbyterians in 1823. These nonconformist denominations were a real threat to the establishment, finding ready ears among the slaves and winning over large numbers to their cause. The loose rituals of these churches—especially the early Methodist and Baptists with their spirit-filled enthusiasm—fit beautifully the exuberant religion of the slaves and brought about an early syncretism between Christianity and various African religions. The slave masters saw, in this amalgamation of the "doctrine of Methodism combined with African superstition," an imminent danger to the community. Every effort, legal and illegal, was utilized to arrest the spread of the nonconformists.

Despite resistance and persecution by the established church, the spread of Christianity continued *unabated* until the emancipation of the slaves in 1835. In that year the slaves celebrated the occasion as the Great Jubilee. Recognizing the considerable effort of the nonconformist churches on their behalf, the slaves flocked to these denominations in great numbers. But as the nonconformist churches gained official recognition, their spirituality diminished, and they began to establish themselves as real denominations with rules, rituals, and structures far removed from the interests of their newly emancipated members. The slaves, sensing a new regimentation of their lives by the Europeans, were not satisfied with the new order. The churches were little prepared for what was soon to develop in Jamaican religion.

The Great Revival of 1860–61

About 1860–61, just over two decades after the emancipation, the missionary religions were in the process of consolidating their religious efforts when a revival similar to the Great Awakening in the United States swept the island. The enthusiasm was so powerful that the missionaries were unable to cope with the demand. Thousands of slaves flocked to the churches day and night—men, women, and children. The behavior patterns of this revival were similar to those observed in New England by Jonathan Edwards, with much singing, crying, dancing, spirit possession, and loud prayers. W. J. Gardner, a Congregationalist minister of that time who evidently relished a more sedate approach to God, described it as follows:

> In 1861, there had been a very remarkable religious movement known as "the great revival." Like a mountain stream, clear and transparent as it sprung from the rock, but which becomes foul and repulsive as impurities are mingled with it in its onward course, so with this most extraordinary movement. In many of the central districts of the island the hearts of the thoughtful and good men were gladdened by what they witnessed in changed lives and characters of people for whom they long seemed to have laboured in vain; but in too many districts there was much of wild extravagance and almost blasphemous fanaticism. This was especially the case where the Native Baptists had any considerable influence. Among these, the manifestations occasioned by the influence of the *myal-men* were common. To the present time what are called revival meetings are common among these people.

Gardner was correct in his observation. He saw practices which were not those of the sedate Congregational Church: to him they were repulsive and extravagant, even blasphemous and fanatic. He saw in these behaviors the influence of *Kumina.*

P. D. Curtain, in his book *The Two Jamaicas,* referred to this Great Revival as the parting of the ways between the missionary churches in Jamaica and the present Afro-Christian sects. As he noted, "What appeared to have been a missionary's hope, turned out to be a missionary's despair."

The Great Revival allowed the African religious dynamic—long repressed—to assert itself in a Christian guise and capture what might have been a missionary victory. Since then, Christianity has been a handmaiden to a revitalized African movement known as "Revival religion."

Afro-Christian Syncretism

At present there are three types of Afro-Christian sects in Jamaica: *Pukumina*, which is mostly African in its rituals and beliefs; the Revival cult, which is partly African and partly Christian; and Revival Zion, which is mostly Christian and the least African in its rituals and beliefs. I place these Revival cults under the broad heading of Afro-Christian religions because all have adopted some aspects of Christianity in their rites, and prefer to be called Christian. All have general characteristics by which they can be analyzed. For example, the leaders of these cults are known as the "shepherd" or "shepherdess," the leader of a *band*. A *band* is a collection of believers from twenty to two hundred members who occupy a *yard*, or a ritual center where meetings and other rituals are held. The *yard* may be an elaborate commune where members build their homes and live together, or just a tabernacle where cult members of the community visit on holy days. Each band possesses a hierarchy of leaders known as shepherds in a graded order. The first or leading shepherd (or shepherdess) can be identified by his (or her) elaborate turban. He (or she) is generally the founder of the *band* and considered to be a person of high spiritual attainment. A shepherd is commonly a *seer* with great clairvoyant powers who serves as preacher, healer, judge, and diviner. If a male shepherd is married, his wife is sometimes known as "the mother" and is as highly respected as her husband in most cases. Below the head shepherd is the warrior shepherd who protects the *band* from the intervention of evil spirits. The water shepherd presides at baptism and sees that water is placed in the tabernacle at all times—water is the avenue through which good spirits enter the service. The wheeling shepherd works around the *yard* counterclockwise to detect any evil, such as witchcraft, which might be present. Many other functionaries operate in a *band*, each distinguishable by dress and role.

Services are called for various occasions, such as birth, death, and illness. Regular services take place on Sundays and weekdays for fasting and especially for healings. A typical service includes singing, drumming, preaching, and Holy Communion. The rituals of the services vary from one *band* to another. Some use the rituals of the Anglican Church, including the *Book of Common Prayer*. These services integrate high-church ritual, dancing, and drumming in which spirit possession, speaking in tongues, and prophecy are tied together. Visitors are amazed at the level of integration that has been achieved. Other *bands* resemble the Baptists with their more free and spontaneous service. All *bands* engage in a special ritual known as "trumping and/or travailing" in the spirit. This consists of dancing counterclockwise in a circle to the beating of drums and chanting. The peak is reached when the singing stops and a peculiar guttural sound begins caused by inhaling and exhaling air while moving the body forward and backward, allowing the air to explode through the lips. It is during this rite that spirit possession is most generally achieved and when many of the dancers attain altered states of consciousness, becoming mouthpieces for gods and spirits. It is often in this same state that members give warnings of imminent dangers such as approaching hurricanes, earthquakes, dangers surrounding births, deaths by accidents—or by revealing to spectators problems which could prove dangerous to them. Such warnings are spoken in English or in "unknown tongues," and are interpreted by other members or by the leader of the *band*. The spectators take these revelations seriously and usually seek the advice of the leaders.

The mountaintop experience of a Revival service is generally followed by a healing service for those who are sick or who need advice on matters which were revealed to them during spirit possession. Usually this service continues late into the night. In some *yards*, healing continues as an ongoing ritual throughout the week. Over 90 percent of the Jamaican peasants depend upon healing centers for their medical needs. Healing and curing involves herbal remedies, baths in herbal mixtures, oils, incense, drinking water blessed by the leaders, and, in recent days, the use of patent medicines.

Revival and Revival Zion sects are closer to Christianity than *Pukumina*. It is believed that the *Pukumina* sect engages in witchcraft and casting spells, while the Revival groups counteract witchcraft and neutralize spells. Many patients observed at Revival services by the author suffered from mental and psychosomatic complaints. Such people generally seek the help of the Revival healers, who are believed to have gifts of clairvoyance and prognosticate psychic problems in a remarkable way. Incidentally, these healers are not only popular with the poorer class; the elite also seek their services, though secretly. In my research, I discovered that people from the highest levels of the society frequent these healers in times of psychic distress, either to be cured of illness or to ensure that the jobs they hold are not easily taken from them. Native spiritualists and herbal healers in Jamaica form an integral part of medical practice and will continue to do so for years to come. One major reason for this is the scarcity of trained physicians in the rural areas. At present, 50 percent of the over-the-counter pharmaceutical drugs purchased are prescriptions written by native healers.

Pentecostalism and Revivalism: A Comparison

As Jamaica experiences rapid social change, its native religions are also undergoing dramatic changes. North America is taking deep root on the island, especially since the advent of the jet age. Beginning about 1929, the native religion received a fresh challenge from the United States of

America in the form of high-voltage, eight-cylinder-type Pentecostal sects. First to appear on the island was the Church of God, headquartered in Cleveland, Tennessee. Then followed the Church of God in Christ and the Apostolic Faith, and finally almost all the Pentecostal churches known in America. These sects have made great headway on the island and have, in some cases, greatly depleted the membership of the missionary denominations. The impact of Pentecostals on Revival sects has been less severe. The similarities and differences between the two movements are complementary, giving advantages to both. Similarities in ritual behavior and organizational structure have probably kept the Pentecostals from completely displacing the Revival sects.

Some other obvious similarities might be mentioned here. The leaders of the Pentecostals are generally charismatic men and women. Like the Revivalist shepherd and shepherdess, they are able to hold an audience spellbound under the most adverse physical setting—whether a crude shack, a storefront, or a street corner. In both sects, healing plays a prominent part in their rituals. Some Pentecostals make use of oils for anointing the sick, and the laying-on-of-hands for exorcisms—practices common to the Revivalists. Both lay great stress on the baptism in the Spirit with the evidence of speaking in tongues. They both believe in baptism by water and place little emphasis on the Lord's Supper.

Oriented toward the lower strata of society, the Revivalists and Pentecostals alike share strong feelings against established denominations and the ruling class. The use of various musical folk instruments—including drums, guitar, cymbals, handclapping—and a worship service with a high emotional overtone are important to both sects. And surprisingly enough, there are close similarities between the native religion of Jamaica and the new charismatic movements imported from America, thereby heightening the religious prestige of the Revivalists who can see their white counterparts in America behaving in the same manner. The result has been a new wave of religious groups, a syncretistic offshoot of Revivalists and Pentecostals on the island. These are identified by the long dress common among American fundamentalists, the clapping of hands, and the ritual ejaculations of the words "Amen," "Hallelujah," and "Praise the Lord."

But with these similarities, we must also speak of the differences between these two sects—differences largely of ideology rather than structure or organization. While the Pentecostals emphasize the baptism in the Holy Ghost, the Revivalists do not limit spirit possession to the Holy Spirit of Acts 2. Myriad spirits may possess the believer. Among these are the ancestors, angels of the New Testament variety, and other spirits of unknown origins—good and bad. For Pentecostals the Bible is central; to the Revivalists, it is peripheral. Their emphasis lies on dreams and visions. The working of miracles and their interpretation are more meaningful as symbols of divine manifestations than biblical words. The great figures of the Bible become spiritual manifestations who often appear in their services; for example, Jeremiah and Ezekiel, and angels such as Michael and Gabriel, and other archangels often appear in their services as real figures.

True Revivalists are nonfundamentalists; that is, the forbidden things taught by Pentecostals seem very strange to them. Abstention from liquor and tobacco, and such things as dancing and a little romancing now and then are very wholesome practices for Revivalists. Sin to them is not what you do, but the spirit in which you do things. So, in a sense, the Revivalists are far more liberal and open to life and living than the Pentecostals. This is not to say they are loose in their spiritual lives, but that they find life more positive than negative.

This short description of Jamaican religions may sound like a chaos of cults running wild on the island. But acquaintance with the island and its people will show that, despite the seeming confusion, a real function is being carried out in the various religious expressions. As I have tried to show historically, the African religious mold, firmly rooted during slavery, has not been dislodged by missionary religions for many reasons. African religious traditions take into consideration not only one's intellect, but also one's emotions, the mental and the visceral. African religion is not a Sunday-go-to-church religion, but one that participates with all of nature—both the living and the dead. An awareness is found not only of the gods and the spirits, but also of demons and powers who can harm the living.

The majority of Jamaicans retain this level of belief. Religion is a total involvement for them, not a mental exercise. Within one's religion one lives, moves, and has one's being. As recently as fifteen years ago, only about a third of the people could read or write; consequently, only a few of the Jamaican masses were able to receive any benefits from the sophisticated liturgies of the missionary churches, which demanded a higher level of literacy to fulfill catechetical requirements for membership. Only the privileged elite became members of the larger denominations and attended these churches with pomp and pride, looking down at the masses who flocked to the Revival *yards*. But, it is in these Revival *yards* that the real Jamaican folk tradition was nourished and preserved. From this folk religion came the charismatic leaders to take over the political leadership of the island before the educated elite succeeded them:

from these *yards* folk painters, sculptors, and musicians emerged. The educated Jamaican elite has remained static and uncreative in most fields of cultural dynamics.

At present, there is an increased availability of education, but most young Jamaicans are choosing to associate with the Revivalists and the Pentecostals, and a large body have opted for the Rastafarian religious expressions. They are finding these religious groups considerably more satisfying and relevant to their spiritual needs. In the 1972 election, the former prime minister—born to the elite—took on the role of a Revival shepherd, calling himself Joshua and carrying a shepherd's staff. He won a landslide victory!

Anyone visiting Jamaica should take the time to go to the prestigious churches in the day, and at night visit the Pocomania *yards* and Pentecostal tabernacles to see the differences. The effervescence of these traditional gatherings confirms that the day of pasteurized religion is over, at least in Jamaica.

The Rastafarian movement of Jamaica is the most recent religious expression of a people who have experienced a bitter history of exploitation and oppression. Its emergence comes as a reaction not only to the native religions which the Rastas see as unreal in the presence of formidable sociopolitical forces, but also against the missionary religions which they view as the religious arm of colonial oppression.

Abdias do Nascimento ◆ Afro-Brazilian Ethnicity and International Policy

One of Brazil's most vocal black activists, Abdias do Nascimento, created the Teatro Experimental do Negro, a black-consciousness movement, in the 1940s. He later became one of the few black congressmen of Rio de Janeiro (1982–1986). Nascimento is responsible for a variety of educational programs that aim to raise consciousness among Brazilians and combat discrimination in Brazilian society. In August 1977 he gave the following speech in Cali, Colombia.

> I, for one, would like to impress, especially upon those who call themselves leaders, the importance of realizing the direct connection between the struggle of the Afro-American in this country and the struggle of our people all over the world. As long as we think—as one of my good brothers mentioned out of the side of his mouth here a couple of Sundays ago—that we should get Mississippi straightened out before we worry about the Congo, you'll never get Mississippi straightened out. Not until you start realizing your connection with the Congo.
>
> *—Malcolm X Speaks*

Here in this historic assembly, the First Congress on Black Culture in the Americas, where for the first time in four centuries the African descendants of the Americas have an opportunity to meet together, I am highly honored and happy to represent, as an Afro-Brazilian, the Project on African Cultures in the Diaspora, of the University of Ife in Ile-Ife, Nigeria. The university is located in the neighborhood of the very city where Obatala, sent by Olorum his father, descended over the inchoate waters of Olokun to create the earth and human beings. Ile-Ife signifies for the black African world not only the cradle of our existence, but also the place where the modes of black artistic creation reached their highest peaks in technique and symbolic significance. It was as if I were practicing a ritual return to my origins, when I stayed there for one year as visiting professor in the Department of African Languages and Literatures. During that stay I was able to witness firsthand what is being realized in that beautiful institution of advanced learning, in the sense of attending to the exigencies of the reconstruction of an Africa that for centuries suffered colonialist destruction. And in this movement to recover the physical and spiritual riches of Africa, the University of Ife, of which I consider

From *Brazil: Mixture or Massacre?* (Dover, MA: The Majority Press, 1979), 178–204. Reprinted by permission of The Majority Press.

myself spiritually a permanent member, in its wisdom included among its preoccupations the Africans of the diaspora: we here reunited and all those whom the circumstances of history scattered to the four corners of the universe. But the diaspora in this epoch of human history has an inverse sense of dispersion: we are the diaspora that turns itself in a concentric rhythm toward the pristine center of historic and spiritual origin of our ancestors. We salute the hour of Africa! We hail the inaugural hour of the ascent of black people of the Americas, and our collective effort to organize the future according to our own definition and determination.

In the terms and space of this informal communication there is not room for a detailed analysis, or an exhaustive one, of the experience of Africans and their descendants in Brazil, who constitute an Afro-Brazilian ethnicity of almost 80 millions of blacks and mulattoes, in a country of 115 million inhabitants. Be it emphasized from the start that this is an ethnic group fenced in by a system of pressures that range from prejudice and discrimination, veiled and dissimulated, to psychological and cultural aggressions, and the open violence of police. This fabric of subtle or explicit violence has transformed Brazilian blacks into victims of an internal colonization of unparalleled cruelty in history. Since the times of slavery, the African and his descendant, the Brazilian black people, have been subjected to a consummate technique of elimination which is characterized by the form of implacable genocide. Thus the Afro-Brazilian—be he *negro* (black), mulatto, *moreno* (brunette), *pardo* (brown), *escuro* (dark), *crioulo* (black Brazilian), or any of those euphemisms of African descent in various gradations of epidermic color and ethnic classification—forms a human group condemned to disappearance. For such is the rhythm, the logic of the racial policies of Brazil.

The aggressions of which blacks are victims can be found on the physical/biological level, in the *ideology of whiteness*, which dictates that they must turn progressively lighter in color, through miscegenation, in order to obtain better living conditions, employment opportunities, social relations and respect, in short, to fully exercise their very human condition and citizenship. On the order of economic aggression operates perhaps the most intensely negative factor, throwing blacks into unemployment and underemployment, subverting their domestic organization and personality, leaving them without resources to attend to their minimal necessities of housing, education, health, etc. The collusion of these factors of criminal and inhuman racism is described and documented in detail in a recent work of the present author (1977), entitled *"Racial Democracy" in Brazil: Myth or Reality?* Here I can only reiterate some of the already divulged notions, which are crystalized in various stereotypes that for centuries have constituted the identity of the African and the image of black people still dominant in Brazilian society. The situation is quite complex, and it looms as an obstacle, almost insuperable, impeding, denying to the African-Brazilian his basic right to a peaceful and creative existence based on self-respect and security.

One of the reasons for the long duration of slavery, which legally lasted in Brazil from 1500 to May 13, 1888—and thus my country was the last in the Americas to abolish this atrocious economic system—was emphasized by historian Nelson Werneck Sodré in his book *Formação economica do Brasil* (Economic development of Brazil): "the African slave is marked by his color, which is like a label." (1970: 248) The obvious implication is that ever since the beginnings of colonization there existed an identification—race/color—marking the presence of the African. It is important to underline this fact because of the great role it shall play when we analyze the factors that produce racism. Various ideologues of racism, whether through mistaken notions, ingenuousness, or maliciousness, make a habit of appealing to conceptual metaphors like "the exclusive relation of *master* and *slave*" which would be possible only on a purely subjective plane. Not by any means can it be said that by coincidence or quirk of fate black Africans are the only people of all times to have been subjected to the chattel slavery of Europeans. It is only futile and facile escapism to deny the fact that the slaves' bondage was inextricably bound up with their *race*, a fact easily confirmed by the enslavement of the white masters' own sons and daughters of mixed blood. Yet many of our own best minds fall into such a fallacy.

What is curious in this treatment of the matter is that the occurrence conjoins researchers, scientists, writers and ideologues of all tendencies, including those of the so-called left. In Brazil they pontificate theories and behave pragmatically, when it comes to the antiracist struggles of the black people, by directly following the models and definitions of the ruling strata, exclusively white or white-aspiring: a society which for centuries has been immersed in a culture that is intrinsically prejudiced and prejudicial to the black. We see reactionaries sustaining the liberal-paternalist myth of "racial democracy," a formula of domestication that is extremely efficient in perpetuating, transfigured, the concepts of inferior race predominant in the past, today out of mode. But let there be no mistake: in essence nothing has changed. For the dominant classes, exploitation, disdain toward the Afro-Brazilian and his aspirations remain inalterable. The Brazilian left, with its endorsement of "racial democracy" or with its systematic refusal to see social facts objectively, implicitly supports the most retrograde positions regarding the possibilities of a society truly multiracial and multicultural. The attempt to mask racism, or better, the custom of substituting its identity by labeling racism as a simple accident in the dialectics of class, in practice becomes a valuable service to the antinational forces that threaten the legitimate interests of the Brazilian people, of whom African descendants are more than half. As such, we constitute a majority to whom is denied not only our inalienable original identity, but also our right to reclaim it.

Those who act in this way reinforce the manipulations of the reactionary right, collaborate with the elites of Aryan origin, in the propagation outside the country of a false image. According to it, blacks, after the abolition of slavery in 1888, in the words of Marxist historian Caio Prado, Jr., would have been integrated and absorbed "by the new social order and economic structure in which they came to participate, and which conditioned them entirely in their culture and personality." (1966: 222) Following this line, assuming such postulates, Brazil goes on to become a rich exporter of models. The model of cruel military dictatorship fancied as democratic revolution. The model of giving away the country's resources to the multinationals, with the blessings of the "economic miracle." The model of ethnic oppression and genocide under the label "racial democracy."

We mentioned previously the constant pressures and threats to which Afro-Brazilians are subjected inside the borders of our country. The opportunity arises to point out that external threats are also configured in this scheme, as of now looming not only before black Brazilians, but also before Africans and their descendants in every part of the world. I refer to an old project, which presently is being once more dynamized by virtue of the contingencies in the dispute for influence and power among the world giants: the Alliance or Treaty of the South Atlantic.

Let us look rapidly at the behavior and attitudes of Brazil in questions and decisions on her international policy. In this area, obviously, blacks have never participated nor had a voice. In fact, as a group or community, Afro-Brazilians have never participated, on any level, in power: be it economic, political, or administrative; be it judicial, executive, or legislative. Never have they belonged to the circles of decision-making, even in matters that affect them immediately, much less in the international policy of the country. For example, blacks have never been heard when in the United Nations the decolonization of the African continent is discussed or voted on. During the entire process of decolonization Brazil voted with Portugal—that is, against independence for the colonies of Guinea Bissau, Angola, and Mozambique. At times, Brazil opted for the recourse of abstention, which in practice is the same as the voting against.

Portugal inaugurated the historical epoch of imperialist aggression in Africa when, in 1482, Diogo Cão "discovered" the Congo. From this point on, until about 1945, the end of the Second World War, European colonizers—large and small—took upon themselves the mission of "civilizing" slices of African territory, which they sacked, terrorized, and enslaved in the name of Christ. Portugal, having been the first to enter, was the last to leave Africa—following, it would seem, a sort of family tradition in which Brazil participated by being the last in the Americas to abolish slavery. . . .

The foreign policy of Brazil is based upon, and indeed subordinate to, colonialist interests of all species and forms. Our own president, Juscelino Kubitchek, declared that Brazil's foreign policy was the same as Portugal's, going to the extreme of stating that our independence had been a "gift" from Portugal. (Rodrigues 1964: 395) Brazil signed a Treaty of Friendship and Consultation with Portugal on November 16, 1953, in the time of Getúlio Vargas's presidency. The treaty favored exclusively the international manipulations of Salazarist colonialism, in radical detriment to Africa. Around this time Portuguese writer Almerindo Lessa stated: "Brazil is and will increasingly be a cornerstone of our Atlantic policy, and specifically in our African action." (Rodrigues 1964: 356) A statement of predictive truth, as we shall see below.

To this line of activity in the United Nations and the wider context of international politics is aligned a tendency of Brazilian thought which has in Gilberto Freyre one of its most conspicuous representatives. Freyre took on a role of veritable justifying ideologue of Portuguese colonialism. He began the praise and valorization of the Portuguese in Brazil with his book *Casa Grande e Senzala* (Mansions and shanties), following with a celebration of Lusian superiority in colonizing the tropics in another work entitled *O Mundo que O Português Criou* (The world that the Portuguese created).

Under such ideological direction Brazil voted in the U.N. in favor of Portugal when, in 1957, the euphemism of Portuguese colonialism designating her colonies in Africa as "provinces" was discussed. (Rodrigues 1964: 366) The Ministers of Foreign Relations of Brazil—be they formally entrenched in the most illustrious reactionarism as a Raul Fernandes, or socialist-laborite as a Hermes Lima, or of liberal-reactionary tendency as Negrão de Lima or Afonso Arinos de Melo Franco—all of them facilitated, with their particular gestures, the expansion or permanence of Portuguese colonialism. One of them, Minister João Neves da Fontoura, with an amazing lack of decency, modesty, or shame, declared in 1957: "Our policy with Portugal is not even a policy. It is family business." (Rodrigues 1964: 357)

In 1969, a Special Committee of the United Nations was created to investigate the implementation of the General Assembly's Declaration on the Granting of Independence to Colonial Countries and Peoples of December 14, 1960. This committee documented and reported on the continuing horrors of the colonial situation in all of Southern Africa (Rhodesia, Namibia, and the Territories under Portuguese Administration). The Committee reported on the bloodletting and atrocities committed by Portugal in Africa, *condemning*

> the persistent refusal of the Government of Portugal to implement General Assembly resolution 1514 (XV) and all other relevant resolutions of the General Assembly, the Security Council and the Special Committee, as well as the colonial war being waged by the Government against the peoples of the Territories under its domination, which constitutes a crime against humanity and a grave threat to international peace and security. (Report 1974: 115)

At the same time, the Committee declared itself

> *Deeply disturbed* by the intensified activities of the foreign economic, financial and other interests which impede the realization of the legitimate aspirations of the African peoples in those Territories to self-determination and independence,

> *Noting further with profound concern* that Portugal continues to receive aid in the form of military training, equipment, weapons and logistic and other assistance from certain States, and in particular from its military allies, which enables it to pursue its military operations against the population of those Territories. (114)

In a section entitled "International Relations of Portugal Affecting the Territories under its Administration," the Report devotes a whole subsection to "Luso-Brazilian relations":

> 101. As reported previously (A/6700/Rev. 1, chap. V, paras. 91–93), in September 1966 Portugal and Brazil signed agreements on trade, technical and cultural cooperation and a joint declaration on economic cooperation. Instruments of ratification in these respects were exchanged between the two Governments only in March 1968, although both countries appear to have considered the provisions of the agreements to have taken earlier effect and the Economic Committee established under the provisions of the new trade agreement, had already met several times before that date.

> 102. In July 1968 Mr. Franco Nogueira noted that within the United Nations, the Governments of Portugal and Brazil took the same positions on the problem of international control of atomic energy, and that as a result, Portugal furnished Brazil with uranium completely free of any conditions. Later, in October, the Minister for Foreign Affairs of Brazil, Mr. Magalhães Pinto, said at a press conference in New York that the links of sentiment and friendship between Portugal and Brazil were very sincere and that in the General Assembly Brazil would vote

against any measures hostile to Portugal; it would abstain on sanctions against Portugal and vote against any proposal of a boycott.

103. For the first time in their history, in August 1968, Portugal and Brazil held joint naval manoeuvres in Brazilian waters. Participating Portuguese naval craft included the newly delivered frigates, the Admiral Pereira da Silva and the Admiral Gago Coutinho. (Report 1974: 149)

These actions and attitudes on the part of Brazil, of course, were in direct violation and persistent noncompliance with the many United Nations General Assembly resolutions condemning Portugal's colonial wars of aggression. Resolution 2395 (XXIII) of November 29, 1968,

5. *Appeals* to all States to grant the peoples of the Territories under Portuguese domination the moral and material assistance necessary for the restoration of their inalienable rights;

6. *Reiterates* its appeal to all States, and in particular to members of the North Atlantic Treaty Organization, to withhold from Portugal any assistance which enables it to prosecute the colonial war in the Territories under its domination;

9. *Urgently appeals* to all States to take all measures to prevent the recruitment or training in their territories of any persons as mercenaries for the colonial war being waged in the Territories under Portuguese domination and for violations of the territorial integrity and sovereignty of the independent African states;

11. *Deplores also* the activities of the financial interests operating in the Territories under Portuguese domination, which obstruct the struggle of the peoples for self-determination, freedom and independence and which strengthen the military efforts of Portugal. (Report 1974: 122)

Brazil ignored this and continued her collaboration with Salazarism.

In return for this collusion, this familiarity with that colonial impotency which imagined itself a potency, according to a denunciation made by Mr. Dadet of the Republic of the Congo (Brazzaville) to the United Nations, Portugal offered Brazil a participation in its colonies as compensation for her help in maintaining the Portuguese Empire. (Rodrigues 1964: 4) José Honório Rodrigues sketches the perfect portrait of these events:

We voted always with the colonial powers in the United Nations, we gave in to all the Portuguese pressure, that of the oligarchical government of Salazar or that which emanated from the colony, and from time to time we would mask our colonial alignment with abstentions. We had not one word of sympathy for African liberty. (1964: 372)

To illustrate this fact we will list a few of the innumerable resolutions discussed and approved by the General Assembly of the United

Nations, underlining the vote of Brazil. Of eleven resolutions supporting the independence of the Portuguese colonies in Africa, there were three votes by Brazil against, six abstentions (these can be counted as votes against), and two votes in favor, one of which, in 1974, took place on the eve of the winning of independence by the Africans, at a time when it was no longer possible to try to impede it.

In its single meaningful vote for independence, Brazil voted in favor of Resolution 2288 (XXII), adopted by the General Assembly on December 7, 1967. (Round-up, Session XXII, Part VI: 13–16) The resolution approves the report of the Special Committee on the Situation with Regard to the Implementation of the Declaration on the Granting of Independence to Colonial Countries and Peoples in Southern Rhodesia, South West Africa, and Territories under Portuguese Domination and reiterates its call to all member states to support Resolution 1514 (XV) and other revelant resolutions calling for decolonization.

A year later, however, when Resolution 2425 (XXIII) was voted on December 18, 1968, repeating essentially the same principles, Brazil abstained: Portugal and South Africa being the only countries to vote against. The United States took the same recourse of abstention along with the United Kingdom. This resolution contains the following clause:

> *Requests* all States to take practical measures to ensure that the activities of their nationals involved in economic, financial and other concerns in dependent Territories do not run counter to the rights and interests of the colonial peoples in conformity with the objectives of resolution 1514 (XV) and other relevant resolutions. (Round-up, Session XXIII, Part VI: 18–20)

This clause was the major difference from the 1967 resolution.

On November 21, 1969, the General Assembly adopted Resolution 2507 (XXIV), the first of these to deal specifically with the Portuguese government itself. A few of its clauses will be instructive here:

> *Condemns* the persistent refusal of the Government of Portugal to implement resolution 1514 (XV) and all other relevant resolutions of the General Assembly and the Security Council; [. . .]

> *Deploring* the aid which the Government of Portugal continues to receive. [. . .] *Urges* all States, and particularly the States of the North Atlantic Treaty Organization, to withhold or desist from giving further military and other assistance to Portugal which enables it to pursue the colonial war in the Territories under its domination. (Resolutions, Session XXIV, VI: 3–5)

The resolution also

> *Reaffirms* the inalienable right of the peoples of Angola, Mozambique and Guinea (Bissau) and of other territories under Portuguese domination to self-determination and independence in accordance with General Assembly resolution 1514 (XV);

> *Reaffirms* the legitimacy of the struggle by the peoples of those Territories for their independence and freedom; [. . .] *Condemns* the collaboration between Portugal, South Africa and the illegal racist minority regime in Southern Rhodesia, which is designed to perpetuate colonialism and oppression in Southern Africa;

> *Deplores* the activities of the financial interests which obstruct the struggle of the peoples under Portuguese domination for self-determination, freedom and independence and which strengthen the military efforts of Portugal. (Resolutions, Session XXIV, VI: 4)

Brazil abstained on this resolution also. (6)

Resolution 2795 (XXVI)—adopted on December 10, 1971—eloquently evokes the deteriorating situation of the Portuguese colonies and the progressively more intense violence and horror of Portuguese attacks on innocent Africans. In it the General Assembly

> *Condemns* the indiscriminate bombing of civilians and the ruthless and wholesale destruction of villages and property being carried out by the Portuguese military forces in Angola, Mozambique and Guinea (Bissau); [. . .]

> *Calls upon* the Government of Portugal to refrain from the use of chemical substances in its colonial wars against the peoples of Angola, Mozambique and Guinea (Bissau), as such practice is contrary to the generally recognized rules of international law embodied in the Protocol for the Prohibition of the Use in War of Asphixiating, Poisonous or Other Gases, and of Bacteriological Methods of Warfare, signed at Geneva on 17 June 1925, and to General Assembly resolution 2707 (XXV) of 14 December 1970;

> *Calls upon* the Government of Portugal to treat the freedom fighters of Angola, Mozambique and Guinea (Bissau) captured during the struggle for freedom as prisoners of war in accordance with the principles of the Geneva Convention relative to the Treatment of Prisoners of War, of 12 August 1949, and to comply with the Geneva Convention relative to the Protection of Civilian Persons in Time of War, of 12 August 1949; [. . .]

> *Calls upon* all States to take immediate measures to put to an end all activities that help to exploit the Territories under Portuguese domination and the peoples therein and to discourage their nationals and bodies corporate under their jurisdiction from entering into any transactions or arrangements that strengthen Portugal's domination over, and

impede the implementation of the Declaration with respect to, those Territories. (Resolutions, Session XXVI, Part VI: 7–12)

And, as the acts of Portugal become graver and more horrible, the support given by Brazil to those acts becomes more adamant: this time Brazil voted against.

On the 20th of December of the same year, the General Assembly passed Resolution 2878 (XXVI), again

> *Strongly deploring* the policies of those States which, in defiance of the relevant resolutions \of the Security Council, the General Assembly and the Special Committee [. . .] continue to co-operate with the Governments of Portugal and South Africa and with the illegal racist minority regime in Southern Rhodesia; [. . .]
>
> *Requests* the Special Committee to undertake a special study on the compliance of Member States with the Declaration and with other relevant resolutions on the question of decolonization, particularly those relating to the Territories under Portuguese domination, Namibia and Southern Rhodesia, and to report thereon to the General Assembly at its twenty-seventh session. (Resolutions, Session XXVI, Part I: 63–68)

Once again, Brazil resorted to her usual recourse of abstention. (68) The resolution further

> *Urges* all States and the specialized agencies and other organizations within the United Nations system to provide [. . .] moral and material assistance to all people struggling for their freedom and independence in the colonial territories. (65)

In 1972, the United Nations General Assembly heard the historic and tragically moving speeches of Amilcar Cabral and Marcelino dos Santos, leaders of the liberation movements of Guinea Bissau and Mozambique, respectively. On the strength of these statements and many other considerations, the General Assembly took the landmark step of recognizing the national liberation movements of Angola, Mozambique, and Guinea Bissau as the "authentic representatives of the true aspirations of the peoples of those Territories." (Resolutions, Session XXVII, Part VI: 2) It recommended that they be included in all matters pertaining to the Territories, "in an appropriate capacity and in consultation with the Organization of African Unity" (2), pending the accession of the Territories to independence. Almost all the other concepts embodied in the aforementioned resolutions were incorporated, along with more specific wording of the condemnation of

> the persistent refusal of the Government of Portugal to comply with the relevant provisions of the aforementioned resolutions of the United Nations, and in particular, the continuation by Portuguese military forces

of the indiscriminate bombing of civilians, the wholesale destruction of villages and property and the ruthless use of napalm and chemical substances in Angola, Guinea (Bissau) and Cape Verde and Mozambique, as well as the continued violations of the territorial integrity and sovereignty of independent African States neighboring Angola, Guinea (Bissau) and Cape Verde and Mozambique, which seriously disturb international peace and security. (2)

Brazil, despite her claims to anticolonialism, voted against this resolution, on November 14, 1972.

About a month later, the General Assembly passed a resolution dealing with the "Activities of foreign economic and other interests which are impeding the implementation of the Declaration on the Granting of Independence to Colonial Countries etc." This resolution, 2979 (XXVII), states that the Assembly,

Deeply disturbed by the increasingly intensified activities of those foreign economic, financial and other interests in the Territories which, contrary to the relevant resolutions of the General Assembly, assist the Governments of South Africa and Portugal [. . .] and impede the realization by the peoples of the Territories of their legitimate aspirations for self-determination and independence; [. . .]

Condemns the policies of the colonial Powers and other States which continue to support those foreign economic and other interests engaged in exploiting the natural and human resources of the Territories without regard to the welfare of the indigenous peoples, thus violating the political, economic and social rights and interests of the indigenous peoples and obstructing the full and speedy implementation of the Declaration in respect of those Territories; [. . .]

Requests all States to take effective measures to end the supply of funds and other forms of assistance, including military supplies and equipment, to those regimes which use such assistance to repress the peoples of the colonial Territories and their national liberation movements. (Resolutions, Session XXVII, Part VI: 18–19)

Brazil, once again, abstained on this point so essential to the decolonization of the Portuguese-dominated African nations. (20)

On December 12, 1973, Resolution 3113 (XXVIII) concerning the "Question of Territories under Portuguese Administration" condemned

the brutal massacre of villagers, the mass destruction of villages and property and the ruthless use of napalm and chemical substances, in order to stifle the legitimate aspirations of those peoples for freedom and independence;

and demanded that the Government of Portugal discontinue its pitiless repression of the inalienable rights of those peoples including the eviction from their homes and the regrouping of the African populations in *aldeamentos* and the settlement of foreign immigrants in the Territories;

and reiterated the demand that Portugal adhere to the Geneva Convention relative to the treatment of prisoners of war; it

invites the International Committee of the Red Cross to continue to maintain close contact with the liberation movements, [. . .] to provide reports on conditions in prisoner of war camps and treatment of prisoners of war detained by Portugal. (Resolutions adopted on the reports of the Fourth Committee, Session XXVIII: 212)

This resolution also contains the points made in the previous sessions on this subject. (210–214) Brazil voted *no* on Resolution 3113. On the same day Resolution 3117 (XXVIII) on the activities of foreign economic and other interests repeated the concepts of the former resolutions on the same subject which we have looked at. Brazil abstained. A year later, in 1974, when it was clear that the wars of liberation were won, Brazil finally voted in favor of Resolution 3299 (XXIX) on the activities of foreign economic and other interests, essentially the same as 3117.

These actions went beyond a simple lack of sympathy or absence of friendship to Africa. They constitute an irreducible position of Brazilian antagonism toward the legitimate aspirations of Africa:

Nothing more, not one message of sympathy, not one solidarity, not one gesture, not to speak of cooperation, as if the spring of African Power were embarrassing to us, as if the other soul that we posssess humiliated us, as if we were ashamed of our common identity, as if it were possible to continue this dichotomy between international policy mandated by a Europeanized elite, which worked for the conservation of the status quo, and the people, whose entrance in the arena of decision-making began only now. (Rodrigues 1964: 372)

Rodrigues wrote this passage before 1964, when at least it was theoretically possible to hypothesize "popular participation" in decision-making. From 1964 on, the military implanted fascism, excluding workers, students, and marginalized poor, from any and all political activity. A good part of the population was excluded from the country, and languish in exile all over the world.

Once more let us reiterate the obvious: neither before nor after 1964 did the black people have any opportunity to form an integral or even minimal part of the significant levels of Brazil's society and conventional institutions. Their destiny was, and continues to be, social marginalization, even in the regions where they are an absolute majority of the population, as illustrates the state of Bahia.

The rejection of this aspect of the Brazilian personality mentioned by Rodrigues—the influence and presence of black African formation in our culture and population—is not a characteristic monopolized uniquely by a Europeanized "elite" which dominates the politics of our country. It is also characteristic of some of the most "progressive" theoreticians, the ideologues of the "Brazilian Revolution." Intellectuals of Marxist orientation are among those who most deny the existence of the racial question as a determinant of social problems, maintaining that the problem is one of confrontation between *master* and *slave*, *oppressed* and *oppressor*, *rich* and *poor*—and not one of race or color. They themselves at times constitute the best proof that the situation of blacks, past and present, results in great part from a *racism* which transcends class conscience. We have a significant example in "revolutionary" historian Caio Prado, Jr. He shows clearly his position on the African soul of the Brazilian people when he writes:

> European immigration constitutes a factor particularly notable in the stimulation of the cultural models of the Brazilian population. A fact which has as easy and immediate proof the great differentiation verified, in this aspect, between the South and the North of the country, and which is due in great if not principal part, to the incorporation in one case, and the absence in the other, of appreciable demographic contingents which were situated in levels sensitively superior to those of the preexistent mass of the working population of the country. (1966: 130)

For those who are not familiar with the geographical traits of Brazil, this statement needs some translating. It refers to the fact that the Northeastern area—especially Bahia—is known for the tremendous wealth and proliferation of African and Afro-Brazilian cultural forms, particularly in its religion, music and dance, and cuisine. The southern areas, especially São Paulo and Rio de Janeiro, are more "advanced"—i.e., more urbanized, industrialized, commercialized, mechanized, impersonalized, and plasticized—with cultural modes *purely imitative of the U.S. and Europe*, which dominate not only the economy but also the ways of life. More importantly, the South was inundated throughout this century by a massive influx of white European immigrants, many subsidized by the State in order to whiten the population. Caio Prado manifestly considers them "sensitively superior" in stock and culture to the "preexistent mass of the working population"—African slaves and their descendants. The unabashed white supremacist grounding of this statement is a representative sample of the mind-set of the Brazilian left while preaching "racial democracy" and workers' unity. . . .

This passage reveals a racism complementary to that other, underlying the Law-Decree No 7969, signed by the dictator Getúlio Vargas in

1945, regulating the entrance of immigrants into the country, which was to obey the "necessity to preserve and develop in the ethnic composition of the population the more convenient characteristics of its European ancestry." (Skidmore 1974: 219) Both, Marxist and dictator, coincide fully in their assumption that African culture is inferior, which, incidentally, reflects the dominant concept held in Brazil about African heritage in the culture and the population of our country. A concept succinctly summed up in the words of Nina Rodrigues, mulatto scientist and influential writer who from the beginning of this century anathematized: "The black race in Brazil shall remain forever as the basis of our inferiority as a people." (1945: 28)

Thus we have an invariable constant: the African, enslaved or "free," is irreducibly an inferior being. The suppression of the slave traffic, in 1850, and the abolition of slavery, in 1888, events which should have furnished opportunities for social integration through salaried labor, became in practice allies to the repressive forces. Afro-Brazilians, whom the ruling classes of white European cast had not allowed to prepare for the system of free market labor, were *rejected* as a source of labor in the new system. Caio Prado talks about the "stimulation" of European immigration of workers to "overcome the lack of labor force." (1966: 128) He doesn't explain how there could be an absence of labor force when millions of blacks recently "freed" could not find means of living or subsistence.

Even before the abolition of slavery, in the year 1882, the black labor force was "leftover," rejected by the system, whose declared objective was the liquidation of the African and his descendant in Brazil. A statistical survey in that year in the important provinces of São Paulo, Minas Gerais, Bahia, Pernambuco, Ceará, and Rio de Janeiro, obtained the following breakdown (Moura 1972: 54):

> Free Workers 1,433,170
> Slave Workers 656,540
> Desocupados (Idle) 2,822,583

These figures reveal that the category of the unemployed was larger than that of free workers and slaves together. The term *desocupado* was the pejorative used for so-called free Africans, ex-slaves to whom the right to life by free labor was denied. Expelled by the dominant society, their strength having been exhausted in the enrichment of that same society, they were cast into a kind of slow death by hunger and all sorts of destitution. An inexorable extermination without drawing blood: very convenient for the system. It is easy to follow the rhythm of this genocidal process by observing the diminution of the number of slaves as the 13th of May—the date of Abolition—approaches (Moura 1972: 52):

Year	Population of Country	Slave Population	Percent Slaves
1850	5,520,000	2,500,000	31
1852	8,429,672	1,500,000	15
1887	13,278,616	723,419	5

Naturally the number of slaves diminishes and that of the "idle" increases. And so we see that nothing really changed for the African: from *legal slavery* he became captive of de facto slavery. The white European immigrant filled what Caio Prado calls the "lack of labor force." The old white Brazilian stock of Portuguese-colonial origin and recent white immigrants came together to build the wall of racial discrimination against blacks.

The contempt of the dominant classes of Brazil toward Africa and Africans is a reality that has lasted from colonial times to the present. The eyes of this Brazil, following the gaze of colonizing interests, turned yesterday to Europe as today they are looking to the United States. Consequently, her foreign policy can only reflect this reality, in which the black is absent, among other reasons because the Ministry of Foreign Relations is, by tradition, one of the strongest bastions of racial discrimination in Brazil: there exists not one black diplomat, in a country whose population is in its majority black. Since 1850, with the suppression of the slave traffic, Brazil has turned its back on Africa, from whence had come those who constructed its economy and peopled its territory which had been emptied, in part, by the massacre of the indigenous peoples, still today in full execution.

During the entire process of discussion and voting in the United Nations around the decolonization of Angola, to whom our historical formation and development owe a debt of blood, labor, and artistic tradition impossible to evaluate in all its extension, Brazil maintained itself, as we have seen above, as the valuable ally of fascist Portugal. At times it attempted to mask its position by resorting to abstention, at times distributing *official notes*, of which we will reproduce an example here in part: a communication of 1961 in which Itamarati (Brazilian Ministry of Foreign Relations) says about the decolonization of Angola,

> the position of our Country results, on the one hand, from the firm anti-colonialist position of the Government, and on the other, from the international commitments and the ties of extremely special nature that unite Brazil and Portugal. (Rodrigues 1964: 380)

Such special ties could as well be inscribed in the Treaty of Friendship and Consultation as they could be found in the "extremely special" agreement denounced in the U.N. by the delegate from the Congo. Nothing can be said in certainty, for silence, secrecy, and conspiracy preside over and envelop the gestures and conjectures of Brazilian diplomats, as if Itamarati functioned as a veritable laboratory of occult acts and sciences.

Here it is appropriate to relate a recent event involving this colonial inheritance of secretiveness that predominates in Itamarati. Researching in the United Nations data with reference to the International Convention on the Elimination of All Forms of Racial Discrimination (General Assembly, December 21, 1965), I went to the respective Committee to see the document submitted by Brazil as justification for her adherence to the Convention. I found only that, even in such a case of general interest, Brazil does not allow her presentation to be divulged—provoking suspicion that she must have adhered with restrictions which she is publicly ashamed of.

All of these events of the foreign policy of Brazil as well as our racial relations inside the country, transform certain declarations by the Brazilian Government into raw material for "white humor." This is what happens with the contents of a letter from President General Ernesto Geisel to the Secretary General of the United Nations on the occasion of the International Day for the Elimination of Racial Discrimination. The president, of good Aryan (German) stock, reinforced the traditional style of Brazilian racism:

> I wish to associate myself, in the name of the Brazilian Government and people, to the universal manifestations of repudiation of the practices of Apartheid and of racial discrimination. [. . .] We Brazilians share the conviction that the rights of the human person are disrespected in those societies where connotations of racial order determine the degree of respect with which individual liberties and guarantees should be observed. We offer, to counter this scheme, which unfortunately endures, the example of a society formed by the spontaneous and harmonious integration of many races: which integration is the very essence of the Brazilian nationality. (*O Estado de São Paulo*, March 22, 1977: 25)

Here we are dealing with a document reiterating the traditional historical position of the dominant strata with relation to African descendants: their systematic liquidation through "whitening." It is necessary to insist on this point in Geisel's letter. The "essence of the Brazilian nationality" is its inalterable ideology and practice of genocide.

Brazil linked herself so faithfully to the imperialist policies of Portugal in Africa, most likely believing in the "Eternity" of colonialism as preached by the Portuguese ambassador in Washington, Pedro Teotonio

Pereira. He emphatically declared in 1961: "We shall continue in our mission in Africa, believing firmly that there we shall still be when all this dust raised by anticolonialism has settled to the earth." (Rodrigues 1964: 348) The association is, in fact, an old one. Let us evoke history. Brazil obtained independence in 1822. Angola was accompanying from the other side of the Atlantic her emancipationist movement. And this is when Brazil signs her first treaty with Portugal, where "she declares to renounce all policies of alliance with Angolan separatist forces." (Clington 1975: 83) And so Brazil remained, up to and after the recent independence of Mozambique, Guinea Bissau, and Angola, servile handmaiden to the most retrograde European colonialism, that of Portugal. Servile to the extent of imprisoning and torturing, in the famous military prisons of the current fascist dictatorship, representative of the MPLA Lima Azevedo. This was one of the first acts of the present regime when it seized power in 1964, giving public proof from the start of its willingness to bear the responsibility of seeing to the "special" tasks of Western civilization and its powers.

It is not surprising that Brazil's immigration policies have been marked always by the preoccupation of prohibiting the entrance of Africans and stimulating, facilitating, even financing the entrance of Europeans of good Aryan stock, including most recently the policy of receiving with open arms the racist whites expelled from Kenya, the ex-Belgian Congo (Rodrigues 1964: 285), and from Mozambique and Angola. Brazil proclaimed herself the hideout of racist and genocidal criminals among whom stand out the names of Antonio Tomás and Marcelo Caetano, the president and prime minister of Salazarist Portugal, the last to disgrace the lives of the Portuguese and African people.

The representative of Belgium in the Commission of Information on Nonautonomous Territories of the United Nations had well-founded reasons when he sustained the thesis of "internal colonialism" supposedly protecting but in reality attacking the Indians of Brazil, to whom we can add millions of African Brazilians subject to all forms of aggression and prohibitions due to their ethnic origins.

The problem of the South Atlantic, its strategic and commercial importance, has been a preoccupation of Brazilian politicians and military men since immediately after the Second World War, when Colonel Golbery do Couto e Silva, currently General-in-Chief of the Civil House of President General Geisel—his closest advisor—advocated the Atlantic as a "peace route," in search of "cooperation and amity." (Rodrigues 1964: 371) It seems that the old dream of a South Atlantic Treaty Alliance, which would include Portugal, South Africa, Brazil, and Argentina, is now on the way to becoming a reality.

In its July 1977 issue, the magazine *Africa* published an article entitled "Pretoria Turns to the Latins," in which it examines the steps being taken by the U.S. to resolve certain strategic and economic problems caused by the historical agony of the racist regime of South Africa, the liberation wars in progress in Zimbabwe and Namibia, and the stabilization of the new governments of Mozambique and Angola. The United States, in no position to intervene directly in these affairs, and reluctant to openly ally itself with white supremacy in South Africa, has found the most convenient path in a South Atlantic Treaty Organization, modelled after NATO. In the words of Zbigniew Brzezinski, Kissinger-surrogate to Jimmy Carter:

> The Southern Atlantic Alliance offers Washington the tool it needs to protect its perceived interests in a post-Vietnam world. Using local allies to serve as proxies is in line with the "Nixon Doctrine." (*Africa*, July 1977: 71, citing Brzezinski article in *Foreign Affairs*)

The object of such a treaty is the integration of South Africa into the perimeters of Western (U.S.) defense, and the "local allies" in this case would be Brazil, Argentina, Chile, and South Africa.

The article in *Africa* relates that "secret talks have been going on since at least 1969 among these countries." It cites a meeting in the Argentine naval base of Porto-Bergano, immediately after the overthrow by the military of Isabel Perón, between the U.S., Argentina, and Brazil, at which naval maneuvers and coordination were discussed along with the general question of security in the South Atlantic. The newspaper *La Nación* of Buenos Aires, recognized mouthpiece of the military regime, commented on this occasion:

> Only three countries, which by their cultures and their traditions are part of the Western World, have a Geographical situation which enables them to play an important role in the control and the protection of the Southern Atlantic: Argentina, Brazil and South Africa. (*Africa*, July 1977: 71)

Soon after this, a joint Argentine-Brazilian military mission arrived at the naval base of Simonstown in South Africa to plan the logistics of future cooperation. South Africa's weakest military force is her navy. The three South American countries have strong naval power which could be of invaluable assistance to the Pretoria regime.

Africa accentuates the recent inauguration of a Buenos Aires-Pretoria air connection, demonstrating the effort on both sides to beef up commerce between an isolated South Africa and the lucrative markets of South America. It goes on to point out that

> Brazil and Argentina are striving to reduce their marked dependency on
> their American suppliers by diversifying their uranium sources. As is
> well known, Pretoria has one of the largest reserves of uranium of the
> world. Using this important bargaining card, it can negotiate its way
> into the Latin American market under favorable conditions. (1977: 71)

Last year, Pretoria's naval commander, James Johnson, was present as a
participant in the Inter-American naval exercises. In Rio de Janeiro in the
summer of 1976, the Eighth Inter-American naval conference highlighted
the threat of the "bridgehead which the pro-Communist countries have
acquired because of the friendly government in Angola."

The dangers of such an alliance have been denounced at the United
Nations by the former Minister of the Exterior of Angola, José Eduardo
dos Santos, who declared that "it is in effect an offensive military pact
against southern Africa and it constitutes a menace to world peace." (1977:
71) And indeed, recent history shows with what efficacy the arms of NATO
aided Portugal in her colonial wars against the people of Angola and
Mozambique. It is but the latest of futile efforts of the repressive forces
of the West against the people of Africa: for, as Samora Machel, leader of
the people of Mozambique in combatting the sophisticated technology of
NATO and Portugal, underlined in his speech to the Symposium in Honor
of Amilcar Cabral held in Conakry on January 31, 1973:

> It was the struggle, the unity of the people in their combat, [. . .] that
> not only permitted the people to forge their personality, but also to as-
> sert themselves on the international level. And it is this that the bullets
> shot by the agents of PIDE [Portuguese intelligence] at Amilcar Cabral
> or the murderous bombs dropped by the airplanes of NATO against the
> population were never able to impede. (1–2)

South Africa's institutionalized policies of apartheid constitute the daily
practice of genocide against the majority of Africans in that country by a
white minority. This criminal act directly affects all peoples of African
origin. To stop its continuation with impunity, to prevent the reinforcement of this destructive force, is a duty of self-defense that imposes itself
on all of us as blacks, as Africans of the diaspora.

This Congress witnesses a historical epoch in which the Africans of
this part of the world, surpassing the phase of lamentation or declama-
tion, are moving in the sense of organizing ourselves to confront the great
battle of our future, of our existence, with liberty and dignity. Consequently I propose that this Congress direct itself to the governments of
the U.S., Argentina, and Brazil as well as Chile, transmitting our repul-
sion and our energetic opposition to the maneuvers, diplomatic and military, and the conservations, meetings, or any other events that could lead

to the concretization of the South Atlantic Treaty Alliance or any other entity under any denomination that attempts to mask the objectives of collaboration with the racist white criminals heading the government of South Africa.

References

Clington, Mário de Sousa (1975) *Angola libre?* Paris: Gallimard.

Machel, Samora (1973) *Falar de Amilcar Cabral é falar de um povo.* Intervention by FRELIMO in Symposium in Homage to Amilcar Cabral, Conakry, January 31, 1973. Lisbon: Edições CEC (mimeograph).

Moore, Carlos (1972) *Were Marx and Engels White Racists?—The Prolet-Aryan Outlook of Marx and Engels.* Chicago: Third World Press.

Moura, Clovis (1972) *Rebeliões da senzala: Quilombos, insurreições, guerrilhas.* Rio de Janeiro: Editora Conquista.

Nascimento, Abdias do (1977) *"Racial Democracy" in Brazil: Myth or Reality?* Ibadan: Sketch Publishing Co., Ltd.

Prado, Caio, Jr. (1966) *A revolução brasileira.* São Paulo: Editora Brasiliense.

"Pretoria Turns to the Latins" (1977) (Special Report), *Africa.* London: Africa Journal Ltd., July (No. 71), 70–71.

Rodrigues, José Honório (1964) *Brasil e Africa: Outro horizonte,* 2nd Edition. Rio de Janeiro: Civilização Brasileira.

Rodrigues, Nina (1945) *Os Africanos no Brasil.* São Paulo: Companhia Editora Nacional.

Skidmore, Thomas E. (1974) *Black into White: Race and Nationality in Brazilian Thought.* New York: Oxford University Press.

Sodré, Nelson Werneck (1970) *Formação economica do Brasil,* 5th Edition. São Paulo: Editora Brasiliense.

United Nations (1974) *Report of the Special Committee on the Situation with Regard to the Implementation of the Declaration on the Granting of Independence to Colonial Countries and Peoples,* Volume II. U.N. Official Records: Twenty-Fourth Session. Supplement No. 23, New York: United Nations General Assembly.

United Nations General Assembly Round-Up and Resolutions, Sessions XXII-XXIX. New York: United Nations General Assembly.

11

Afro-Brazilian Women, Civil Rights, and Political Participation

Darién J. Davis

The task of integrating women into the history of Africa, Asia, and Latin America poses the same challenges as including women in European and U.S. history. That is, say Cheryl Johnson-Odim and Margaret Strobe, the effort must involve "the expansion of conceptual categories that in explaining male, rather than integrated, human experience, have treated women as anomalies." Many scholars attempting to explore women's roles in Latin America have either stereotyped them as exotic or victimized or have presented them in monolithic categories, such as Third World women.*

Chandra Talpade Mohanty, in particular, has criticized feminists in the United States and Europe for erroneously lumping all women in Third World nations into the "oppressed" category, suggesting that this practice displays a paternalistic view by Western women who see their position as superior. Any discussion of race and gender requires an understanding that all systems have their own dynamics, sets of values and resources, and mechanisms of justice and punishment. Furthermore, paradigms that divide a society into strict categories of oppressed and oppressors ignore the possibility that subordinates create their own destinies, even with the limited resources at their disposal. Such analyses perpetuate the idea that women and the poor, for example, are helpless victims rather than actors who take part in the construction of their lot.†

*See Cheryl Johnson-Odim and Margaret Strobe, *Restoring Women to History* (Bloomington, IN: Organization of American Historians, 1988), 1–30.

†Chandra Talpade Mohanty, "Under Western Eyes: Feminist Scholarship and Colonial Discourse," *Boundary 2* 12, no. 3 and 13, no. 1 (Spring and Fall 1984): 333–57.

The involvement of Afro-Creole women in civil rights movements and politics provides an object lesson. Civil rights can be defined in many ways by members of different groups and genders.* For many Afro-Creole women, they mean eliminating poverty and class oppression. The struggle against latent and overt day-to-day discrimination notwithstanding, many Afro-Creole women have more immediate concerns, such as their children's welfare, upkeep of their homes, fair salaries, health, and education. Previous histories of civil rights in Latin America have focused on the campaign for economic and political opportunities, thus overlooking these concerns of women.

In this chapter, Darién J. Davis, professor of history at Middlebury College, looks at the issues of class, race, and gender and the involvement of women such as Ruth de Souza and Lélia Gonzalez in the civil rights movements and politics in twentieth-century Brazil. Examining the lives of Afro-Creole women, it provides an overview of participation in the Black Brazilian Front (FNB), the Black Experimental Theater (T.E.N.), and the Unified Black Movement (MNU). It reproduces an interview with Ruth de Souza and reviews the political activities of Benedita Souza da Silva. In November 1992, sixty years after the creation of the Black Brazilian Front, da Silva became the first Afro-Brazilian woman candidate for mayor of Rio de Janeiro. Great changes have occurred in Brazil as a result of the consciousness-raising movements throughout the twentieth century, and women like da Silva have helped forge this transformation.

African and Afro-Creole women are often marginalized in national literatures and histories in general as well as in scholarship that focuses on the African dimension of Latin America, Caribbean cultures in particular. Yet they have played crucial roles in the construction of modern American societies. As slaves, African women served as mothers for their own families as well as surrogate mothers for the children of the white masters. They were the central figures of the Afro-Creole matriarchal families as well as wet nurses for white infants. Furthermore, the manumission of slave women far outnumbered that of men. Women often formed extended families based on social and economic relationships and liaisons with free blacks, people of color, and whites.

Women also played a key role in the *quilombos*, the escaped-slave communities. Felippa María Aranha was a leader of one such community that joined together with Amerindians in Trombates, a region of the Amazon, to resist Portuguese domination. Other Afro-Brazilian women were famous as trustees of African traditions and customs in Brazil. Priest-

*Gerda Lerder, "Re-conceptualizing Differences among Women," *Journal of Women's History* 3 (Winter 1990): 106–22.

esses (*mae de santos*) were important leaders in the *candomblé* religion, for example.[1] Sinhá Inocência was a famous Bahian who has become legendary. A slave in the nineteenth century who had an extraordinary talent as a storyteller, she often told her stories in Nago, the language of the Yoruba people. Storytelling was an important art form through which Afro-Creoles preserved their heritage. Scholars continue to uncover the contribution of women like Sinhá Inocência to Latin American culture.

The struggle and contribution of Afro-Creole women in the social movements for equality and justice throughout the twentieth century stand out vividly in Brazil. The 1920s and 1930s marked the beginning of a new generation with greater working-class consciousness. Several movements emerged proclaiming the rights of their members. Issues of women's suffrage, workers' representation, working conditions, and fair wages were all a part of the demands of these new groups.

The principal objective of these movements was integration, based on the request that rights be allocated to a sector of society from which they had been withheld. The major civil rights movement of the 1930s, the Frente Negra Brasileira (FNB), founded in São Paulo, emphasized this integrationist goal.[2] The FNB was well informed on local as well as international conditions, keeping a watchful eye on social movements around the world. Yet its focus was decidedly national, in the spirit of cooperation and not defiance. The principal aim was to build and strengthen ties and to influence the political process. Civil rights for the Frente meant equal treatment under the law and the right to work free of discrimination.[3]

The FNB—founded in 1930 and the first national civil rights organization in Brazil—saw race and gender rights as intimately related. As a result, a women's department was created within the movement. This subcommittee, called the Departamento Feminino da FNB (Women's Department of the Black Brazilian Front) served as a forum for the promotion of the ideas of women of color in Brazil. Women of the FNB opposed sexual discrimination, harassment, and exploitation, and called upon their male counterparts to work with women for the procurement of rights for all.[4]

Many of the women involved in the FNB came from the working class. Even though the Women's Movement had procured the right to vote in 1932, Afro-Brazilian and popular-class women felt alienated from this increasingly elitist effort. At the Second National Feminist Convention, held in Bahia in July 1934, the delegates present resolved to support women in their quest for political office. However, the convention endorsed only upper- or middle-class women with prestigious family backgrounds.[5]

Many Afro-Brazilian women saw the FNB as more in line with their goals. Together they forged a sense of pride and dignity, promoting a forum for mutual support. Many of the women worked as domestics, as clerks in stores, and in the growing manufacturing and transport industries. By 1933 those who joined the movement were known as *frentenegrinas* and were considered strong, assertive, dependable women who would not tolerate sexism or racism. This reputation had both its advantages and disadvantages. Many employers specifically asked for *frentenegrinas*. Others would not hire them because of their involvement in a movement that many conservatives thought of as disorderly and reactionary.

The political aspirations of the Frente were thwarted due to the creation of Getúlio Vargas's Estado Novo in 1937, which banned all political organizations, including the Women's Movement. By the early 1940s national attention, in any event, had turned to World War II. Five years after the war had ended, the second major civil rights movement emerged: the Teatro Experimental do Negro (T.E.N.). In May 1949, T.E.N., along with several other Brazilian interest groups, organized the First National Negro Congress in an attempt to foster research on black issues. T.E.N. went on to take part in the psychological polarization of Brazilian thought.

Members of T.E.N. demanded proper treatment of all citizens in the fields of politics, economics, and, especially, education. T.E.N. deemed it indispensable to include women's issues in its struggle against the status quo. Like the Frente, T.E.N. created a forum for the promotion of ideas that concerned women. It was important to inform Brazilians of the national and regional accomplishments of Afro-Creoles in particular. One of the cofounders of T.E.N. was the formidable actress Ruth de Souza, only seventeen years old at the time. T.E.N. published several articles on Souza and on a number of other Afro-Brazilian women who were viewed as role models for the population at large.[6]

Women used *Quilombo*, the journal of T.E.N., for the dissemination of their ideas. A regular column, "Fala Mulher" (Woman speaks), appeared in *Quilombo*, and the columnist María Nascimento dedicated her energies to giving the woman's perspective. She reminded readers of the importance of Afro-Brazilian women of all backgrounds and classes to society. Particular emphasis was given to women from the popular classes. Many domestics who reared middle-class and elite children and many women who lived in the cities' *favelas* (slums) were lauded as good, humble, hard-working Brazilians.[7]

T.E.N. began as a theatrical group that aimed at promoting black issues through the arts. The intimate relationship between art and politics in the history of Brazil led many graduates of T.E.N. to utilize their art as a symbol of their personal struggle in society. Such was the case of Ruth de Souza. Her long and accomplished career as an actress spanned from 1945 to 1989. In 1988, she was honored with the Order of Rio Branco for her contribution to the arts.

Souza's voice is another example of the diversity of the African diaspora in the Americas. She is well respected in Rio and throughout Brazil. She does not speak for all women nor does she represent the Afro-Brazilian population. Her comments come from the struggles of her own life, her own career, and her very personal political philosophy.

I began my work in the theater along with a group of black actors creating the Teatro Experimental do Negro. At the time (1940s) there were very few black actors and actresses. There was only Grande Otelo, a great Brazilian actor. Many blacks were involved in musical theater and dance groups, but not in cinema or theater. T.E.N. proved, really, that blacks could be actors. We began with many great works: works by Eugene O'Neill and of course by Brazilian dramatists as well. After five years of struggle and experience with T.E.N., I went on to do cinema and later television. Haroldo Costa[8] and I were two of the first blacks to begin work in television. Haroldo, who was also in T.E.N., is a great director and actor.[8]

One of the first plays that we did was *Emperor Jones* by Eugene O'Neill. This was superb—we performed it in the Municipal Theater which was reserved for the greatest operas and foreign troupes. A group of blacks performing *Emperor Jones* was a great occurrence. Everyone commented at the time that it was a great event.

I think that all my life I have had a passion for acting. When I was young, I was afraid that I could never be an actress because at the time we were very influenced by the images from Hollywood. Everyone was very blonde, very pretty, and the participation of blacks, even in the United States, was very limited. I always wanted to be an actress, but I was afraid because of my color. T.E.N. changed all that. It gave the initial space to actresses like me. I was the first, yes, I think, the first black actress to perform theater in Brazil.

My dream was to continue to perform in a theater group, but we had so few possibilities. Many blacks don't have educational possibilities. The few that do aren't particularly interested. Blacks don't have a high level of culture, not because they are black but because of the conditions that don't allow them to go to school. Theater? Why go? It is difficult when blacks are suffering from underemployment and unemployment. It's amazing, I've tried very hard and I have forty-three years of experience behind me.

T.E.N. did not only create a theatrical movement. The director, Abdias do Nascimento, was involved in many things—politics, beauty competitions, etc.[9] We began doing too many things in my opinion. But in one sense, the theater was a way to call attention to the black movement. When we began there were three hundred people. Many small groups eventually broke off to form other groups. Brasilianse, for example, was a dance group that eventually traveled to Europe. Solano Trinidade founded the popular Brazilian theater group interested more in folklore, so even though we began united, different interests separated us.

But from the beginning T.E.N. was very diverse. I was a student when I joined the group, like Haroldo Costa, but there were many different types of people involved, domestic workers, some even unemployed. Many were illiterate.[10] They were humble people and didn't really have an understanding of theater.

After T.E.N., I turned professional along with many others. Today, some people consider me one of the most well known black actresses in Brazil. I even won a scholarship to study in the United States for one year. I went to Cleveland, Ohio, to participate in a theater group. I also visited New York and Washington, DC. When I returned I had already decided to be a professional. There are few actresses that live from acting in Brazil. I love cinema, it's such an important part of my life.

I spent a wonderful time in the U.S. In New York, I went to the great shows on Broadway, and in Washington, DC, I visited Howard University. Let me tell you a story about Howard. When I was a child, I saw an article in *Life* magazine that showed a photograph of the entrance to Howard University. And I thought, how wonderful it would be to attend such a university. I kept the magazine and when the directors of the Rockefeller Foundation came to Brazil, I asked them if they would give a black actress the scholarship. When I eventually won the scholarship, they asked me where it was that I wanted to go. Now, I had very little knowledge of the U.S. So I mentioned several places, but I also said that I would like very much to go to Howard University.

When I was in Cleveland, I took a train to Washington, DC. From the train station, I took a taxi to Howard University. When we passed through the entrance it was as if I were entering the photograph from *Life*. It was a dream come true. At Howard, I had contact with students. I did everything. It was such a different experience from Brazil. It was so difficult just to create a black theater in Brazil, so you can imagine that I took advantage of the opportunities at a black university.

When I returned to Brazil, I did a very important film, *Sinhá Moça*.[11] That was in 1954. I was nominated for best actress for that film at the Venice Film Festival in 1954. Lilli Palmer, Michelle Morgan, and Katharine Hepburn were also nominated for the award. I was very, very happy. Who could imagine a South American black woman competing for an award with such well-known actresses? Even though I didn't win, I was very happy. Being nominated was an award in itself.

Although I eventually left T.E.N., it was the first cultural and artistic movement to give a space to black artists. Although today it is still a fight. There was a time when I was really tired of playing roles of a slave woman, domestic servant—marginals, you know. One has to fight against these stereotypes. My story is not a happy one, but I never look at the negative side. My mother washed clothes for a living, but she enjoyed the cinema and always took me with her. You see, I learned everything I know from intuition, I never really had a formal education in Brazil, and of course I was very insecure, but when I went to the United States and returned, I knew that I was on the right track.

It was difficult though and I never had any heroes or heroines or role models. But I always try my hardest. We have to! An actress is an actress—regardless of race. Later I worked on television and also adapted to that medium. Through my work, I have made a contribution to the black movement. Politically, there are many groups that have formed, but I hate politics. I try to be a good citizen, but I don't believe in endorsing any agenda. I believe that the artist has to use his work as a form of protest, but politics should not destroy the artist.[12]

Although Ruth de Souza did not participate directly in many of the organizations of the 1950s, she recognized the importance of politics and was deeply aware of the unique struggles of women in Brazilian society. Debates between the importance of individual versus collective action are endemic to every social movement. Souza chose to use her work to represent her individual contribution to the Afro-Brazilian movement. In the period after Souza left T.E.N., several women followed her tradition, including Lea Garcia, another well-known actress in Brazil today. This was also the period in which T.E.N. became more politicized. Several organizations were formed within T.E.N. that represented the concerns of women. One was the Congresso Nacional das Mulheres Negras (Black Women's National Congress), which served as a center mainly for professional women, domestic workers, and female artists. The female sector of T.E.N. called for the integration of women of color into social life. In the spirit of self-help, it carried out several major activities: a literacy campaign, a children's theater for the recreation and education of young people, and several educational seminars for mothers.[13]

Since the 1950s, Afro-Brazilian women have continued to develop and forge identities as members of the struggle for justice in their country, and several organizations have emerged in the postauthoritarian period. One well-known organization was the Black Women's Collective, which focused on the care and education of children as well as providing legal assistance to women in a variety of matters. On July 2, 1975, a group of women signed the "Manifesto of Black Brazilian Women," which declared opposition to the exploitation of women of color.

Individuals like Souza have continued to rise, gaining recognition in the arts, society, and politics. The diverse mosaic that is the Afro-Brazilian experience continues to be formed with the contribution of these women. Lélia de Almeida Gonzales, for example, ranks among the most important Afro-Brazilian women in the post-1950 period. She was one of the first to hold an academic position at the Federal University of Rio de Janeiro, and she was one of the cofounders of the Unified Black

Movement against Racial Discrimination. This organization, founded in São Paulo, achieved national attention with a public demonstration against racial discrimination on May 13, 1979, the anniversary of Brazil's 1888 abolition of slavery. It was also the precursor of the most organized black civil-rights movement to date, the Unified Black Movement (MNU).

The MNU, more so than its predecessors, recognized its multiple dimensions. Women played and continue to play key roles in the forging of the movement's agenda. Although many of the issues remained the same—discrimination, prejudice, lack of jobs, and low salaries—the 1980s brought a different focus: police brutality, health care, violence against women, the rights of children, and the right to religious expression. Women like Gonzales recognized that in order to change attitudes it was necessary to begin with education. In 1976, Gonzales had organized the first course on African culture in Brazil ever to be taught in an institution of higher education.

The MNU has attempted to form associations and liaisons to promote its ideas throughout the nation. In the northeastern state of Bahia, Arani Santana was a professor and actress involved in the formation of the MNU there. Bahian women started the Black Women's Front, which had concrete aims in the area of education. Many times there were conflicts with the men of the movement. Women believed that often the focus was too concentrated on political protest and demonstrations of solidarity to the detriment of long-term transformational goals such as education. The MNU women in Bahia organized classes of adult education based on the ideas of Paulo Freire, who laid down the foundations of a grass-roots campaign for education and consciousness-building.[14] Initially this proposal did not receive much attention from the men in the movement. Nonetheless, the women of Bahia went into neighborhoods such as the Fazenda Grande do Retiro to begin their campaign, and after six months met with much success.[15]

In other regions of Brazil, education became a forum of protest for women, independent of the MNU. Leda María Martins represents another part of the mosaic. A young professor, poet, and essayist from the rich mineral state of Minas Gerais, Martins resides in Belo Horizonte but teaches in the Faculty of Letters at the Federal University of Ouro Preto. She has done comparative studies of black identity and culture in the United States and Brazil. She is particularly interested in the theatrical representation of black culture in each country and believes that in both the United States and Brazil theater and art in general have served an important function in the expression of identity and self-affirmation. Her experience with the two cultures is extensive. Like Ruth de Souza's, Martins's consciousness was heightened by her experiences in the United

States. She has held a visiting professorship at the University of California, Berkeley, and has taught at Indiana University. She has played an important role in demystifying the negative images of blacks throughout history, and her voice continues to echo on the importance of diversity and the reconstruction of a national identity.

Throughout the 1980s, individual voices and organizations continued to be heard. According to Paulo dos Santos, researcher for the Centro dos Estudos Afro-Asiaticos, the end of the 1970s signified a watershed for civil rights in Brazil. Much of the consciousness-raising and fighting for civil rights was related to the emergence of the national liberation of Luso-African republics such as Angola and Mozambique.[16] Brazilians were also affected by the Women's Movement and civil rights in North America. Groups coming forward in the late 1970s and 1980s were characterized by ideological flexibility and political pluralism. By 1985 more than four hundred separate but related civil rights groups had emerged in different regions throughout the country, with the MNU becoming the overall umbrella organization.[17]

The MNU encouraged and endorsed Afro-Brazilian men and women to run for political office through alliances with leftist parties. Two of the stronger ones were the Workers' Party (PT) and the Democratic Workers' Party (PDT).[18] Many Afro-Brazilians benefited from this close alliance. A primary example was the Rio de Janeiro politician Benedita Souza da Silva. Although women emerged from many classes and backgrounds, da Silva is a unique representation of the Afro-Brazilian presence in the political arena, one of the areas that has been less penetrated by the popular classes. Political institutions have been most resistant to change, retaining the patriarchal heritage of colonial times. In Rio de Janeiro alone, only four of the forty-two members of the state congress are Afro-Brazilians.

For this reason, Benedita Souza da Silva is a remarkable political force who challenges the establishment on many fronts. She is a living testimony to the gains that Afro-Creoles have made in the sphere of Latin American politics. At the age of fifty, she made history by becoming the first Afro-Brazilian woman to run for mayor of Rio de Janeiro in the elections of November 16, 1992. Born into an impoverished family of thirteen children, da Silva comes from the poor neighborhood of Chapeu de Mangueira. She became politically active during the Goulart regime, speaking out on the hardships of the *favelas* and on the need for better education and health care. Da Silva had two strong family role models in her life: her mother, a *macumba* priestess, and her grandmother, an ex-slave. At the age of twenty-six, she became an Evangelical Protestant when she joined the Assembly of God Church, and in the 1970s, when leftist and progressive associations began to protest the injustices of the authoritarian regime, she joined the PT.

The MNU had emerged with the growing protest against the policies of the military dictatorship. Even within the ruling regime there was a desire for transition to democracy or, as some called it, a "redemocratization." General Ernesto Geisel (1974–1979) was a relative moderate who guaranteed free congressional elections. His successor, João Figueiredo (1979–1985), continued in his footsteps, leading to the first general elections of November 1982. The following year da Silva was elected to Rio de Janeiro's city council on the Workers' Party ticket. In 1987 she became the first Afro-Brazilian woman ever elected to Brazil's Congress. She was also chosen as national vice president of the Workers' Party.

In the primary elections for mayor of Rio de Janeiro, Brazil's second largest city, da Silva received much more support from voters than did the ruling party's candidate, but in the final election her opponent, Cesar Maia of the moderate Democratic Movement Party, won by a slim margin. Despite this outcome, da Silva's political activity remains a watershed in modern Brazilian history. Her political aspirations, motivated by a real desire to alleviate the problems of the popular classes of the cities and the *favelas* from which she comes, have inspired the nation.

Notes

1. See Chapter 6 in this volume on African religious influences in Latin America, especially in Haiti.

2. Several documents provide rich sources of information for regional studies. Magazines and newspapers with such names as *O Bandeirante*, *Senzala*, and *Libertade* attempted to address national issues related to blacks in a manner similar to the groups in Cuba.

3. "A lei do Lynch," *O Clarim d'Alvorada*, 28 September 1930, n.p. See also "Destroe o paternal imperialismo norteamericano," ibid.

4. "Associação cívico feminina," *A Voz da Raça*, December 1936, n.p.

5. Morris J. Blachman, "Selective Omission and Theoretical Distortion in Studying the Political Activity of Women," in *Sex and Class in Latin America*, ed. June Nash and Helen Icken Safa (South Hadley, MA: J. F. Bergin, 1980), 245–57.

6. "Romances de Jorge Amado," *Quilombo* 1, no. 1 (December 1948): 6.

7. María Nascimento, "Crianças Racistas" ("Fala Mulher"), *Quilombo* 1, no. 3 (June 1949): 3.

8. Haroldo Costa also is the author of the collection of interviews entitled *Fala Criolo* (Rio de Janeiro: Editora Record, 1986).

9. The beauty contests were designed to encourage "black beauty." There were two major contests: the queen of the mulattas and "The Tar Baby." For a critical assessment of these contests see Dorris J. Turner, "The Teatro Experimental do Negro and Its Black Beauty Contests," *Afro-Hispanic Review* 11, no. 1–3: 76–81. For more on Abdias do Nascimento see Chapter 10, fourth selection, in this volume.

10. T.E.N. also conducted literacy classes in which many of the members were taught how to read and write.

11. *Sinhá Moça*, directed by Tom Payne, received national and international recognition. It won three Brazilian awards: Saci, O Indio, and Governador do Estado de São Paulo.

12. This is a direct translation of Ruth de Souza's words with slight editing for added clarity. The excerpt is taken from the author's interview with Souza in her home in Rio de Janeiro in the summer of 1990.

13. "Instalado a Conselho Nacional das Mulheres Negras," *Quilombo* 2, no. 7–8 (March–April 1950): 4.

14. Freire is closely linked with the liberation theology movement. He is professor of history and the philosophy of education at the University of Recife, in northeastern Brazil. He believes that the educational system in Brazil was created with built-in stereotypes and prejudices against the majority of the students and proposes a system that develops dignity and self-esteem.

15. See *1978–1988: Dez anos de luta contra o racismo* (São Paulo: Movimento Negro Unificado, 1988), 13–15.

16. Chapter 12 in this volume looks at the role of Latin American nations, especially Cuba, in the struggles for independence in Africa.

17. Paulo Roberto dos Santos, "Conciência negra, conciência nacional," *Bandeirantes* 58, no. 6 (December 1985): 1.

18. John Burdick, "Brazil's Black Consciousness Movement," *NACCLA Report on the Americas* 15, no. 4 (February 1992): 23–27. The PT was led by Luis da Silva, former president Fernando Collor's principal opponent in the 1989 election, while the PDT was led by the charismatic Rio de Janeiro politician Leonel Brizola. For a good overview of race relations in São Paulo see George Reid Andrews, *Blacks and Whites in São Paulo, 1888–1988* (Madison: University of Wisconsin Press, 1991).

12

Cuban Policy for Africa

Armando Entralgo and
David González López

National governments employ a number of strategic tools in international relations to promote or discourage cooperation with other nations or to exert influence over them. Four major international policy instruments are: 1) diplomatic relations; 2) geopolitical treaties and agreements; 3) military aid; and 4) economic and humanitarian aid. Governments pursue relations based on goals that may change depending on the regime in power. Given their lack of political and economic power, Latin American nations have focused on establishing good relations with developing countries rather than with one another.

Despite the historical bond between Latin America and Africa discussed in this volume, few countries in the Americas had established relations with African nations prior to the decolonization that began in the 1960s. Cuba, whose involvement with the continent had been nonexistent before the 1959 revolution, was one of the first to announce its solidarity with African peoples in their struggle for liberation. Elaborated in the interest of Cold War ideological politics, Cuba's African policy provided Fidel Castro with both prestige and visibility. It made him an important force in Third World politics, although he failed to displace the nonaligned leadership of Marshal Josip Tito of Yugoslavia. Castro asserted that Cuba had a revolutionary obligation to assist in the creation of a just society free of imperialist exploitation and to eradicate all forms of institutional racism that allegedly plagued colonial societies. As early as 1962, Cuba established diplomatic relations with several African countries; and, in 1963, Castro sent combat troops to Algeria. Involvement grew with the

From Jorge I. Dominguez and Rafael Hernández, eds., *U.S.-Cuban Relations in the 1990s* (Boulder: Westview Press, 1989), 141–53. Reprinted by permission of Westview Press.

*establishment of the Organization of African Unity in 1963, and Cuba
began to offer numerous scholarships to black students from Angola and
Zimbabwe.*

*Cuba's commitment provoked other nations in the West into paying
greater attention to Africa. Prior to the 1970s the U.S. Department of
State had paid scant attention, but Cuban activities as well as other causes
drew its notice. The Cubans repeatedly voiced their solidarity with blacks
in white-ruled South Africa, and their involvement in Namibia and Angola
helped secure the independence of both countries. Policymakers in
Havana reiterated that their solidarity with these nations resulted from
the historical impact that Africa has had on the culture of Cuba.*

*The following essay—by Armando Entralgo, former Cuban ambas-
sador to Ghana, and David González López, director of the Department
of Sub-Saharan Africa of the Center of African and Middle Eastern Studies in Havana—outlines Cuba's commitment to Africa from the 1960s to
the 1980s. Both Entralgo and González López have written extensively
on African issues.*

Cuban revolutionary praxis with respect to Africa has often been perceived by successive U.S. administrations as running counter to its
interests and those of its allies. Therefore, many Western views of the
subject have tended to distort Cuba's objectives, dramatize its impact,
and misrepresent the essence of its actions, especially over the past twelve
years. It has now become standard for any meeting of U.S. and Cuban
scholars on the general subject of relations between the two countries to
include the question of these links (which Cuba and a good number of
African countries have been establishing, exercising their respective sovereignty) as an "issue of conflict" between these two countries of the
American continent.

However, a quick review of a comparison of declarations and deeds
over thirty years of revolutionary policy allows us to formulate the hy-
pothesis that the execution of Cuba's Africa policy has been coherent
with respect to the principles stated, and continuous on the basis of postulates that have been maintained throughout the period in question, beginning in 1959. This, of course, does not exclude adjustments, appropriate
clarifications, adaptations to particular circumstances, or even changes
of perspective or assessment of a concrete situation.

That is, while preserving its essential principles, easily identified
throughout these three decades, Cuba's policy, far from [being] immo-
bile, has adopted nuances under the effect or the circumstances of the
historical moment. Based on this adaptation, its relations with a given
country might have changed. The most frequent cases can be generally
classified in two kinds of circumstances. The first includes some African
governments that at a given moment and notwithstanding a platform of

progressive policies, made certain concessions that were inappropriate from the viewpoint of Cuba's policy toward Africa. In most of these cases, these governments' actions brought them nearer to their own extinction and isolation. The case of the Somali regime is the paradigm of this first category (particularly after its opportunist aggression in 1977 against the nascent revolutionary process in Ethiopia). Also in the first category are Morocco and post-Nasser Egypt, whose policy turnabout stifled relations with more than one Third World country.

The second category groups the African countries perceived by Cuba as extremely dependent on capitalist countries but that, at a given moment, began to take—or actually took—clear nationalist and anti-imperialist stands. Thus, they received the support of socialist countries, notably Cuba. This category includes Cuba's good relations with successive Nigerian military governments, or the gradual establishment of diplomatic and other normal relations with governments that are ideologically different from that of Cuba (such as Zaire and the Ivory Coast) as well as the slow but steady renewal of contacts with Hosni Mubarak's Egypt that appears to have—according to Cuban perspectives—more pragmatism in foreign policy than its predecessor, in spite of persisting profound differences.

The Bases of Cuban Policies

There is an old history of the human links between Cuba and Africa and, as a result, there has been a significant impact of African culture on Cuban culture. Nonetheless, relations between Cuba and Africa were quite limited until the Cuban revolutionary government expanded them after 1959. This happened only to a small degree as a result of this cultural background or as a consequence of the fact that only after 1960 did the massive decolonization of Africa begin: Latin America—including that part of Latin America with a heavy black influence—barely had relations with Africa in the 1960s and the 1970s, due fundamentally to an orientation similar to that of Cuban governments before 1959. This factor also delayed the incorporation of the official Latin American world into the Nonaligned Movement. What mainly motivated the development of Cuba's relations with African countries after 1959 was the nature of Cuban foreign policy, the principles that sustain it, and its evident acceptance on a continent recently liberated from colonial occupation and that is still the victim of colonialism's effects.

The principles of Cuba's policy toward Africa are clearly put forward in many fundamental documents of the Cuban revolution. They can be summarized as follows:

1. *Denunciation of colonialism and support for national liberation struggles.* From the first statement by the new representative of the Cuban revolutionary government to the United Nations in 1959, Cuba's solidarity with the cause of the Algerian patriots was made evident. Beginning thereafter, Cuba repeatedly condemned the Portuguese colonial presence during the entire period of its existence.

2. *Denunciation of institutionalized racism in southern Africa in the form of apartheid in South Africa, its extension to Namibia, and its expression in the Rhodesian regime.* Hence, Cuba's support for the nationalist movements in the three countries was made known early on.

3. *Denunciation of the neocolonial policy of the leading capitalist powers in Africa.* This principle encompasses the firm solidarity with the cause of Patrice Lumumba and with the countries of the "Casablanca Group" since its inception in 1961. The Cuban revolutionary government identified this group of countries as the most committed to the struggle for real decolonization and for positive nonalignment, in the founding of which they were coparticipants.

4. *Support for the cause of anti-imperialist unity among African states, culminating in 1963 with the creation of the Organization of African Unity (OAU) with the essential aim of eradicating the powerful colonial-racist remnants and neocolonial interference.* These aims were consistent with those of the Cuban revolutionary government. Therefore, Cuba offered active and unlimited support for African unity, regardless of the OAU's limitations, particularly in its first years of existence.

5. *Establishment of diplomatic relations and mutually beneficial collaboration with any number of the OAU, irrespective of its political regime.* Relations were first established with the governments of the "Casablanca Group" and later with Congo-Brazzaville and Tanzania. By the late 1960s and early 1970s, diplomatic ties and collaborative links were developed with a considerable number of countries that were very active in the UN and in the Nonaligned Movement in the search for converging interests worldwide.

It must be remembered that during all these years Cuba lacked, and still lacks, the capacity that would allow it great volumes of commercial exchange or financing for large-scale projects with its African counterparts. However, in connection with the principles previously stated, the revolutionary government developed an increasingly strong policy of collaboration.

While the military aspect of Cuba's collaboration with the African countries—and particularly the presence of its troops—monopolized the attention of Western mass media from 1975 on, Cuba's civilian collaboration has been more continuous and extensive than its military counterpart in terms of its economic worth, the variety of its forms, and the growing number of beneficiary countries. The main characteristics of Cuban civilian collaboration are:

1. *Concentration in spheres of social impact in which Cuba has achieved notable progress, essentially those of health and education.* Cuba sent its first group of doctors and other health personnel to Africa (specifically, to Algeria) in 1963. Since then, Cuba's civilian collaboration has expanded and diversified. But health and education continue to be the two favored spheres. In the 1980s, the number of African scholarship students in Cuba exceeded thirteen thousand, a substantial number in absolute terms and even more so relative to Cuba's total population.

2. *Grants without profit motive or conditionality.* The departure of the first Cuban doctors for Algeria—just when the exodus of this professional group from Cuba forced the new revolutionary government to stretch its resources while launching its domestic projects to increase access to these services at home—set a precedent in the nature of Cuban technical collaboration: it was intended as an act of solidarity having a local, positive impact. It would not be a lucrative arrangement nor an attempt to place excess personnel abroad. Cuba's civilian collaboration was generally offered free of charge until 1977. In 1978, Cuba began to charge modest sums for some of the services offered mainly to oil-exporting countries whose incomes gave them the ability to pay. But the essential principle was not altered. Most African countries, which suffer from serious economic problems, continued to receive the assistance free of charge.

   In general, the host government covers the Cuban technicians' lodging and food expenses and gives them a modest per diem fee. The living conditions of these Cubans are much more austere than those of the typical foreign technicians; therefore, the host country can afford them more easily. Afterward, at the beginning of the 1980s, when the economic crisis struck Africa hardest, most of the countries that were being charged modest sums were exempted from payment, given the financial adversities that they were facing. Suffice it to mention the most important case in terms of the amount of the aid offered: from 1983 onward, Angola was again exempted from payment. Cuba's main gain from this type of collaboration lies essentially in the ideological and professional development of its specialists because they face particularly difficult working conditions, which they must overcome.

3. *Ability to respond and to adapt to local conditions.* On occasion, Cuba's granting of civilian assistance—in rapid response to urgent needs—even preceded the formal establishment of cooperation agreements, as was the case of Algeria (1963), Guinea-Conakry (1965), Congo-Brazzaville (second half of the 1960s), and Angola (1976), among others. Furthermore, aspects such as the austere life-style of the Cuban collaborators and the special programs adapted to the needs of the African students on Cuba's Isle of Youth point to the serious Cuban effort to adjust its collaboration to the requirement of the recipients.

4. *Good local acceptance and compatibility in the spirit of South-South cooperation.* The above-mentioned peculiarities have made Cuban cooperation very popular in Africa; local sources have often described it as an example of collaboration among developing countries.

Nevertheless, much of Western attention focused on the military aspect of the collaboration. But here, too, it would be fitting to recall its origins and patterns of occurrence. The most common manifestation of this type of collaboration consisted in the training of African cadres; sometimes, this type of cooperation led to small numbers of Cuban advisers being posted on African soil. In truly exceptional circumstances, military collaboration has led to the dispatch of combat forces. Although their appearance in Algeria in 1963 to assist that country in its war with Morocco—the first example of this exceptional situation—did not give rise to much controversy, more than a decade later the provision of a similar kind of assistance, albeit of larger proportions, to the governments of Angola and Ethiopia has remained in the headlines for several years.

In the case of Angola, the nature and extent of Cuba's commitment have been thoroughly explained from the Cuban perspective. Solidarity with the cause of the Angolan revolution was built on the basis of a shared history of oppression, rebellion, and heroism. But an outstanding factor was the way in which African governments, as well as African public opinion, accepted both the amount and the nature of Cuban assistance. In general, this Cuban military support for Angola was perceived in Africa as an active example of the defense of the juridical principles contained in the UN Charter and reaffirmed in that of the OAU, especially the exercise of the right to self-determination and the protection of national sovereignty in the face of an act of aggression by the South African racist regime against Angola.

In the case of Cuban military support for Ethiopia, which faced an invasion from Somalia in 1977–78, some of the factors of the Angolan scenario were not present, but African objections were not raised in this case either, owing to the fact that here another fundamental, very sensitive principle, peculiar to the OAU, was involved: that which precluded the use of force to change the borders inherited from colonialism. Of course, this does not exclude that governments such as that of Somalia (feeling directly affected by Cuban actions in Ethiopia) and others would have encouraged or promoted some of the actions that caused Cuba's military presence in Angola or Ethiopia. But the truth is that no significant objections were made, and Pan-African policy readily and clearly accepted Cuba's actions. These Cuban actions received important support, publicly stated, from governments ideologically quite distant from Cuba.

The arrival of Cuban military contingents on African territory and their permanence in Angola and Ethiopia over more than a decade allows for specific conclusions to be drawn concerning the circumstances in which these actions take place and the principles governing them:

1. *The action takes place following the breaking off of negotiations, of a pledge, or of an agreement by one of the parties, which decides to opt for a quick military victory through foreign intervention, unlawfully crossing internationally recognized boundaries.* Often Cuba's initiatives—initiatives that make clear its persistent effort to encourage peaceful solutions—have been ignored, even when these initiatives may necessarily imply concessions on the part of friendly forces.

2. *Cuba's favorable reply to the African request for aid has had generalized support among the governments of the continent and has been accepted by the OAU.* Respect for—and defense of—the objectives and principles of the OAU have been at the heart of Cuban concerns.

3. *The Cuban presence responds exclusively to situations of concrete aggressions or threats of aggression originating in other countries.* Both the continued behavior patterns of Cuba's troops within the borders of the host countries and the circumstantial

fluctuations of the number of its forces according to the situation prove the point.

4. *The permanence of Cuban troops depends on the sovereign decision of the host government and does not in any way hinder continued negotiations between the conflicting parties, who seek a lasting solution that would make said presence unnecessary.* In all the cases of conflict in which the military presence has been maintained, the host government has entered into negotiations of its choice—bilateral or multilateral, with or without Cuban participation—with a view to a definitive and honorable settlement for all parties involved. The recent evolution of the conflict in southern Africa, given its particular complexity, is probably the best example of this modus operandi.

The Negotiated Settlement in Southern Africa

In the early 1980s, the prospects for just solutions to the problem of Namibia and for the generalized crisis in southern Africa receded. From the perception of Cuba and of the black-majority governments of southern Africa—supported by the OAU—the paralysis stemmed in good measure from the attempts to establish a link between the independence of Namibia and the presence of Cuban military forces in Angola, the first being conditioned on the prior unilateral cessation of the second. According to the point of view of Cuba and the African governments, the paralysis was further complicated by the renewed and strong Western support for the South African regime and the considerable overt assistance granted to the Angolan counterrevolution after 1985, two matters in which the U.S. government has played a leading role.

Taking stock of the most recent years, the crucial element to be considered when analyzing future prospects is the fact that, contrary to many Western predictions, the African "Front Line" states facing South Africa have resisted pressures and acts of aggression of exceptional dimensions. Cuba's positions in the region, instead of being eroded, have enjoyed a growing endorsement in Africa and in other parts of the world. Even Western sources that earlier criticized the "intransigence" of the Angolan and Cuban positions now consider that the joint communiqués and common actions show signs of "realism" and "flexibility," despite the fact that the underlying principles have remained unchanged.

Some of the milestones on the road to the definition of common Angolan-Cuban positions bear this point out. After the signing of the Lusaka Accords between Angola and South Africa with the mediation of the United States—accords that were violated repeatedly by South

Africa—a Cuban-Angolan Joint Communiqué was issued in March 1984. It stated the principles that could have served as a basis, at that stage, for a "negotiated, fair, and honorable" agreement for all the parties. "Negotiated, fair, and honorable" are three key words to be taken into account to understand all the public positions taken by Cuba before and after this date. However, shortly afterward, the resumption of the arms supply to UNITA [Uniâo Nacional para Independência Total de Angola] by the United States stopped the talks, which had been going on for many months, between that country and Angola.

More recently, and just when Angola and Cuba were compelled to reinforce their military defenses due to the increase in South Africa's acts of aggression, Cuba and Angola formed a joint delegation, which participated in talks in Luanda with a U.S. delegation on January 28 and 29, 1988. According to the editorial published in Cuba's daily newspaper *Granma*,[1] at the meeting Angola and Cuba maintained that the indispensable conditions for a settlement were:

- the cessation of foreign intervention in the internal affairs of Angola (which was expressed in U.S. and South African logistical aid to UNITA);
- the withdrawal of South African forces, which have systematically raided Angola;
- implementation of Resolution 435 of the UN Security Council that leads to Namibia's independence; and
- international guarantees that there will be no more attacks on Angola.

The editorial added that, upon reaching an agreement on these bases, Cuba and Angola would be prepared to implement a "timetable for a gradual withdrawal of the Cuban internationalist contingent until all our combatants are repatriated." As in other statements that elaborate on the Cuban positions, the editorial adds that these are based on international law, on the UN Charter, and on successive UN Security Council resolutions. However, at that time the clear and precise Angolan-Cuban position referred to a scenario in which numerous elements of ambiguity still remained with regard to the positions of the other actors involved in the regional conflict, and which gave rise to a good number of doubts.

In the first place, toward late 1986 and early 1987, there were indications that some type of revision of U.S. policy for Africa was under way that might later facilitate the resumption of talks in the search for a settlement. It remained to be seen, however, whether this change of attitude was sufficiently comprehensive in the U.S. policy-making circles, and (even assuming that the shift reflected something more than a characteristic posture of a government nearing its end, and with that perspective alone in mind) whether U.S. diplomacy could at this time maintain its momentum and its ability to take the initiative, to make decisive progress along the difficult road to a settlement in the few months remaining in Ronald Reagan's presidency.

Other factors that fostered doubt were those introduced by the South African regime. At a time when preparations were being made for the dialogue between the joint Angolan-Cuban delegation and the U.S. delegation, toward the end of 1987, the South African army launched an attack deep into Angolan territory. It was the most important act of aggression since 1976. In addition, in an unprecedented action, high officials of the apartheid regime for the first time confirmed that their intention was to block an imminent UNITA military defeat.

These elements seriously threatened progress in the negotiations that seemed about to begin. In the military sphere, the unprecedented South African action forced Angola and Cuba to proceed with a major military reinforcement, which increased the number of Cuban troops in Angola to approximately fifty thousand. It also meant the urgent deployment of advanced military technology to Angola. In the diplomatic field, South Africa also jeopardized what remained of the U.S. project of so-called constructive engagement, since its actions also cast doubt on the presumed U.S. mediation ability to exercise a "moderating influence" on South Africa.

The above-mentioned *Granma* editorial foresaw alternative scenarios, in each of which the positions of South Africa and the United States would be decisive. It observed that "the solution now depends, fundamentally, on the position adopted by the government of the United States" regarding noninterference in the internal affairs of Angola and the firmness with which it commits itself to a political solution. This proposition was based on the conviction that "South Africa could not defy the entire world community if the United States were to join in the unanimous demand for implementation of Resolution 435."

The editorial does not rule out the alternative scenario of South Africa's seeking a military solution. This option would be extremely dangerous, but it posed a real, though latent, threat to be taken into account. In such a scenario, the editorial anticipated that the final outcome could very well be "the swan song of the odious apartheid regime," and for that reason it represented a much costlier risk for South Africa, "much more than what it would have to grant in order to find a negotiated solution as has been urged upon" all the parties.

The second scenario, according to the editorial, would foresee a negotiating process that would make unlikely the occurrence of the first scenario. In line with the principles that have characterized nearly a quarter of a century of the Cuban revolution's policy with respect to Africa, in good faith Cuba proposed the only course of action that could lead to a satisfactory settlement for all the parties. With Cuba's many years of experience based on excellent links with the African continent, and with complete confidence in the future, the editorial concluded [that] "a solution in a relatively short time is, in reality, objectively possible."

During the first months of 1988, the South African offensive against Cuito Cuanavale was stopped. Angolan, Cuban, and SWAPO [South West African People's Organization] troops carried out a counteroffensive that took their forces well to the south near the Namibian border. The reaction to these developments unleashed within South Africa itself was among the main reasons why South Africa decided, for the first time, to try to negotiate a just and lasting agreement that would encompass all of southwestern Africa. The four-party meetings, begun in London in May 1988, ended with the signing of the peace agreements for southwestern Africa on December 22, 1988, at UN headquarters in New York. These meetings were proof of the joint Cuban-Angolan delegation's will to negotiate in spite of "the deliberate hesitations and arrogant stands of the South Africans, and, at times, of the inconsistencies of the mediator [the U.S. government], an unmistakable ally of South Africa."[2]

The speech of Isidoro Malmierca, Cuba's minister of foreign relations, at the signing of the Tripartite Agreement was especially clear when he referred to Cuba's assessment of the importance of and the circumstances that made possible this agreement. He stated that "at long last it may be possible that the illegal occupation of Namibia may end and that this land may cease to be a South African colonial dependency and become instead a sovereign and independent country." Together with the withdrawal of South African forces from Angola, this creates "some of the fundamental bases to guarantee the security of the People's Republic of Angola and to permit the Angolan people to find the means and the ways to solve the conflicts that have led to a fratricidal war."[3]

Days later, Cuba's president Fidel Castro expressed his views on the talks and on the agreements reached: "The most wonderful outcome is to have reached all the goals that we set for ourselves without shedding even one drop of blood beyond what was necessary in order to solve the difficult military situation that appeared at the end of the past year. Though great were the accomplishments of the Cuban internationalist troops and of the courageous Angolan fighters on the battlefields, great, too, were the accomplishments in the diplomatic realm." He went on: "We have negotiated seriously and we have reached a serious accord."[4] From Cuba's point of view, the signing of the Tripartite Agreement "successfully ends one of the most glorious pages" of Cuban history.[5]

In summary, for the Cubans, the return of their fifty thousand troops from Angola represents the successful culmination of what has been the most important page in the history of these last thirty years of relations between Cuba and Africa. At the same time, it is a good opportunity to reaffirm the principles, objectives, and actions of Cuba's policy toward Africa. Cuban leaders have underlined that, once all the soldiers are back, "humanity will have witnessed the loyalty to principles that explain and encourage the policy of solidarity of the Cuban Revolution."[6] For Cubans, this aid "represented a modest but certain contribution to the struggle of the African peoples against colonialism, racism, and apartheid,"[7] and, at the same time, the "opportunity to honor our debt with Black Africa, one of the roots of the Cuban nation."[8] Our loyalty to these principles determined the firm decision to remain on African soil for as long as was needed, actively helping to strengthen the sovereignty of a sister nation against foreign aggression. The same commitment to principle was evident in our unwavering readiness to search for lasting solutions to the complex conflicts by means of negotiations "in close and creative brotherhood with the government of Angola, both acting fully independently and with the resolute will to favor a negotiated solution."[9]

This sustained, firm position eventually affected the "will of all parties" to the conflict—mainly South Africa and the United States—to contribute to, and it was the indispensable element to facilitate, an agreement acceptable to all interested parties participating in the negotiations. The Cuban government in particular rejects the versions that "grossly simplify what has happened, trying to present it as a simple understanding between the great powers, as if the rest of us were only the obedient implementors of their plans."[10] In response to the analysis that attributed to Cuba the wish to perpetuate its presence in Angola—and that, therefore, considered the withdrawal of Cuban troops a "failure" of Cuba's alleged aspirations—Cuba's leaders have reiterated what they have invariably stated since 1975:

> We did not go to the People's Republic of Angola in search of economic benefits, nor to defend strategic interests to which, as a small Third World country, we cannot aspire. Cuba does not leave behind in that sister nation military bases, or properties of any kind, or rights over Angola's riches. As we said twelve years ago, from Angola we will take only the love and the respect of its long-suffering and heroic people and the remains of the sons of the people of Cuba, who fell defending Angola's sovereignty and integrity against external aggression and apartheid.[11]

The Front Line states, the OAU, the Nonaligned Movement, and other important international actors have understood and welcomed not only the actions carried out by Cuba in 1975, but also Cuba's policy toward Africa in general. Thus, a growing number of countries are willing to accept Cuba's offer, presented by its minister of foreign relations, Isidoro Malmierca, in the following terms:

> We will work without fail to achieve peace and security in southwestern Africa and in any other part of the world where we may make a contribution to the opening and the consolidation of a potential of independence and development for all peoples without exception. Toward those ends, we will be ready to work with all those prepared to undertake real and specific actions, in the absence of a search for hegemony and of the ambition to profit.[12]

Notes

1. "¿Cuál sería la esencia de una solución negociada a los problemas de Angola y Namibia?" *Granma* (February 4, 1988), 1.

2. "La historia de Africa será diferente antes y después de Cuito Cuanavale," *Granma* (December 23, 1988), editorial on 2.

3. "Cuando el último combatiente internacionalista retorne a su patria, la humanidad habrá sido testigo de la lealtad a los principios que explican la política solidaria de la revolución cubana." Speech by Isidoro Malmierca, minister of foreign relations, in *Granma* (December 23, 1988), 7.

4. "Efectuado el VIII pleno del Comité Central," *Granma* (December 16, 1988), 1.

5. Ibid.

6. "Cuando el último," 7.

7. "La historia de Africa," 2.

8. "Cuando el último," 7.

9. Ibid.

10. Ibid.

11. Ibid.

12. Ibid.

Glossary

cafuso
Offspring of African and native American parents. Synonym for *zambo* in the Spanish-speaking world.

candomblé
Thriving Brazilian religion, practiced in Bahia, which was influenced by Catholicism and African folk religion.

Code Noir
French colonial law passed on March 10, 1685, that mandated the baptism and conversion of African slaves.

criollo (creole)
Historical term referring to person born in the Americas.

encomienda
Royal grant of tribute-paying Indians to a favored individual, often a conquistador, usually for one lifetime but sometimes extending over several generations.

Lusotropicalism
Theory, proposed by Gilberto Freyre, that the Portuguese colonizers developed a special ability to adapt and survive in the tropics and identify with other races and cultures as a result of their constant contacts with peoples of the tropics. The prefix "Luso" means "Portuguese."

macumba
General term referring to Afro-Brazilian cults and rituals, including *candomblé* (in Bahia), *Shangô* (in the extreme northeast), *Pajelança* (northeast), and *Batuque* (south).

mariñera
Popular dance that originated in the poor mulatto areas of Lima, Peru. Originally called the *Cueca Chilena* because of its popularity in Chile,

the name was changed in honor of the Peruvian marines during the War of the Pacific (1870–1880), when Peru fought against Chile.

mayoral
Literal translation is" mayor," but the mayoral was a local leader who had less power than modern-day mayors of towns.

merengue
National dance of the Dominican Republic with roots in African rhythms.

mestizaje
Mixing of cultures, peoples, and customs.

mestizo
Person of mixed stock; sometimes used as a euphemism for mulatto.

moreno
Person of brown complexion; synonym of *pardo* or mulatto.

mulatto
Offspring of the union of an African and a European. The children of mulattoes are also considered mulattoes. In Spanish and Portuguese America, often used to refer to a skin color between black and white; synonym of *pardo* or *moreno*.

Negrismo
Philosophical literary movement in Hispanic America that promoted the contribution of African culture to Latin America.

Negritude
Philosophical literary movement, originating in French-speaking countries in Africa and the Caribbean, that celebrated the contribution of African culture to the West.

orisha (orixá)
Spirits or deities of *candomblé*.

palenques
Runaway slave communities in Spanish America, equivalent to Brazilian *quilombos* or maroons in the English colonies.

pardo
Synonym of mulatto, but indicates person of color between black and white or yellow and brown; also called *moreno*.

patria

Homeland, often applied to a particular region within a broader national territory.

peninsulares

Term referring to persons born on the Iberian Peninsula (that is, in Spain and Portugal) to distinguish them from Creoles.

portero

Gate opener or guard. In colonial times, when many cities were surrounded by walls, the *portero* controlled traffic going in and out of the city.

pregonero

An official town crier who, in colonial times, proclaimed the news, usually in the town square or at some predetermined location.

pretos (**Port.**)/*prieto* (**Sp.**)

Black person of very dark color.

Rastafarianism

Afro-Creole religion with origins in Jamaica. "Rastafarians," as the members of the sect are called, believe in the divinity of Ethiopia's Haile Selassie and look to Africa as their spiritual homeland.

samba

Umbrella name that refers to a variety of Brazilian popular musical forms. The ballads with a samba beat are called *samba cancão*. The best-known one, associated with the merriment of Carnival, is called *samba de enredo*.

Santería

Afro-Creole religion practiced in the Caribbean region, associated especially with Cuba.

tango

National music of Argentina that developed in the mulatto sections of Buenos Aires.

transculturation

Coined by Cuban Fernando Ortiz, the term refers to the process by which a group of people carry or transport their cultural values, systems, and beliefs to another place or region.

umbanda
> Urban Afro-Creole spiritualist religion of Brazil.

vecino
> Literally "neighbor," but in colonial times the word referred to a citizen who had gained the right to inhabit a neighborhood according to the laws of the period.

vodun/voodoo
> Afro-Creole religion originating in Haiti but practiced throughout the Caribbean.

zambo
> Offspring of the union of a native American and an African.

Suggested Readings

Literature on the African presence in Latin America has grown tremendously over the last three decades. It is possible only to suggest some starting points for further reading and research. Two dictionaries may be helpful: Robert M. Levine, *Race and Ethnic Relations in Latin America and the Caribbean: A Historical Dictionary and Bibliography* (Metuchen, NJ: Scarecrow Press, 1980), is a good general volume of racial terminology, dates, and important events that affected race relations in the region. With more than four thousand entries, Benjamin Nuñez, *Dictionary of Afro-Latin America* (Westport, CT: Greenwood Press, 1980), focuses exclusively on the African experience, including select biographies, generic terms, and significant historical events. Organized alphabetically, both dictionaries conclude with impressive bibliographies of books and articles on race and race relations from the major Latin American countries.

Understandably, information on Brazil and the Caribbean basin predominate. The following list of suggested readings is drawn mostly from published manuscripts, although some periodical citations are included. Fewer works are available on the period of exploration prior to European colonization and on the period immediately following abolition, but the number of provocative and insightful works on Africans in the Americas is beginning to fill the gaps. Five general areas of scholarship may be identified: 1) slavery, 2) abolition, 3) cultural influences, 4) contemporary race relations, and 5) African-Latin American relations.

Slavery

The abundance of work available on slavery is due to several factors: the duration of the slave societies (almost three centuries, from circa 1500 to 1860; the availability of meticulous Spanish, Portuguese, and British documents on the trade; and the fact that race relations between masters and slaves, although varied, represented the most dramatic human aspect of colonial society. Slave riots, rebellions, runaway settlements (maroons), and accounts of abuse and torture add heroic social tension to the history of the period. Most important, many believe that modern racism, racial exclusion, and prejudice are grounded in the experience of slavery. The quantity of works available is made manageable by John Davis Smith, *Black Slavery in the Americas: An Interdisciplinary Bibliography, 1860–1980*, 2 vols. (Westport, CT: Greenwood Press, 1982). More recent material must be gleaned from bibliographical essays that often accompany surveys of the subject and sources cited in the latest monographs.

North American scholarship on slavery began with comparative studies of the slave experience in North and South America. One of the forerunners of research on slavery and race relations in this vein was Frank Tannenbaum, who portrayed the African slave of Latin America in a positive light in comparison to the slave in the southern United States. In *Slave and Citizen: The Negro in the Americas* (New York: Vintage Books, 1946), he painted the picture of a repressive Southern plantation while pointing out that Latin American slavery was milder as evidenced by laws on manumission and christianization.

The best critical work on Tannenbaum's thesis is Carl N. Degler, *Neither Black nor White: Slavery and Race Relations in Brazil and the United States* (New York: Macmillan, 1971). Degler refused to accept that Latin American slavery was milder than that in the United States. There was, as far as he was concerned, a marked difference between the law and actual practices within the society. A good compilation of essays on differing slave experiences in Latin America is Robert Brent Toplin, ed., *Slavery and Race Relations in Latin America* (Westport, CT: Greenwood Press, 1974). This volume contains fourteen chapters that investigate distinct aspects of the slave society from Mexico to Chile and Brazil.

A number of important works provide a clear understanding of Afro-Creoles under Spanish rule, among them Frederick P. Bowser, *The African Slave in Peru, 1524–1650* (Stanford: Stanford University Press, 1974), and Colin A. Palmer, *Slaves of the White God: Blacks in Mexico* (Cambridge: Cambridge University Press, 1976). For Brazil, Katia M. de Queirós, *To Be a Slave in Brazil, 1550–1888* (New Brunswick: Rutgers University Press, 1989), provides a good overview of the institution and those who struggled to survive its harsh reality. Patrick J. Carroll, *Blacks in Colonial Veracruz: Race, Ethnicity, and Regional Development* (Austin: University of Texas Press, 1991), is an excellent study of an often-forgotten Afro-Creole population in central Mexico.

Stuart B. Schwartz, "Resistance and Accommodation in 18th-Century Brazil: The Slaves' View of Slavery," in *Hispanic American Historical Review* 57, no. 1 (February 1979): 69–81, has contributed to the historiography on race relations in pre-abolition Brazil. Schwartz charters the changing aspirations of both slaves and masters as well as the moral-political pressures from other nations that eventually led to abolition. He also examines the various forms of resistance that altered traditional master-slave relations and the importance of external influences such as the Haitian slave uprising of 1791. C. L. R. James, *The Black Jacobins* (New York: Vintage Books Edition, 1989), is a revision of the much-acclaimed work on the Haitian Revolution led by Toussaint Louverture from 1791 to 1803. James provides the best account of the events, ideas, and individuals that inspired the Haitians to rise up against the French, abolish slavery, and create the second independent republic in the Americas. (The United States was the first.)

Abolition

The mechanics of the slave trade itself and an assessment of the numbers involved may be drawn from Philip D. Curtin, *Atlantic Slave Trade: A Census* (Madison: University of Wisconsin Press, 1970), and Colin A. Palmer, *Human Cargoes: The British Slave Trade to Spanish America, 1700–1739* (Urbana: University of Illinois Press, 1981). The process of ending the trade is presented by Leslie Bethell in *Abolition of the Brazilian Trade* (New York: Cambridge University Press, 1970). Among the studies on the abolition of slavery, Rebecca Scott, *Slave Emancipation in Cuba* (Princeton: Princeton University Press, 1985), is one of the most persuasive. While traditionally slavery was cast as an economic, political, or moral problem, Scott treats it as a way of life rather than merely as an institution.

Works on abolition in the second half of the twentieth century tend to debunk notions of ideal race relations espoused by writers such as Tannenbaum and Gilberto Freyre (see *The Masters and the Slaves*, 1933; reprint ed., 1986 [Berkeley: University of California Press, 1986]). These works present complex systems comprised of blacks, Indians, and whites and various combinations of the three. This is not to imply that there is a consensus in the emerging historiography. For example, Robert Brent Toplin, in *Freedom and Prejudice* (Westport, CT: Greenwood Press, 1940), documents the abolitionist movement, demonstrating that abolition in Brazil was rushed through by often violent means in order to avoid a social revolution or anything similar to what had occurred in Haiti. On the other hand, Robert Conrad, *The Destruction of Brazilian Slavery, 1850–1888* (Malabour, FL: Krieger, 1993), stresses that abolition was a gradual process.

Seymour Drecher, "Brazilian Abolition in Corporate Perspective," in *The Abolition of Slavery and the Aftermath of Emancipation in Brazil*, ed. Rebecca J. Scott et al. (Durham: Duke University Press, 1988), 429–60, describes a heterogeneous multiracial and multiclass society. The author argues that slavery lingered on in Brazil until 1888 because there was no tradition of mobilization and a lack of a strong opposition, such as the church or a well-defined abolitionist movement. Other insightful articles appear in the same volume. Colin M. MacLachlan, in a perceptive essay "Slavery, Ideology, and Institutional Change: The Impact of the Enlightenment on Slavery in Late-Eighteenth Century Maranhão," *Journal of Latin American Studies* 2, no. 1 (May 1979): 1–17, notes the eighteenth-century roots of Luso-Brazilian abolition evident in changing judicial views of the slave institution. His work provides an early indication of the importance of ideology and the courts in the process of altering social and racial realities—a phenomenon well demonstrated in our own time.

A recent provocative essay by David Eltis, "Europeans and the Rise and Fall of African Slavery in the Americas: An Interpretation," *American Historical Review* 98, no. 5 (December 1993): 1399–1423, also looks at philosophical factors to explain the use and continuation of African slavery in the New World. A general survey of the end of slavery may be found in Leslie B. Rout, Jr., *The African Experience in Spanish America* (New York: Cambridge University Press, 1970). For studies of the process in various countries see John Lombardi, *The Decline and Abolition of Negro Slavery in Venezuela, 1820–1854* (Westport, CT: Greenwood Press, 1971); the excellent analysis by Peter Blanchard, *Slavery and Abolition in Early Republican Peru* (Wilmington, DE: SR Books, 1992); and Christine Hunefeldt, *Paying the Price of Freedom: Family and Labor among Lima's Slaves, 1800–1854* (Berkeley: University of California Press, 1994).

Cultural Influences

Verena Martínez Alier examines the resistance and accommodation between slaves, free men and women, and Spaniards in *Marriage, Class, and Colour in Nineteenth-Century Cuba: A Study of Racial Attitudes and Sexual Values in a Slave Society* (Ann Arbor: University of Michigan Press, 1989). Martínez Alier elucidates the plight of the black and mulatto women in a changing society, explicating the differences between laws and actual practices during the epoch. For example, although there was a rigid law in Cuba that prohibited interracial marriages, widespread concubinage occurred. Women are not presented as passive victims of the system but rather as active participants who sought to increase their well-being within the system. Barbara Bush, *Slave Women in Caribbean Society, 1650–1832* (Bloomington: Indiana University Press, 1990), and Marietta Morissey, *Slave Women in the New World: Gender Stratification in the Caribbean*

(Lawrence: University of Kansas Press, 1989), provide a wealth of information on the economic and social importance of slave women.

A sensitive and remarkably insightful analysis of the complexity of the Cuban slave society is presented by Franklin W. Knight, *Slave Society in Cuba during the Nineteenth Century* (Madison: University of Wisconsin Press, 1970). Impressions by foreign travelers of Cuban slavery and society provide a much-appreciated human aspect in the carefully selected accounts in Louis A. Pérez, Jr., ed., *Slaves, Sugar, & Colonial Society: Travel Accounts of Cuba, 1801–1899* (Wilmington, DE: SR Books, 1992). Anthropologist Sidney W. Mintz, in *Caribbean Transformations* (Chicago: Aldine, 1974), helps place the larger economic and political views in daily context. He focuses on both historical and contemporary societies of Puerto Rico, Haiti, and Jamaica.

The Cuban Fernando Ortiz and the Brazilian Gilberto Freyre were two pioneers writing in the 1930s who explored transculturation, or the transfer of African culture to Latin America. Scholars following in their footsteps have investigated the African influence on Latin American myth, customs, food, childbearing, literature, language, music, and social values. This body of literature can be divided into three subfields: 1) language and literature, 2) religious influences, and 3) music and dance.

Three general volumes of essays on African cultural influences should be a point of departure. Sidney W. Mintz and Sally Price have produced an insightful collection of essays on the Caribbean region. *Caribbean Contours* (Baltimore: Johns Hopkins University Press, 1985) underscores the importance and value of looking at the Caribbean as a cultural unit, despite the differing ties that individual nations may have with a range of European traditions. Decidedly comparative, this volume emphasizes regional trends from the development of politics and race relations to linguistic patterns and musical traditions, highlighting the Afro-Creole dimension.

Margaret E. Crahan and Franklin W. Knight, eds., *Africa and the Caribbean: The Legacies of the Link* (Baltimore: Johns Hopkins University Press, 1979), expresses the complexity and variety of the African experience in the Caribbean region. This volume covers themes from slavery to contemporary times with particular emphasis on the English-speaking Caribbean, although Lorna V. Williams ends the collection with an excellent analysis of the poetry of Afro-Cuban Nicolás Guillén.

Scholarship on the African and Afro-Creole presence in Caribbean and Latin American prose and verse is growing, but for too long it has been difficult to find general works in English which are both balanced and comprehensive. Needed are more works that treat the African cultural presence cross-nationally within the region. William Luis, ed., *Voices from Under: Black Narrative in Latin America and the Caribbean* (Westport, CT: Greenwood Press, 1984), does just that. An impressive collection of essays dealing with the Caribbean basin as a unified region with recurring literary themes as presented in its prose, the volume is divided into six sections that focus on the Spanish, English, and French Caribbean, Central America, Spanish South America, and Portuguese South America. Luis has enlisted experts in the field for this first-rate venture.

Language and Literature

In addition to these three volumes of essays, readers would do well to consult O. R. Dathorne, *Dark Ancestor: The Literature of the Black Man in the Caribbean* (Baton Rouge: Louisiana State University Press, 1981), and his *African Literature in the Twentieth Century* (Minneapolis: University of Minnesota Press, 1976). Dathorne, a Guyanese-born scholar and founder of the Association of Caribbean Studies, is well respected for his numerous publications on literary and cultural themes in the region.

Richard Jackson's work is also indispensable: *The Black Image in Latin American Literature* (Albuquerque: University of New Mexico Press, 1976) investigates the portrayals of blacks in the region's literature. In *Black Writers in Latin America* (Albuquerque: University of New Mexico Press, 1979) and *Black Literature and Humanism in Latin America* (Athens: University of Georgia Press, 1988), Jackson presents and examines an impressive list of Afro-Creole writers. Mariam DeCosta, ed., *Blacks in Hispanic Literature: Critical Essays* (Port Washington, NY: Kennikat Press, 1977), is a good overall survey that examines the African presence in essays, prose, and poetry in Spanish Latin America. Among the plethora of insightful articles and manuscripts on the black cultural movement dubbed Negritude are James A. Arnold, *Modernism and Negritude* (Cambridge: Harvard University Press, 1981); and Lewis Nkiosi, "Negritude: New and Old Perspectives," in *Tasks and Masks*, ed. Lewis Nkiosi (Essex, England: Longman, 1981).

Pedro Pérez Sarduy and Jean Stubbs, eds., *Afrocuba: An Anthology of Cuban Writing on Race, Politics, and Culture* (New York: Ocean Press/Center for Cuban Studies, 1993), is a much-needed contribution to the literature on the African experience in Cuba. This anthology includes original essays, extracts from novels, poetry, and scholarly articles on Afro-Cuban culture. It is an indispensable source, especially for the non-Spanish speaker, as it provides English translations of several works on and about Afro-Cubans that were previously available only in Spanish.

Several other sources on Afro-Caribbean literature also should be consulted. Selvyn Cudjoe, *Resistance in Caribbean Literature* (Athens: Ohio University Press, 1980), is a well thought-out assessment of the Afro-Caribbean writers of the twentieth century, and G. R. Coulthard, *Race and Color in Caribbean Literature* (London: Oxford University Press, 1962), outlines several themes that are elaborated upon by subsequent literary works. For Luso-Brazilian literature, Russell G. Hamilton, *Voices from an Empire: A History of Afro-Portuguese Literature* (Minneapolis: University of Minnesota Press, 1975), is a good source that contains a dated but useful bibliography. David T. Haberly, *Three Sad Races: Racial Identity and National Consciousness in Brazilian Literature* (New York: Cambridge University Press, 1983), examines racial identity, mixture, and ethnic diversity as depicted in Brazilian literature. Flora Edwards Mancuso furnished a provocative work on national identity and literature in her doctoral dissertation, entitled "The Theater of Black Diaspora: A Comparative Study of Drama in Brazil, Cuba, and the United States" (New York University, 1975). Mancuso convincingly showed the importance of art and theater in particular in forging a racial consciousness in the three countries under study.

Religious Influences

Well-written works on Afro-Creole religious practices are not as available as those on literature. Popular and uninformed visions of religions such as voodoo and Santería continue to be propagated. Three of the leading scholars on African religious experiences in the Americas—Pierre Verger, Fernando Ortiz, and Lydia Cabrera—have yet to be translated into English. Several works have nonetheless illuminated the role of African religion in society.

Jean Price-Mars, *So Spoke the Uncle*, trans. Magdaline Shannon (Washington, DC: Three Continents Press, 1983), ranks high among them. First published in 1928, Price-Mars's work emphasizes the religious nature of voodoo, while explaining its sociological importance to Haitian folklore. Although criticized by later scholars for idealizing the Haitian peasant's life, this is a well-written book that must be consulted for information on Haitian life during the first half of this century. Haitian anthropologist Remy Bastien, in *Religion and Politics in Haiti* (Washington, DC: Institute of Cross-Cultural Studies, 1966), provides a more critical approach to voodoo and its use and abuse in the political arena.

Arthur Ramos, "Acculturation among the Brazilian Negroes," *Journal of Negro History* 26, no. 2 (April 1941): 244–50, is a dated but good essay on the religious culture of Bahia. Roger Bastide, *African Civilizations in the New World* (New York: Harper Torchbooks, 1971), is an objective and insightful standard resource, as is his *The African Religions of Brazil: Towards a Sociology of the Interpretations of Civilizations*, trans. Helen Sebba (Baltimore: Johns Hopkins University Press, 1987). Santería's popularity has grown within the United States with the migration of Cubans to this country. Raul Canizares, *Walking with the Night: The Afro-Cuban World of Santería* (Rochester, VT: Destiny Books, 1993), reflects this growing interest. Canizares, a Cuban émigré, religious scholar, and Santería initiate, provides a good anthropological study from an insider's perspective. Somewhat more sensationalist but nonetheless provocative is Migene González-Wippler, *Santería: African Magic in Latin America* (Garden City, NY: Doubleday/Anchor, 1973). Consult also Joseph Murphy, *Santería: An African Religion in America* (Boston: Beacon Press, 1988). Isabel Mercedes Castellanos's unpublished dissertation on the role of language in the African religions in Cuba, "The Use of Language in Afro-Cuban Religion" (Georgetown University, 1977), provides a wealth of detail. For further information on Rastafarianism see, among others, Tracy Nicholas and Bill Sparrow, *Rastafari: A Way of Life* (New York: Doubleday, 1979).

Music and Dance

Two good general surveys on the African influence on the region's music include Billy Bergman, ed., *Hot Sauces: Latin and Caribbean Pop* (New York: Quill, 1985). Bergman's study is an excellent overview of the musical tradition of Latin America and the Caribbean. Focusing on the major rhythms familiar to North American audiences, such as salsa, reggae, *soca*, and Latin Jazz, Bergman has assembled an impressive series of essays that always attempts to understand the sociocultural context from which such music emerges. He underscores the importance of African rhythms and style to music in Cuba, Puerto Rico, Panama, Jamaica, Haiti, and Brazil. Irene V. Jackson, ed., *More than Drumming: Essays on African and Afro-Latin Music and Musicians* (Baton Rouge: Louisiana State University Press, 1980), and Gerhard Kubik, *Angolan Traits in Black Music, Games, and Dances of Brazil: A Study of African Cultural Extensions Overseas* (Lisbon: Junta de Investigacões Científicas do Ultramar, 1979), investigate the links between the two continents. Popular music magazines such as *Beat* (see vol. 10, no. 2 [1991], for example) and *Musart* (see vol. 26, no. 3 [Spring 1974]) contain an abundance of material on Latin American music and its African roots and influences.

Contemporary Race Relations

Works on contemporary race relations focus on a variety of topics, from blacks in the workplace to national identity and modern prejudice. Just as studies in the pre-abolition society focused on differences from the North American system, studies on contemporary race relations often attempt to compare practices in Latin America with those in the United States. Such is the case of Marianne Masferrer and Camelo Mesa Lago, "The Gradual Integration of Blacks in Cuba: Under the Colony, the Republic, and the Revolution," in *Slavery and Race Relations in Latin America*, ed. Robert Brent Toplin (Westport, CT: Greenwood Press, 1974). They argue that racial prejudice in Cuba was always milder and never as harsh as it existed in the United States.

The seminal work on race relations in Brazil is undoubtedly Florestan Fernandes, *The Negro in Brazilian Society*, trans. Jacqueline D. Skiles (New York: Columbia University Press, 1969). This study focuses on the status of blacks in São Paulo. Fernandes maintains that the rapid industrialization in São Paulo marginalized blacks and mulattoes, who were ill prepared for assimilation into modern society owing to prejudice and pauperization caused by the slave experience. Fernandes produced many articles and books on race and national culture in Brazil. Numerous scholars follow in Fernandes's footsteps, examining race relations from a sociohistorical perspective in various Latin American nations. A study conducted by Annani Dzidziendo and Dr. Lourdes Casal, *The Position of Blacks in Brazilian and Cuban Society* (London: Minority Rights Group, 1979), analyzes the status of blacks in Cuba and Brazil.

Two works that have looked at the black movements in Brazil and their views on national identity are also worth mentioning. Thomas Skidmore, who is well known for his studies on race in Brazil, has examined race in the context of the political development of the modern Brazilian nation. Skidmore explores nationality and the idea of whitening in that country in *Black into White: Race and Nationality in Brazilian Thought* (New York: Oxford University Press, 1974). In another publication, "Race and Class in Brazil: Historical Perspectives," in *Race, Class, and Power in Brazil*, ed. Pierre-Michel Fontaine (Los Angeles: University of California, 1980), Skidmore states that the decision to omit race from the national census in the 1960s was due to political expediency and the desire to avoid facing potential problems.

Several studies have looked at the concept of race in Latin America in general. Richard Graham, ed., *The Idea of Race in Latin America, 1870–1940* (Austin: University of Texas Press, 1990), includes two important essays. Thomas Skidmore investigates racial attitudes and social policy in Brazil in "Racial Ideas and Social Policy, 1870–1940," while Aline Helg, "Race in Argentina and Cuba, 1880–1930: Theory, Policies, and Popular Reaction," focuses on the desire of both countries to whiten the population. George Reid Andrews, *The Afro-Argentines of Buenos Aires, 1800–1900* (Madison: University of Wisconsin Press, 1980), restored an important diaspora group to our historical consciousness. Studies such as these provide a framework for comparative approaches to different regions in Latin America. See also George Reid Andrews, *Blacks and Whites in São Paulo, 1888–1988* (Madison: University of Wisconsin Press, 1989).

A handful of works have examined the relationship between race, ethnicity, and gender as it relates to the Afro-Creole experience; among them, Filomina Chioma Steady, *The Black Woman Cross-Culturally* (Cambridge, MA: Schenkman, 1981), contains a section on women in the Caribbean and Latin America. Gerder Lerder, "Reconceptualizing Differences among Women," in *Journal of Women's History* 3 (Winter 1990): 107–22, although not specific to Latin America, provides an excellent appraisal of the relationship of gender and race to American societies in general. Edna Acosta Belen and Christine E. Bose, eds., *Researching Women in Latin America and the Caribbean* (Boulder: Westview Press, 1993), contains several excellent bibliographical lists for further research. Nancy Leys Stephan, *"The Hour of Eugenics": Race, Gender, and Nation in Latin America* (Ithaca: Cornell University Press, 1991), examines "eugenics," the 1883 term coined to refer to the movement to improve the race, as it relates to Latin American nations; Chapter Four, entitled "Matrimonial Eugenics: Gender and the Construction of Negative Eugenics," may prove useful. Rosemary Geisdorfer Feal, "Feminist Interventions in the Race for Theory: Neither Black nor White," in *Afro-Hispanic Review* 3 (Summer 1991): 11–20, examines the interpretations of Afro-Creole texts in the North American press.

The relationship between race and national identity is further elaborated upon in Winthrop R. Wright, *Café con Leche: Race, Class, and National Image in Venezuela* (Austin: University of Texas Press, 1990). Wright examines the role of intellectuals in the construction of a national image in Venezuela. More studies of this nature are needed for other countries of the region.

African-Latin American Relations

Finally, Africa's role in Latin American politics has been highlighted by Cuba's political and military involvement in that continent. Nonetheless, African-Latin American ties should be seen in historical contexts. As modern nation-states seek closer relations with each other in the creation of regional communities based on economics, politics, and culture, relations between Africa and Latin America may further develop. A few scholars have already examined the historical, political, and cultural reasons and consequences of these ties. A very detailed account of Cuba's involvement is David Deutschmann, *Changing the History of Africa: Angola and Namibia* (Melbourne, Australia: Ocean Press, 1989). This volume contains contributions by Fidel Castro and Gabriel García Márquez, among others. Three articles on Cuba are also helpful: Gordon Adams and Michael Locker, "Cuba and Africa: Politics of the Liberation Struggle," *Cuba Review* 8, no. 3–4 (October 1978): 3–9; Nelsón Valdés, "Cuban Foreign Policy in the Horn of Africa," *Cuban Studies/Estudios Cubanos* 10, no. 1 (January 1980): 49–80; and Jorge I. Domínguez, "Political and Military Limitations and Consequences of Cuban Policies in Africa," *Cuban Studies/Estudios Cubanos* 10, no. 2 (July 1980): 1–35.

José Honorio Rodrigues, *Brazil and Africa*, trans. Richard A. Mazzara and Sam Hileman (Berkeley: University of California Press, 1965), is essential for anyone interested in Brazil's foreign relations with Africa. Chapter Eight of this book looks at the country's Africa policy and Luso-Brazilian living in Africa, as well as Brazil's line in the United Nations vis-à-vis African issues. More current analysis of Brazil is needed.

Another interesting factor that has affected international relations between Africa, Latin America, and the Caribbean is the Pan-African movement. Many Afro-Creoles have emerged, sharing their views on the importance of closer relations with peoples of African descent throughout the diaspora. One such writer and activist already well published is Abdias do Nascimento. His *Brazil: Mixture or Massacre?* (Dover, MA: Majority Press, 1979) is a disconcerting perspective on race relations in that country. The volume also contains reflections on the Pan-African movement. Writings by the world-renowned Pan-Africanist Franz Fanon are essential readings. Fanon, a Martinican and psychiatrist by profession, worked in Africa during the Franco-Algerian war. He eventually joined the revolution on the side of the Algerians and became one of their most articulate spokesman. Students should consult *Black Skin, White Masks*, trans. Charles Lam Markmann (London: Paladin, 1972), and *The Wretched of the Earth*, trans. Constance Farrington (New York: Grove Press, 1968).

Students also should consult works by and about Marcus Garvey, Henry Sylvester Williams, and Dr. J. Robert Love, among others. As the literature grows, we will come closer to understanding and appreciating the greater Afro-Creole contribution to American societies beyond the institution of slavery.

◆ ◆ ◆

Despite the growing interest in the African diaspora and Africa's culture and impact on Latin American societies, researchers seeking information from journals will detect an unanticipated void. Fewer than five deal exclusively with Afro-Latin American history and culture. In the last decade, however, several useful scholarly journals have emerged that attempt to provide a forum for the discussion of these themes. Although Afro-Latin American history and historiography are slowly expanding to include issues beyond slavery, the majority of journals focus on contemporary cultural and religious studies, and on literature in particular. It is hoped that this trend will broaden and continue to explore the racial complexity of the region. The following list cites the major journals that center on issues of the African diaspora in Latin America.

The Afro-Hispanic Review
Editor: Marvin A. Lewis
Publisher: University of Missouri, Columbia

This is one of the first journals to be dedicated solely to the exploration of African culture and values in Latin America. Published jointly by the Department of Romance Languages and the Black Studies program at the University of Missouri, the *Review* focuses mainly on literary criticism but nonetheless has produced several articles of social, historical, and sociological merit. The interdisciplinary approach of the journal has fostered a pluralistic view of both foreign languages and cultural studies in academia.

Callaloo
Editor: Charles H. Rowell
Publisher: Johns Hopkins University Press

One of the most respected literary scholarly productions, *Callaloo* focuses on critical studies of the African experience in the Americas, the Caribbean, and on the African continent. Quarterly issues include an array of insightful and controversial articles on fiction, poetry, drama, folklore, and cultural studies. From time to time, the journal publishes special issues on the lives and works of noted black authors from the diaspora.

Caribbean Monthly Bulletin
Editor: Dale Mathews
Publisher: University of Puerto Rico, Institute of Caribbean Studies, Rio Piedras

Although not well known in the continental United States, this Puerto Rican journal provides a forum for the discussion of Caribbean relations, culture, and aspects of the Caribbean diaspora. Published in both English and Spanish.

Caribbean Quarterly
Editor: Rex Nettleford
Publisher: University of the West Indies, Kingston, Jamaica

This periodical contains articles and essays of relevance to the Caribbean experience; and issues of race and race relations, although not an explicit part of its mission, are common themes. *Caribbean Quarterly* is a good general source of information on the region's relations, much like its Trinidadian counterpart, *Caribbean Affairs*, which is edited by Owen Batiste.

Caribbean Review
Editor: Robert B. Levine
Publisher: Florida International University

The *Review* features articles of interest on the wider Caribbean basin and the Caribbean diaspora, often highlighting the African dimension of these societies. Topics range from politics to the arts and music to human relations, often with illustrations in black and white.

Ethnology
Editor: Leonard Plotnicov
Publisher: Department of Anthropology, University of Pittsburgh

Although this quarterly does not focus exclusively on Latin America or the Caribbean, it has published several articles and reviews related to Latin American cultural anthropology. It boasts an impressive list of international editors, including Roberto Cardoso de Oliveira from Brazil.

The Journal of Afro-Latin American Studies and Literatures
Editor: Rosangela María Viera King
Publisher: Journal of Afro-Latin American Studies and Literatures

Committed to promoting the contribution of peoples of African descent to the cultures and societies of Spanish, French, English, and Portuguese America, the *Journal* aims to publish both creative and informative works. Its editorial goal is to present alternative views to the patterns of racial tensions that have plagued American societies.

Journal of Black Studies
Editor: Molefi Kete Asante
Publisher: Sage Publications

This periodical publishes articles of rigorous research in the social sciences, providing an intellectual forum for discussions of economic, political, sociological, historical, and sometimes literary and philosophical issues of the African diaspora. Concentrating on African Americans, the *Journal* has a highly respected editorial staff and an international group of scholars who often focus on issues of relevance to the African experience in the Caribbean and Latin America.

Présence Africaine: Revue Culturelle du Monde Noir
Editors: Geoffrey Jones and Voahangy Rajaonah
Publisher: Société Africaine de Culture, Paris, France

A prominent and well-respected journal of the Francophone nations, *Présence Africaine*, which began in 1947, now publishes articles, poems, short stories, documents, and book reviews in English and French. Latin Americanists may find it helpful for comparative research. In addition, the journal also has produced a considerable body of literature on the French-speaking Caribbean, particularly Haiti, Martinique, and Guadeloupe.

Race and Class
Editors: A. Sirvanandan and Eqbal Ahmad
Publisher: Institute of Race Relations, London, England

This English periodical has an international focus but often publishes articles on Latin America and the Caribbean as well as comparative studies. Quarterly issues contain essays that comment on diverse topics, often from contradictory points of view and from a variety of disciplines.

Sage: A Scholarly Journal on Black Women
Editors: Patricia Bell-Scott and Beverly Guy-Sheftall
Publisher: Sage Women's Educational Press

A scholarly journal for the discussion of issues related to women of the African diaspora, *Sage* is geared toward a broad audience, publishing articles, critical essays, interviews, reviews, research reports, and announcements relating to black women in the United States, Africa, Latin America, and the Caribbean.

Suggested Films

The Latin American film industry has developed rapidly over the past few decades, with Brazil, Argentina, Cuba, and Mexico leading the way. Cuba and Brazil have produced the most films on the African experience in Latin America, but several Hollywood movies are also included. The following list of films in English (or with English subtitles) that may aid in the study of the Afro-Creole dimension of Latin American culture is organized by title, year of release, director, and running time. Directors of documentaries are not given. For those films that are difficult to acquire, I have added the distributor at the end of the citation.

A Samba da Criação do Mundo (The samba of the creation of the world). 1979. Director: Vera de Figueiredo. (56 minutes) A highly imaginative musical that tells the story of the creation of the world by the Yoruba (Nago) people, who represent the largest African ethnic group of slaves taken to Brazil. It is not well edited but contains actual footage from Carnival scenes from Beija Flor, one of Brazil's top samba schools.

Benedita. 1991. (30 minutes) This short documentary examines the life of Benedita Souza da Silva, the first black woman elected to Congress in Brazil. Benedita narrates her life and her attempts to organize the Rio de Janeiro neighborhood of Chapeu de Mangueira. (International Media Resource Exchange)

The Bob Marley Story. 1986. (100 minutes) This documentary explores the life, music, and philosophy of one of the Caribbean's most acclaimed personalities. The film chronicles the importance of Rastafarianism in Jamaica, shedding some light on the religious and spiritual aspects of the movement. With the help of interviews with friends and family, as well as live footage of Bob Marley's life and reggae music, we have a clear vision of the man. (Island Visual Arts)

Burn! 1970. Director: Gillo Pontecorvo. (112 minutes) This U.S. film starring Marlon Brando is about a fictitious Caribbean island called Quemada (Burn). It recounts the conflict between the British and

Portuguese over the colony prior to independence and the creation of a black republic. The story follows loosely the struggle of Haiti for independence.

Cecilia. 1981. Director: Humberto Solás. (114 minutes) Based on the nineteenth-century *costumbrista* novel by Cirilo Villaverde, the film, despite some cryptic scenes, is a good representation of Cuban race relations during that time period.

Chico Rei. 1986. Director: Walter Lima, Jr. (115 minutes) Set in Minas Gerais in the eighteenth century, *Chico Rei* centers on the life of Chico, a member of African royalty who is sold into slavery. The film shows the hardships of slavery in Brazil but also illustrates how some slaves were able to buy their own freedom and become prosperous members of a society in transition.

Cimarrones. 1982. Director: Carlos Ferrand (30 minutes) This docudrama looks at slavery in an understudied region of Latin America—Peru. It is a rare production that takes us back to a *palenque* in the eighteenth century.

De Cierta Manera (One way or another). 1977. Director: Sara Gomez. (79 minutes) This black-and-white documentary brings to the surface the problems of the consolidation of the revolution in Cuba. It focuses on the marginalized sectors of society in the 1960s when the revolution had already begun to achieve some success. The film illustrates the challenges that many of the marginalized black sectors posed for the Cuban revolution. (Unifilm)

Ganga Zumba. 1963. Director: Carlos Diegues (99 minutes) This is the story of the first successful American slave revolt. In 1641 escaped slaves created a *quilombo* that developed into the Republic of Palmares, which became a symbol of resistance to white rule as its leader attempted to create a more just society for Afro-Brazilians. (New Yorker Films)

La Ultima Cena (The last supper). 1977. Director: Tomás Gutiérrez Alea (120 minutes) In the eighteenth century, during the celebration of Easter, a Cuban slaveholder decides to treat his slaves better by inviting them to participate in the Passover meal. It proves to be his last supper as it ultimately leads to a rebellion and the destruction of the plantation. This movie is a good source of information on race relations in pre-abolition Cuba. (New Yorker Films)

Las Américas. 1992. Part III. (55 minutes) The third part of this PBS series looks at race and national identity in Bolivia, the Dominican Republic, and Haiti. The histories of Haiti and the Dominican Republic, which share the same island, are intimately related. Raul Julia narrates the perceptions of race, color, and identity in both Caribbean nations. (PBS)

"Macumba, World of the Spirits." 1984. Producer: Madelaine Richeport. (30 minutes) This short documentary deals with the different religious influences in Brazil by following the many believers of the Afro-Brazilian sects. The film should follow a discussion of African religions in Latin America rather than precede it, as images from the film may be met with confusion and disbelief by students. (National Geographic Special)

Macunaíma. 1969. Director: Joaquin Pedro de Andrade (103 minutes) Based on Mario de Andrade's modernist novel of the same name, *Macunaíma* is a comedy starring the famous Brazilian actor Grande Otelo. The film parodies race and class relations in Brazil, putting close emphasis on the migration between rural and urban centers. (Globo)

Marcus M. Garvey and Booker T. Washington: Theory of Self-Reliance. 1986. Director: John Henrick Clarke. (120 minutes) This documentary chronicles the lives of two prominent African-American spokesmen. Their philosophies and endeavors to promote civil rights for peoples of African descent are reviewed and compared. (Blacast Productions)

O Pagador de Promesas. 1962. Director: Anselmo Duarte (95 minutes) A good film for the discussion of the nature of syncretism in Latin America. Zé do Burro, a peasant from the Northeast, has made a promise to Yemanja, the Afro-Brazilian deity associated with Saint Barbara. He does not distinguish between the two. On arrival at church, he is not allowed to enter and his faith is dismissed by the priest as witchcraft. (Globo)

Oggún. 1992. Director: Gloria Rolando (57 minutes) This wonderfully produced documentary introduces the viewer to the Afro-Cuban deity Oggún and his Santería followers in Cuba. Lázaro Ross, *santero* and blessed son of Oggún, narrates and explains his love of the Afro-Cuban religion. Best for adult audiences, this film is most helpful if students are familiar with the history, rites, and practices of Santería. (Center for Cuban Studies)

Orfeu Negro (Black Orpheus). 1958. Director: Marcel Camus (103 minutes) This French production is based on the myth of Orpheus and Eurydice but is set during Carnival in Rio de Janeiro. Brought up to date, Orpheus is an Afro-Brazilian train conductor who meets Eurydice, a beautiful mulatta. Although the film won the Grand Prize in Cannes and the Oscar for best foreign film, it gives an often stereotypical vision of Brazil. It may be used for a discussion of stereotypes of Latin America and visions of Afro-Brazilian culture.

Portrait of America: Puerto Rico. 1991. (55 minutes) This documentary chronicles the history and geography of Puerto Rico. Although it often lends itself to stereotypes, the film discusses the ethnic diversity of the island and reviews the political opinions that Puerto Ricans have of themselves and of the United States. (PBS)

Quilombo. 1984. Director: Carlos Diegues (90 minutes) This classic Brazilian film won praise from international critics. It is the story of a community of escaped slaves and its struggles for survival. (New Yorker Films)

Routes of Rhythm. 1990. (60 minutes, each part) This three-part documentary narrated by Harry Belafonte explores the Spanish and African influences on Latin American music. Special focus is given to the African element in Cuban music and the transfer of this music to the United States. (PBS)

The Serpent and the Rainbow. 1987. Director: Wes Craven (110 minutes) Listed in *Variety's Complete Home Video Guide* as a horror film, this motion picture is a good springboard for a discussion of voodoo in Haiti. The film does little to describe the complex religious system but focuses instead on the sensational aspects of zombies in Haiti. Discussion could center around North American perceptions of Haiti and voodoo.

Sugar Cane Alley. 1983. Director: Euzhan Paloy. (106 minutes) Set in Martinique in 1931, this film follows the life of a young black boy under colonialism. Conflicts between rural and urban society on the island are emphasized, with assimilation as another major theme. (New Yorker Films)

Xica da Silva. 1976. Director: Carlos Diegues (120 minutes) Zeze Mota plays the title role of a slave who becomes the mistress of a powerful and influential estate owner. She is an excellent example of a woman who is able to improve her situation despite the odds against her. The film underscores the fact that slaves were not mere victims of the system but actors who were often able to pursue their own interests, within bound-aries. It may serve as a good point of discussion since many viewers have criticized the film for portraying women in a stereotypical manner. (New Yorker Films)